This challenging collection of new essays by an international group of scholars aims, through the critical concept of "context," to put the work of James Joyce in its "place." The four sections explore a range of contexts, offering significant perspectives – historical, theoretical, feminist, cultural, and linguistic – on Joyce's writing. Essays on the modernist context place Joyce alongside contemporaries like Woolf, Ford, and Freud, re-evaluating accepted notions of literary relationship and ideology. The context of the "other" is invoked in essays drawing on recent developments in feminist, poststructuralist, and psychoanalytic literary theory, and taking Joyce's work as a site for provocative investigations into the nature of sexual, national, ethnic, and cultural marginality. Next, original rereadings of Joyce's relationship to particular writers, critics, and cultural traditions draw him into proximity with Homer, Lacan, the comic strip, and Irish popular literature. Finally, in essays that examine aspects and evolutions of his distinctive style, Joyce is considered within the parameters of his own œuvre.

JOYCE IN CONTEXT

JOYCE IN CONTEXT

EDITED BY VINCENT J. CHENG
AND TIMOTHY MARTIN

CAMBRIDGE
UNIVERSITY PRESS

Published by the Press Syndicate of the University of Cambridge
The Pitt Building, Trumpington Street, Cambridge CB2 1RP
40 West 20th Street, New York, NY 10011–4211, USA
10 Stamford Road, Oakleigh, Victoria 3166, Australia

First published 1992

Printed in Great Britain at the University Press, Cambridge

A catalogue record for this book is available from the British Library

Library of Congress cataloguing in publication data
Joyce in context / edited by Vincent J. Cheng and Timothy Martin.
p.   cm.
Papers presented at the 1989 James Joyce Conference held in
Philadelphia, Pa.
ISBN 0–521–41358–3 (hardback)
1. Joyce, James, 1882–1941 – Criticism and interpretation –
Congresses.   I. Cheng, Vincent John, 1951–   .
II. Martin, Timothy Peter, 1950–   .
III. James Joyce Conference (1989: Philadelphia, Pa.)
PR6019.09Z6647 1992
823'.912–dc20   91–31584 CIP

ISBN 0 521 41358 3 hardback

CE

Contents

Illustrations

Notes on contributors

BERNARD BENSTOCK is Professor of English at the University of Miami and editor of the *James Joyce Literary Supplement*. He is author or editor of many books on Joyce, including *Joyce-again's Wake* (1965), *The Seventh of Joyce* (1982), *Critical Essays on James Joyce* (1985), and, with Shari Benstock, *Who's He When He's at Home* (1980). A former president of the James Joyce Foundation, his most recent book is *Narrative Con/Texts in "Ulysses"* (1991), and his *Narrative Con/Texts in "Dubliners"* is forthcoming.

VINCENT J. CHENG, editor, teaches English at the University of Southern California. He is author of *Shakespeare and Joyce: A Study of "Finnegans Wake"* (1984); of *"Le Cid": A Translation in Rhymed Couplets* (1987); and of numerous articles on modern literature and on Joyce. He has been awarded a Guggenheim Fellowship for 1991–2 and is working on a book about "Joyce, Race, and Empire."

IAN CRUMP, a graduate student in English at the University of California, Berkeley, is completing a dissertation entitled "Disselving the Individuone: Joyce's Narrative Representations of the Self."

DENIS DONOGHUE has taught at University College Dublin and is now Henry James Professor of English and American Letters at New York University. He is author of many books on Irish, English, and American literature, including *We Irish* (1986), *Reading America* (1987), and *England, Their England* (1988). His memoir *Warrenpoint* was published in 1990.

JOHANNA X. K. GARVEY teaches English and Comparative Literature at Fairfield University. She is completing a book entitled "City Voyages: Gender and Reflexivity in the Modern Novel," and has published an article on *Mrs. Dalloway* in *College English*. She has begun a study of women writers and the city, tentatively entitled "Building Con/texts."

ROY GOTTFRIED teaches English at Vanderbilt University. He is the author of *The Art of Joyce's Syntax in "Ulysses"* (1980), and he is currently at work on a manuscript provisionally entitled "The Dis-lexic *Ulysses*."

SUZETTE HENKE is Morton Professor of Literary Studies at the University of Louisville. She is author of *Joyce's Moraculous Sindbook* (1978) and co-editor, with Elaine Unkeless, of *Women in Joyce* (1982). Her most recent book, *James Joyce and the Politics of Desire*, was published in 1990.

DI JIN, Professor of English at the Foreign Languages Institute in Tianjin, China, is currently a Visiting Fellow at the University of Virginia. Since 1979 he has been working on a Chinese translation of *Ulysses*: a number of episodes have appeared in books and periodicals in China. A collection of his recent essays in English is being prepared under the title of "The Great Sage and James Joyce."

COLLEEN R. LAMOS is Assistant Professor of English at Rice University. She is the author of articles on Joyce, Eliot, and feminist theory, and she is currently at work on a book, "Going Astray: Gender as Errancy in Modern Literature."

GARRY M. LEONARD is Assistant Professor at the University of Toronto. He has published essays on Joyce in *Novel*, *Modern Fiction Studies*, *James Joyce Quarterly*, and *Joyce Studies Annual*, and his book *Re-Joycing "Dubliners": A Lacanian Perspective* is forthcoming from Syracuse University Press.

TIMOTHY MARTIN, editor, teaches English at Rutgers University in Camden. He has published numerous articles on Joyce, Faulkner, and Henry James, and his book *Joyce and Wagner: A Study of Influence* was published by Cambridge in 1991. He was Director of the 1989 James Joyce Conference in Philadelphia.

THERESA O'CONNOR has studied in Galway and is a doctoral candidate at the University of Connecticut. She is completing a dissertation, "Teangas of Babblers: Joyce's Linguistic Grail Myth," in the library of the Ecole Pratique des Hautes Etudes at the Sorbonne. A winner, in 1991, of the first annual Graduate Student Scholarship of the International James Joyce Foundation, she has chaired panels and delivered papers at several Joyce conferences.

DAN SCHIFF is a cartoonist for the *Ampersand* and a founding member of the Berkeley Tuesday Night *Wake* Group. He is currently working on a series of illustrations for *Ulysses*.

BONNIE KIME SCOTT is Professor of English at the University of Delaware. She is author of *Joyce and Feminism* (1984) and of *James Joyce* (1987). She is editor of *New Alliances in Joyce Studies* (1988), the volume from the 1985 Joyce conference in Philadelphia, and of *The Gender of Modernism: A Critical Anthology* (1990).

FRITZ SENN is Director of the Zurich James Joyce Foundation, with its annual workshops, and co-editor of *European Joyce Studies*. He is author of books and articles in German and in English, including *Nichts gegen Joyce* (1983) and *Joyce's Dislocutions* (1984). Until 1983, he was co-editor of *A Wake Newslitter*.

BRIAN W. SHAFFER is Assistant Professor of English at Rhodes College. He recently published an essay on Joyce's *Exiles* in *James Joyce Quarterly*. Forthcoming are articles on Joseph Conrad in *PMLA* and *Conradiana* and on Virginia Woolf in *Journal of Modern Literature*.

CONSTANCE V. TAGOPOULOS is a doctoral candidate in Comparative Literature at the Graduate Center of the City University of New York, specializing in classical and modern Greek literature. She teaches at CUNY, Queens College.

Acknowledgments

This book assumes two classes of debt: to those who helped make the 1989 James Joyce Conference possible and to those who helped with the book itself. The former have been acknowledged in other contexts, but some of them must be mentioned once again. We owe thanks to an aggregation of some 141 Joyceans who made up the academic program and especially to the large number who allowed us to consider their work for this volume. We owe renewed thanks to the ten universities in the Philadelphia area which helped underwrite the conference. Most notable among these were Drexel University and Rutgers University, Camden, which supported the roles of the conference's two main organizers with secretarial help, release time, graduate student assistance, and the use of office facilities and supplies, in addition to substantial monetary contributions. Among conference organizers, Denise Buzz and David Borodin deserve special citation for attention to detail, for imagination, and for unstinting willingness to help. A belated thanks is due Mort Levitt and Carol Shloss, whose directorship of the 1985 Philadelphia conference opened so many doors to this one. Finally, and above all, we thank Academic Program Chair Michael O'Shea, without whose foresight, patience, diplomacy, and hard work there would have been no academic program.

In putting this volume together, we have profited from the experience and expertise of Richard Yarborough, Allan Casson, Mort Levitt, Melvin Friedman, Michael Gillespie, Bonnie Scott, and especially Kim Devlin and Margot Norris. At Rutgers, we were ably assisted by Phyllis Triestman, who provided secretarial support, and by Susan Skand, who acted as editorial assistant. We express deep appreciation to Peter Blake for his kind permission to use the image on the book jacket. And finally, among those at Cambridge University Press we thank Josie Dixon, Kay McKechnie, and especially, for his diligence in persuading us to keep reshaping and improving the collection, Kevin Taylor. Thank you all.

Abbreviations

Quotations from the following works are cited in the text, parenthetically:

CP   Joyce, James. *Collected Poems*. New York: Viking, 1957.

CW   Joyce, James. *The Critical Writings of James Joyce*. Ed. Ellsworth Mason and Richard Ellmann. New York: Viking, 1959.

D   Joyce, James. *Dubliners*. New York: Viking, 1967. Joyce, James. *"Dubliners": Text, Criticism, and Notes*. Ed. Robert Scholes and A. Walton Litz. New York: Viking, 1969.

FW   Joyce, James. *Finnegans Wake*. New York: Viking, 1939.

JJ   Ellmann, Richard. *James Joyce*. Rev. edn. New York: Oxford University Press, 1982.

JJA   *The James Joyce Archive*. Ed. Michael Groden et al. 63 vols. New York: Garland, 1978.

Letters Joyce, James. *Letters of James Joyce*. 3 vols. Vol. 1, ed. Stuart Gilbert. Vols. 2 and 3, ed. Richard Ellmann. New York: Viking, 1966.

P   Joyce, James. *A Portrait of the Artist as a Young Man*. New York: Viking, 1964. Joyce, James. *"A Portrait of the Artist as a Young Man": Text, Criticism, and Notes*. Ed. Chester G. Anderson. New York: Viking, 1968.

SH   Joyce, James. *Stephen Hero*. Ed. John J. Slocum and Herbert Cahoon. New York: New Directions, 1963.

SL   Joyce, James. *Selected Letters of James Joyce*. Ed. Richard Ellmann. New York: Viking, 1975.

U   Joyce, James. *Ulysses: A Critical and Synoptic Edition*. Ed. Hans Walter Gabler with Wolfhard Steppe and Claus Melchior. 3 vols. New York: Garland, 1986.

Joyce, James. *Ulysses: The Corrected Text*. Ed. Hans
Walter Gabler with Wolfhard Steppe and Claus
Melchior. New York: Random; London: Bodley
Head; Harmondsworth: Penguin, 1986

Passages from *Ulysses*, following its editor's suggestion, are identified by episode and line number. Sections of *Finnegans Wake* are
identified by book (roman numeral) and chapter (arabic), as in
"II.4." Quotations from the *Wake* are identified by page and line
number – "313.21–35" – except that lines in footnotes in II.2 are
numbered separately. Thus, "*FW* 279fn.21" designates the
twenty-first line of footnoted material on page 279 of *Finnegans
Wake*. *The James Joyce Archive* and the *Letters of James Joyce* are
cited by volume and page number.

These conventions follow, with minor exceptions, the format
prescribed by the *James Joyce Quarterly*.

Editors' introduction

To introduce is, in part, to contextualize, and what follows is the context of *Joyce in Context*. A collection of new essays developed from the academic program of the 1989 James Joyce Conference in Philadelphia, this book marks a particular point in the history of Joyce studies and represents some of the best current work in this large and vigorous field. As the international Joyce community has continued to grow, the annual Bloomsday conferences and symposia have increased in scale and comprehensiveness and acquired new importance as catalysts for scholarly exchange. The 1989 conference drew over four hundred scholars to Philadelphia; 141 Joyceans from around the world made, officially, 181 presentations. Each of the sixteen essays in this volume traces its origin to one of these contributions to the program: to a panel, paper session, or workshop, and in one case to the keynote address. Since its original presentation in Philadelphia, each has been extensively revised in accordance with the editors' suggestions and with the author's own sense of its relation to its ideal form.

In giving shape to a collection of essays chosen for individual merit rather than for adherence to any a priori theme, we have sought a rationale that is sensitive to contemporary critical currents and flexible enough to accommodate the rich diversity of Joyce criticism in the 1990s. Reading the many submissions for this volume, we saw how frequently the essays, and especially the best of them, could be described as contextual studies, situating Joyce's work in relation to a cultural field, a related discipline, a contemporary writer, or some other "text." As criticism has moved its emphasis from the hermetic study of individual works to a broader conception of what a "text" is, and to the poststructuralist notion of "intertextuality," much critical interest now centers on the way in which the "literary" text is derived from, reflects, responds to, is

illuminated or even exposed by, or interacts "with" other texts,
those "con-texts" – autobiographical, historical, social, psychological, ideological, literary – in which they are historicized or situated.
The table of contents of *Joyce in Context* offers one possible metastruc-
ture for Joyce studies, identifying four approaches – four general but
by no means exhaustive "contexts" – through which our contributors, and students of Joyce generally, are now investigating Joyce's
work. "The Modernist Context" situates Joyce within a literary and
historical period; "The Context of the Other" considers him from
the perspective of those on the social margins; "ConTexts for Joyce"
places him in relation to particular literary, cultural, or theoretical
"texts"; and "Joyce in His Own Context" considers the individual
work as part of the entire body of Joyce's work, "the Joycean Text."
Among the contributors to *Joyce in Context*, readers will find the
international flavor characteristic of Joyce studies today as well as a
balance between established scholars offering a link to critical tradition and emerging Joyceans bringing new insights and perspectives.

After a brief essay by conference director Timothy Martin, com-
memorating the 1989 conference itself, the first group of essays, in
"The Modernist Context," pursues from new perspectives the
enduring interest in Joyce's place alongside his contemporaries.
Denis Donoghue opens the volume, as he did the conference, with
his provocative keynote address "Is There a Case against *Ulysses*?"
Donoghue examines in detail two recent attacks on *Ulysses*: Fredric
Jameson's allegation, seen in the context of a long-standing Marxist
case against the major modernist works, that *Ulysses* represents "a
retreat to privacy, a refusal of history, a blatant privileging of
subjectivity"; and Leo Bersani's contention that *Ulysses* isn't the
challenging, subversive, avant-gardist work that it pretends to be.
Both attacks allege in Joyce a "philosophic idealism" and "a conservative ideology of the self." Drawing on the work of Saussure,
Derrida, and Levinas, and particularly on Deleuze and Guattari's
notion of "the social character of enunciation" and on Emile Benveniste's idea of the "middle voice," Donoghue examines the
"Eumaeus" episode of *Ulysses*. He argues that Joyce's free indirect
discourse consists not of individualized speech acts but of "secondary gestures" ruled by a "posited collectivity." Such discourse may
not be accused of sustaining a politics of inwardness and retreat from
social and historical conditions. "Eumaeus," Donoghue writes,
"makes much of the fact that individuality need not be construed as

inaugural, but as issuing from an assemblage of possibilities embodied in a language." In "Woolf and Joyce: Reading and Re/Vision," Johanna X. K. Garvey takes up the question of Woolf's own case against Joyce and offers a corrective to the widespread critical acceptance of Woolf's supposedly negative responses to *Ulysses*. Using feminist methodology and drawing on Woolf's *Ulysses* notebook, on unpublished drafts of *Jacob's Room*, and on *Jacob's Room* itself, Garvey discusses not only Woolf's developing appreciation of the innovations of Joyce's novel but also Woolf's response to elements in it that she as a woman writer judged more negatively. Vincent J. Cheng encourages further dialogue about a long-neglected topic by initiating critical investigation into the relationship between "Joyce and Ford Madox Ford," two close friends and important modernist writers living and working in Paris. Based on research into letters and memoirs by the two authors and their many mutual friends, this is a study of a neglected literary friendship, within the context of an important moment in literary history (Paris in the Twenties), focusing particularly on Ford's role as the "godfather" (as Joyce himself called him) of *Finnegans Wake*. Brian W. Shaffer's "Joyce and Freud: Discontent and Its Civilizations" rereads Joyce's texts in dialogue with the work of another great modernist, situating Joyce's Irish characters within the context of late Freudian and Frankfurt School ideas – from *The Future of an Illusion* and *Civilization and Its Discontents* – that link narcissism, civilization, and the social determination of subjectivity. Focusing on two of Joyce's characters, Little Chandler and Gerty MacDowell, Shaffer shows how Freud's later work offers an intriguing new perspective on Irish "paralysis": specifically, that a culturally encouraged narcissism keeps these characters from comprehending, much less altering, the inequalities they face with respect to wealth, power, and social opportunity. Through the mechanism Freud has termed the "narcissism of minor differences," each of Joyce's characters mentally rewrites his or her own life, with the aid of forms provided by popular literature and culture, in order to obscure an otherwise unbearable reality.

The essays in the second grouping, "The Context of the Other: Joyce on the Margins," reflect some of the most innovative and exciting recent work in critical studies, the investigation into the nature of marginality, exclusion, and authority. This area of interest combines issues of gender, ethnicity, culture, race, nationality,

colonialism, subjectivity, and psychoanalysis. As one of the writers
most consciously aware of the complex interdynamics of marginality
and exclusion, Joyce offers a promising site for such investigation.
Colleen R. Lamos opens this section with "Cheating on the Father:
Joyce and Gender Justice in *Ulysses*." Drawing on recent French
feminist, deconstructive, and psychoanalytic theory (in particular,
on Lacan, Kristeva, Lyotard, and Derrida), Lamos argues that
Molly's monologue in "Penelope" represents Joyce's attempt to
evade the law of the father by forging the signature of the mother.
According to Lamos, Joyce appropriates a "feminine" pre-symbolic
in order to attack the father, but, like the masochist, he does so on
the father's terms. The forgery of Molly's "countersignature" to
Ulysses permits Joyce to include her as a sign of the novel's supposed
transcendence of sexual difference. In "Demythologizing Nationalism: Joyce's Dialogized Grail Myth," Theresa O'Connor reads
Ulysses and Irish nationalism within the contexts of Christian and
Celtic fertility myths and of Bakhtin's notion of the "dialogic
imagination." She argues that Joyce has "demythologized" the
monological discourse of Irish cultural nationalism, which in *Ulysses*
is associated with the christianized myth of the Holy Grail, by
confronting it with "its own occulted prototype," a body of (pre-
Christian) Celtic myth that opposes the nationalist myth in preach-
ing a doctrine of regeneration not through blood sacrifice but
through love. The "chalice" of new life in *Ulysses* is the product of a
dialogic oscillation between the Grail and the womb, symbol of
cyclic life. Joyce thus decenters the monologic voice of Irish chauvi-
nism onto the multi-vocal margins: "In the place of dogmatic
nationalism, [Joyce] offers 'plurabilities'; in the place of sacrificial
death, [he] offers a vision of cyclical life." In "Joyce and Michelet:
Why Watch Molly Menstruate?" Bonnie Kime Scott takes up a hint
in *Ulysses* that Joyce read Jules Michelet on "the nature of women"
and rereads the Joycean feminine in light of Michelet's construction
of female nature. Her approach, in this speculative and suggestively
intertextual essay, is to show what Michelet's statements on gender
and his studies in history, including his studies of medieval witches,
have meant to writers like Marguerite Duras, Xavière Gauthier,
and Roland Barthes, towards an understanding of what Michelet
may have meant to Joyce. Scott examines the romantic identification of woman with nature, and she redefines the concept of the male
gaze with the help of Barthes's notion of the Micheletian male as

chambermaid. Molly Bloom, Scott concludes, resists such a specular male construction of the Other; but her reader may be the ultimate voyeuristic Micheletian chambermaid. Finally, Suzette Henke completes this grouping with her essay in revisionary feminism "Re-Visioning Joyce's Masculine Signature." Using the terms, tools, and texts of poststructuralist feminist theory and probing Joyce's various constructions of the feminine (such as Mother, Eve, Virgin, and Whore), Henke suggests how resisting feminist readers can find in Joyce's "masculine signature" something beyond misogyny and patriarchal appropriation.

The third group of essays, "ConTexts for Joyce," presents Joyce literally "with texts," offering original rereadings of Joyce in relation to particular cultural, psychological, literary, and even pictorial texts. The range of particular contexts here extends well beyond those normally considered within the English literary canon, and it attests to the increasing critical interest in a broader conception of the idea of "text." Roy Gottfried, in "'Scrupulous Meanness' Reconsidered: *Dubliners* as Stylistic Parody," extends our image of Joyce as a parodist and mimic of "literary" styles to his earliest fiction. Gottfried reads *Dubliners* in the context of popular Irish letters at the turn of the century; he argues that what Joyce understood as "mean" style was that of the Literary Revival, a style "neither good nor bad." His essay examines the prose of the Revival, including that of Standish O'Grady, Lady Gregory, and William Carleton, in order to identify the features which, for Joyce, would define the "mean" style and from which Joyce would develop the style of his own stories as parodies of popular Irish literature. Garry M. Leonard's "Joyce and Lacan: The Twin Narratives of History and His[$]tory in the 'Nestor' Chapter of *Ulysses*" applies to Joyce's schoolroom episode Lacan's ideas on the relationship between history, subjective identity, and the subject's need to create a fable of his or her own identity – what Leonard calls "His[$]tory" – that necessarily displaces and denies the experiential "reality" beyond the self. "Both narratives," Leonard writes, "operate upon one another like a see-saw of which the subject is the fulcrum: the privileging of one sets in motion the deconstruction of the other." In "Joyce and Homer: Return, Disguise, and Recognition in 'Ithaca,'" Constance V. Tagopoulos refutes the commonplace of Joyce criticism that considers the Homeric parallels in *Ulysses* idiosyncratic, arbitrary, and noninstrumental to the work. Reading

Joyce's "Ithaca" in close comparison to Homer's own "Nostos," she demonstrates the ways in which the Homeric themes of return, disguise, and recognition are embedded, assimilated, and trans- formed – both structurally and linguistically – in Joyce's text. The intertextual "return" of Homer in Joyce, Tagopoulos sug- gests, liberates Homer's terms from their ideological and cultural weight and reactivates meaning for Joyce's own purposes. Finally, in "James Joyce and Cartoons," Dan Schiff documents, with illustrations, Joyce's knowledge of such cartoon and comic strip characters as Ally Sloper and Iky Moses, Mutt and Jeff, Popeye and Olive Oyl, and Mickey and Minnie Mouse, and he discusses their appearance and significance in *Ulysses* and *Finnegans Wake*. Lively and original, this essay by a working cartoonist corrects several earlier misidentifications and assumptions and advances our knowledge of Joyce's well-known affection for popular culture.

The final group of essays, "Re-reading Joyce: Joyce in His Own Context," depends not on intertextual contexts, as in the other groupings, but on an intratextual context; these essays examine aspects of Joyce's own literary signature and consider the Joycean Text within its own parameters. Ian Crump's "Refining Himself out of Existence: The Evolution of Joyce's Aesthetic Theory and the Drafts of *A Portrait*" combines genetic and narratological modes of critical analysis to explore the connection between the development of Joyce's early aesthetic theory and the several versions of *A Portrait of the Artist as a Young Man*. Joyce's troubles with his early auto- biographical efforts, Crump argues, resulted from his difficulties with *style indirect libre* – what Crump identifies as "represented speech and thought" – difficulties which, in turn, were caused by his problem in achieving "aesthetic distance" from the past self who was to become the protagonist of his fiction. Only when Joyce developed "a disinterested interest" in his hero was he able to rely entirely on interior monologue and on represented speech and thought, and thus to complete, in 1914, the novel he had begun a decade before. Next, what are we to make of the tendency in Joyce's prose to drift into catalogue, into a series of items that develops an agenda of its own and threatens to usurp the entire narrative? Fritz Senn's witty "Entering the Lists: Sampling Early Catalogues" sets aside the longer and more obvious lists of *Finnegans Wake* and the later chapters of *Ulysses* in favor of the more subtle but nonetheless

Joycean lists of *Chamber Music, Dubliners, A Portrait,* and the earlier *Ulysses.* Senn trumpets a challenge to other scholars to enter the lists, as did his workshop sessions in Philadelphia, and join him in an exploration of this distinctive feature of Joyce's prose. The first challenger to enlist is Bernard Benstock, who, in "Cataloguing in *Finnegans Wake*: Counting Counties," accounts for some of Joyce's playfully oblique ways of counting and listing, and unearths a tantalizingly incomplete list of the thirty-two Irish counties buried at *FW* 595.10–17. Finally, the collection is rounded out – and itself placed in an entirely new context – by Di Jin's essay "Translating *Ulysses,* East and West." Currently engaged in the task of translating *Ulysses* into Chinese, Jin here discusses German, Danish, French, and Spanish translations of sample passages from *Ulysses* and compares them to his own Chinese translations of the same passages, arguing for large rather than simple equivalence, for the closest approximation in the "target language" of the total effect available to readers in the original. Jin's essay illuminates the context of the non-English reader trying to make sense of Joyce's highly inflected text; it offers new perspectives on the intricacies of Joyce's language; it provides numerous insights into the nature of literary translation itself; and it helps explain why no one has heretofore attempted the Herculean task of translating the century's greatest novel for the world's most populous audience, an audience for which it is still only partially available.

On one level, the effect of *Joyce in Context,* as each essay attempts to elaborate more precisely the historical, ideological, and cultural positions in which Joyce is situated, may be to help put the Irish author in his place, to "localize" him, even sometimes to expose his limitations. However, the heterogeny of approaches to Joyce, in this book as a whole and, in some cases, within individual essays, has the simultaneous effect of placing each critical angle of investigation within a larger context, testifying at once to the durability of more traditional approaches to Joyce criticism as well as to the compelling presence of new ones. Thus, *Joyce in Context* offers not only a contextualized Joyce but also a contextualized and many-faceted Joyce criticism, each methodology informed and conditioned by its fellows. In keeping with the nature of both Joyce studies and Joyce's works themselves, a unitary centralized authority (textual and otherwise) is frequently removed to the margins, to an-other context or other contexts; *Joyce in Context* thus tries to maintain the parallactic,

multi-visioned, pluralistic (and plurabelletristic) Joycean ability to
– in the words of Leopold Bloom – "See ourselves as others see us"
(*U* 8.662). To put Joyce into context, ultimately, is to help locate the
collective position that is uniquely his.

CHAPTER I

The 1989 conference: a retrospect

Timothy Martin

To be a student of James Joyce in the 1990s is to watch the calendar as closely as the bibliographies. Gatherings of Joyce scholars have proliferated much as Joyce scholarship has done, and though the Irish writer remains second to Shakespeare in total entries in the annual *MLA Bibliography*, he outstrips everyone in organized meetings. Workshops in August at the James Joyce Foundation in Zurich, a James Joyce Birthday Conference in February at the University of Miami, the Paris *Colloques* in the spring: each of these annual events takes up a current issue in Joyce studies, applies a development in literary theory to Joyce's work, or focuses on a particular text. Other conferences – on Joyce and Vico in Venice, for example, on the 1984 *Ulysses* in Monaco, and on *Finnegans Wake* at Leeds and at Berkeley – sprout less predictably. The most catholic of these events, the focal point and catalyst for Joyce studies since 1967, has been the Bloomsday meeting, now a week-long event alternating between a European "symposium" and a North American "conference."

If Joyce is the most democratic of writers – he is supposed to have boasted that none of his characters is worth more than one hundred pounds – the Bloomsday meetings are the most democratic of gatherings of Joyceans. By tradition, the call for papers is broadcast widely, and the academic program expands to accommodate the wide variety and large number of substantive proposals elicited. Often conference organizers advertise a theme in advance – "The Languages of Joyce," for example, or "Joyce and the Law" – but any such theme is calculated to inspire rather than to inhibit, and it is quietly – and quite sensibly – set aside whenever a worthy proposal for a panel, individual paper, or workshop does not follow the topic. Space on the program is equally available to the most junior and the most senior of Joyceans, and to the occasional serious

9

amateur as well as to the professional academic. Diverse in subject and critical methodology, responsive rather than prescriptive in its construction, and thoroughly international in its constituency, the academic program offers an excellent cross-section of what is of current interest in Joyce studies.

The year 1989 marked the return of the Bloomsday conference to Philadelphia and to the Curtis Institute of Music, after a memorable meeting there in 1985. In the early years of the European symposium, organizers felt it desirable to convene in Joyce's home cities, where they might trace his footsteps, and this practice persisted through 1982. When this tradition came to be seen as a restriction, the feeling remained that the site should be made to seem "appropriate" in some way. Thus organizers of the Copenhagen symposium in 1986 took pains to point out that Joyce had been there fifty years before, that Scandinavians were the founders of Dublin, and that a Scandinavian writer was one of Joyce's earliest enthusiasms. Organizers of the North American conferences have been harder pressed, but a case for Philadelphia and Curtis can nonetheless be made. A slight pretext is provided by the frequent appearance in *Finnegans Wake* of the plucky song "Off to Philadelphia," which served as a conference motto in 1985; and Curtis itself, it turns out, is a friend of a friend. Joyce's students will remember the writer's association with American composer George Antheil in Paris in the 1920s. In 1930 Antheil set to music Joyce's "Nightpiece," a poem published a few years before in *Pomes Penyeach*, and he dedicated the piece to Mary Louise Curtis Bok, the founder of the Curtis Institute. However, a more direct and more significant connection between James Joyce and Philadelphia is found just a few blocks from Curtis at the Rosenbach Museum and Library: the holograph manuscript of *Ulysses*, purchased by A. S. W. Rosenbach from John Quinn in 1924.

Dedicated to mythologist Joseph Campbell and to bookseller Frances Steloff, the 1989 conference drew some 400 Joyceans to Philadelphia from across the United States, Canada, Europe, and Asia. The conference met not in a university setting but in congenial surroundings in the heart of the city on Rittenhouse Square, a business and residential district surrounding a tree-lined park. Most sessions took place at Curtis, as gracious and elegant a conference host as it had been in 1985. (See the facade of Dan Aykroyd's private club in the film *Trading Places*.) One of the most important conservatories of music in the world, Curtis numbers Leonard Bernstein, Jorge Bolet, Samuel Barber, Anna Moffo, Gian Carlo Menotti, and Ned Rorem among its most distinguished graduates. The Rosenbach hosted a welcome reception, and Assistant Curator Eileen Cahill arranged, with the assistance of David Borodin, an exhibition of books, manuscripts, and other Joyceana. In addition to selected pages of the *Ulysses* manuscript, this included the copy of the first edition of *Ulysses* that Joyce set aside expressly for Dijon printer Maurice Darantiere; first editions of *The Mime of Mick, Nick and the Maggies* and *Storiella as She is Syung*, both with art work of Lucia Joyce; and a 1904 letter, on Hely's stationery, that Joyce wrote James Starkey and signed "Thine purgatively, Stephen Daedalus." Among the guests of the conference was American composer Otto Luening, a former Director of the Columbia–Princeton Electronic Music Center in New York. Mr. Luening knew Joyce during 1918 and 1919 in Zurich, where he divided his time between studying at the Zurich Conservatory of Music, playing flute in the Tonhalle and opera orchestras, and acting with Joyce's English Players. The traditional Bloomsday dinner, for 151 on this occasion, took place in the Lower Egyptian Gallery at the University of Pennsylvania Museum.

The academic program of the 1989 conference, chaired and organized by Michael O'Shea, was nearly twice the size of its 1985 predecessor, with fifty sessions and, officially, 141 presenters. To the tradition of democracy in the Bloomsday meeting, Philadelphia contributed an additional element. With the exception of Denis Donoghue's keynote address, no speeches were singled out for special emphasis; all participants assumed equal positions on the program. In one respect, however, the 1989 conference marked an important departure from tradition: for the first time, participants were asked to focus their efforts on a single formal paper, or, as the call for papers put it, "to read no more than one paper from typescript." Then, instead of preparing a second or a third formal presentation, participants were urged to organize and join less formal and more interactive workshops and discussions, as in the Zurich symposium in 1979. Eventually, twenty sessions were organized in this way, with five or more participants speaking continuously for no more than a few minutes and with a good deal of extemporaneous discussion. A number of essays in this volume would grow out of these workshops and discussions. Our intent in structuring the program as we did was to take better advantage of the opportunities that any scholarly gathering presents: to sharpen the sense of audience, free criticism from isolation, and encourage revision and collegiality. But the ultimate effect was to relieve the pressure that, in the burgeoning Joyce industry, the academic program is beginning to feel. For example, the Venice symposium, one of the largest conferences to date, filled an entire week with five and six concurrent sessions, and many of these attempted to accommodate five or six speakers.

A glance through the official program gives some indication of the subjects that were of particular interest to Joyceans in Philadelphia. Topics like "Joyce and Bakhtin," "Joyce and the Visual Arts," "Joyce and History," and "Joyce and the Moderns" attracted enough presenters to require double sessions. A number of sessions extended discussions begun at other conferences: "Computer-Assisted Joyce Studies," "Advertising in *Ulysses*," "Joycean Parody," "Joyce and Milton." Several sessions assessed Joyce's work in the context of feminist literary theory, and two sessions considered Joyce with the assistance of the poststructuralist notion of "intertextuality." Two workshops were of such general interest and importance that they were allotted two time slots apiece. "A Practical Exercise in Editing *Ulysses*," conducted by Hans Gabler and Claus Melchior, demonstrated the computer program used in creating the 1984 *Ulysses*. Energetic discussion between the presenters and their audience underlined the fact that Joyceans were still struggling to come to terms with the new *Ulysses* five years after its appearance. "Joycean Cataloguing," orchestrated by Fritz Senn, allowed each speaker a few minutes to discuss this feature of Joyce's literary signature before permitting discussion among panelists. One innovation on the program was the Authors Revue, an amicable alternative to the Living Book Review, which focused on the writing of books on Joyce rather than the reading of them. Also of special interest were Denis Donoghue's keynote address, sessions given in memory of John Hannay and in honor of Robert Boyle, and a panel arranged by the James Joyce Society of New York in memory of its "guardian angel" Frances Steloff. One of the most compelling events, and certainly the most moving, was Di Jin's lecture on the challenges of translating *Ulysses* into Chinese, with a reading from "Penelope" by Professor Jin's daughter Jeanette, delivered within days of the massacre of demonstrators in Tiananmen Square.

Special artistic programs are traditional at meetings of Joyceans, and the cultural resources of Philadelphia and generous grant support for the conference made possible an artistic program of breadth and quality. Such events may do more than simply relieve a long day in the conference room; ideally, they help us see Joyce's work afresh. Two of Philadelphia's distinguished musicians, soprano Paula Brown and pianist Andrew Willis, gave us a concert of musical allusions in Joyce. Ms. Brown's performance of Dido's Lament from *Dido and Aeneas* persuaded us of the perfect suitability of that aria for the last few lines of *Finnegans Wake*, and her rendition of "I Dreamt that I Dwelt in Marble Halls" showed us by how much poor Maria's "tiny quavering voice" (*D* 106) must have missed the mark. Maria's host praises the music, the composer, and the "old times," but he has nothing to say for the performer. Various sorts of "musicality" have been claimed for Joyce's prose, and readings by Irish actress Sorcha Cusack and Philadelphian Michael Toner showed the sensitivity to tone and rhythm that makes the Irish writer's work as satisfying to hear as that of any prose stylist. Ms. Cusack, whose father's recordings of passages from *Finnegans Wake* are widely known, read "Eveline" and excerpts from "Nausicaa" and from Anna Livia's final monologue. Mr. Toner read the Prank-quean's tale as well as excerpts from the first sermon on hell in *A Portrait* and from "Cyclops."

Twentieth-century writers have found Joyce's legacy almost over-whelming, and many have complained of the difficulty of writing in his wake. After Joyce, what remains to be done? But if writers of fiction have sometimes found Joyce's achievement suffocating, painters, composers, and even dancers and filmmakers have found it liberating. Not least among the artists who, without anxiety, take Joyce as a precursor is DeLoss McGraw, who created, especially for the conference, several dozen paintings in collage and gouache on themes inspired by "Cyclops" and "Nausicaa." Shown at the Gian-netta Gallery and reproduced in the official conference program and poster, McGraw's paintings captured Joyce's exuberance and allusiveness and evoked his heterogeneity of styles. Relâche, Phil-adelphia's ensemble for contemporary music, presented a program of music inspired by Joyce, featuring work by John Cage, John Buller, Vincent Persichetti, and Teijo Ito. Dancer and choreogra-pher Jean Erdman discussed her adaptation of *Finnegans Wake* in the Obie-winning *Coach with the Six Insides*. (*Ulysses*, she told us parenthetically, was Joseph Campbell's favorite, not *Finnegans Wake*.) In a letter to *James Joyce Quarterly* published shortly before the conference, Stephen Joyce, whose affection for his grandfather's earlier work is well known, suggested that a profitable use of a Joycean's time might be to arrange a roundtable discussion on the meeting between "two giants, John Huston and James Joyce." An approximation of such a discussion took place in Philadelphia, when screenwriter Tony Huston hosted a screening of *The Dead* and discussed the making of the film as what he called the Huston family's "valentine" to Ireland. Taking forty-five minutes of surprisingly tactful questions, Huston explained some of the liberties the film medium required the makers of *The Dead* to take: the relocation of the story of Patrick Morkan, the elimination of Gabriel's glasses, the curing of Bartell d'Arcy's cold. Collectively, these varied responses to Joyce's achievement may suggest that the anxiety of influence dissipates when it crosses disciplinary lines.

The Philadelphia conference was the beneficiary of a high degree of support by both individual and corporate members of the community. The conference earned competitive grants from three public bodies, all in the context of significant budget restrictions: the Pennsylvania Humanities Council (our major supporter), the Pennsylvania Council on the Arts, and the Fund for Philadelphia. Faculty from a number of the many colleges and universities in the area served, informally, on the conference Host Committee, and many Philadelphians outside the academic community registered for the conference and attended sessions. A remarkable degree and variety of media coverage reflected this general public interest. Di Jin, interviewed on National Public Radio's "Performance Today," discussed the history of Joyce's official reputation in China and some of the complexities of rendering *Ulysses* in Chinese. Jin illustrated the sort of difficulties he has encountered and overcome by discussing his attempt to evoke the black Mass in his translation of "Circe" and his efforts to capture the subtleties of Molly's final "Yes." Marti Moss-Coane of WHYY, one of Philadelphia's NPR affiliates, talked with Jean Erdman about the relationship between *The Coach with the Six Insides* and *Finnegans Wake* and about the founding of the Theatre of the Open Eye by Ms. Erdman and Joseph Campbell in 1972. In acknowledgment of Bloomsday and of the conference, WHYY also broadcast a brief reading by Michael Toner from the Robert Emmet section of "Cyclops." The *Philadelphia Inquirer* ran a feature story with photographs, Radio Israel interviewed Hans Gabler, and New York's WBAI, known for its battles with the FCC over broadcast readings from *Ulysses*, conducted a twenty-minute retrospective.

There is a certain risk in public exposure, and in his opening remarks on June 12, Michael O'Shea reminded us of the coverage the 1985 conference had received in *Philadelphia* magazine. A writer for this organ of yuppie Philadelphia had dropped by the welcome reception at the Rosenbach and shared a pitcher of Guinness at the Irish Pub. Most of us had left town by the time her article came out in the September issue, but those who remained found their colleagues and themselves reduced to the stereotypes of academe, to "Foremost Authorities" and "Young Lions," and satirized for indifferent grooming and poor table manners, and for dropping names and crushing them underfoot. The *Inquirer*, in 1985, even got a few indignant letters. One came from a movie-lover nursing an old grievance: years before, he had been "duped" by the title of Joseph Strick's *Ulysses* into expecting "a pleasant story about the renowned Greek hero and explorer." But, this writer and his wife discovered, "It was nothing but literary filth and [the] lewdness of modern-day people. We couldn't get the connection and felt betrayed." Another, protesting Joyce's continued "glorification" by such events as the conference then in the news, offered the public a colorful history of a man who had been kicked out of Belvedere College for "vulgarity and scandalous behavior," whose alleged masterpiece was recently exposed as containing 5,000 errors, and whose body was exhumed from its grave in Zurich and transported to "a newly Christened James Joyce Park adjacent to Trinity College." There is some evidence, however, that after two major conferences Philadelphians have begun to take us in stride, perhaps even to absorb us into their culture. In seeking sites for conference meetings and planning special events, I encountered only one person who, on principle, wanted nothing to do with Joyce, and just one other who, on principle, wanted nothing to do with Joyceans. Indeed, David Iams of the *Inquirer* dropped by the Bloomsday Dinner, and a few days later several Joyceans, for the first and possibly the last time of their careers, appeared in the Society column of a great metropolitan newspaper. Rearriving in Philadelphia in 1989, Joyce and Joyceans were warmly received.

The principle of democracy in the Bloomsday conference, in the context of a vigorous and growing community of Joyce scholars, presents a considerable challenge to its organizers. But it creates a windfall for the editors of a collection, who may offer their readers not only what is current and representative in Joyce criticism but also what is exemplary. What follows represents the best of what Joyceans were talking about in 1989.

PART I

The modernist context

CHAPTER 2

Is there a case against Ulysses?

Denis Donoghue

This exists that isits after having been said we know.

FW 186.8–9

So far as I can judge, Joyce's reputation is as high as it ever was: he seems to have been exempted from the various attacks directed upon other masters of Modernism, notably Eliot, Pound, and Yeats. No one doubts that *Dubliners, A Portrait of the Artist as a Young Man*, and *Ulysses* constitute a major achievement. *Exiles* is not much admired: only one critic known to me, Stanley Kauffmann, thinks it a superb play. *Finnegans Wake* hasn't broken out of the seminar room: it is studied rather than read. But those who study it give every sign of enjoying it. Perhaps we can agree on so much. But during the past few years a number of readers whom one might have expected to think well of *Ulysses* have been speaking harshly of it. It is always a matter of interest, and sometimes of concern, when a critic one admires turns against a book one loves. So I propose to consider two such turnings, and to see whether or not they are justified.

I first came across Fredric Jameson's reflections on *Ulysses* in an essay, "Wyndham Lewis as Futurist," which he published in the *Hudson Review* in July 1973. It was surprising to find a Marxist critic praising Wyndham Lewis's novels, but it soon emerged that for Jameson the great merit of *The Apes of God, Tarr, The Wild Body, The Childermass*, and *The Revenge for Love* consisted in their antithetical relation to the particular version of Modernism which Jameson associated with Joyce and Eliot. That version, as Jameson described it in the first chapter of his book on Wyndham Lewis, *Fables of Aggression* (1979), amounted to an impressionistic aesthetic. "The most influential formal impulses of canonical modernism," Jameson wrote, "have been strategies of inwardness, which set out to reappropriate an alienated universe by transforming it into personal

19

styles and private languages." Such "wills to style," he said, "recon-
firm the very privatization and fragmentation of social life against
which they meant to protest" (2). Lewis's novels, on the contrary,
refuse to engage in the impressionism of "style," and direct the
enormous energy of their satire against the inwardness which Lewis
sees as a pathetic surrender to mere conditions. Eliot's J. Alfred
Prufrock and the Stephen of Joyce's *Portrait* deal with their alienated
environments by deriving from them certain private gestures and
intimations; of self-disgust or *hubris*, it hardly matters which.

It could be said that Jameson's attack on Eliot and Joyce, his
repudiation of the strategies of inwardness to be found in their early
writings, is merely the latest in a long-established Marxist attack on
the major works of Modernism; attacks of which Lukács's was the
chief example. The gist of the Marxist case has always been that the
major works of Modernism represent a retreat to privacy, a refusal of
history, a blatant privileging of subjectivity. When Marxist critics
refer to solipsism and inwardness, we know how predictably the rest
of the argument will follow. But Jameson differs from his Marxist
colleagues in one respect. He finds in a notoriously right-wing,
indeed Fascist artist the qualities he admires: a deliberate discrepancy of tone between Lewis's sentences and the human reality they
advert to, a Cubist insistence on the friction of lines and forms, visual
rather than oral analogies, recourse to metonymy rather than to
metaphor, the separation of subject from object in rigorously maintained hostility, and the notion of characters as mere functions of
their situation, the *gestalt* coming first. I assume that Jameson
proposes to use these qualities in Lewis against opposite qualities in
Joyce and Eliot and then, in a second phase of his programme, to
appropriate the favored qualities for a politics of the Left. I take it
that this is what is attempted in his later book, *The Political
Unconscious*.

In the essay on Lewis, Jameson quotes a passage from the "Circe"
chapter of *Ulysses* to show that the details, while they may appear to
be as external as any in Lewis's novels, are "unified by the stylistic
tone in which all contradictions are ironically resolved as well as by
the overall unity of Mr. Bloom's personality" ("Lewis as Futurist"
318). Where Lewis composes by phrase, each phrase jarring upon
the next one to such an extent that the phrases are never subdued by
the sentence, Joyce composes by tone and allows every discrepancy
to be resolved within the mind that suffers it. Joyce, according to

Jameson, keeps faith with the illusions of subjectivity; and meanwhile the social conditions at large are free to remain unchanged. In a later essay called "*Ulysses* in History," Jameson develops these points into a full-scale attack not only on that novel but on the entire tradition of Symbolism in which, allegedly, it is implicated. He starts by referring to "the modern" or "modernity" as involving a crisis, "something like a dissociation between meaning and existence" (128). His authority, for the moment, is Roland Barthes, whom he quotes on "the great mythic opposition between the *vécu* [the "lived experience"] and the intelligible" (129). Jameson extends the alleged opposition between what exists and what means into an attack on symbolism: it involves, he says, "the illicit transformation of existing things into so many visible or tangible meanings" (129). He means that if Nature has now been trans- ⌐ formed into Culture, and if cultural artifacts and events are still felt as meaningless, then it is monstrous that we should try to take the harm out of this situation by endowing any of these artifacts or events with a halo of significance.

This argument of Jameson's may remind you of another version of it, in Paul de Man's *Blindness and Insight*, in which de Man refers to "the contradictory relations between natural being and the being of consciousness." Romanticism is the phase or mode of literature in which writers seek either to resolve the contradiction or to persuade us to reside in it. The romantic symbol has long been understood as sign of a possible reconciliation between man and nature, the being of consciousness and natural being. Wordsworth's "spots of time" are moments in which the burden of consciousness seems to be lifted. Now de Man has an interest in showing that these moments of apparent harmony are delusions, and that the most honorable figure of thought is not symbol but allegory; because allegory testifies to the gap between experience and meaning:

Whereas the symbol postulates the possibility of an identity or identification, allegory designates primarily a distance in relation to its own origin, and, renouncing the nostalgia and the desire to coincide, it establishes its language in the void of this temporal difference. In so doing, it prevents the self from an illusory identification with the non-self, which is now fully, though painfully, recognized as a non-self. (207)

The upshot of Jameson's argument is that we should read *Ulysses* differently; not taking pleasure in the chapters of abundant human interest or those of lived experience which seems rich enough to

remove from the agenda the question of its meaning: that is not it at
all. We are to read the chapters which Jameson regards as the two
most boring in the book, "Eumaeus" and "Ithaca," on the assumption that Joyce means us to register, in those chapters, everything in
the world that is finally stifling to us. "Eumaeus" is to be our text for
"the problematic of the centred subject, of the closed monad, of the
isolated or privatised subjectivity" (*"Ulysses* in History" 139).
"Ithaca" is to be our text for the reified object, "a form of discourse
from which the subject ... is radically excluded" (139). Jameson
says of this chapter:

> And if it is observed that even this seemingly sterilised alternation of
> question and answer turns increasingly, towards the end of the chapter,
> around Mr Bloom's private thoughts and fantasies, in other words, around
> the subjective rather than the objective, then I will reply by noting the
> degree to which those fantasies ... are henceforth inextricably bound up
> with objects, in the best consumer society tradition. These are falsely
> subjective fantasies: here, in reality, commodities are dreaming about
> themselves through us. (*"Ulysses* in History" 139)

II

I propose to remove Jameson's argument and place it for the
moment, like Leopold Bloom's saucepan, on the left hob while I look
at another objection to *Ulysses*, this one by Leo Bersani. Not a
Marxist, so far as I know, Bersani's sense of the book isn't entirely
different from Jameson's.

The basic argument is that *Ulysses* isn't what it pretends or claims
to be, a challenging, subversive work of Modernism. On the contrary, Bersani says, it is a nineteenth-century realistic novel of
character and personality; it is predicated upon a "conservative
ideology of the self" (29). Nothing in the book undermines Joyce's
claim that in his mind, at least, not only has nature become culture
but culture has become man. "Joyce is faithful to our humanist
tradition," Bersani says, "in his reenactment of its assumptions and
promise that the possession of culture will transcend anxiety and
perhaps even redeem history" (32). Joyce "gives us back our culture
as *his* culture" (31). Ultimately, *Ulysses* domesticates the forces with
which it deals, and shows us the form a serene possession of cultural
acquisitions would take.

The book is not, then, according to Bersani, a great *avant-garde* work. The contrast is made between Joyce and Beckett; though Bersani also glances at other writers whom he regards as genuinely *avant-garde*, notably Lawrence and Bataille:

Sociability in Joyce is a function of realistically portrayed characters, and not, as in Beckett, the fascinatingly anachronistic remnant of the disappearance of such characters. Beckett's authentic avant-gardism consists in a break not only with the myths fostered by cultural discourse, but more radically, with cultural discourse itself. The mystery of his work is how it is not only sustained but even begun, for intertextuality in Beckett (the echoes of Descartes and of Malebranche in the early works, for example) is not a principle of cultural continuity (as it is in Joyce, in spite of the parodic nature of the repetitions), but the occasion for a kind of psychotic raving ... [In Joyce] the parodistic replays of Homer, Shakespeare, and Flaubert – not to speak of all the authors "quoted" in "Oxen of the Sun" – are neither subversive of nor indifferent to the fact of cultural inheritance; rather, Joyce relocates the items of that inheritance with *Ulysses* as both their center and belated origin. (20–1)

III

Jameson and Bersani agree in repudiating Joyce's subjectivity and the conservative ideology of the self which it apparently entails. They find it a scandal that Joyce gives Bloom, Stephen, Molly, Gerty, and every other important character in the book – except, notably, Buck Mulligan – virtually unrestricted access to their inner lives. It doesn't matter that the materials of those lives are often trivial, banal, and derivative. My own view is that any constituents of one's inner life are good enough if they enable one to fend off the external conditions. Gerty's musings are not at all invalidated by the fact that they are not as fine as Isabel Archer's; they serve much the same purpose, at a lower level of pressure and intensity. It would be monstrous to deny to Gerty, or to anyone else, the consolation of an inner life. Marxists have never been able to avoid the snobbery of thinking that their soliloquies are fine but that mine are sordid functions of late capitalism. But surely Levinas is right and just to say, as he does in *Totality and Infinity*, that "the inner life is the unique *way* for the real to exist as a plurality" (58), and again that "interiority is the very possibility of a birth and a death that do not derive their meaning from history" (55). Interiority "institutes an order different from historical time in which totality is constituted, an order where everything is *pending*, where what is no longer possible

historically remains always possible" (55). I assume that the
capacity by which what is no longer possible historically remains
always possible is what we call the human imagination.

The second form of snobbery that Jameson shows is his assumption that wherever in modern literature we see two characters failing
to achieve full communication, it is because each is a closed monad,
a victim of privative subjectivity. The superior alternative to this
condition, apparently, is that of being an undifferentiated part of a
collectivity. But again Levinas is right and just to say, as he does in
an essay on Proust, that the collectivity must not be sought as a
fusion:

> One begins with the idea that duality must be transformed into unity, and
> that social relations must culminate in communion. This is the last vestige
> of a conception that identifies being with knowledge, that is, with the event
> through which the multiplicity of reality ends up referring to a single being
> and where, through the miracle of clarity, everything that encounters me
> exists as coming from me. It is the last vestige of idealism. ("The Other in
> Proust" 164)

Proust's most profound vision, on the contrary, "consists in situating
reality in a relation with something which for ever remains other,
with the Other as absence and mystery, in rediscovering this relation
in the very intimacy of the 'I'" (165).

IV

The obvious chapter to think of in this context is "Eumaeus,"
especially as Jameson and Bersani have reflected sadly upon it, but I
propose to postpone saying anything about it till I have considered
the question of individuation; or rather, the status we give to
particular acts of speech.

Suppose we start with Saussure's concept of language as a set of
relations, indefinitely large indeed, between *langue* and *parole*; that is,
between the body of a language as it exists and is available at this
moment and the particular acts of speech which one chooses and
performs within the limits of the language as a whole. One of the
problems entailed in Saussure's system is that it inevitably sets up
oppositions where, in the common practice of speech, no such
oppositions are felt. I mean the oppositions that arise from the
differentiation of *langue* and *parole*; constraint and freedom, the

unconscious and the conscious, absence and presence, passivity and activity. It is possible, but invidious, to emphasize one of these forces at the expense of the other. In Saussure's linguistics every act of speech is made to appear an intervention, and the speaker is required to justify it. Claims are vested in the speaker which amount to claims of autonomy. But suppose one were to ground a linguistics not upon the speech acts of *parole* but upon a more inclusive consideration of *langue*; of language before – or as if before – any differentiations or dualities. Something like this is sketched in a chapter of *A Thousand Plateaus* by Gilles Deleuze and Félix Guattari:

If language always seems to presuppose itself, if we cannot assign it a nonlinguistic point of departure, it is because language does not operate between something seen (or felt) and something said, but always goes from saying to saying. We believe that narrative consists not in communicating what one has seen but in transmitting what one has heard, what someone else said to you. Hearsay. It does not even suffice to invoke a vision distorted by passion. The "first" language, or rather the first determination of language, is not the trope or metaphor but *indirect discourse*. The importance some have accorded metaphor and metonymy proves disastrous for the study of language. Metaphors and metonymies are merely effects; they are a part of language only when they presuppose indirect discourse. (76–7)

Another passage will make the position clearer:

The social character of enunciation is intrinsically founded only if one succeeds in demonstrating how enunciation in itself implies *collective assemblages*. It then becomes clear that the statement is individuated, and enunciation subjectified, only to the extent that an impersonal collective assemblage requires it and determines it to be so. It is for this reason that indirect discourse, *especially "free" indirect discourse*, is of exemplary value: there are no clear, distinctive contours; what comes first is not an insertion of variously individuated statements, or an interlocking of different subjects of enunciation, but a collective assemblage resulting in the determination of relative subjectification proceedings, or assignations of individuality and their shifting distributions within discourse. (80)

If this collective assemblage were merely notional, it would be of little significance. It is not enough to call it *langue*, in Saussure's term. The merit of the emphasis, in *A Thousand Plateaus*, on the collective assemblage is that it is also given a founding form of articulation, that of free indirect discourse. Every speech act thereafter can be understood as a concession or a determination, something

permitted by the collective assemblage, called forth under its jurisdiction. A speech act, if understood in this way, would not be
required to account for itself as if it were an intervention, an act of
will, performed upon its own authority, or upon an authority that
could only be located in the individual self. It would be seen as
operating under the jurisdiction of the collective assemblage. Nor
would the assemblage be open to the charge which we have seen
Levinas directing against any collectivity that is sought as a fusion; if
only because the linguistic assemblage does not identify being with
knowledge but with lore, repetition, what Deleuze and Guattari call
hearsay.

V

You may be recalling at this point that in *Joyce's Voices* Hugh
Kenner made much of the free indirect style and called it the Uncle
Charles Principle on the strength of several sentences including this
one –

Every morning, therefore, uncle Charles repaired to his outhouse but not
before he had creased and brushed scrupulously his back hair and brushed
and put on his tall hat. (*P* 60)

– an example, according to Kenner, of something apparently new in
fiction, "the normally neutral narrative vocabulary pervaded by a
little cloud of idioms which a character might use if he were
managing the narrative" (17). That is a way of putting it, but I'm
not sure that any vocabulary is ever neutral. A vocabulary is like
poetic diction, inasmuch as it issues from a choice, however unasser-
tive the choice may be.

I'm not claiming that Kenner is wrong about the Uncle Charles
Principle, but that his description of it is incomplete. For instance: it
requires him to posit an Uncle Charles sufficiently separable from
the action to be capable of describing it; as if to say, "I repaired to
the outhouse every morning, but not before ... " As the consider-
ations I have in mind will be useful to us when we come to
"Eumaeus," I'll look at them now. The specification needed, to
make Kenner's account of the Uncle Charles Principle satisfactory,
is that of the voice not in Joyce but in grammar.

In grammar, voice denotes the form of a verb by which the
relation of the subject to the action implied is indicated. Gram-

marians distinguish three voices, active, passive, and middle. In
1950 Emile Benveniste published an essay on this matter which has
exerted immense influence on linguists, philosophers, and critics.
Briefly, the distinction between the three voices is that in the passive,
the subject is affected by the action of someone else. "I was kicked by
John." In the active, as Benveniste says, "the verbs denote a process
that is accomplished outside the subject." In the middle voice, "the
verb indicates a process centering in the subject, the subject being
inside the process" (148). The classical distinction between the
active and the middle voices is given in the verb *to sacrifice*. The verb
is in the active voice if the priest sacrifices the victim on my behalf.
He offers the sacrifice but he is not affected by it. But the verb is in
the middle voice if I seize the knife and make the sacrifice for myself.
In "To Write: An Intransitive Verb?" Roland Barthes took up
Benveniste's account of the three voices, and of the process by which
transitivity becomes a necessary product of the conversion from
middle to active voice. As Benveniste explained it: "Thus, starting
from the middle, actives are formed that are called transitives, or
causatives, or factitives, and which are always characterized by the
fact that the subject, placed outside the process, governs it
thenceforth as agent, and that the process, instead of having the
subject for its seat, must take an object as its goal" (149). Barthes
uses these distinctions to say that "it is subjective writings, like
romantic writing, which are active, because in them the agent is not
interior but *anterior* to the process of writing" (143). The one who
writes, in such a case, "does not write for himself, but, as if by proxy,
for a person who is exterior and antecedent (even if they both have
the same name)" (143). Barthes also uses the distinction to claim
that a certain kind of writing, modern indeed, is an instance of the
middle voice, in the sense that the distance between the writer and
the language is notably diminished. "[T]he subject is immediately
contemporary with the writing, being effected and affected by it.
The case of the Proustian narrator is exemplary: he exists only in
writing" (143).

Barthes took romantic writing as his example of the active voice,
but it applies just as well to realism. In a realistic novel, the novelist
tries to make the reader feel that the characters exist outside the
fiction and have existed prior to it; such that the novel merely
transcribes their anterior lives. This is the aspect of *Ulysses* that
Jameson and Bersani alike resent, the sense that Bloom, Stephen,

and Molly exist and may be liked or disliked. Jameson and Bersani resent this impression, because it endorses what Bersani calls a conservative ideology of the self, and it asks the reader – a request Jameson especially rejects – to take an interest in extremely commonplace events, such as Bloom's boiling the kettle.

The sentence about Uncle Charles now calls for a somewhat different description. In that sentence, and in the sentences that follow it, Joyce is effecting a disjunction between grammar and diction. The grammar is that of the active voice, we are encouraged to believe that Uncle Charles has lived before going to the outhouse, and that his going to the outhouse merely confirms his prior existence, just as the manner of his going enhances it. But the diction the sentence and its neighboring sentences use is such that if Uncle Charles were to exist, he would exist chiefly, perhaps solely, through such words as these: repaired; salubrious; mollifying; arbour. According to the grammar, the action of going to the outhouse is accomplished outside the subject who goes there; according to the diction and the rhetoric of the middle voice, the subject is contemporary with the enunciation, and lasts while the enunciation lasts.

VI

In 1968, Jacques Derrida resorted to Benveniste's account of the middle voice to say what he had in mind by *différance*. It is neither a word nor a concept, he said:

Différance is not simply active (any more than it is a subjective accomplishment); it rather indicates the middle voice, it precedes and sets up the opposition between passivity and activity. With its *a, différance* more properly refers to what in classical language would be called the origin or production of differences and the differences between differences, the *play* [*jeu*] of differences. (130)

A few pages later:

Here in the usage of our language we must consider that the ending -*ance* is undecided between active and passive. And we shall see why what is designated by "*différance*" is neither simply active nor simply passive, that it announces or rather recalls something like the middle voice, that it speaks of an operation which is not an operation, which cannot be thought of either as a passion or as an action of a subject upon an object, as starting from an agent or from a patient, or on the basis of, or in view of, any of these *terms*. But philosophy has perhaps commenced by distributing the middle voice, expressing a certain intransitiveness, into the active and the passive voice, and has itself been constituted in this repression. (137)

It would be misleading – though I feel tempted – to bring Derrida's notion of *différance* close to Deleuze and Guattari's idea of free indirect discourse as the ground of language. *Différance* is that which precedes differentiation and makes it possible. Let us suppose, with Derrida, that *différance* is then suppressed and its force distributed, in consideration of simplicity, into active and passive voices, a strategic simplification. From that mythic day to now, the use of these simple oppositions and polarities has been punished; with bad faith in those who use them, and categorical inadequacy in the opposing vehicles themselves. Derrida regards the history of metaphysics as the story of that bad faith, that incapacity. It is not my business to agree or disagree with him. But consider, in the light or shadow of his *différance*, Deleuze and Guattari's notion of the social character of enunciation, enunciation as collective assemblage, and free indirect discourse as founding mode of utterance. Add to earlier quotations this sentence from *A Thousand Plateaus*:

Indirect discourse is not explained by the distinction between subjects; rather, it is the assemblage, as it freely appears in this discourse, that explains all the voices present within a single voice. (80)

And this one:

My direct discourse is still the free indirect discourse running through me, coming from other worlds or other planets. That is why so many artists and writers have been tempted by the séance table. (84)

Of course the crucial difference between *différance* and free indirect discourse is that the first has been suppressed, the second hasn't. As we'll see in "Eumaeus," free indirect discourse is acknowledged on virtually every page. But the reference to the séance table is enough to alert us to the fact that literary criticism, hermeneutics, and critical theory have not been pursued on the basis of free indirect discourse as foundation; but on the basis of individual speech acts as the objects of study.

What difference does it make? Chiefly this: Jameson's attack on ⌄ certain speech acts – Prufrock, Stephen Dedalus, let's say – makes sense only if acts of that kind are deemed to sustain a corresponding politics, and to be answerable for doing so. Such acts are exemplary only if they are claimed to be – or accused of being – inaugural and therefore privileged. But suppose they are merely concessions, secondary gestures permitted by "the social character of enunciation" and subject to its jurisdiction: then they should attract to themselves a far more temperate commentary. By a temperate commentary I mean the uninvidious tone of, say, Bakhtin on dialogism or Auerbach on "mixture of styles."

VII

If there is a case against *Ulysses*, the main evidence for it must be "Eumaeus," a chapter commonly claimed to be the most boring part of the book, its sole contender the nearby "Ithaca." That the chapter is a plethora of clichés is the substance of common report. In mitigation, it is sometimes mentioned that Bloom is stunned by the events of the evening and, worse still, by a certain event presumed to have taken place at Eccles Street in the afternoon; and that Stephen is sunk in drink and exhaustion.

Notwithstanding its relation, such as it is, to a certain episode in the *Odyssey*, "Eumaeus" is first and last the story of the Good Samaritan, as we are told, preparatory to anything else, in the first sentence. Stephen, much fallen among thieves, is rescued by Bloom, a practical as well as a kindly man, who brings him to the cabman's shelter and buys him, at a cost of four pence, a cup of undrinkable coffee and a stale bread roll. After a long pause for rest and recuperation, he brings him up the hill to his home at 7, Eccles Street. What more could a fellow do for son or brother?

"Eumaeus" might well have been written to illustrate the main argument of *A Thousand Plateaus* in the matter of language, that the contents of our minds are quotations from earlier minds, and that free indirect discourse is the paradigm of their disclosure. As in Skin-the-Goat's reported animadversions upon the British Empire:

But a day of reckoning, he stated *crescendo* with no uncertain voice, thoroughly monopolising all the conversation, was in store for mighty England, despite her power of pelf on account of her crimes. (16.997–1000)

Each of us takes the words out of another's mouth. Other voices, other rooms: those voices have preceded us to become our voices, in notional relation to our eyes, hands, face. In the following passage we are to understand that the organs in question belong to Leopold Bloom, but in respects not worth defining:

The eyes were surprised at this observation because as he, the person who owned them pro tem. observed or rather his voice speaking did, all must work, have to, together. (16.1149–51)

Received phrases, not received ideas, set Bloom's mind astir: the ideas bring up the rear and constitute, when seen as a farrago of lore, received wisdom.

It has been held, notably by Hugh Kenner, that "Eumaeus" is written in the style Bloom would use if, pen in careful hand, he were in charge of the narration. I agree that it's a written style, its main source the daily newspaper, and that it sustains a man writing at the kitchen table rather than a man thinking or talking:

So saying he skipped around, nimbly considering, frankly at the same time apologetic to get on his companion's right, a habit of his, by the bye, his right side being, in classical idiom, his tender Achilles. The night air was certainly now a treat to breathe though Stephen was a bit weak on his pins.
– It will (the air) do you good, Bloom said, meaning also the walk, in a moment. (16.1714–19)

The decorum of the written word sustains these sentences, commas and interpolated phrases permitting niceties of adjudication and concession beyond the resources of larynx and facial muscles. The comedy of the passage arises from the fact that the phrases buzzing around Bloom's ears before settling upon his pen may have suited some earlier occasions admirably but not this one. The decorum of conversation does not permit the swift, retrospective clarification by which "It" (presumably beginning a sentence) is detained long enough to have its noun supplied – (the air). "Tender Achilles" ends its sentence with a hum of kindred phrases in undeclared relation to vaguely recalled motifs – Achilles heel, and "the tendon referred to" (16.1006).

But the style, so far as it is Bloom's, is not that of narrative script or even of Anglo-Irish journalism but, specifically, of Letters to the Editor:

A great opportunity there certainly was for push and enterprise to meet the travelling needs of the public at large, the average man, i.e. Brown, Robinson and Co. (16.536–8)

And, two hundred lines later:

Whoever embarked on a policy of the sort, he said, and ventilated the matter thoroughly would confer a lasting boon on everybody concerned. (16.745–7)

The editor of a newspaper is an institution rather than a person; anonymous, and therefore magisterial, a function of historical process rather than of psychological constitution. Communications addressed to that institution are supposed to be in a correspondingly formal style; it is not an occasion for the colloquial note. It is an error, therefore, to dismiss as a dead thing the sentence just quoted; it occupies a zone between two forms of life, personal and institutional, and it protects the writer from incurring an entirely personal judgment.

It follows that the narrative voice in "Eumaeus" should be similar in kind to Bloom's, but higher in degree; that is, complete in its editorial, letter-writing style where Bloom's is merely partial. So an adequate if brief description of the narrator, or of the intimations we gather under that designation, is that he is omniscient in the mode of a Dublin gossip. Omniscient, as demonstrated by the fact that he knows what Stephen's mind's eye is engaged upon, even though no evidence is forthcoming:

... Stephen's mind's eye being too busily engaged in repicturing his family hearth the last time he saw it with his sister Dilly sitting by the ingle, her hair hanging down, waiting for some weak Trinidad shell cocoa that was in the sootcoated kettle to be done ... (16.269–72)

The narrator can even keep up with Stephen in a bout of synesthesia:

He could hear, of course, all kinds of words changing colour like those crabs about Ringsend in the morning burrowing quickly into all colours of different sorts of the same sand where they had a home somewhere beneath or seemed to. (16.1142–6)

Not that omniscience is enough to turn its adept, a supreme Dublin gossip, into a competent reporter by the standards of the *Evening Telegraph*. Even more scrupulous than Bloom – whom he resembles in this respect – in trying to get the details right, he has to take advantage of the second-chance resources of print to keep the sense of his narrative going:

He, B, enjoyed the distinction of being close to Erin's uncrowned king in the flesh when the thing occurred on the historic fracas when the fallen leader's, who notoriously stuck to his guns to the last drop even when clothed in the mantle of adultery, (leader's) trusty henchmen to the number of ten or a dozen or possibly even more than that penetrated into the ... (16.1495–1500)

Similarly, while the distinction between Parnell and Captain O'Shea is clear to Bloom, the narrator finds difficulty in keeping the clauses of the relevant sentence correspondingly lucid:

A magnificent specimen of manhood he was truly augmented obviously by gifts of a high order, as compared with the other military supernumerary that is (who was just the usual everyday *farewell, my gallant captain* kind of an individual in the light dragoons, the 18th hussars to be accurate) and inflammable doubtless (the fallen leader, that is, not the other) in his own peculiar way ... (16.1388–93)

Still, the story gets told, in much the same way as Stephen gets delivered to the Bloom residence in Eccles Street; not perhaps the shortest way, but it comes out alright in the end. As generally in Joyce, the reader's interest is held by apparently minor disjunctions, sentence by sentence. A short list would include these: the difference in degree between Bloom as the man in charge and the narrator who is officially in charge, a difference comparable to that between the active voice and the middle voice, since Bloom has indeed an anterior existence and the narrator comes into temporary existence only with these words in this chapter: the discrepancy between Bloom (sober) and Stephen (sobering up, but not quickly enough); Bloom nearly as garrulous as the redbearded sailor, Stephen mostly silent; Bloom, forthcoming on issues social, political, and historical, Stephen breaking silence only in favor of metaphysics (the nature of the simple soul), linguistics ("Sounds are impostures ... like names" [16.362–3]) and the development of the Elizabethan song ("the lutenist Dowland who lived in Fetter lane" [16.1762–3]). The crucial disjunction, like a toothache the tongue can't avoid probing, is the motif of the faithless wife. Bloom probes it on at least six occasions: when he asks the sailor, "Have you seen the rock of Gibraltar?" (16.611); when he muses silently about "those love vendettas of the south, have her or swing for her" (16.1061); when he thinks he sees Boylan's name in the *Telegraph* (16.1238); when he broods on Molly's being Spanish "or half so, ... passionate abandon of the south, casting every shred of decency to the winds" (16.1409–10); when he ponders "the life connubial" (16.1384); and when he recalls Tom Moore's poem, "I looked for the lamp which she told me/Should shine when the Pilgrim returned" – "Suppose she was gone when he? I looked for the lamp which she told me came into his mind but merely as a passing fancy of his ... " (16.1470–1). To make matters worse, Stephen mentions "Boylan, the billsticker" (16.199) and the sailor claims to have a wife waiting in Queenstown: "She's waiting for me, I know" (16.420).

VIII

So we have two motifs, neither of them original to their adepts. The dominant one is the Good Samaritan: it carries the story forward, and associates Bloom and Stephen with one of the most popular of Christ's parables. The secondary motif, that of the-returning-husband-and-the-faithless-wife, is nearly as visible as that of the Good Samaritan, and Bloom spends the chapter obsessively internalizing it. Virtually every occasion brings his mind back to it. When he shows Stephen the photograph of Molly, the "slightly soiled photo" (16.1465), as he is deemed to say, the words "soiled" and "soiling" (16.1468) send his mind back to slightly soiled linen and Molly's soiled undergarments (16.717), the "soiled drawers" (4.321–2), and the "striped petticoat, tossed soiled linen" (4.265–6) which, many hours ago, Bloom transferred from the chair to the foot of Molly's bed. The motif is an ironic reversal of the story of Hero and Leander, Hero whose lamp guided a fated lover to her bed.

We appear to choose, then, between two ways of reading the chapter. Jameson and Bersani read it invidiously or prejudicially by assuming that "the dominant" is a speech act performed by each character, on the authority of philosophic idealism and a conservative ideology of the self. Everything apparently external in the cabman's shelter finds its expressive destiny in someone's mind. But it is also possible to read the chapter on the lines recommended for other purposes by Deleuze and Guattari. By this method, we start with a posited collectivity, represented in this chapter by the narrative voice we hear as gossip, lore, received wisdom, an attribute of sundry Dubliners. Call this voice Mr. Dublin. We then regard every apparent intervention of an individual voice – Lord John Corley's, Stephen's, Bloom's, Jack Tar's, and so forth – as an act of individuation permitted or ordained by the collectivity, the assemblage. The merit of this way of reading the chapter is that the clichés, the stock phrases, mark a communal way of being alive in the world. Only a snob would think such a life the same as death. A further merit of this way of reading is that it doesn't put us under any obligation to hit these characters over the head with an ideology. Whether we call them characters or not; whether we find each of them manifesting the active, the passive, or the middle voice, is a decision we can take at leisure and without intimidation.

I choose a passage which includes many of the resources made available by the particular collective assemblage we call the Dublin of 1904:

> All kinds of Utopian plans were flashing through his (B's) busy brain, education (the genuine article), literature, journalism, prize titbits, up to date billing, concert tours in English watering resorts packed with hydros and seaside theatres, turning money away, duets in Italian with the accent perfectly true to nature and a quantity of other things, no necessity, of course, to tell the world and his wife from the housetops about it, and a slice of luck. An opening was all that was wanted. Because he more than suspected he had his father's voice to bank his hopes on which it was quite on the cards he had so it would be just as well, by the way no harm, to trail the conversation in the direction of that particular red herring just to.
>
> The cabby read out of the paper he had got hold of that the former viceroy, earl Cadogan, had presided at the cabdrivers' association dinner in London somewhere. Silence with a yawn or two accompanied this thrilling announcement. Then the old specimen in the corner who appeared to have some spark of vitality left read out that sir Anthony MacDonnell had left Euston for the chief secretary's lodge or words to that effect. To which absorbing piece of intelligence echo answered why.
> – Give us a squint at that literature, grandfather, the ancient mariner put in, manifesting some natural impatience. (16.1652–70)

The passage begins as if it were (or might be) detached, omniscient narration. The cadence of fastidious revision is established by way of second thoughts diligently inserted, newspaper-style, directly after the first – "his (B's) busy brain," "education (the genuine article)." But the sentence then steadies itself into the mode of free indirect discourse, picking up Bloom's phrases (which he, in turn, has picked up from hearsay and gossip) and letting them do the work of reportage: "with the accent perfectly true to nature." The stability of print enables the reader to divine that in the sentence that begins with "Because" the first "he" refers to Bloom and the second to Stephen. The new paragraph is as close as the passage comes to detached narration, but the sentence about silence and yawns restores matters to Mr. Dublin, who treats with appropriate disdain anything read aloud from a newspaper. "To which absorbing piece of intelligence echo answered why." The collective assemblage utters itself in that sentence by assembling several cognate tones: affected pedantry ("To which"), sarcasm ("absorbing"), a finical phrase ("piece of intelligence"), and a tag from Byron's "Bride of Abydos" ("echo answered why"). There ensues the individuation called diversely Jack Tar, the ancient mariner, the seafarer, the sailor, and so forth, who takes the occasion to say, "Give us a squint of that literature, grandfather." Whereupon "And welcome" maintains the decency of the occasion and postpones, briefly, the restoration of the discourse to Mr. Dublin, who takes charge again with "answered the elderly party thus addressed" (16.1671).

The decorum of the newspaper is just as much to the point of "Eumaeus" as it is of "Aeolus": source of the information, accurate or not, on which Dublin social life kept itself going. The authority of the daily printed word is acknowledged even when the details of its lore are mocked. Indeed, the chapter embodies the process by which print becomes hearsay, and hearsay the speech of individual speakers. Bloom moves equably in that world, borrows its hearsay, and passes its phrases along. He does not complain about the quality of the lore. Stephen complains; but so did (and still does) every member of the intelligentsia, a professionally disgruntled class invented in France, exported to Russia, and only recently (in 1904) arrived in Dublin. In 1904, however, Dublin was still for most of its citizens a feasible city; it was not yet, as London and Paris were, anonymous and unknowable. Newspapers were still the means by which information, news, and gossip were distributed; adequately, on the whole, if the criterion in such matters is the degree to which Dublin lore permitted people to go on talking to one another without having much to say. In 1904 there was no sign of "the revolt of the masses" or indeed of "the masses": there was a proletariat, and there was trouble enough between workers and management to cause Jim Larkin, in 1913, to lead a strike against William Martin Murphy. But *Ulysses* testifies to a moment in the public life of Dublin when, perhaps for the last time, the daily printed word gave its readers the lore they required. There is no sign, in "Aeolus," "Eumaeus," or the book as a whole of the exacerbations to come: the masses, facelessness, *anomie*, corporate power.

IX

If "Eumaeus" is, as I contend, neither foolish nor dull, the argument against *Ulysses* as a whole seems to fail; the book is as fine as anyone has ever deemed it to be. Further debate on the matter would have to turn upon questions of principle and of ideology. It is not a matter of setting oneself against Marxism. Indeed, I find persuasive, on the disputed issue of subjectivity, the following passage which I quote without comment from Marcuse's *The Aesthetic Dimension*:

The deterministic component of Marxist theory does not lie in its concept of the relationship between social existence and consciousness, but in the reductionist concept of consciousness which brackets the particular content of individual consciousness and, with it, the subjective potential for revolution.
  This development was furthered by the interpretation of subjectivity as a "bourgeois" notion. Historically, this is questionable. But even in bourgeois society, insistence on the truth and right of inwardness is not really a bourgeois value. With the affirmation of the inwardness of subjectivity, the individual steps out of the network of exchange relationships and exchange values, withdraws from the reality of bourgeois society, and enters another dimension of existence ... And today, in the totalitarian period, [subjectivity] has become a political value as a counterforce against aggressive and exploitative socialization. (4–5)

X

But there is another issue. In an essay, "Heroic Styles," Seamus Deane has adverted to the two great "ways" by which an Irish imagination responded to the conditions it had to meet. Yeats's way was to seek a single style, grand indeed, as the expression of the true history of Ireland; it is the way of Parnell and de Valera as well as Yeats. Joyce's way was to produce "a multitude of equivalent, competing styles, in which the atomisation of the community is registered." Deane doesn't propose, even with the condition of Northern Ireland as his incentive, that we learn to suspect Yeats and to endorse Joyce. Yeats surrendered to the appeal of violence, but he also "conceded the tragic destiny this involved." As for Joyce:

Joyce, although he attempted to free himself from set political positions, did finally create, in *Finnegans Wake*, a characteristically modern way of dealing with heterogeneous and intractable material and experience. The pluralism of his styles and languages, the absorbent nature of his controlling myths and systems, finally gives a certain harmony to varied experience. But, it could be argued, it is the harmony of indifference, one in which everything is a version of something else, where sameness rules over diversity, where contradiction is finally and disquietingly written out. In achieving this in literature, Joyce anticipated the capacity of modern society to integrate almost all antagonistic elements by transforming them into fashions, fads – styles, in short. (16)

There are logical problems with this argument. Indeed, it is surprising that Deane, having observed the paratactic character of Joyce's writing, goes on to say that his styles are equivalent and yet somehow in competition. There is nothing especially modern in parataxis; as Peter Levi has shown by examining a passage from the ninth book of the *Iliad* (27–8). If the mode of organization is paratactic, there is no cause of competition. There may be a resultant indifference, but I can't see evidence of it. "Eumaeus" comes into the case. While it goes about its business, lowly indeed, it doesn't claim any privilege, it is one chapter among many. Deane is right in this respect: neither in *Finnegans Wake* nor in *Ulysses* did Joyce seek a single, authoritative style, corresponding to the will one might try to impose upon one's material.

So where are we? I have not even glanced at the several other objections which have been brought to bear upon *Ulysses* since 1922. I think of Jung, Forster, Wyndham Lewis, Shaw, and Woolf. But these objections have receded, they issued from spontaneities of taste rather than from principle. Yeats's sense of *Ulysses* is a more demanding matter, but I can't say anything about it now. So, to give the gist of my argument. "Eumaeus" is one perspective, one style, among eighteen. It makes light of the fact that our words are old; it doesn't hanker after "firstness." Instead, it makes much of the fact that individuality need not be construed as inaugural, but as issuing from an assemblage of possibilities embodied in a language. No insult to inwardness is proposed.

WORKS CITED

Barthes, Roland. "To Write: An Intransitive Verb?" *The Languages of Criticism and the Sciences of Man: The Structuralist Controversy.* Ed. Richard Macksey and Eugenio Donato. Baltimore: Johns Hopkins Press, 1970. 134–56.

Benveniste, Emile. "Active and Middle Voice in the Verb." *Problems in General Linguistics.* Trans. Mary Elizabeth Meek. Coral Gables, Fla.: University of Miami Press, 1971. 145–51.

Bersani, Leo. "Against *Ulysses.*" *Raritan* 8.2 (1988): 1–32.

Deane, Seamus. *Heroic Styles: The Tradition of an Idea.* Derry: Field Day, 1984.

Deleuze, Gilles, and Félix Guattari. *A Thousand Plateaus: Capitalism and Schizophrenia.* Trans. Brian Massumi. London: Athlone, 1988.

de Man, Paul. *Blindness and Insight: Essays in the Rhetoric of Contemporary Criticism.* Theory and History of Literature 7. Minneapolis: University of Minnesota Press, 1983.

Derrida, Jacques. *Speech and Phenomena and Other Essays on Husserl's Theory of Signs.* Trans. David B. Allison. Evanston, Ill.: Northwestern University Press, 1973.

Jameson, Fredric. *Fables of Aggression: Wyndham Lewis, the Modernist as Fascist.* Berkeley and Los Angeles: University of California Press, 1979.

"*Ulysses* in History." *James Joyce and Modern Literature.* Ed. W. J. McCormack and Alistair Stead. London: Routledge, 1982. 126–41.

"Wyndham Lewis as Futurist." *Hudson Review* 26 (1973): 295–329.

Joyce, James. *Ulysses: The Corrected Text.* Ed. Hans Walter Gabler et al. London: Bodley Head, 1986.

Kenner, Hugh. *Joyce's Voices.* Berkeley and Los Angeles: University of California Press, 1978.

Levi, Peter. *A History of Greek Literature.* Harmondsworth: Penguin, 1985.

Levinas, Emmanuel. "The Other in Proust." Trans. Séan Hand. *The Levinas Reader.* Ed. Séan Hand. Oxford: Blackwell, 1989. 160–5.

Totality and Infinity: An Essay on Exteriority. Trans. Alphonso Lingis. Duquesne Studies, Philosophical Series 24. Pittsburgh: Duquesne University Press, 1969.

Marcuse, Herbert. *The Aesthetic Dimension: Toward a Critique of Marxist Aesthetics.* Trans. Herbert Marcuse and Erica Sherover. Boston: Beacon, 1978.

CHAPTER 3

Woolf and Joyce: reading and re/vision

Johanna X. K. Garvey

"Here we come to Joyce. And here we must make our position clear
as bewildered and befogged. We don't pretend to say what he's
trying to do. We know so little about the people" ("Modern
Novels").[1] One could easily interpret these words of Virginia Woolf
as an admission of a lack of understanding or appreciation for the
revolution in fiction that James Joyce was performing in *Ulysses*.
Indeed, commentators have often cited Woolf's criticisms of Joyce's
novel ("pretentious," "underbred," "a queasy undergraduate
scratching his pimples") to demonstrate her perceived ignorance of
his achievement, as well as her alleged snobbishness and prudery.[2]
Moreover, when critics move beyond disparagements of Woolf's
evaluations, their attempts at drawing parallels between the two
writers often rest on the belief that Woolf was imitating a superior
artist; such is the case, for instance, in a recent article that concludes
(after a series of juxtaposed passages from *Mrs. Dalloway* and
Ulysses), "Woolf, subconsciously in a quasi-Jungian sense, permitted
herself to be influenced by that which she ostensibly rejected. Woolf
should be included among those who have accorded Joyce's great
work the recognition it deserves" (Jenkins 519). Thus, according to
many, not only did Woolf inexcusably dismiss Joyce, but her novels
remain pale imitations, when set beside a "master" text like *Ulysses*.

A study of Woolf's reading notes for *Ulysses*, however, reveals a
much more complex reaction to the novel, as she responds to this
"something new" with questions, exclamations, and assessments not
only negative but also directly appreciative of the innovations he
was introducing into modern fiction.[3] In an insightful discussion of
this "*Ulysses* notebook," Suzette Henke states that Woolf "had
always regarded Joyce as a kind of artistic 'double,' a male ally in
the modernist battle for psychological realism" (41). Similarly,
Bonnie Kime Scott notes, in her wide-ranging study of *Joyce and*

Feminism, that Woolf seems to see herself "as Joyce's literary rival as well as his critical admirer" (122). Thus we must balance Woolf's contemptuous comments about *Ulysses* against her clear comprehension that it was a major work, and we should likewise acknowledge that she perhaps did perceive him as a sort of counterpart.[4] Nevertheless, Woolf's engagement with the text of *Ulysses*, combined with her own developing narrative strategies, led her to offer not imitations but dramatic re/visions of his novel in several of her own fictions, including *Jacob's Room*, *Mrs. Dalloway*, and *Orlando*. For present purposes, *Jacob's Room* (1922) offers telling examples of Woolf's discourse with *Ulysses*.

Woolf's first references to Joyce's text occur in both her diary and her letters of April 1918, after Harriet Weaver had brought her the manuscript to consider for publication by the Hogarth Press. And from this evidence alone Woolf may indeed appear prudish and judgmental, referring to the book's "filth" and perceiving Joyce's "attempt to push the bounds of expression further on" but not in any new direction (*Diary* 1: 140). Though the notebook in which Woolf's comments on *Ulysses* appear is undated, on one of the first pages she wrote "April 1918," indicating that she is here recording her first assessments of Joyce's novel. The essay draft on "Modern Novels" that follows these notes was eventually revised and published before *Jacob's Room*, Woolf's third novel, written between April 1920 and November 1921.[5] This work, the first extended prose fiction that Woolf wrote after reading at least the initial seven episodes of Joyce's book, thus reveals in significant ways that she was not merely influenced by *Ulysses* but in fact was arguing with it and developing her own strategies of narration, characterization, description. Furthermore, her letters from this period and particularly her diary entries show her returning again and again to *Ulysses*, and to her close friend T. S. Eliot's praise of it, even as she, too, attempted to create a unique form for the novel.

Several diary entries indicate that Joyce's book (and the author himself) loomed large in Woolf's mind during the composition of *Jacob's Room*. She writes, for instance, of her "idea for a new form for a new novel ...: no scaffolding, scarcely a brick to be seen," and continues: "I suppose the danger is the damned egotistical self; which ruins Joyce & [Dorothy] Richardson to my mind; is one pliant & rich enough to provide a wall for the book from oneself..." (*Diary* 2: 14). Later the same year, her own novel now underway, she records one of Eliot's visits and his admiration for Joyce, and then observes: "Ulysses according to Joyce is the greatest character in history[.] Joyce himself is an insignificant man, wearing very thick eyeglasses, a little like Shaw to look at, dull, self-centred, & perfectly self-assured" (*Diary* 2: 68). The following entry is perhaps the most telling, for she notes that Eliot's visit has brought a halt to her own writing (after two months of solid work on "Jacob"): "Eliot coming on the heel of a long stretch of writing fiction ... made me listless; cast shade upon me; & the mind when engaged upon fiction wants all its boldness & self-confidence. He said nothing – but I reflected how what I'm doing is probably being better done by Mr. Joyce. Then I began to wonder what it is that I am doing ..." (*Diary* 2: 68–9). Despite such "anxiety of influence," however, Woolf soon returned to her own "experiment" and drafted large portions of *Jacob's Room* in the next few months, as one can ascertain from the dates in her holograph notebook.[6] When one considers these drafts as well as the finished version, three central and related preoccupations emerge, especially if one reads her text as a dialogue with Joyce's: the problematic enormity of the male ego, the distressing lack of recognition for women's writing, and the question of how to deal with what she terms "indecency."

In both her "*Ulysses* notebook" and her diary Woolf criticizes the "egotism" she perceives in Joyce and his male contemporaries, a self-centered and self-absorbed attitude that she later condemns in *A Room of One's Own*.[7] Reading "Hades," for instance, she suggests that "perhaps this method gets less into other people and too much into one." Her response in *Jacob's Room* is to take that ego as ostensible subject and then to refuse almost all knowledge of it, to present Jacob often only in parentheses and his rooms in little detail, to empty out the male center just as she empties the purported "room" of any identity or individuality. And in fact, the comments of a first-person female narrator force us to realize that Jacob is already dead at the start of the book, which becomes a sort of anti-biography, a non-portrait of a not-great young man, a radical act of deconstruction.[8]

Early in the novel, we learn that Betty Flanders, Jacob's mother, is a widow, and that she has in a sense forged her dead husband's identity: "'Merchant of this city,' the tombstone said; though why Betty Flanders had chosen so to call him when, as many still remembered, he had only sat behind an office window for three months, and before that had broken horses ... – well, she had to call him something. An example for the boys" (*Jacob's Room* 16). Her fiction replaces or rewrites the dead father, just as her presence fills in his absence. Similarly, the narrator's first-person voice continually draws our attention to the story-teller, who asserts the difficulty of knowing someone else and of conveying any such knowledge, while also questioning why we should even want to know others.

> It seems that a profound, impartial, and absolutely just opinion of our fellow creatures is utterly unknown ... And why, if this and much more than this is true, why are we yet surprised in the window corner by a sudden vision that the young man in the chair is of all things in the world the most real, the most solid, the best known to us – why indeed? For the moment after we know nothing about him. (72)

And all becomes "guesswork." In her notes on *Ulysses*, Woolf stresses that Joyce is advancing narrative technique particularly in terms of psychology, yet she also says of his characters that "[t]heir minds lack quality – and as you get nothing *but* their minds!" In *Jacob's Room*, the narrator approaches the character from numerous angles and perspectives, external views of Jacob as well as sequences from his words and thoughts, yet the result is often ambiguity rather than clarity, erasure rather than portraiture – a denial of the importance, interest, or relevance of the masculine subject.

One way of rendering void the patriarchal ego is to devalue that which it idealizes. Throughout *Jacob's Room*, men turn to Greece as the ultimate standard; when they do, however, disappointment follows, as when Jacob travels from Paris to Italy, then Greece, and experiences a let-down, finding gloom and boredom: "(This violent disillusionment is generally to be expected in young men in the prime of life, sound of wind and limb, who will soon become fathers of families and directors of banks)" (151).[9] Overtly linking Jacob to those who will inherit the powers of patriarchy (as she has already done in choosing his biblical name), the narrator deflates the visions of (male) grandeur via a rejection of Greece and things Greek. Given not only its title but also the manifold references to the Hellenic in the early episodes of *Ulysses*, Woolf's argument against the heroic ego seems at least in part inspired by her reading of Joyce.[10]

Perhaps the most direct reference to Joyce's text comes when a young woman infatuated with Jacob attempts to hold onto her impressions of him:

Sustained entirely upon picture post cards for the past two months, Fanny's idea of Jacob was more statuesque, noble, and eyeless than ever. To reinforce her vision she had taken to visiting the British Museum, where, keeping her eyes downcast until she was alongside of the battered Ulysses, she opened them and got a fresh shock of Jacob's presence, enough to last her half a day. But this was wearing thin. (170)

The direct comparison of Jacob to the Greek epic hero and the suggestion of hollowness in both indicates a subtle rejection of Ulysses as model – or if a model, it is one that the narrative is shattering, a sightless, and ego-less, statue rather than an inspiring heroic ideal. The text abounds with other references to Greek, including a passage that recalls Bloom's investigations in "Lestry-gonians": "'And the Greeks, like sensible men, never bothered to finish the backs of their statues,' said Jacob, shading his eyes and observing that the side of the figure which is turned away from view is left in the rough" (149). So will Jacob, as well as his various "rooms," be left very much in the rough, for (as the narrator says), "It is no use trying to sum people up. One must follow hints, not exactly what is said, not yet entirely what is done ... There is also the highly respectable opinion that character-mongering is much overdone nowadays. After all, what does it matter?" (154). But if Woolf works to silence Jacob, she nevertheless also strives to introduce women's voices into her narrative.

In her initial notes for the novel, Woolf wrote that it should be "free" and that the style should change "at will." In the final version, we indeed find constant shifts but more of perspective than of style – a major difference from *Ulysses* with its multiple styles and "voices."[11] The many fragmentary points of view as well as the frequent use of night scenes do not fill in the character, however, but instead render Jacob a shadowy, often voiceless figure. Female characters, of varying age, class, occupation, take over the narrative; the text becomes an attempt to confront the exclusion of women from patriarchal institutions, to open doors that have long kept women on the outside. Another scene in the British Museum illustrates the rage – albeit contained – of those on the margins, which Woolf would go on to express at length in *A Room of One's Own* and *Three Guineas*. While Jacob sits transcribing Marlowe, Julia Hedge – "The feminist" – waits for her books: "She wetted her pen. She looked about her. Her eye was caught by the final letters in Lord Macaulay's name. And she read them all round the dome – the names of great men which remind us – 'Oh damn,' said Julia Hedge, 'why didn't they leave room for an Eliot or a Brontë?'" (106). This "room" is precisely what Woolf's text allows women's writing – and women's voices more generally; among the books in Jacob's library, alongside Spinoza, Dickens, a Greek dictionary, all the Elizabethans, we find the works of Jane Austen – "in deference, perhaps, to someone else's standard" (39). Women's writing thus infiltrates the masculine space of Jacob's rooms at Cambridge, just as Woolf clearly insists on a literary canon more inclusive than the male-centered one that fills the thought and speech of Stephen Dedalus in the first sections of *Ulysses*.[12] Framed by Betty Flanders, whose words both open and close the novel, the male character is continually forced into contact with women, ostensibly the narrator's "reporters" but actually presented in more detail than Jacob himself.

The first draft of the novel begins with Jacob as a small boy trotting on the beach, and the description suggests that along with "Hades" (which Woolf found especially successful), the third episode of *Ulysses* also made a strong impression on her. In the draft version, Jacob investigates an enormous rock, peers into a pool of water, discovers a couple lying on the sand, and finds a weathered jawbone; waves, tides, sand and gulls create a backdrop for a scene in which we observe not a self-conscious young man strolling on the beach but a frightened young boy anxious to return to his mother. Woolf eventually revised the opening, so that the book begins with Betty Flanders, sitting on the sand and looking over a bay in Cornwall as she writes a letter. In this revisioning, the author is also perhaps responding to the "Proteus" episode, when Stephen walks along Sandymount Strand and proclaims, "Signatures of all things I am hear to read," and later proceeds to write a poem.[13] Throughout *Jacob's Room*, women write, belying one critic's comment that women do not write in Woolf's texts until *A Room of One's Own* (DiBattista 109); in fact, in this early novel women's writing proliferates, while Jacob's literary productions seem as lifeless as he is. And Woolf perhaps appropriates *Ulysses* itself to her own presentation of the cityscape: the signs for tube stops are written in "eternally white letters upon a blue ground" (67). Meanwhile, throughout the novel we see women write – and not just the educated, middle-to-upper classes: a small girl posts a letter in the first scene set in London; a young woman, though semi-literate, pens sincere notes to Jacob; Julia Hedge pursues her scholarship in the British Museum; and what will remain in Jacob's room after his death are women's letters, including those his mother has steadily sent him. The text implicitly states that women's writing not only abounds but may be somehow equally if not more significant than the published work of men. The narrator calls attention to the "unpublished works of women, written by the fireside in pale profusion, dried by the flame, for the blotting-paper's worn to holes and the nib cleft and clotted" (91), and comments that "[l]ife would split asunder without [letters]" (93). Furthermore, our view of Jacob – such as it is – usually comes framed by a female speaker or observer, the most important of whom is the narrator herself.

Many of the chapters begin with the words, thoughts, or actions of a female character, such as the old woman who shares a railway carriage with Jacob on his way to Cambridge. While she is apprehensive and prepared to defend herself if necessary, he seems unaware of her presence – "youthful, indifferent, unconscious," like other young men who "see themselves" (30–1).[14] Since there is no direct interaction between the two, as the narrator says, one "must do the best one can with her report. Anyhow, this was Jacob Flanders, aged nineteen." And in fact she can give no report, as we see one of the many erasures of Jacob: "this sight of her fellow-traveller was completely lost in her mind, as the crooked pin dropped by a child into the wishing-well twirls in the water and disappears for ever" (31). While a reader expecting to follow an orderly, developed portrayal of a young male character will meet with frustration, the narrator relentlessly imposes her own presence just as she subverts traditional concepts of authorial power. Her female allies often find Jacob lacking, as when he is hung with glass grapes and looks "like the figure-head of a wrecked ship," or when an older woman with whom he had fallen in love thinks of him as a "mere bumpkin." In respect to this non-affair, the narrator comments that Jacob "had in him the seeds of extreme disillusionment, which would come to him from women in middle life" (159). And such a woman is the narrator herself, constantly undermining the supposed "centre" or "magnet" of the text and inserting her own presence: "Whether we know what was in his mind is another question. Granted ten years' seniority and a difference of sex, fear of him comes first; this is swallowed up by a desire to help – overwhelming sense, reason, and the time of night; anger would follow close on that ..." (94–5). I suspect that Woolf had similar reactions to Joyce's characters – specifically Buck Mulligan and Stephen Dedalus – as she read the first episodes of *Ulysses*.

One sees numerous instances of the impact Joyce's book had on Woolf, including minor details such as references to Home Rule in Ireland, a book on "Diseases of the Horse," and a belief in the "transmigration of souls," the more significant re/visioning of scenes such as "Proteus," and the much larger concerns *Ulysses* clearly raised for her. As her reading notes indicate, one of the latter was her response to its "indecency," what she perceived as an "indifference to public opinion," a "desire to shock." Yet what might appear to be a rejection on Woolf's part in fact emerges as a strong effort to deal with "indecencies" – particularly sexual ones – in her own next novel. In this respect, as well as in her experiments in narrative technique, *Jacob's Room* marks a radical departure from *The Voyage Out* and *Night and Day*.[15] The first draft shows her struggling with words such as "gelded" (which she would have found in the "Hades" episode) and "copulation," some of which she censored in the final draft while retaining others. Thus, for instance, she initially recorded Betty Flanders's thoughts on receiving a proposal of marriage after several years of widowhood: "It was, probably, that the idea of copulation had now become infinitely remote from her. She did not use the word; and yet as she sat darning the boys clothes that night it annoyed her to find that it was so." The published version reads, "She had always disliked red hair in men, she thought" (21), with no reference to sexuality. The two "dislikes" are connected, however; the draft shows Woolf's attempts to include "indecencies," as Mrs. Flanders observes her cat Topaz. She remembers having had him gelded and thinks of red-headed men: "– both thoughts coming on top of each other & making her smile, though she had not used the word 'gelded' or consciously connected the two ideas in her mind – indeed she never used words when she thought indecent thoughts." Some of the passage remains in the final version: "and she smiled, thinking how she had had him gelded, and how she did not like red hair in men. Smiling she went into the kitchen" (22–3). It is interesting to note here a line in *Ulysses* that may have struck Woolf: "Redheaded women buck like goats," Buck Mulligan comments to Stephen near the end of "Telemachus."[16]

Besides sexuality, other references to the body clearly disturbed

Woolf as she read *Ulysses*, yet she would go on to incorporate such topics into her own fiction. Two letters from April 1918, for instance, recognize Joyce's "experiment" and sophisticated "method," but also find fault: "First there's a dog that p's – then there's a man that forths, and one can be monotonous even on that subject"; "I dont know that he's got anything very interesting to say, and after all the p---ing of a dog isn't very different from the p---ing of a man. Three hundred pages of it might be boring" (*Letters* 2: 234). Nevertheless, in a scene set in King's College Chapel, Cambridge, Woolf writes: "No one would think of bringing a dog into church. For though a dog is all very well on a gravel path, and shows no disrespect to flowers, the way he wanders down an aisle, looking, lifting a paw, and approaching a pillar with a purpose that makes the blood run cold with horror . . ." (33). Woolf is capable not only of including "indecency" in her own manner but of having great fun as she does so.

Thus Woolf does deal with the more purely "animal" aspects of what at first seemed inappropriate to her in Joyce's text, but she also works in human sexuality and incorporates a much wider range of female behavior than she had in previous novels. In her "*Ulysses* notebook," Woolf comments as follows: "Also seems to be written for a set in a back street. What does this come from? Always a mark of the second rate. Indifference to public opinion – desire to shock – need of dwelling so much on indecency. Whole question of indecency a difficult one. It should be colourless; but this we can't quite manage yet." Nevertheless, she herself does indeed "manage," taking us to back streets in Soho, where the lamps "made large greasy spots of light upon the pavement. The by-streets were dark enough to shelter man or woman leaning against the doorways" (81). And indeed among the characters in the novel Woolf includes prostitutes, both young and old, as when we see Jacob sitting by the fire with "Laurette," then putting coins on the mantle as he leaves. In both draft and novel, the author does reveal some repugnance (the madame not only displays a "leer" and "lewdness" but is compared to a "bag of ordure"); by the very fact of inclusion, however, such scenes are new for Woolf and seem to a great extent motivated by her reading of Joyce.

"No escaping the body," she notes in the draft of an episode that she censored even as she penned it, crossing out lines such as the following: "all that veils & places in the shadows these natural functions of the body"; "These functions & desires would assert themselves. All these functions and desires would press become prominent"; "Whether The small room is altogether filled with the body." (Most of this episode disappears in the novel itself, but in the draft it *may* refer to an out house – shades of Bloom?) In a much-rewritten scene that does remain, Woolf cleverly uses one of Mrs. Flanders's letters to follow Jacob and a young woman into his bedroom; while he leaves the envelope in the sitting-room, the letter takes on the maternal persona, as if she stands outside listening. The draft indicates extreme distress at the sounds from within: "Behind the door knives cut human flesh from the bone, on(?) death alight." The references to "knives" and "surgeons" Woolf removed, so that the novel reads, "But if the pale blue envelope lying by the biscuit-box had the feelings of a mother, the heart was torn by the little creak, the sudden stir. Behind the door was the obscene thing, the alarming presence" (92). Besides allowing the narrative to include sex, if indirectly, putting such a response into the mother's perspective also can serve to free the narrator from accusations of prudery.[17]

Finally, we have Jacob's essay, which is the one literary work we see him produce (besides the mendacious letters he writes home from Europe and a note on history that the narrator says should be burnt). He writes to correct the "outrage" a professor has committed in editing a volume of Wycherley, "without stating that he had left out, disembowelled, or indicated only by asterisks, several indecent words and some indecent phrases" (69–70). Jacob calls this "a breach of faith; sheer prudery; token of a lewd mind and a disgusting nature," ways Woolf may have feared her own reaction to *Ulysses* might be interpreted. Several journals reject the essay and it ends in a black wooden box, painted with Jacob's name, "the lid shut upon the truth" (70). Bonnie Kime Scott notes Woolf's recollections late in life of Harriet Weaver's visit and her own initial response to Joyce's manuscript: "And the pages reeled with indecency. I put them in the drawer of the inlaid cabinet" (Scott 123–4, 226 n.32). This "shutting away" of the text of *Ulysses* is re-enacted in the fate of Jacob's essay, tossed into the black box when he is confirmed in the belief that "no one would ever print [the pages]" (70). The word "truth" rings facetiously on one level, the echo of Jacob's own self-importance; from Woolf's perspective, however, we may read this line as an admission that Joyce in fact was capturing the "truth" of human experience in ways unknown in previous fiction.

The small black casket also prefigures the final scene in the novel, just as Jacob's surname has predicted his demise; though we are not told the manner of his death, he has clearly perished in the Great War, perhaps on Flanders fields.[18] We are left with his best friend, Bonamy, and his mother surveying the empty room, as she queries what to do with her son's old shoes. Ironically, we have arrived just where the title has indicated and as the narrator has often reminded us that we would: "What do we seek through millions of pages? Still hopefully turning the pages – oh, here is Jacob's room" (97). As noted, it is significant that letters are strewn about, all from women; but why end with a question about Jacob's shoes? Certainly we can read an elegiac note, as do Gilbert and Gubar: "it seems that, along with pain at this mother's loss, the novelist may have half-consciously wondered who, or what, might now step into those empty shoes of the doomed heir" (315). But Jacob has been fatherless throughout the book and the only money he inherits is from an old *woman* (the money that allowed him to make his pilgrimage to Greece). Turning to *Ulysses* once more, we find that from the moment when Stephen walks on the beach, men's presence is often emphasized and their positions established by their boots – including those Stephen has borrowed from Buck and the "rusty boot" he observes in the sand. Woolf turns this characteristic into a leitmotif, such that boots help to identify male characters – young boys, journalists, a painter, a fix-it man, a traveler, a philosopher, as well as Jacob – and may have caused the death of Jacob's father, who refused to remove his wet boots after a hunting expedition and expired. Early in *Jacob's Room*, the narrator takes us into King's College Chapel and observes the owners and inheritors of male privilege: "how airily the gowns blow out, as though nothing dense and corporeal were within. What certainty, authority controlled by piety, although great boots march under the gowns" (32). As in *Ulysses*, heavy boots often announce masculine presence and punctuate men's actions, but Woolf subverts such authority, renders it void – ultimately in the image of Jacob's empty shoes, which serve not to characterize but to immobilize him.[19] In addition, just as Betty Flanders opens the novel, penning one of the myriad letters that insist on the universality of women's writing, so her words and gesture close the book, the female (and maternal) presence thus framing the absence of the masculine subject.

In *Jacob's Room*, Virginia Woolf entered into an argument with male writers, Joyce primary among them, about the content and direction of modern fiction. In doing so, she produced not only an extremely complex response to *Ulysses* but also began to liberate herself from conventions, to experiment with her own methods. She wrote in her diary as the publication date of *Jacob's Room* drew near: "There's no doubt in my mind that I have found out how to begin (at 40) to say something in my own voice; & that interests me so that I feel I can go ahead without praise"; "I think Jacob was a necessary step, for me, in working free" (*Diary* 2: 186, 208). Woolf's discourse with *Ulysses* contributed in major degree to that discovery of her own voice; the process continues in *Mrs. Dalloway* and *Orlando*, further examples of Woolf's re/visioning of Joyce's text.

NOTES

1 I am grateful both to the New York Public Library and to Professor Quentin Bell for permission to quote from this manuscript and from the unpublished holograph notebook "Jacob's Room". I also thank Patrick B. Miller for his invaluable comments on several versions of this essay.

2 Most of these statements come fairly late in the sequence of Woolf's readings of *Ulysses*, from August 1922, or later – when *Jacob's Room*, the novel I am examining in some depth, was already revised and with the publisher. See *Diary*, vol. 2.

3 Her reading notes for *Ulysses* are included at the start of the holograph notebook cited above.

4 For instance, she refers to him as a "he-goat," perhaps a parallel to her own nickname "the goat." For more on this nickname, see note 16 below. See also her diary comments on his death, as quoted by Henke.

5 Virginia Woolf, "Jacob's Room" holograph notebook. The first entry is dated Thursday, April 15, 1920. Woolf herself noted in her diary that she finished this novel on November 11, 1921, but there are a few additions as well as the draft of the final chapter, dated March 12, 1922, in part three of the holograph.

6 Woolf does not mark the date for every portion of the draft; the dates she does note fall in November 1920, January and April 1921.

7 See the famous passage on mirrors, which begins: "Women have served all these centuries as looking-glasses possessing the magic and delicious power of reflecting the figure of man at twice its natural size" (35–6).

8 As with Woolf's other commentaries (fictional as well as essayistic) on biographies of "great men," her father's endeavors in biography probably stand in the background, so that she is also reacting to a direct paternal (and patriarchal) example. On this aspect in *Jacob's Room* see Blain.

9 Woolf's reaction to patriarchal behavior begins with her first novel,

written when she was ten years old, the second half of which is titled
"The Experiences of a Pater-familias." For an illuminating discussion
of this early work see DeSalvo, especially ch. 5.

10 One thinks immediately of Buck and Stephen's banter in the first
pages of "Telemachus," with references to the latter's Greek name
and the former's Hellenic one, to a project to "Hellenise" Ireland, and
so forth.

11 The references here are multiple – Kenner and Lawrence are crucial
starting points. In her diary Woolf wonders about what she had
intended as changes of style in her own text: "I am not satisfied that
this book is in a healthy way. Suppose one of my myriad changes of
style is antipathetic to the material? – or does my style remain fixed?
To my mind it changes always" (*Diary* 2: 94).

12 Woolf would have found few if any allusions to women writers in the
early episodes, though we do see women write letters – including the
secretary who types the full date for the events of Joyce's novel.
Orlando will offer a further re/visioning of this situation.

13 Other parallels to the early episodes include the Roman fortress over-
looking the Bay, like the Martello tower, the description of the rocks
and tides and seaweed, and a dog (in the draft version).

14 For an insightful interpretation of this scene as a means of turning
Jacob into a "type" see Bowlby, ch. 6.

15 Each of these previous works is much closer to a realistic novel in
structure and style; *Night and Day* (1919), though set in London, has a
drawing-room quality and contains no direct references to sexuality –
or indeed to the body, "indecencies," obscenities, and so forth. *The
Voyage Out*, Woolf's first novel (1915), shows attempts to include such
material but does so very obliquely: the main character has been
"kept entirely ignorant as to the relations of men with women," and is
thus extremely disturbed when an older man kisses her (80). Similarly, mention of prostitutes in London labels them "terrifying" and
"disgusting." Throughout, the narrative evinces an uneasiness with
any such subjects and an effort more to avoid than to explore them.

16 Again, besides responding to "indecency" Woolf may have been
offended by the (unintentional) reference to "goat," her nickname
among family and close friends. Also, throughout "Telemachus" she
might have read a homosociality between Stephen and Buck, and
responded in *Jacob's Room* with her depiction of Jacob's "good friend"
– Bonamy. In the draft she often writes that the latter "despises" or
"hates" women, and lets stand in the text some oblique references to
Bonamy's homosexuality.

17 For another crucial way of looking at what has often been considered
Woolf's somewhat Victorian reticence in writing about sexuality see
DeSalvo's careful delineation of the degree to which sexual abuse,

beginning when Woolf was six or seven, influenced her life and writing.

18 The only direct reference comes in an aside concerning two very minor characters: "And now Jimmy feeds crows in Flanders and Helen visits hospitals" (97). On his first name, it is interesting to note that it is a form of the name "James"; Vince Cheng has also pointed out to me *FW* 1.7, "Shem is as short for Shemus as Jem is joky for Jacob." And in "Aeolus," Woolf herself would have read "Then the twelve brothers, Jacob's sons."

19 It is interesting to note that among the first brief ideas Woolf enters in her notebook for *Jacob's Room* is the phrase "Intensity of life compared with immobility." Cryptic in itself, the phrase does suggest that Woolf from the outset envisioned a "center" for the novel that might remain static, passive, silent.

WORKS CITED

Blain, Virginia. "Narrative Voice and the Female Perspective in Virginia Woolf's Early Novels." Clements and Grundy 115–36.

Bowlby, Rachel. *Virginia Woolf: Feminist Destinations.* New York: Blackwell, 1988.

Clements, Patricia, and Isobel Grundy, eds. *Virginia Woolf: New Critical Essays.* London: Vision, 1983.

DeSalvo, Louise. *Virginia Woolf: The Impact of Childhood Sexual Abuse on Her Life and Work.* Boston: Beacon, 1989.

DiBattista, Maria. "Joyce, Woolf and the Modern Mind." Clements and Grundy 96–114.

Gilbert, Sandra M., and Susan Gubar. *Sexchanges.* Vol. 2 of *No Man's Land: The Place of the Woman Writer in the Twentieth Century.* 2 vols. to date. New Haven: Yale University Press, 1988–.

Henke, Suzette A. "Virginia Woolf Reads James Joyce: The *Ulysses* Notebook." *James Joyce: The Centennial Symposium.* Ed. Morris Beja et al. Urbana: University of Illinois Press, 1986. 39–42.

Jenkins, William D. "Virginia Woolf and the Belittling of *Ulysses.*" *James Joyce Quarterly* 25 (1988): 513–19.

Kenner, Hugh. *Joyce's Voices.* Berkeley and Los Angeles: University of California Press, 1978.

Lawrence, Karen. *The Odyssey of Style in "Ulysses."* Princeton: Princeton University Press, 1981.

Scott, Bonnie Kime. *Joyce and Feminism.* Bloomington: Indiana University Press, 1984.

Woolf, Virginia. *Diary.* Ed. Anne Olivier Bell. 5 vols. New York: Harcourt, 1977–84. Vols. 1 (1915–19) and 2 (1920–4).

"Jacob's Room." [Holograph notebook, in three parts.] Henry W. and Albert J. Berg Collection, New York Public Library.

Jacob's Room and The Waves. New York: Harcourt, 1959.
"Modern Novels." [Holograph notebook, unsigned and undated.]
    Henry W. and Albert J. Berg Collection, New York Public Library.
A Room of One's Own. New York: Harcourt, 1929.
The Voyage Out. New York: Harcourt, 1915.

CHAPTER 4

Joyce and Ford Madox Ford

Vincent J. Cheng

James Joyce and Ford Madox Ford were two of the great early Modernist writers, both living in Paris in the 1920s and 1930s: one was the greatest prose writer of the century; and the other one of the most influential critics and editors of the age, as well as one of its most respected and prolific authors. Joyce and Ford would seem to present a naturally promising topic for critical investigation – yet there has been, to my knowledge, no formal published work focusing on their relationship.[1] This neglect is all the more surprising considering that Joyce and Ford were two of the major figures on that Parnassian literary scene that was Paris and the Left Bank in the 1920s; that both were self-exiled Catholic cosmopoles, pursuing a Continental (rather than a narrowly British) literary tradition; that they were good friends, meeting frequently for dinner, writing many letters and postcards to each other. Furthermore, their artistic interests were similar: both were disciples of the Flaubertian school, experimental prose stylists, novelists whose fictions were less interested in external action than in internal psychology, especially in the relationships between sex, religion, repression, consciousness, and subconscious thought. Ford – like his good friend Ezra Pound – was one of Joyce's staunchest defenders in the two decades when *Ulysses* was causing world-wide controversy and even supporters of Joyce were giving up on him as they became aware of Joyce's *new* "Work in Progress." Most importantly, Ford played a role in the genesis of *Finnegans Wake*: as editor of one of the leading literary magazines of the time, the *Transatlantic Review*, he published "mamalujo" in 1924, the very first fragment of "Work in Progress" to be printed; in fact, it was Ford who provided Joyce with the title "Work in Progress." Joyce later wrote that, for these reasons, he considered Ford to be the "godfather" of *Finnegans Wake* (*JJ* 563). This paper, then, intends

55

to be a beginning study and overview of the neglected literary relationship between Joyce and Ford.

Much of what we know about the nature of their friendship comes from a number of surviving letters between them, and from accounts in the memoirs of and letters to/from various mutual friends in those years (Pound, Sylvia Beach, Harriet Weaver, Robert McAlmon, Djuna Barnes, and so on). All of these sources suggest that the two men knew each other quite well, and there are several repeatedly recounted anecdotes in these accounts.

In August 1922, just months after the publication of *Ulysses*, Ford and Stella Bowen (the woman – succeeding Elsie Martindale and Violet Hunt – Ford then considered to be his "wife") left the small cottage they had been inhabiting in the British countryside and came to Paris. They were pleased to find and be welcomed by old friends in the artistic community: as Ford wrote, "I had not been ten minutes in Paris before I was invited to a *lunch d'honneur* at the Paris branch of the Pen Club" (*Nightingale* 201); "Ezra is here, going very strong; Joyce going rather weak" (letter to Edgar Jepson; Ford, *Letters* 146–7). Sylvia Beach recalls that Ford "was a jolly creature, and popular with his fellow writers ... The first thing he and his wife did was to invite 'the Crowd' to a party ... Ford invited me to dance with him, first making me take off my shoes ... I saw Joyce watching us from the side-lines with great amusement ... On another occasion, Ford and Stella invited me to supper" (*Shakespeare and Company* 137–8). Stella recalled that Joyce was "the most courteous and unassuming of guests" (*Drawn from Life* 112).

Ford was trying to decide whether to stay on and live in Paris, or whether to return to England. He later recalled reaching his decision one evening on which he had a dinner engagement with Joyce at one of Ford's favorite restaurants: "I had a date with Mr. Joyce at the old Lavenue's which used to be one of the best restaurants in Paris. As I stood outside it the clock on the Gare Montparnasse marked five and twenty past seven ... I had asked Joyce for seven-thirty; so I bought an English newspaper and sat down to an aperitif outside the restaurant in an evening of golden haze ... " As he waited, Ford considered the attractions of settling in Paris and the nuisances of living in England. After some time, Sylvia Beach and Nina Hamnett walked past:

> "We shall see you at Joyce's dinner at nine. Opposite!"
> I said: "No: he's dining with me here at 7.30 ... " It was then 8.37.
> They said: "Joyce never dines with anybody, anywhere but opposite and never at seven-thirty."
> I said: "He is dining with me to-night to try the *Chateau Pavie, 1914.*"
> They said: "He never drinks anything but white wine."
> I said: "Anyhow I am never going back to England."
> They said: "How nice!" and passed on. (*Nightingale* 259–67)

Like Joyce, Ford had chosen exile from his homeland.

Ford wrote that "For Mr. Joyce's work I had the greatest admiration and for his person the greatest esteem. I also liked his private society very much. He made then little jokes, told rather simple stories and talked about his work very enlighteningly" (*Nightingale* 290). In any event, the two men got along well – in spite of Ford's half-serious habit of lecturing Joyce on the ills of white wine: "I used to beseech Mr. Joyce to drink red, not white wine. I was really very much in earnest and not quite without official warrant" (*Nightingale* 290–1) – going on to cite some dubious medical arguments. But, as Ford good-humoredly notes, it was to no avail: "So when on the boulevards I would meet one or other of [Joyce's followers] and told them that Joyce was dining with me at 7.30 in order to taste my *Chateau Mouton Rothschild* 1885 they would cry with one accord: 'Mr. Joyce never dines with anybody. He never dines before 9.30. He never drinks anything but white wine ... ' " (*Nightingale* 292).[2]

A month or so after the dinner engagement at Lavenue's, both Joyce and Ford were guests at a dinner party given by Lloyd Morris; so was an unfrocked priest named Edwards. As Morris himself recounts (in the third person): "Soon after Edwards' arrival, [Morris] became aware that Joyce and Ford had deserted the party. He went in search of them, and finally found them irately pacing the garden path in the darkness. It developed that the presence of an unfrocked priest was an affront to their piety, and the venom of their indignation left Morris stupefied ... The matter was somehow patched up, but Morris was to receive another shock when, a few days later, he entered a favorite restaurant, and was summoned to a table where Joyce and Ford and Edwards were peaceably enjoying luncheon" (Morris 244). Both Joyce and Ford *were* lovely mummers.

Ford and Joyce's correspondence over the years is full of the tones and concerns of easy friendship. For example, in January 1923, Joyce recommends that Ford, then staying in the south, should visit a good eye doctor in Nice, the same oculist that had operated on Joyce's eyes; and he asks Ford (*Letters* 3: 70; Maddox 215, 218) to bring back for him a favorite ten-franc shell-cameo souvenir sold only by the hawkers on the souvenir bridge between France and Italy. (Ford later reported that, "on Joyce's own recommendation" he had gone to the "great oculist in Nice" who had "operated on Joyce," and that the doctor "told me that there was nothing the matter with the eyes" but to "never drink white wine. It is ruinous to the eyesight"; *Nightingale* 291). Or, for example, in July 1924 Ford wrote Joyce after another of Joyce's eye operations: "I am very glad you are through with your operation: it must be a long drag to have one hanging over the head. I feel quite confident that it will be successful" (Ford, *Letters* 161).

In April of 1928, Joyce accepted Ford's offer of "a little house [Ford] has in Toulon"; the Joyces moved to Ford's house within days, and were happy with the situation; as Joyce wrote Harriet Weaver (from Toulon), "I am here by Fr. Ford's advice and am very pleased with it, him, and myself" (Joyce, *Letters* 3: 176). Meantime, Ford and Stella had asked Joyce to be godfather to their daughter Julie; as Joyce reports to Harriet Weaver, "Ford has invited me to be godfather to his daughter ... who is to be baptised a R.C. on Friday next" (*Letters* 3: 175); "Ford's child has to be instructed in Xian doctrine, it seems ... I don't see much use for a sponsor at all if the child (who is a nice little girl anyhow) can remove the devil etc on her own account but I accepted his invitation as an act of friendliness" (*Letters* 3: 176). This concession must have been an act of personal friendliness indeed, by a man of such rigid religious principles as Joyce. In 1929 Joyce presided at a P.E.N. dinner in Paris in honor of Ford (*JJ* 622n), an act of more formal, professional friendship.

In November 1930, Joyce met Janice Biala, Ford's new "wife" ("an eighth or eighteenth," as Joyce reported to Harriet Weaver) for the first time. Joyce was struck by Ford's obvious appeal to attractive young women, and (remarking that Ford's six wives were one less than Earwicker's) penned to Harriet Weaver two stanzas of doggerel to the tune of "Father O'Flynn" (*JJ* 635–6n):

O Father O'Ford, you've a masterful way with you,
Maid, wife and widow are wild to make hay with you,
Blonde and brunette turn-about run away with you,
You've such a way with you, Father O'Ford.

That instant they see the sun shine from your eye
Their hearts flitter flutter, they think and they sigh:
We kiss ground before thee, we madly adore thee,
And crave and implore thee to take us, O Lord.

Ford responded good-naturedly with his persistent *shtick*, writing
from Toulon where he now lived with Janice: "I hope you have
given up white wine and prosper, though naturally I do hope you
prosper whether or no. Still le premier devoir du vin est d'être
rouge. I am sure the wine of Cana must have been" (Ford, *Letters*
199). Soon after, Ford requested from Joyce a few words in tribute of
Ezra Pound for a pamphlet of testimonials Ford was assembling to
help boost the American edition of the *Cantos*; Joyce, while normally reluctant to comment on his contemporaries, responded with
uncharacteristic willingness to his friend's request by generously
acknowledging the debt he owed Pound for "discovering" him (see
Ford, *Letters* 212, and *JJ* 661) – thus still avoiding direct comment
on Pound's work and maintaining a separation between personal
friendship and professional opinions.

PROFESSIONAL OPINIONS

As he did with Pound, Joyce carefully refrained from commenting
on Ford's own writings; and it is not clear how many of Ford's many
volumes he had read. But there is certainly plenty of evidence of
Joyce's respect for Ford's professional abilities, influence, and judgment. In January 1924, for example, Joyce wrote (*Letters* 3: 86) Italo
Svevo to suggest that he send his book *Zeno* to T. S. Eliot and Ford –
presumably as the influential editors of *Criterion* and of the new,
Paris-based *Transatlantic Review* (Ford had also been the founding
editor of the *English Review*). Three months later Joyce wrote Ford to
ask the latter's advice on a publishing contract tendered by Jona-
than Cape: "[Cape] has forwarded a contract to me and suggests
that I submit it to you. May I trouble you to let me know what you
think of it. The royalty 15% seems to me rather low" and so on
(*Letters* 3: 93). A few days later Joyce wrote to Sylvia Beach that "At
Mr Cape's suggestion I discussed the contract with Ford who, I

must say, gave me many useful hints" and then goes on to detail Ford's points of advice (*Letters to Sylvia Beach* 35). The following year, when a piratical journal no one knew anything about, named *Two Worlds*, appeared and published some of "Work in Progress" and *Ulysses* without Joyce's consent, Joyce wrote Harriet Weaver that "Nobody here, not even Mr Ford, can solve the problem of *Two Worlds*" (*Letters* 3: 131); obviously if anyone could figure out this vexing enigma, Joyce thought Ford could; he seemed to consider "Father O'Ford" a godfather of not only the *Wake*. In 1931, Mrs. Svevo asked Joyce to write a preface for the English translation of her late husband's *Senilità*, but Joyce (who, as *JJ* 635 notes, "had made a point of refusing to comment formally on the work of other writers") suggested Ford instead; he had Lucia write to Signora Svevo: "[My father] spoke to his friend Mr Ford Maddox [sic] Ford ... Mr Ford is perhaps the best known and most successful lecturer among english authors in the United States. He is also of a certain age himself and can write an admirable 'causerie'" (*Letters* 1: 299). That same year, Joyce even asked Ford to write the preface for Joyce's own *Tales Told of Shem and Shaun* in the event that Joyce's first choice, C. K. Ogden, refused (Ford agreed willingly, but so did Ogden; *JJ* 614).

If Joyce was reluctant to comment formally on Ford's writing, Ford had no such hesitations in turn. As early as 1914 Pound had reported to Joyce Ford's high opinion of *A Portrait of the Artist as a Young Man* (*Pound/Joyce* 25; *JJ* 354), an admiration that Stella Bowen shared.[3] Ford himself recalled: "I had my view of foreign literary life in Paris through Miss Sylvia Beach. That untiring lady battered me without ceasing. She demanded that I should write innumerable articles about 'Ulysses' and, with lance in rest, slaughter all [Joyce's] English detractors. I did!" (*Nightingale* 200). He certainly tried to offset *Ulysses*'s many detractors, writing at least three different times in 1922 alone: in the *Yale Review* (11 [July 1922]: 714–17) he wrote that

Mr. Joyce is a writer of very beautiful composed English ... *The Portrait of the Artist as a Young Man* is a book of such beauty of writing, such clarity of perception, such a serene love of and interest in life, and such charity that ... one was inclined to say: "This surely must be a peak! It is unlikely that this man will climb higher!" But ... *Ulysses* contains the undiscovered mind of man; it is human consciousness analyzed as it has never before been analyzed. Certain books change the world.

In August he wrote Jepson that "I'm quite content to leave to Joyce the leading novelist-ship of this country, think he deserves the position, and hope it will profit him" (Ford, *Letters* 143). In December 1922 he wrote in an essay on *Ulysses* in the *English Review* (35 [December 1922]: 538–48):

even though the great uninstructed public should never read *Ulysses*, ... no writer after to-day will be able to neglect *Ulysses* ... [F]or the first time in literature on an extended scale, a writer has attempted to treat man as the complex creature that man – every man! – is.

Ford defends Joyce's frankness of language, in self-aware contrast to Ford's own heavily elliptical style: "I ought to say that in Mr. Joyce's pages the epithets that my more coy pen has indicated with dots are written out in full. I don't see why they should not be" – and ends by calling *Ulysses* "a book of profound knowledge and of profound renderings of humanity" which is nevertheless unlikely to find a large reading public.

In 1929, in his study of *The English Novel*, Ford refers to "the author of 'Ulysses' who is certainly the greatest of all virtuosos of the word" (125). In 1932, in *Return to Yesterday* (171) he discusses "the road ... of English letters between *Gulliver's Travels* and Joyce's *Ulysses*" – obviously accepting *Ulysses* as one of the great modern literary landmarks; he notes in the same work that "I do not see why you should not write more than one review of a book for which you have a great admiration. I have written several times about *Ulysses*" (366). In *It Was the Nightingale* (1933) Ford wrote that "My sympathies are altogether with revolutionary work ... I would rather read work of Miss Stein or Mr. Joyce or look at the work of Picasso" (181); Joyce he refers to as "the most distinguished Anglo-Saxon writer in Paris" (203). In the testimonials for the edition of Pound's *Cantos* Ford (as editor) amassed in 1932, including one from Joyce, Ford refers to "Mr. Joyce, the most unrivalled virtuoso, [who] leads the vanguard of the green, westernmost shores of Europe" (*Pound/ Ford* 114–15).

As to *Finnegans Wake*, which drew an even more hostile (if less controversial) reaction from the literary world, it found in Ford not only a rare admirer but one of the first critics to appreciate the musical and rhythmic qualities of Wakean language. As early as 1924, with the publication of "mamalujo" in Ford's *Transatlantic Review*, Ford writes that "the whole thing is to be taken as a nonsense rhythm and that the reader should abandon himself to the sway of it" (*Letters* 3: 103); this quoted paraphrase is by Stannie, to whom Joyce, obviously pleased, had sent a copy of Ford's article; he also sent one to Harriet Weaver (*Letters* 3: 92). The essay itself had appeared in the *Chicago Tribune Sunday Magazine* (April 6, 1924), including Ford's comments that: "For myself then, the pleasure – the very great pleasure – that I get from going through the sentences of Mr. Joyce is that given me simply by the cadence of his prose, and I fancy that the greatest and highest enjoyment that can be got from any writing is simply that given by the cadence of the prose." Enthusiasm for the rhythmical music of *Finnegans Wake* is a response and argument that many more critics (such as J. Mitchell Morse) would take up later on. As Ford was again to say in his very last book – in 1938 – his excitement in reading Joyce comes from "'[Joyce's] skill in juggling words as a juggler will play with many gilt balls at once" (*The March of Literature* 324). And finally, in 1939, after the recent publication of *Finnegans Wake* had drawn a negative review in *The Saturday Review of Literature*, Ford wrote a long letter to the editor in protest, arguing the "full joy ... of Mr. Joyce's polychromatic fugal effects of language" (*Saturday Review* 20 [June 3, 1939]: 9) and that Joyce's magnificent experiments with language "affords us lesser navigators in the sea of words a chart to show us how far we may go."[4]

"MAMALUJO" AND THE "TRANSATLANTIC REVIEW"

Certainly the central element in the relationship between Ford and Joyce is the story of the first publication of a fragment from the "Work in Progress" that was to be *Finnegans Wake*; this was the "mamalujo" section (the opening pages of *FW* II.4, including the Tristan and Isolde section) printed in the April issue of the new *Transatlantic Review* in 1924. Here is the story.

In October 1923 Joyce wrote to Harriet Shaw Weaver that "Mr John Quinn [one of the financiers behind the new proposed review] has been in Paris for the past fortnight but I have not seen him. Mr Hueffer [Ford] has been made editor of a new Paris review. The editorship was offered by a financial group on condition that nothing of mine was published in it. Mr Hueffer then declined it. Finally the group gave in. Mr Pound (to whom I had shown the pieces I have written) came round to say that the front pages of the first issue were to be reserved for me with a trumpet blast" (*Letters* 1: 204). A few days later Joyce wrote again to say that "Mr Hueffer is very insistent I should give him the Earwicker episode"; that "Part of the opposition [to publishing work by Joyce], it appears, came from the British consul-general here. Perhaps that official thinks I am a popular figure in my native land"; and that "Mr Quinn invited me to dinner" (*Letters* 1: 206). Obviously some time between those two letters (October 9 and October 23) Joyce had met with Quinn and Ford: Bernard Poli (20) places the date of that famous meeting, orchestrated by Pound and taking place at Pound's studio, as October 12, 1923; it is also the meeting which produced the well-known group photographs of Joyce, Ford, Pound, and Quinn (one of which provided the model for Peter Blake's etching, reproduced on this book's dust jacket). A little while later that afternoon (after the photos were taken), Hemingway, whom Ford had never met before, also arrived, and started shadow-boxing in another room – as Ford reports (*Nightingale* 295) – with an old Chinese silk bonze of Pound's ("That young man," I said to Ezra, "appears to have sinophobia"). Meanwhile Ford pulled Joyce aside and "took the occasion to tell him that I would like to print in my review some pages of the book he was writing. I was going to devote a section of my magazine to Work in Progress of persons like himself and Picasso" (*Nightingale* 295, 292). Joyce was at first reluctant, feeling that the piece was not ready (he had earlier declined to give it to Eliot's *Criterion*), but by early 1924 he wrote (to Robert McAlmon) that "Ford has come so often to the well and talked about support given me in the past that I have consented to give him the four masters bit ... for his next number" (*Letters* 1: 209).

But Ford was at the same time concerned that Joyce's contribution might be censored or suppressed, a fear Joyce also shared; this was not an unrealistic concern, for both had in mind the recent Folkestone seizure of *Ulysses* (the 500 copies printed in Paris by John Rodker for the Egoist Press) as criminally indecent. Joyce reported in a letter to Quinn that "[Ford] fears prosecution and seizure on the charge of blasphemy" and then in a letter to Harriet Weaver: "Mr Ford in the new Transatlantic Review is taking up [in an editorial column] the question of the Folkestone seizure which he hopes to bring under government notice, I think. I have consented to give him for the next issue the Mamalujo episode"; but, with obvious relief, he reports that "The correspondent of [the] *Times* here was appealed to and, having examined it, gave his opinion that it would not lead to prosecution for blasphemy" (*Letters* 1: 210).

This correspondent was Sisley Huddleston (1883–1952), a literary journalist and the Paris correspondent for the *London Times*, who was appealed to by Ford as the "most representative official Englishman that we could find" (as Ford wrote in the *Transatlantic Review* 1.4 [April 1924]: 201). The three men met, and Joyce read the manuscript for this arbitration; as Huddleston reported:

Joyce read as only he can read: and I waited in vain for the obscenity and blasphemy ... They were not apparent to me. If they were they were carefully concealed. I reported to Ford that whatever impropriety there might be would not be visible to the naked eye of a British or American policeman. (Huddleston 264)

(One wonders if Huddleston could make anything at all of "mamalujo.") With that obstacle removed, then, the "mamalujo" fragment (now *FW* II.4, 383–99) appeared in April, in a Literary Supplement of "Work in Progress" that also included some work by Tristan Tzara (Joyce must have enjoyed the coincidence, since these pages were on Tristan and Isolde) and Hemingway.

It was the world's first glimpse of Joyce's new work-in-progress. Joyce grew fond of Ford's title "Work in Progress," which remained the working title until *Finnegans Wake*'s publication in 1939. Joyce later said (to Harriet Weaver) that Ford was thus the book's godfather (having named it and presented it to the world), and that he had "reciprocated by acting as godfather ... to one of Ford's daughters" (see *JJ* 563 and *Letters* 3: 175).

THE "FORD" IN THE "WAKE"

Not only was Ford the "godfather" of the *Wake*, it seems to me that he figures in at least several passages of *Finnegans Wake* (the first two below are admittedly speculative).

(a) Even Ford's daughter (Joyce's godchild) may be here – for Joyce, soon after telling Harriet Weaver that he has just godfathered Ford's daughter, again writes (April 28, 1928): "As regards Ford and his daughter who, by the way, is named like her mother 'Stella' I shall write soon as I have waded through a half dozen of my notebooks of revision" (*Letters* 3: 177). Does he mean he will write about "Stella" to Harriet Weaver (he had already done so on April

8 and April 16), or write about "Stella" (after doing his revisions) in "Work in Progress"? Significantly, Ford's daughter's name was *Julie*: Joyce is confusing the name of the mother, named Stella (née Esther Bowen), with the daughter, Julia (Esther Julia Ford) – whom Ford and Stella (and everyone) referred to as Julie. But in blurring "Julie" and "Stella" just days after her christening, at which he was the godfather, surely Joyce, whose memory was prodigious and precise, is not simply consciously conflating mother and daughter. Rather, he must have been amused by the resonances of the mother–daughter equivalences/transformations he was beginning to work out for himself in *Finnegans Wake*, and especially by the echoes of the daughter-figure in Swift's *Esther* VanHomrigh, *Stella* and *Vanessa* (*Stella* Bowen and *Esther* Julia Ford are *both*, in Joyce's mind, at once Esther and Stella – and perhaps even Romeo's Juliet). The coincidences may not have only been a source of amusement; it is even possible that Julie becomes one of Joyce's models for Issy – for Joyce had previously written Harriet Weaver about Julie ("who is a nice little girl"): "Ford has invited me to be godfather to his daughter (see Shaun's sermon) who is to be baptised a R.C. on Friday next" (*Letters* 3: 175–6). Is Shaun's sermon to Issy in *Finnegans Wake* (431 ff.), so full of misplaced parental advice, written by godfather Joyce partly with Julie Ford in mind? Therein lies perhaps another avenue (or dead end) of scholarly inquiry.[5]

(b) In 1923, Ford wrote a pantomime, a short and surreal poetic drama – for which Thomas C. Moser suggests that "perhaps the Nighttown section of *Ulysses* with its surreal vaudeville routines was a catalyst" (Moser 243). In turn, I might speculate that Ford's own pantomime may have gone into the creation of II.1, *Finnegans Wake*'s Mime episode ("The Mime of Mick, Nick and the Maggies") – certainly the playbills contain similar elements common to pantomimes: "*Mr. Bosphorus and the Muses, A Short History of Poetry in Britain*: Variety Entertainment in four acts ... with harlequinade, transformation scene, cinematographic effects, and many other novelties, as well as old and tried favourites" (compare *FW* 219ff.). While this is pure speculation, its plausibility is enhanced by the likelihood that Joyce read Ford's pantomime, for Ford presented Joyce with an inscribed copy of *Mr. Bosphorus* when it was published in November 1923 (Harvey 57, Moser 327n).

(c) *FW* 512.30–1: "You've soft a say with ye, Flatter O'Ford, that, honey, I hurdley chew you." This line, spoken by ALP to her

66 VINCENT J. CHENG

husband, obviously combines the songs "Father O'Flynn" and "Johnny, I Hardly Knew Ye" (both frequent in the *Wake*) with Dublin, "Town of the Ford of the Hurdles" (see also below on "Hurdlestown" and Ford). Joyce, in appreciation of Ford's parental care in lending him Ford's house in Toulon, had previously referred to Ford as "Father Ford" (*Letters* 3: 176: "I am here by Fr. Ford's advice"); and he had written doggerel stanzas about Ford as "Father O'Flynn," referring to Ford's appeal to his young and attractive "wives": the two references combine here in "Flatter O'Ford," who with his honeyed words of flattery can appeal (as HCE to his wife ALP) to young women like Janice Biala or Stella Bowen.

(d) Ford also appears several times in *Finnegans Wake* in conjunction with Sisley Huddleston. Joyce would naturally associate them together in his mind as being responsible for the first publication of Work in Progress; and he must have been struck by how their combined names were echoed in the translated name of Dublin, *Baile Atha Cliath*: "Town of the Ford of the Hurdles." The frequent Wakean plays on "Hurdlestown" are particularly suited to the pun of Huddleston.

A number of such possible references occur in the *Wake*: "Blurry works at Hurdlesford" (14.5, describing the *Wake*); "Humphrey's fordofhurdlestown" (203.6–7); "He fould the fourd; they found the hurtled stones" (224.5–6). If these references to "fourd" and "hurtled stones" are not fully convincing, the references to Dublin in 447.30 as "our town of the Fords in a huddle!" and in 481.28 as "Huddlestown" should be – for here we find the spelling of "hurdles" changed clearly to "huddles" and Huddleston. Most interesting, perhaps, is 570.32–4 (first noticed by Adaline Glasheen, 96–7), which lines include: "ford ... hurdley ... crimstone in the face." To me, "crimstone" seems to combine Folkestone (the reason for consulting Huddleston), crime, criminal indecency, and the resulting brimstone (and turning crimson in the face).

(e) Finally, page 382 of *Finnegans Wake* includes the following passage:

the Litvian Newestlatter is seen, sold and delivered and all's set for restart after the silence ... and the very boxs in all his compass, whereuponce, behome the fore for cove and trawlers, heave hone, leave lone, Larry's on the focse and Faugh MacHugh O'Bawlar at the wheel, one to do and one to dare, par by par, a peerless pair ...

William York Tindall (206) first suggested that "Faugh MacHugh O'Bawlar" (382.22) refers to Ford Madox Ford. As Roland McHugh (another "MacHugh") and others have accurately noted, the name echoes two different songs – "Follow Me Up to Carlow" (with a hero named Feagh MacHugh Byrne) and "To Ladies' Eyes a Round (Faugh a ballagh)," also referred to in 5.31 ("fargobawlers"), in 398.18 ("to Ladyseyes"), and in 541.18–19 ("Fugabollags! ... eyeball"). *Faugh a Ballagh*, the song's refrain, is Irish for "Clear the Way." If it is Ford pictured in this nautical passage, what is he clearing the way for?[6]

Certainly "Faugh MacHugh O'Bawlar" has a verbal configuration similar to "Ford Madox Ford" and is a plausible Wakean transformation. But there is also, it seems to me, some external evidence to support Tindall's speculation: 1) For, when the *Saturday Review* printed a negative review of *Finnegans Wake* upon the book's publication in 1939, Ford immediately took up his lance again to slay Joyce's detractors – his long letter to the editor, published in *Saturday Review* on June 3, 1939, was signed *"Faugh an-Ballagh Faugh"* (and not "Ford Madox Ford"; my italics). While it is conceivable that Ford remembered the name from *Finnegans Wake* and intuited that it referred to him, it is more likely that there had already been some understanding between the two friends that this should be a pet reference to Ford. This seems even more likely when one considers the position and the content of this passage on page 382. This is the page immediately preceding "mamalujo" (and was in fact the very first passage of *Finnegans Wake* composed, just prior to "mamalujo") and thus "clears the way" for the first published pages of the *Wake*. The nautical references suggest the nautical launching of the *Wake* as a vessel on its maiden voyage of publication: the "Litvian Newestlatter" (Joyce's newest Liffeyian Newsletter) to be "seen, sold and delivered" in Ford's magazine, where "all's set for restart after the silence" since the publication of *Ulysses*, with "Faugh MacHugh O'Bawlar" at the wheel (Ford as editor; I have no idea who "Larry's on the focse" refers to), editing Joyce's paragraphs "par by par," "clearing the way" for the publication and maiden voyage of Work in Progress. Furthermore, as David Dow Harvey writes (in reference to the repeated nautical allusions): "one must remember that the seal of the *Transatlantic Review* was a storm-tossed ship and its motto an abbreviated form of the Paris motto, 'Fluctuat' [Let it sail]. The magazine also was published

The Transatlantic Review

EDITED IN PARIS BY

FORD MADOX FORD

(Ford Madox Hueffer)

CONTRIBUTORS

Joseph Conrad	Thomas Hardy	A. E. Coppard
E. E. Cummings	Ezra Pound	Mary Butts
Luke Ionides	R. Descharmes	Jean Cassou
D. Chaucer	Philippe Soupault	V. Larbaud
T. S. Eliot	Jeanne Foster	R. McAlmon
H. G. Wells	Ford Madox Ford	James Joyce

PARIS   **NEW YORK**   **LONDON**

literally on the banks of the Seine" (Harvey 541–2; see frontispiece, taken from Poli 38, reproduced above) – so that the *Transatlantic Review* (whose very name is nautical) could be seen as a ship, or as the *Wake*, on her maiden voyage.

In the letter to the editor of *Saturday Review*, Ford defends Joyce and *Finnegans Wake* passionately, concluding by picking up the nautical references himself:

And the world owes gratitude to [Joyce's] huge prodigality, since not only does his prose prove how magnificently hued our language may be but it affords us lesser navigators in the sea of words a chart to show us how far we may go. It maps the verges of the word user's habitable universe.

Thus "Finnegans Wake" stands up across the flat lands of our literatures as does the first Pyramid across the sands of Egypt, and its appearance at this moment [in 1939, with War seeming certain] is almost the one event of amazing importance sufficient to withdraw our attention from public events.

The letter is signed "Your obedient servant, Faugh an-Ballagh Faugh."

This letter was printed in the *Saturday Review* on June 23. Ford and Janice, who had been living in America, were themselves on a transatlantic voyage home to Paris, having set sail from New York May 30 on the *Normandie*. Ford got ill on the voyage, and died in Deauville on June 26. A month later Joyce wrote to Frank Budgen, enclosing a copy of Ford's letter to the *Saturday Review* and acknowledging Ford's loyalty and Joyce's debt to his old friend: "[Enclosed is] a letter signed Faugh-à Ballaugh-Faugh ... possibly the last public act of his life. The first instalment of *F.W.* appeared in his *Transatlantic Review* (your 4 old men) and it was he who called it 'Fragment from *Work in Progress*'" (*Letters* 1: 405). Very likely, Ford's letter defending the *Wake was* "the last public act of his life."[7]

NOTES

1 This essay was written in spring 1989 and accepted for publication in the summer of 1989. I am adding this endnote to clarify that very recently (summer 1991), with this volume already in press, I have learned of the publication of an essay by Joseph Wiesenfarth on the relationship between Joyce and Ford, titled "Fargobawlers: James Joyce and Ford Madox Ford," just published (Summer 1991) in *Biography* 14.2: 95–116, much too late for me to make substantive reference to in this essay. In summer 1989 Robert L. Caserio had published a much more narrowly focused essay arguing that there is evidence in Ford's later novels of some

influence by *Finnegans Wake*; Caserio, "Ford Madox Ford, His Fellow Writers, and History: Another Tale of Shem and Shaun," *Contemporary Literature* 30.2 (Summer 1989): 280–98.

2 While Joyce never liked to dine early or drink red wine, he did in fact occasionally meet Ford at L'Avenue. Robert McAlmon describes one such gathering "at L'Avenue, across from the Gare Montparnasse," at which Joyce and Nora joined Ford, Stella, and Nina Hamnett, among others (McAlmon 247–8; also Brenda Maddox 248).

3 As Stella recalled from her days as a young painter and acquaintance of Pound's in London (*Drawn from Life* 50):

But there were lovely things for us to admire – Eliot's "Prufrock," Ezra's "Lustra" – Gaudier Bjeska's [sic] stone carvings and drawings of animals, and Wyndham Lewis's drawings ... There was also James Joyce's "Portrait of the Artist." Joyce and Lewis were Ezra's twin gods, before whom we were bidden to bend the knee most deeply. I did not meet Joyce, until years later, in Paris, when I found him to be far less alarming than Wyndham Lewis, whose conversation held so many traps for the unwary ...

4 In addition to his admiration for Joyce's works, Ford may have found himself strongly influenced, in his own writing, by Joyce's example. Some commentators on Ford have speculated in this vein: for example, Ann Barr Snitow argues the influence of *Ulysses* and *Finnegans Wake*, especially in terms of their myths and in terms of their epical-human conflations, on *Parade's End* (Snitow 210); and Charles G. Hoffmann suggests *Ulysses* and *Mrs. Dalloway* as models for both the stream-of-consciousness style and for the narrative structuring of *Last Post* (Hoffmann 97).

5 Julie grew up eventually to marry and become Mrs. Julia Loewe of Pasadena, California; she owns the largest cachet of Ford's letters, including seven to Joyce. I don't know if she is still alive and living in Pasadena; if so, she has thus far eluded my efforts to locate her.

6 Interestingly, "Faugh a ballagh" is also referred to once in *Ulysses* – also in a nautical context, as Bloom thinks in "Nausicaa": "Dreadful life sailors have too. Big brutes of oceangoing streamers floundering along in the dark, lowing out like seacows. *Faugh a ballagh*! Out of that, bloody curse to you! Others in vessels, bit of a handkerchief sail, pitched about like snuff at a wake when the stormy winds do blow" (13.1148–51).

7 Yeats had died in January 1939; Joyce would be gone two years later. Pound, in the *Pisan Cantos*, would later remember (*Pound/Joyce* 275) these three buried "companions" together:

Lordly men are to earth o'ergiven
these the companions:
Fordie that wrote of giants
and William who dreamed of nobility
and Jim the comedian singing:
"Blarrney castle me darlin'
you're nothing now but a StOWne."   (Canto 74)

WORKS CITED

Beach, Sylvia. *Shakespeare and Company.* New York: Harcourt, 1959.
Bowen, Stella. *Drawn from Life: Reminiscences by Stella Bowen.* London: Collins, 1941.
The Chicago Tribune Sunday Magazine, April 6, 1924.
The Criterion. Literary journal.
Deming, Robert H. *James Joyce: The Critical Heritage.* 2 vols. New York: Barnes, 1970.
Ellmann, Richard. *James Joyce.* Rev. ed. New York: Oxford University Press, 1982.
The English Review. Literary journal.
Ford, Ford Madox. *The English Novel.* Philadelphia: Lippincott, 1929.
  It Was the Nightingale. Philadelphia: Lippincott, 1933.
  Letters of Ford Madox Ford. Ed. Richard M. Ludwig. Princeton: Princeton University Press, 1965.
  The March of Literature. New York: Dial, 1938.
  Mr. Bosphorus and the Muses. London: Duckworth, 1923.
  Return to Yesterday. New York: Liveright, 1932.
  Thus to Revisit: Some Reminiscences. New York: Dutton, 1921.
Glasheen, Adaline. *Third Census of "Finnegans Wake."* Berkeley and Los Angeles: University of California Press, 1977.
Hart, Clive. *A Concordance to "Finnegans Wake."* Minneapolis: University of Minnesota Press, 1963.
Harvey, David Dow. *Ford Madox Ford: A Bibliography of Works and Criticism.* Princeton: Princeton University Press, 1962.
Hoffmann, Charles G. *Ford Madox Ford.* New York: Twayne, 1967.
Huddleston, Sisley. *Bohemian Literary and Social Life in Paris.* London: Harrap, 1928. Published in America as *Paris Salons, Cafés, Studios.* Philadelphia: Lippincott, 1928.
Joyce, James. *Finnegans Wake.* New York: Viking, 1939.
  James Joyce's Letters to Sylvia Beach, 1921–1940. Ed. Melissa Banta and Oscar A. Silverman. Bloomington: Indiana University Press, 1987.
  Letters of James Joyce. 3 vols. Vol. 1, ed. Stuart Gilbert. Vols. 2 and 3, ed. Richard Ellmann. New York: Viking, 1966.
  Ulysses: The Corrected Text. Ed. Hans Walter Gabler et al. New York: Random, 1986.
Maddox, Brenda. *Nora: The Real Life of Molly Bloom.* Boston: Houghton, 1988.
McAlmon, Robert. *Being Geniuses Together.* Rev. Kay Boyle. Garden City, N.Y.: Doubleday, 1968.
McHugh, Roland. *Annotations to "Finnegans Wake."* Baltimore: Johns Hopkins University Press, 1980.
Mizener, Arthur. *The Saddest Story: A Biography of Ford Madox Ford.* New York: World, 1971.
Morris, Lloyd. *A Threshold in the Sun.* New York: Harper, 1943.

Morse, J. Mitchell. "On Teaching *Finnegans Wake.*" *Twelve and a Tilly.* Ed. Jack P. Dalton and Clive Hart. Evanston, Ill.: Northwestern University Press, 1965. 65–71.

Moser, Thomas C. *The Life in the Fiction of Ford Madox Ford.* Princeton: Princeton University Press, 1980.

Poli, Bernard J. *Ford Madox Ford and the "Transatlantic Review."* Syracuse, N.Y.: Syracuse University Press, 1967.

Pound, Ezra. *Pound/Ford, The Story of a Literary Friendship: The Correspondence between Ezra Pound and Ford Madox Ford.* Ed. Brita Lindberg-Seyersted. New York: New Directions, 1982.

Pound/Joyce: The Letters of Ezra Pound to James Joyce, with Pound's Essays on Joyce. Ed. Forrest Read. New York: New Directions, 1967.

The Saturday Review of Literature 20, June 3, 1939.

Snitow, Ann Barr. *Ford Madox Ford and the Voice of Uncertainty.* Baton Rouge: Louisiana University Press, 1984.

Tindall, William York. *A Reader's Guide to "Finnegans Wake."* New York: Farrar, 1969.

The Transatlantic Review. Literary journal.

The Yale Review 11 (July 1922): 714–17.

CHAPTER 5

Joyce and Freud: discontent and its civilizations

Brian W. Shaffer

I seriously believe that you will retard the course of civilisation in Ireland by preventing the Irish people from having one good look at themselves in my nicely polished looking-glass.
                    Joyce, defending *Dubliners*, in a letter to Grant Richards

Evidently she had been unfit to live, without any strength of purpose, an easy prey to habits, one of the wrecks on which civilisation has been reared.
                    James Duffy on Emily Sinico in Joyce, "A Painful Case"

It has long been a truism of Joyce studies that the critique of Irish civilization in Joyce's works centers upon its representative subjects – "paralyzed" Dubliners.[1] Pointing to the author's avowed intention to "write a chapter of the moral history of my country" (*Letters* 2: 134), critics typically view Joyce's fiction as "an attempt to represent certain aspects of the life of one of the European capitals" (*Letters* 2: 109). While Joyce insists that the *raison d'être* of a volume like *Dubliners* is "to betray the soul of that hemiplegia or paralysis which many consider a city" (*Letters* 1: 55) – Dublin seeming to him the very "centre of paralysis" (*Letters* 2: 134) – there has been little scholarly attention to the psychosocial and the broadly cultural nature and determinants of this crippling discontent.

Two notable expositions of Joycean paralysis in *Dubliners*, and, by extension, other of Joyce's fictions, have been advanced. The first, and still most popular, might be called the "thematic unity" theory: that "the theme of paralysis serves as a unifying concern which embodies the value of the material out of which the stories were shaped" (San Juan 17), that "the basic pattern underlying all others is a paralytic process: *Dubliners* has a pathological unity more subtle than is immediately apparent" (Walzl, "Pattern" 22). The second most popular explanation attributes this paralysis to spiritual enervation. Brewster Ghiselin has argued this perspective succinctly.

73

"When the outlines of the symbolic pattern have been grasped," he writes, "the whole unifying development will be discernible as a sequence of events in a moral drama, an action of the human spirit struggling for survival under peculiar conditions of deprivation, enclosed and disabled by a degenerate environment that provides none of the primary necessities of spiritual life" (318). Frequently accompanying this view is the insight that the Irish suffer inexorably simply because they deserve it: that "the timelessness of Irish paralysis reinforces ... mythic, religious and legendary patterns that Joyce seems to place so frequently at the very center of each story ..." (Torchiana 9). Yet both of these perspectives neglect the fact, as Florence Walzl has shown, that "Joyce's picture of Dublin social life is solidly based on historical reality" (*"Dubliners* Women" 53). Moreover, both of these explanations, while convincing up to a point, fail to address the psychosocial dimension of the paralysis represented in Joyce's fiction.

To this end, I seek to bring certain late Freudian ideas to bear on the paralysis represented in *Dubliners* and *Ulysses*. Let me state at the outset that I advance ideas from Freud's *The Future of an Illusion* (1927) and *Civilization and Its Discontents* (1930)[2] neither to apply these critiques to Joyce's fiction without qualification nor, still less, to argue any (chronologically impossible) influence between these theoretical works and the fiction. Instead, I will discuss *Dubliners* and *Ulysses* in light of Freud's critique of civilization in order to reveal what might be called a Joycean critique of modern Irish civilization. Moreover, by bringing Joyce's texts to bear on Freud's contribution to the "hermeneutics of suspicion," the critical limitations, as well as the critical power, of this contribution are broached.

Freudian interpretations of Joyce's texts have tended to concentrate either on character or author psychology, on what Joyce thought of Freud, or on speculations of what portion of Freud's work was known to Joyce.[3] This has led to the critical neglect of certain important intersections of Joycean and Freudian thinking. For one thing, both writers view the path of individual development as a trope for the process of civilization – that "civilization," as Patrick Brantlinger characterizes late Freudian thought, "is no more than the mature individual writ large" (163). "I perceived even more clearly," Freud declares late in life, "that the events of human history" and of "cultural development" are "no more than a reflection of the dynamic conflicts between the ego, the id, and the super-ego . . . are the very same processes repeated on a wider stage" (cited in Levi 174). Likewise, Joyce opens his essay, "Ireland, Island of Saints and Sages," with the statement that "Nations have their ego, just like individuals" (*CW* 154), and, in his 1904 sketch "A Portrait of the Artist," speaks of paralysis not in individual terms but in terms of the "general paralysis of an insane society" (*P* 266).

Second, both Joyce and Freud unceremoniously push aside the possibility of autonomous subjectivity. As Gerald Levin succinctly puts it of Freud's work, the individual therein is "a diminished being, ridden with conflicts that civilization heightens rather than alleviates" (142–3). And Jeremy Hawthorn points out of Joyce's fiction that "few novels show their characters less as free, autonomous beings or more tied to their society and its history" (116). Whatever else one may say of the characters who inhabit Joyce's *Dubliners, A Portrait of the Artist as a Young Man, Exiles, Ulysses,* or *Finnegans Wake,* none of them, it is clear, accomplish that task set by Stephen Dedalus: to "fly by those nets" of "nationality, language, religion" (*P* 203) – indeed, these fictions are among other things *about* this impossibility.[4]

Third, both Joyce and Freud indicate the possibility of a mental "liberation" which their works can provide their readers. "By withdrawing their expectations from the other world and concentrating all their liberated energies into their life on earth," Freud, here reminiscent of Marx, optimistically asserts of his readers toward the end of *The Future of an Illusion,* "they will probably succeed in achieving a state of things in which life will become tolerable for everyone and civilization no longer oppressive to anyone" (50). Joyce is equally direct about the therapeutic function of *Dubliners,* even if his rhetoric is smug and self-serving: "I believe that in composing my chapter of moral history in exactly the way I have composed it I have taken the first step towards the spiritual liberation of my country" (*Letters* 1: 62–3). However, more important than this common ground between them – and despite Joyce's avowed disdain of Freud (whom he at one point refers to as "the Viennese Tweedledee" [*Letters* 1: 166])[5] – is the great degree to which late Freudian thinking supplies us with the tools to uncover a neglected critique of civilization in Joyce's fiction.

The Future of an Illusion and *Civilization and Its Discontents* are of particular interest to me here because it is in these works that "Freud's psychology is as much a social psychology as an individual psychology" (Levi 180). While Freud's approach to the problem of civilization is not "historical" in any thoroughgoing way – to the extent that he psychoanalyzes civilization much as he would a patient – these two texts, unlike most of Freud's earlier ones, take up the health of Western civilization as a whole rather than that of individuals within it.[6]

But what, for Freud, is civilization? His answer: "the whole sum of the achievements and the regulations which distinguish our lives from those of our animal ancestors and which serve two purposes – namely to protect men against nature and to adjust their mutual relations" (*CD* 36). For Freud this first purpose concerns our capacity to extract wealth from nature in order to satisfy human needs, and the second one concerns the regulations used to adjust human relations, particularly with respect to the distribution of available wealth (*FI* 6). While one might expect that this civilizing trend leads to an harmonious human community which can devote itself at last to the acquisition and enjoyment of wealth, in fact, for Freud, "It seems rather that every civilization must be built up on coercion and renunciation of instinct . . ." (*FI* 7). And herein lies the true purpose of religion for Freud: by maintaining the illusion of a divine order, civilization can continue to demand the instinctual renunciations necessary for its survival. In this way, for him, religious ideas amount to little more than expressions of childhood neurosis and illusion.

However, for Freud, it is not religion alone but what he calls "the narcissism of minor differences" as well by which civilization is able to dispel the aggressive feelings generated by its own repressiveness. This concept is particularly valuable for our purposes as it suggests an important link between civilization and narcissism – a link represented repeatedly in Joyce's fiction. In *The Future of an Illusion* Freud maintains that:

The narcissistic satisfaction provided by the cultural ideal is . . . among the forces which are successful in combating the hostility to culture within the cultural unit. This satisfaction can be shared in not only by the favoured classes, which enjoy the benefits of the culture, but also by the suppressed ones, since the right to despise the people outside it compensates them for the wrongs they suffer within their own unit. No doubt one is a wretched plebeian, harassed by debts and military service; but, to make up for it, one is a Roman citizen, one has one's share in the task of ruling other nations and dictating their laws. This identification of the suppressed classes with the class who rules and exploits them is, however, only part of a larger whole. For, on the other hand, the suppressed classes can be emotionally attached to their masters; in spite of their hostility to them they may see in them their ideals; unless such relations of a fundamentally satisfying kind subsisted, it would be impossible to understand how a number of civilizations have survived so long in spite of the justifiable hostility of large human masses. (*FI* 13)[7]

In *Civilization and Its Discontents* Freud puts this phenomenon in even plainer terms: "It is always possible to bind together a considerable number of people in love, so long as there are people left over to receive the manifestation of their aggressiveness" (61). It is difficult to overestimate the importance of Freud's concept of a culturally encouraged narcissism – as a means of diffusing aggressive feelings within civilization – when attempting to understand Joyce's representation of Irish paralysis.[8]

Gerty MacDowell in the "Nausicaa" episode of *Ulysses* (and her two predecessors in *Dubliners* who closely resemble her: Eveline, in the story of that name, and Maria, in "Clay") is a case in point.[9] While it is hardly innovative to attribute to Gerty a narcissistic perspective – Kimberly Devlin deems her "narcissistic and yet highly self-conscious" (141), and Mark Shechner speaks of her as "the narcissistic phase of Irish Catholic adolescence" (161) – none has linked Gerty's narcissism, as late Freudian thinking would urge, with the preservation of civilization: as a means of allaying the discontent which arises from its contradictions. Indeed, most attention to Gerty's narcissism has settled on the style of narrative discourse associated with her. Fritz Senn, for example, notes that this discourse "is manifestly unable to characterize anything outside itself." "It reflects only its own vacuity," he continues, "it hardly illuminates or communicates, its glitter is narcissistic, its essence is self-gratification" (309). Apt though this assessment is, the psychosocial context which necessitates Gerty's text demands further clarification.[10]

To say the least, Gerty, like Eveline and Maria, experiences her "present naively, as it were, without being able to form an estimate of its contents" (*FI* 5), due to her need to dress an otherwise unbearable existence in the narcissistic garb of self-celebratory discourse. Consider the images in "Nausicaa" which suggest Gerty's narcissistic delusion: her placement on Sandymount Strand like Narcissus, "near the little pool by the rock" (*U* 13.355), and her memory of standing before the bedroom mirror – "what joy was hers when she tried [new attire] on then, smiling at the lovely reflection which the mirror gave back to her!" (*U* 13.161–2). She "knew how to cry nicely before the mirror. You are lovely, Gerty, it said" (*U* 13.192–3).[11] Introduced as self-absorbed, "lost in thought, gazing far away into the distance" (*U* 13.79–80), Gerty accepts a narcissistic orientation toward her experience in order, as Freud would have it, "to re-create the world; to build up in its stead another world in which its most unbearable features are eliminated and replaced by others that are in conformity with [her] wishes." The victim "corrects some aspect of the world which is unbearable" to her, Freud continues, "by the construction of a wish and introduces this delusion into reality" (*CD* 28). Because Gerty is not able, despite her avowed desire, to "throw my cap at who I like because it's leap year" (*U* 13.590), she therefore resorts to slighting her friends Cissy Caffrey and Edy Boardman – engaging in the narcissism of minor differences – in order to keep potentially crippling realizations about her future amatory life at bay.

Gerty's narcissism of minor differences manifests itself in her suspiciously fluctuating appraisals of her friends. Sometimes finding Cissy "a girl loveable in the extreme" (*U* 13.37–8) and "sincerity itself, one of the bravest and truest hearts heaven ever made" (*U* 13.278–9), and other times finding her a "confounded little cat" (*U* 13.581) (and Edy a "little spitfire" [*U* 13.221], an "Irritable little gnat" [*U* 13.523]), Gerty attempts to deflect the misery of her experience onto others: no matter how bad it is for her it is worse for her friends; no matter how good they look she looks better. Gerty's new clothes, she reasons at one point, will "take the shine out of some people she knew," and her shoes, "the newest thing in footwear," will also contribute to her unparalleled beauty ("Edy Boardman prided herself that she was very *petite* but she never had a foot like Gerty MacDowell, a five, and never would . . .") (*U* 13.164–7). Gerty's narcissism – because of the blinders it applies and the limited focus it therefore enforces – allows her to evade, or at least to ignore, the dimensions of her own material hopelessness. It allows her to explain away her competitiveness with Cissy and Edy as due to *their* "jealousy," to the "little tiffs" that "from time to time" afflict even the best of "girl chums" (*U* 13.93–4). Further, she can insist on her superiority over her "fallen women" friends because they date "soldiers and coarse men" (*U* 13.662–3) while she is "adored" exclusively by "gentlemen" (like Bloom). However, Gerty's narcissism of minor differences pertains not only to physical appearance but to religious difference. She makes much out of the difference between Catholics, who know "Who came first and after Him the Blessed Virgin and then Saint Joseph" (*U* 13.139–40), and Protestants, such as the mysterious "gentlemen" (Bloom is Jewish), who nevertheless might "convert" if they "truly loved her" (*U* 13.434). By fetishizing the difference between Catholics and Protestants, rather than focusing on her own social oppression, Gerty's self-knowledge remains severely limited. Gerty will keep her mind off that which oppresses her as long as other distracting tensions, religious and otherwise, exist to claim her attention.

While the nature of Gerty's narcissistic delusion is, above all else, sexual, it is also related to her internalization of religious rhetoric, its "external coercion gradually becom[ing] internalized" (*FI* 11). As Joyce himself insists in "Ireland, Island of Saints and Sages," "individual initiative is paralysed by the influence and admonitions of the church ..." (*CW* 171). Freud would explain this phenomenon by suggesting that Gerty feels that she will enjoy, if she only has patience, the perfection that she is presently being denied. Because – as Freud explains the Western religious understanding – "In the end all good is rewarded and all evil punished," Gerty can assume that "all the terrors, the sufferings and the hardships of life are destined to be obliterated" (*FI* 19). This is represented most clearly in Gerty's description of the "men's temperance retreat conducted by the missioner," in which the assembled men, "after the storms of this weary world, kneeling before the feet of the immaculate" – as in death – are "*gathered together without distinction of social class*" (*U* 13.282–7, my emphasis). For Gerty this socio-economic equality is clearly the final and just state of things for which she must patiently wait.

Freud's critique of eros and civilization speaks to Gerty's sexuality as well. Indeed, Freud himself asks the question, "is it not the case that in our civilization the relations between the sexes are disturbed by an erotic illusion or a number of such illusions?" (*FI* 34). His answer, of course, is a resounding "yes": "I am ... speaking of the way of life which makes love the centre of everything, which looks for all satisfaction in loving and being loved" (*CD* 29). In his "On Narcissism: An Introduction" Freud makes clear, in his characteristically misogynistic prose, the role of narcissism in this illusion: "Strictly speaking, such women love only themselves with an intensity comparable to that of the man's love for them" (46). Yet what better way to characterize Gerty's obsession than this way: her obsession with "loving and being loved" ("Nothing else mattered. Come what might she would be wild, untramelled, free" [U 13.672–3]), both as tantalizing lover ("a womanly woman" [U 13.435]), and as nurturing daughter/mother ("A sterling good daughter was Gerty just like a second mother in the house ..." [U 13.325–6]). Indeed, for Gerty, love is "a woman's birthright" (U 13.200), "her dream" and "master guide" (U 13.671–2). "[S]he could make him fall in love with her" (U 13.438), Gerty at one point thinks of Reggy Wylie, for "he who would woo and win Gerty MacDowell must be a man among men" (U 13.206–7). As for Bloom, the "mystery man on the beach," Gerty can miraculously tell "without looking" that he never takes "his eyes off of her" (U 13.495–6). Replete with "sweet flowerlike face" (U 13.764), with the most seductive "bluest Irish blue" eyes (U 13.108), and with her "wealth of wonderful hair" (U13.116), Gerty MacDowell fancies herself no less than "as fair a specimen of winsome Irish girlhood as one could wish to see" (U 13.80–1) in "God's fair land of Ireland" (U 13.122). In this way Gerty mistakes Bloom's lust for love, his "passionate gaze" for "undisguised admiration" (U 13.565): "It is for you, Gerty MacDowell, and you know it" (U 13.566–7).

Freud's critique of love centers on the contradictory and ambiguous role of eros within civilization, on the "careless way in which language uses the word 'love.'" "People give the name 'love' to the relation between a man and a woman ... but they also give the name 'love' to the positive feelings between parents and children, and between the brothers and sisters of a family ..." (CD 49). For Freud, because "love comes into opposition [with] the interests of civilization," on the one hand, and because "civilization threatens love with substantial restrictions," on the other, the relation of love to civilization becomes ambiguous (CD 50). For him, whereas the commandment to "Love thy neighbor as thyself" is fundamental to the development of civilization, it is nevertheless "impossible to fulfill; such an enormous inflation of love can only lower its value, not get rid of the difficulty." "Civilization pays no attention to all this," Freud continues, "it merely admonishes us that the harder it is to obey the precept the more meritorious it is to do so" (CD 90). If Gerty MacDowell's perspective on love can be seen as the ideal fictionalized representation of Freud's revealed contradiction, then the narrator's perspective on it in "Cyclops" can be seen as its ideal parody:

Love loves to love love. Nurse loves the new chemist. Constable 14A loves Mary Kelly. Gerty MacDowell loves the boy that has the bicycle. M. B. loves a fair gentleman ... Jumbo, the elephant, loves Alice, the elephant ... You love a certain person. And this person loves that other person because everybody loves somebody but God loves everybody. (*U* 12.1493–1501)

Trite, sentimental, and defensive, this narcotic view of love, Joyce's text seems to be suggesting, cannot help but encourage Gerty's placid acceptance of the hopelessness that she faces. Whatever else Freud's critique of civilization tells us of Joyce's paralyzed subjects, it precludes perspectives such as the following, that "no specifically Irish paralysis is to blame for the fact that Maria is man-hungry and is not fed" (Glasheen 106), and that "Joyce indicates why Eveline will not, in fact, be able to escape. Paralysis will win because she is not worthy to defeat it" (Hart 50). Indeed, Freud's critique of civilization tempers, rather than emphasizes, our sense of Gerty, Eveline and Maria as weak, self-defeating, and worthless.[12]

To the extent that Freud's critique of civilization provides insights into the paralysis of Joyce's female subjects, it sheds light on the discontent of Joyce's male subjects as well. In the case of Little Chandler, the protagonist of "A Little Cloud," for example, late Freudian theory reveals a related aspect of Joyce's critique of Irish civilization. Beyond the conventional wisdom that Little Chandler's state of paralysis is due to his own sentimentality and delusions of grandeur,[13] this discontent is more convincingly explained in psychosocial terms.

R. B. Kershner has pointed out that "Little Chandler's story, more than that of any other character, works upon a framework of massive oppositions." "Of all the Dubliners," Kershner continues, "he and his opposite, Gallaher, are perhaps the closest to stock characters; the two seem to exist only in order to complement one another" (96). To be sure, such oppositions as East/West and England/Ireland (Ghiselin 327) dominate the symbolic and metaphoric architecture of the narrative. The story of an encounter, after eight years, between "two friends" who meet at Corless's – a Continental-style hotel and restaurant in Dublin – "A Little Cloud" opens by suggesting the nearly total opposition of Thomas ("Little") Chandler, a 32-year-old clerk (and would-be poet) at the

Kings' Inns, and Ignatius Gallaher, a successful, ex-patriot journalist of the London Press who returns home for a business visit.

Whereas the "divide" which separates Chandler and Gallaher – derivative poet versus derivative journalist – is ultimately engulfed in irony, it is not undercut thoroughly enough to negate the relevancy of this distinction between them. Little Chandler has remained a petty clerk in "old jog-along Dublin" (D 78) with its "poor stunted houses," a "band of tramps" (D 73), and with its "horde of grimy children" who populate the street "like mice," like "minute vermin-like life" (D 71). Gallaher, on the other hand, who years ago Chandler thought possessed a "future greatness" (D 72) and rare talent, has since escaped to the "great city London" (D 70) in order to pursue a "triumphant life" (D 80). In comparison with Gallaher's "travelled air, his well-cut tweed suit and fearless accent" (D 70), his "large gold watch" (D 80), and his career, which takes him not only to London and Berlin but to Paris with its "gaiety, movement, excitement" (D 76), Chandler cuts a pious and a "modest figure" (D 71), is a "melancholy" (D 73) and timid man who merely "pull[s] along" (D 74), vacationing no further from "dull" Dublin than the Isle of Man. In contrast to Gallaher, Chandler feels he possesses a "sober inartistic life" (D 73) of "tiresome writing" (D 71). While Little Chandler allows his whiskey to be "very much diluted" (D 75) and slowly sips at the drink (D 76), Gallaher finishes his "boldly" (D 76), drinking it "neat" (D 75). Dublin, Little Chandler comes to feel, is a slow, small, and watered-down version of London, a still backwater for those too weak to leave. To Little Chandler's "stale" marriage (D 82), unromantic and constraining (he now regards Annie as cold and passionless), Gallaher speaks of his freedom to sample from among the wealthy, exotic, passionate, and voluptuous women of Europe, "Hot stuff!" (D 76).

While Hélène Cixous is certainly correct to note that "'A Little Cloud' symbolizes the fallen dream, the idea of powerlessness" (90), it is Freud's insights into the mystifying powers of civilization that best explain the paralysis represented in "A Little Cloud." For what better way than through "the narcissism of minor differences" to explain Little Chandler's new-found discontent at the prospect of seeing Gallaher again: "For the first time in his life he felt himself superior to the people he passed. For the first time his soul revolted against the dull inelegance of Capel Street. There was no doubt about it: if you wanted to succeed you had to go away. You could do nothing in Dublin" (*D* 73).[14] Too close for comfort in wealth and station to the Dubliners around him, Little Chandler can distinguish himself only by patronizing Ireland ("the old country" [*D* 75]) as Gallaher does him ("old hero" [*D* 74]). Despite the fact that Chandler is anything but satisfied with his lot, he nevertheless vainly attempts to contrast his "refined" manners, appearance, and literary sensibility with those base ones of the "crowd" (70, 74): perhaps he has little to boast about, but his compatriots have even less.

Freud's critique of civilization also speaks to Little Chandler's resignation to fate and his "dull resentment against his life" (*D* 83): "He felt how useless it was to struggle against fortune, this being the burden of wisdom which the ages had bequeathed to him" (*D* 71). Germane to this attitude Freud writes that in addition to the constraints imposed by civilization on the individual "are added the injuries which untamed nature – he calls it Fate – inflicts on him. One might suppose that this condition of things would result in a permanent state of anxious expectation in him and a severe injury to his natural narcissism" (*FI* 16). For this reason, Little Chandler (like Gerty, Eveline, and Maria) conjures an escape fantasy ("Could he not escape from his little house? . . . Could he go to London?" [*D* 83]), even though his narcissistic impulse, which limits options rather than makes them possible, checks this notion immediately ("It was useless, useless! He was a prisoner for life" [*D* 84]). Despite the fact that he comes to "feel somewhat disillusioned" with Gallaher (*D* 76–7), he nevertheless proceeds to engage in self-victimization by internalizing his own aggression, by making himself his own enemy. As Theodor Adorno puts it, linking Freudian narcissism with the internalization of social sanctions, "This repression of . . . powerlessness points not merely to the disproportion between the individual and his powers within the whole but still more to injured narcissism and the fear of realizing that [individuals] themselves go to make up the false forces of domination before which they have every reason to cringe" ("Sociology and Psychology" 89). In Adorno's Freudian scenario, the civilization-inspired superego is triumphant, rendering the subject his or her own jail-keeper.[15]

In Little Chandler's case, not only does civilization, as Freud would view it, master the individual's dangerous desire for aggression by weakening it and by setting up an agency within him to guard it, "like a garrison in a conquered city" (*CD* 70–1), but civilization offers two other means of evading its own shortcomings, both of which are reflected in "A Little Cloud": isolation and intoxication (*CD* 24–5). Clive Hart has described Little Chandler's fundamental solitude – "he cannot emerge from the hell of loneliness in which he is trapped" (92) – yet neglects to point out that it is a feeling of isolation verging on paranoia: "The bar seemed to him to be full of people and he felt that the people were observing him curiously" (*D* 74). The function of intoxication in this story is even more obvious. Not only does Chandler become "warm and excited," the "three small whiskies" having "gone to his head," and the cigar having "confused his mind" (*D* 80), but earlier Gallaher is described as "emerging after some time from the clouds of smoke in which he had taken refuge" (*D* 78). Hence, Joyce's fiction suggests, "intoxicants" too function as mystifiers of Ireland's imposed contradictions. They permit Little Chandler, paradoxically, both to admire and to despise Gallaher. In spite of Chandler's hostility toward Gallaher, he sees in the ex-patriot the English ideal he (and Ireland) seeks but cannot embody. He can only lamely wish to "vindicate himself in some way, to assert his manhood" (*D* 80) – even if he remains fundamentally "paralyzed."

W. J. McCormack has most vociferously bemoaned the widespread "refusal to acknowledge the metaphorical nature of Joycean 'paralysis'" (94). To begin to redress this imbalance, this reading of Gerty, Chandler and Gallaher seeks to demonstrate the extent to which Joycean "paralysis" is part and parcel of an entire critique of Irish civilization, rather than simply a thematic unifying principle or an attack on the "inherent spiritual enervation" of Dubliners. Yet Joyce's texts are far more knowing than Freud's in at least one respect: for their understanding and demonstration of the complex relationship between the discourse of culture and the language of the mind, between the "social text" and the "streaming of consciousness."[16] To be sure, one of this fiction's most provocative qualities is that it forcefully shows us just how much an impoverished public discourse can effect, detrimentally, the subjects who speak and think it. Helmut Bonheim argues that "Joyce's style is indeed admirably suited to his central theorem: that the more positive and creative aspects of civilization are developed by those who, by fighting against society as it is, fight for it, by those who envision the future as substantially different from the present" (15). If Bonheim is correct, then it is arguable that such "paralyzed"

Dubliners as Gerty MacDowell and Little Chandler represent for Joyce various extremes to which the "civilized" will go, not in fighting society, but in fighting themselves.

NOTES

1 Craig Werner, for example, has recently written that "competing approaches to [*Dubliners*] generally center on disagreements concerning the implications of what nearly all critics have recognized as Joyce's central theme: the paralysis permeating Irish life"(33). This paralysis is no less an issue in *Ulysses*, a novel which can be viewed as an elaborate and lengthy *Dubliners* story.

2 Hereinafter abbreviated as *FI* and *CD*, respectively.

3 For insightful Freudian interpretations of Joyce's works see Anderson, Brivic, Gose, Kimball, and Shechner.

4 See Herr, *Joyce's Anatomy of Culture*, for the most sustained and sophisticated argument that Joyce's subjects are the products, not of their own autonomy, but of the competing discourses of their culture.

5 Joyce also disparagingly refers to Jung, with whom he eventually corresponds over Lucia and *Ulysses*, as "the Swiss Tweedledum" (*Letters* 1:166).

6 Unlike Nietzsche, Freud scorns "to distinguish between culture and civilization" (*FI* 6). Nevertheless, Freud, in these texts, clearly means "civilization" rather than "culture" if we take seriously his delineation of "barbarous," "which is the opposite of civilized" (*CD* 40).

7 This idea of a "narcissism of minor differences" dates from Freud's *Group Psychology and the Analysis of the Ego* (1921) in which he writes: "In the undisguised antipathies and aversions which people feel towards strangers with whom they have to do we may recognize the expression of self-love – of narcissism" (34).

8 For more on Freud's critique of civilization see Brantlinger 154–83, Levi 173–83, and Levin 124–45.

9 Gerty and Eveline share a number of salient characteristics. Each is an aging, female adolescent (Gerty is twenty-one, Eveline nineteen), religious, impoverished, and ill-educated, who fears the passing of time. Moreover, each comes from a home in which the mother is absent and the father (who refuses to give his daughter freedom) is frequently violent and intoxicated. He is unemployed and manipulative, and has his daughter do the household chores. In each case there is little chance of escaping from this state of affairs, yet each conjures an escape fantasy – centered around males – to mask the paralyzing hopelessness of her situation: for Eveline it is Frank who will save her; for Gerty it is "the dark stranger" (Bloom) who will alleviate her discontent. Finally, both Gerty's and Eveline's predicaments are glimpsed by twilight: in each case the seated Dubliner witnesses the arrival of evening and the dimming of hopes.

10 For more on the relationship between Gerty's discourse and pre-
dicament see Richards, and Norris, "Modernism, Myth, and Desire in
'Nausicaa.'" These two culturally-oriented approaches nicely complement Joyce's familiar description of the style of "Nausicaa" (that it is
"written in a namby-pamby jammy marmalady drawersy (alto-là!)
style" [*Letters* 1: 135]) as well as Hugh Kenner's ingenious formulation
of "The Uncle Charles Principle" (*Joyce's Voices* 15–38) at work in
Joyce's texts.

11 In "Clay" Maria too stands "before the mirror" and looks "with quaint
affection at the diminutive body which she had so often adorned . . .
[S]he found it a nice tidy little body" (*D* 101). Craig Werner aptly notes
of this story that "implicitly commenting on the absence of real communication in spoken language, Joyce transforms conversation into internal
monologue, emphasizing his characters' self-absorption" (44). For a
masterful reading of "Clay" see Norris, "Narration under a Blindfold."

12 Gerty's boundless conventionality has led Suzette Henke to note correctly that Gerty is "a pawn of social self-definition" the "pathetic
victim of social and religious enculturation," and, hence, that "Nausicaa" is in fact directed "less against Gerty than against the manipulative society of which she is a product" (147, 132, 134).

13 For Hélène Cixous Little Chandler "suffers, as do all Joyce's Dubliners,
from a sickness which acts as the unifying theme of the fifteen stories,
paralysis" (89).

14 In his essay, "Ireland, Island of Saints and Sages," Joyce appears to
agree with Chandler: "No one who has any self-respect stays in
Ireland," he writes, "but flees afar as though from a country that has
undergone the visitation of an angered Jove" (*CW* 171).

15 This notion is also reflected in Joyce's "After the Race," in which the
Dublin "sightseers," who gather "in clumps to watch the cars" race
homeward, are described as raising "the cheer of the gratefully
oppressed": "through this channel of poverty and inaction the Con-
tinent sped its wealth and industry" (*D* 42).

16 As Cheryl Herr puts the relationship between style and subjectivity in
Joyce's fiction, "one of the things that Joyce's insistent alluding makes
clear is that thinking, the streaming of consciousness, the content of
interior monologue, the very shape of the self are woven from the
materials of one's culture" ("Art and Life, Nature and Culture, *Ulysses*"
25).

WORKS CITED

Adorno, Theodor W. "Sociology and Psychology." *New Left Review* 46
(1967): 67–80, and 47 (1968): 79–91.
Anderson, Chester. "Leopold Bloom as Dr. Sigmund Freud." *Mosaic* 6
(1972): 23–43.

Bonheim, Helmut. *Joyce's Benefictions.* Berkeley and Los Angeles: University of California Press, 1964.

Boyle, Robert. "A Little Cloud." Hart 84–92.

Brantlinger, Patrick. *Bread and Circuses: Theories of Mass Culture as Social Decay.* Ithaca: Cornell University Press, 1983.

Brivic, Sheldon. *Joyce between Freud and Jung.* Port Washington, N.Y.: Kennikat, 1980.

Cixous, Hélène. *The Exile of James Joyce.* Trans. Sally A. J. Purcell. New York: David Lewis, 1972.

Devlin, Kimberly J. "The Female Eye: Joyce's Voyeuristic Narcissists." *New Alliances in Joyce Studies.* Ed. Bonnie Kime Scott. Newark: University of Delaware Press, 1988. 135–43.

Freud, Sigmund. *Civilization and Its Discontents.* Trans. James Strachey. New York: Norton, 1961.

The Future of an Illusion. Trans. James Strachey. New York: Norton, 1961.

Group Psychology and the Analysis of the Ego. Trans. James Strachey. New York: Norton, 1959.

"On Narcissism: An Introduction." *Collected Papers.* Ed. Joan Riviere. 5 vols. London: Hogarth, 1950. 4: 30–59.

Ghiselin, Brewster. "The Unity of Joyce's *Dubliners.*" Joyce, *Dubliners* 316–32.

Glasheen, Adaline. "Clay." Hart 100–6.

Gose, Elliott B., Jr. *The Transformation Process in Joyce's "Ulysses."* Toronto: University of Toronto Press, 1980.

Hart, Clive. "Eveline." Hart 48–52.

Hart, Clive, ed. *James Joyce's "Dubliners": Critical Essays.* New York: Viking, 1969.

Hawthorn, Jeremy. "*Ulysses,* Modernism, and Marxist Criticism." McCormack and Stead 112–25.

Henke, Suzette. "Gerty MacDowell: Joyce's Sentimental Heroine." Henke and Unkeless 132–49.

Henke, Suzette, and Elaine Unkeless, eds. *Women in Joyce.* Urbana: University of Illinois Press, 1982.

Herr, Cheryl. "Art and Life, Nature and Culture, *Ulysses.*" *Joyce's "Ulysses": The Larger Perspective.* Ed. Robert D. Newman and Weldon Thornton. Newark: University of Delaware Press, 1987. 19–38.

Joyce's Anatomy of Culture. Urbana: University of Illinois Press, 1986.

Joyce, James. *"Dubliners": Text, Criticism, and Notes.* Ed. Robert Scholes and A. Walton Litz. New York: Viking, 1969.

"Ireland, Island of Saints and Sages." *The Critical Writings of James Joyce.* Ed. Ellsworth Mason and Richard Ellmann. New York: Viking, 1959. 153–74.

Letters of James Joyce. 3 vols. Vol. 1, ed. Stuart Gilbert. Vols. 2 and 3, ed. Richard Ellmann. New York: Viking, 1966.

"A Portrait of the Artist." Joyce, *Portrait* 257–66.

"*A Portrait of the Artist as a Young Man*": *Text, Criticism, and Notes*. Ed. Chester G. Anderson. New York: Viking, 1968.

Ulysses: The Corrected Text. Ed. Hans Walter Gabler et al. New York: Random, 1986.

Kenner, Hugh. *Joyce's Voices*. Berkeley and Los Angeles: University of California Press, 1978.

Kershner, R. B. *Joyce, Bakhtin, and Popular Literature: Chronicles of Disorder*. Chapel Hill: University of North Carolina Press, 1989.

Kimball, Jean. "Freud, Leonardo, and Joyce: The Dimensions of a Childhood Memory." *The Seventh of Joyce*. Ed. Bernard Benstock. Bloomington: Indiana University Press, 1982. 57–73.

Levi, Albert William. *Philosophy in the Modern World*. Chicago: University of Chicago Press, 1959.

Levin, Gerald. *Sigmund Freud*. Boston: Twayne, 1975.

McCormack, W. J., and Alistair Stead, eds. *James Joyce and Modern Literature*. London: Routledge, 1982.

McCormack, W. J. "Nightmares of History: James Joyce and the Phenomenon of Anglo-Irish Literature." McCormack and Stead 77–107.

Norris, Margot. "Modernism, Myth, and Desire in 'Nausicaa.'" *James Joyce Quarterly* 26 (1988): 37–50.

"Narration under a Blindfold: Reading Joyce's 'Clay.'" *PMLA* 102 (1987): 206–15.

Richards, Thomas Karr. "Gerty MacDowell and the Irish Common Reader." *ELH* 52 (1985): 755–76.

San Juan, Epifano, Jr. *James Joyce and the Craft of Fiction: An Interpretation of "Dubliners."* Rutherford, N.J.: Fairleigh Dickinson University Press, 1972.

Senn, Fritz. "Nausicaa." *James Joyce's "Ulysses": Critical Essays*. Ed. Clive Hart and David Hayman. Berkeley and Los Angeles: University of California Press, 1974. 277–311.

Shechner, Mark. *Joyce in Nighttown: A Psychoanalytic Inquiry into "Ulysses."* Berkeley and Los Angeles: University of California Press, 1974.

Torchiana, Donald T. *Backgrounds for Joyce's "Dubliners."* Boston: Allen, 1986.

Walzl, Florence L. "*Dubliners*: Women in Irish Society." Henke and Unkeless 31–56.

"Pattern of Paralysis in Joyce's *Dubliners*." *College English* 22 (1961): 221–8.

Werner, Craig Hansen. "*Dubliners*": *A Pluralistic World*. Boston: Twayne, 1988.

PART II

The context of the other: Joyce on the margins

CHAPTER 6

Cheating on the father: Joyce and gender justice in Ulysses

Colleen R. Lamos

In Joyce's now-famous words, Molly's monologue is "the indispens-able countersign to Bloom's passport to eternity" (*SL* 278). Molly's "last word" to *Ulysses* hardly ends the story, though, and the ambiguity of her signature is troublesome. Does Molly *underwrite* Bloom's Odyssean voyage, her affirmative flesh the "breasts, arse, womb, and cunt" (*SL* 285) that warrant his immortalization in *Ulysses*? Or does she sign *counter* to Bloom's signature, her menstrual mark controverting the narrative that Bloom has endorsed? Or does she simply *write over* it, blotting with her famed indifference the story that Bloom tells? As Patrick McGee points out, Molly's counter-signature could only be construed to legitimate Bloom's – if indeed it does – "because [his] first signature lacks authenticity without the second to endorse it" (171). Hence, Molly's signature, along with its representation of female sexuality, has the structure of a supplement in the Derridean sense, one which calls into question the authority and integrity of that "first signature."

The sexual economy of the novel is initially governed by Stephen's division of women into virgins and madonnas, on the one hand, and whores on the other, an economy reproduced in the debate over how many lovers Molly *really* has had and thus whether she is a "good" or "bad" girl. Yet the complications introduced in every episode undermine the confidence Stephen exhibits in a male eye that surveys and appraises female sexuality, and in a unified male subject who takes woman as the vehicle for transcendence. Instead of a symmetry of sexual difference, *Ulysses* demonstrates that difference is reproduced *within* the regimes of gender, and that the apparently simple terms of the male/female opposition are intern-ally divided. Among the effects of this doubling (of what should no longer strictly speaking be called *sexual* difference) is that Molly's discourse cannot be appealed to as resolving – either in the sense of concluding or dissolving – difference within a monologue that has, for so many, been read as the conjunctive, incorporative moment of *Ulysses*, as the utterance in which addresser and addressee acquiesce, in which "I" and "you" converge into a communal "we" and say "yes" to love.

Whether or not it is "the word known to all men," *love* is at least the word invoked by Bloom in his definition of justice as "the opposite of hatred" (*U* 12.1485). Bloom's vision of a community in which the addressers and addressees are able to utter divergent phrases, free from "force" and "hatred" (*U* 12.1481), is ironically contrasted to the patriotic myth promoted by the Irish citizen of the pub for whom community is defined and legitimated by a "we" determined by race and nation.[1] "Love," on the other hand, is not national but international, articulated by the multiracial Bloom and Molly. Yet the equivocations raised both in "Cyclops" and "Circe" (e.g., the "new Bloomusalem") suggest that Bloom's "we" without a "them" is a utopian fantasy of harmonious assimilation. What *appears* to legitimate Bloom's defence of love as the basis for community, for a collectivity which would merge men and women as "children of nature" (*U* 15.1687) – "Free money, free rent, free love" (*U* 15.1693) in a union of differences, of "mixed races and mixed marriage" (*U* 15.1699) – is Molly's discourse. Her "language of flow" (*U* 11.298), according to Bonnie Kime Scott, is like the "feminine language" of ALP in *Finnegans Wake*, and "is what provides the umbilicus," circulating and recirculating among continuous subjects, thus "offer[ing] a new politics of relationship and authority" (129). Such a notion locates the exchange and circulation of phrases in a homogeneous language, thereby seeking redemption in a nonalienated site figured by women's bodies in much the same way as do Stephen and Bloom.

Stephen's self-constitution as a son is blocked by his deep ambivalence toward his mother. As the female "other," she is "the womb of sin," the Eve/Anne Hathaway who seduces and betrays. But, on the other hand, Stephen insists on the naturalness and immutability of the maternal bond as opposed to the arbitrariness and contingency of the "mystical estate" of fatherhood: "*Amor matris*, subjective and objective genitive, may be the only true thing in life. Paternity may be a legal fiction" (*U* 9.842–4). The symmetry of the objective and subjective genitive (the mother's love/love of the mother) would render this phrase the perfectly closed circuit of an addresser and addressee who exchange places and share the same referent: tautological and thus incontrovertible. However, it is the reproachful ghost of the mother whom Stephen cannot love as she would have him, for motherhood is neither reciprocal nor "true," but just as much of a "fiction" as that of the madonna "which the cunning Italian intellect flung to the mob of Europe" (*U* 9.839–40). Maternity is Stephen's nocturnal resource and his nightmare, a fathomless origin and fatal destiny, as though the mute female body gestured from beyond the pale of the symbolic order in some unspeakable, undecidable infinity. His enigmatic formula, "In woman's womb word is made flesh but in the spirit of the maker all flesh that passes becomes the word that shall not pass away" (*U* 14.292–4), renders the womb a figure for a nonfigurable origin, the source of eternal art in perishable forms, the material ground of the immaterial word. As such, the womb is, in McGee's explanation, "undecidable, even though Stephen tries to make a decision" (103–4) between the virgin and the whore, between the spiritual and the fleshly woman, between the first Eve whom "we are linked up with by successive anastomosis of navelcords," who "sold us all . . . for a penny pippin," and the second Eve, who will save us (*U* 14.300–1). This difference between the good and the bad woman brings Stephen to an aporia. And although Bloom does not express himself in Stephen's theological terms, and while his attitude toward femininity is significantly more complex than Stephen's, he is likewise troubled and fascinated by the divergence between female carnality and, in his words, "sacred, lifegiv[ing]" motherhood (*U* 15.4648–9).

   Both Stephen and Bloom, along with many of their critics, arbitrate sexual difference by enclosing difference within one of the parties – the female. The determinate male self is defined against the female, who embodies in herself the opposition between definition and indefinability, between flesh and spirit. Thus, the difference which separates male and female – that long string of metonymies by which man distinguishes himself from his "other" – is transferred or displaced onto the female who contains an *internal* self-difference that renders her undecidable. Male subjectivity initially seems assured by such a move – he, at least, is what is known – but at the price of surrendering woman to an ungraspable zone beyond the symbolic order, to a region where, he fears and hopes, the Name of the Father does not govern.

Such a configuration of Stephen's and Bloom's relation to women is common to both traditional scholars and recent feminists, the latter of whom find in the feminine pre-symbolic what they consider an alternative space outside paternal authority. Thus, employing Kristeva's terms, Scott endorses what she believes to be the "semiotic pre-speech" of *Finnegans Wake* and, shifting to Cixous, Molly's "writing the body," both of which spring from a "generative principle positively associated with the river, the primordial mud, and the mother" (109, 117). However, this positing of a female space not only provides no leverage with which to dislodge that authority, but accepts on its own terms the Law of the Father and its supposed governance of the symbolic code. Furthermore, such a strategy reinstates precisely the sexual difference it set out to question, and in virtually identical terms. This recuperation is also at work in McGee's and Colin MacCabe's readings of *Ulysses*.

After describing the figure of the womb as the "unfinalized frame" in opposition to the defined male phallus, for the former "insists on the representation of what has been foreclosed by the symbolic construction of the body of man" (101), McGee transfers this feminine undecidability onto the privileged male characters in the novel. Stephen is said to exist on the margins of the symbolic order, for "he subverts the law of the father not by standing in the place of its imaginary opposition [the female position as such], but by standing on the edge of the symbolic" (68). Likewise, as the "spermatazoon" in "Oxen of the Sun," "Bloom is a masculine figure, [yet] he enters into a process that is indeterminate as to sex. He is not the phallus ... because, in some sense, he is there [in the womb] as an indeterminate part of what frames and is framed" (104). In short, Bloom's identification with Mrs. Purefoy in her labors enables him to become like, or even "part of" the mother.

Indeed, these male characters become even better "women" than the female characters, at least those like Gerty and Mrs. Purefoy who are prisoners of their sex. Locked in her conventional discourse, "Gerty is finalized and imprisoned by the language that speaks for her," incapable of transcending the limits of her gender, whereas Bloom, according to McGee, is "unfinalized" (95).[2] Framed (in every sense of the word) by Joyce's style into precisely the gender opposition that femininity as a trope supposedly transcends, Gerty occupies the *male* position of determinacy and definition, while Bloom is the "womanly man" (*U* 15.1799). The location of the indeterminacy of gender difference in one of the parties to the opposition thus neutralizes the force of femininity and confirms the opposition it set out to overthrow.

According to MacCabe, what enables Bloom to "become a woman" (128) is his "perverse" acknowledgment of castration. Rather than shielding himself from castration by taking refuge in the phallus as a fetish, as though it were a stable signified, Bloom releases himself to the movement of signification. "This submission to the signifier is a submission to writing, and writing functions . . . as the very exemplar of perversion. The crucial feature of perversion . . . is the instability of sexual position" (123). Thus, in "Circe," Bloom partially succumbs to the "pressure of the feminine," lets go of the fetishized potato, and gives voice to the woman within him. But the woman he becomes, as McGee correctly notes, is *"what he imagines a woman to be"* (147).

MacCabe's argument that the gender confusion of "Circe" constitutes a "bisexuality" through which Bloom transcends the limitations of his own gender to become a multivoiced subject is premised on the prior bisection of woman into a pre-symbolic, pre-oedipal maternal plenitude (a whole) and the castrated female under the law of the father (a hole). This ambivalent construction reproduces sexual difference *within* the female subject who is thus thought to contain a fundamental, internal undecidability, an inherent doubleness; the female is accordingly the very *untruth* of the truth of sexual difference, and *her* body is the privileged site of the "suture" or folding in upon itself of male and female.[3] This projection of difference onto the female in turn permits the male subject to appropriate female undecidability as a means of attacking the father *in the name of woman*. Becoming female in *Ulysses*, a gesture that reaches its apogee in "Penelope" when a male pen writes a woman's desire, is thus not a matter of denying or dismantling or even inverting sexual difference, but of the male introjection of a projected femininity, which seems to stand ambiguously on the edge of paternal authority. This, again, is a strategic move by the son attacking the father, and the "bisexuality" or "androgyny" or "intermediate sex" that issues is a kind of male drag show.[4]

The strategic function of this drag style is evident in the scene of masochism in "Circe." This scene is often cited as evidence of Bloom's bisexuality – after all, he and Bella Cohen switch genders. Yet Bloom's "femininity," including his transvestism, is the

masochist's script for rebellion against the father, not an "identification" with women or somehow becoming female. According to
Deleuze in his interpretation of Sacher-Masoch's *Venus in Furs* – the
subtext of the scene in Joyce – the masochist abjures the father and
transfers the paternal functions onto the mother, especially the oral
mother. In order to challenge the father's authority and to exorcise
the repression he exercises over sexuality, the masochist engages in
an alliance with the mother. Having expelled the father, "the
masochist experiences the symbolic order as a . . . maternal order in
which the mother represents the law . . .; she generates the symbolism through which the masochist expresses himself. It is not a case
of identification with the mother" (63). Investing the *mother* with the
symbolic power of the law, so that she becomes the "ideal phallus,"
the masochist in effect punishes the father, for, according to Deleuze,
in the masochistic scene it is *"a father that is being beaten"* (68).
Masochism thus achieves an ironic, even humorous, overthrow of the
paternal prohibition, for by strictly applying the law – now in the
hands of the mother – the masochist is able to feel the pleasure that
the law had denied. The mother remains plumped full of the riches of
the pre-symbolic, and yet assumes the authority of the symbolic law.

Just as the masochist, by sealing a pact with the mother and
investing her with the paternal law, tries to expel the father's
authority, Joyce attacks the father in the name of the mother, thus
appropriating a female pre-symbolic in order to neutralize the
father, but finally on the father's terms. This move succeeds in
placing woman in cosmic exile from the symbolic, powerful only
insofar as she can return *in the place of the father* as the fantasy of the
woman with the whip. Molly and Bella are versions of the same
woman: "massive, potent, and self-possessed" (Brown 101).[5] The
similarity between the monstrous Bella and the effusive Molly suggests that we analyze the *male* subject who produces the female as
both this side of and beyond the law of the father.

There are many ways of cheating at the father's game, including
masochism – laughing at the paternal proscription by scrupulously
submitting to its rules. Another way, equally ironic in its pyrrhic
victory, has been forging the mother's signature with the father's
hand. Whether the author be male or female, the sanction of such
écriture féminine is a system of gender difference in which woman is the
limit and margin of the articulate. Such a writing obeys the law that
it abjures.

Rather than conclude that there is no exit from the circuit of paternal authority, one might try a different move: questioning the status of the judge of this game – the law of the father. The judge is also a player in the game, yet he must disguise his play (Weber 105). The penis in the masquerade of the phallus has been one of his more successful disguises, masking the discursive investments of what purports to be a *meta*discursive "truth" of language. For the notion that sexual difference, and concomitant access to the symbolic order, is instituted by the law of the father rests upon the crucial distinction – and confusion – between the phallus and the penis, between the symbolic and the empirical. The basis of the Lacanian game, the phallus/penis distinction not only sacralizes the phallus as the privileged signifier, but, according to Jean-François Lyotard, mystifies the *discursive* status of the phallus.[6] Unveiling the phallus by insisting on its corporeal reference deprives it of metalinguistic authority, revealing it to be "one signifier among others, prey to the contingencies of the letter" (Gallop 99). Joyce from time to time seemed to recognize that phallic law is materially contingent, and that sexual difference need not be acknowledged in terms of a lack. "Funny spot to have a fingey," Issy says in *Finnegans Wake* (*FW* 144.35), and Molly is equally dismissive of the phallus as the arbitrator of sexual difference and its pretension to place its signature on the female body: "they always want to see a stain on the bed ... a daub of red ink would do" (*U* 18.1125–8).

Nevertheless, Joyce's attempt to write women's desire as though from the other side of the symbolic, like recent feminists' theorizing of an *écriture féminine*, plays along with the father by appearing to renounce the paternal symbolic through an alliance with the mother, yet that alliance is simply the reappropriation of an imaginary construction. This game of projection and introjection is the psychological equivalent of Joyce's textual strategy of incorporation. By including within itself its own measure, *Ulysses* does not thereby abandon the distinction between discourse and meta-discourse, but installs itself as a self-interpretive supertext, a meta-metadiscourse. This operation depends upon the internal articulation of the "other" of the text, the creation of an interior alien, in a process analogous to the creation and incarceration of madness by and in the service of that which wishes to call itself reason (Derrida, "Cogito" 31–44). The forgery of Molly's discourse permits Joyce to include her as a sign of *Ulysses*'s transcendence of sexual difference.

The apparent relinquishment of phallic authority is thus managed by the invention and sublation of "woman." Likewise, the interiorization of metalanguages in *Ulysses* consolidates its own authority while denying the difference that it subsumes.

NOTES

1 For a critique of such national myths in terms of their "phrasing" or structures of address, see Lyotard, *The Differend* 147.
2 Instances of such a reading abound. For example, Phillip Herring condescendingly comments, "Poor Gerty ... is held captive on her ventriloquist's knee, laboriously scribbling her letter to the world while her master howls with laughter" (193). But it is Herring who is laughing.
3 Philippe Sollers, quoted by McGee (145). The theme of woman as "the untruth of truth" is developed most fully in Nietzsche's texts – e.g., *Beyond Good and Evil* and *The Gay Science* – and analyzed at length by Derrida in *Spurs*.
4 "Bisexuality" is MacCabe's term; "androgyny" is McGee's; and "intermediate sex" is borrowed by Richard Brown from turn-of-the-century sexologists (103).

   Brown quotes Joyce's praise of Ibsen and his female characters: "*he seems to know them better than they know themselves.* Indeed, if one may say so of *an eminently virile man*, there is a curious admixture of the woman in his nature. His marvelous accuracy, his faint traces of femininity, his delicacy of swift touch, are perhaps attributable to this admixture" (*CW* 64, emphasis added). Ibsen is a better woman than a woman, as Bloom is a better woman than Gerty.

   McGee argues that "the only desire speaking in 'Penelope' is Joyce's masquerading as female" (175), although he does not pursue the implications of that performance.

   Cheryl Herr notes the "pantomime transvestism" of "Circe" and claims that, "instead of yearning for a true androgyny, Bloom seems always to have gravitated toward only a stereotyped femaleness composed of clothing, makeup, hairstyle and mannerism" (152), yet she fails to analyze the difference between true and simulated "femaleness," or Bloom's motives for such a simulation.
5 Brown describes Molly as a "phallic woman" in these terms but does not link Molly with Bella Cohen.
6 Lyotard argues: "When a 'feminist' is reproached for confusing the phallus, symbolic operator of meaning, and the penis, empirical sign of sexual difference, it is admitted without discussion that the metalinguistic order (the symbolic) is distinct from its domain of reference (realities). But if the women's movement has an immense impact ... it is that this movement solicits and destroys the (masculine) belief in meta-

statements independent of ordinary statements" ("On One of the Things at Stake" 15).

WORKS CITED

Brown, Richard. *James Joyce and Sexuality*. Cambridge: Cambridge University Press, 1985.

Deleuze, Gilles. *Coldness and Cruelty*. Trans. Jean McNeil. New York: Zone, 1989.

Derrida, Jacques. "Cogito and the History of Madness." *Writing and Difference*. Trans. Alan Bass. Chicago: University of Chicago Press, 1978. 31–63.

Spurs: Nietzsche's Styles. Trans. Barbara Harlow. Chicago: University of Chicago Press, 1979.

Gallop, Jane. *The Daughter's Seduction: Feminism and Psychoanalysis*. Ithaca: Cornell University Press, 1982.

Herr, Cheryl. *Joyce's Anatomy of Culture*. Urbana: University of Illinois Press, 1986.

Herring, Phillip F. *Joyce's Uncertainty Principle*. Princeton: Princeton University Press, 1987.

Joyce, James. *The Critical Writings of James Joyce*. Ed. Ellsworth Mason and Richard Ellmann. New York: Viking, 1959.

Finnegans Wake. New York: Viking, 1939.

Selected Letters of James Joyce. Ed. Richard Ellmann. New York: Viking, 1975.

Ulysses: The Corrected Text. Ed. Hans Walter Gabler et al. Harmondsworth: Penguin, 1986.

Lyotard, Jean-François. *The Differend: Phrases in Dispute*. Trans. Georges van den Abbeele. Minneapolis: University of Minnesota Press, 1988.

"On One of the Things at Stake in Women's Struggles." Trans. Deborah J. Clarke et al. *Sub-Stance* 20 (1978): 9–17.

MacCabe, Colin. *James Joyce and the Revolution of the Word*. London: Macmillan, 1978.

McGee, Patrick. *Paperspace: Style as Ideology in Joyce's "Ulysses."* Lincoln: University of Nebraska Press, 1988.

Scott, Bonnie Kime. *James Joyce*. Brighton: Harvester, 1987.

Weber, Samuel. Afterword. *Just Gaming*. By Jean-François Lyotard and Jean-Loup Thébaud. Trans. Wlad Godzich. Minneapolis: University of Minnesota Press, 1985. 101–20.

CHAPTER 7

Demythologizing nationalism: Joyce's dialogized Grail myth

Theresa O'Connor

> Hot fresh blood they prescribe for decline. Blood always
> needed. Insidious.   (*U* 8.729–30)

"For many centuries," Conor Cruise O'Brien observed in a recent article on nationalist ideology, "the grand legitimizer of hatred in our culture was called Religion. Then after the great surfeit of the Wars of Religion, the power of religion to legitimize war and persecution began to fade and the cult of Nationalism took its place ... Henceforward, it was in the name of the nation that men would be most likely to feel it legitimate to hate and kill other men, and women and children" (27). Linking nationalism with religion, O'Brien argues that both creeds serve to legitimize war and bloodshed because both are rooted in the perverse notion that renewal comes through blood sacrifice. It is precisely this belief that Joyce sets out to decode in *Ulysses*. Like O'Brien, he was convinced that – as he himself put it – nationality "must find its reason for being rooted in something that surpasses and transcends and informs changing things like blood and the human word" (*CW* 166). In *Ulysses* he sets out to demythologize the discourse of Irish nationalism, a discourse rooted in what is undoubtedly the most powerful narrative script embodying the doctrine of sacrificial renewal in the history of Western culture, the legend of the Holy Grail. To do this, he confronts the hegemonic nationalist myth with the Celtic myth in which it had its origins. Joyce's revisionary Grail myth slowly takes on form by means of a continuous series of dialogic encounters between antithetical Grails.

The chief architect of the Irish nationalist discourse was William Butler Yeats. For Yeats, as John Hutchinson points out, "Irish culture was seen in essentially a passive role as material to be moulded by an artistic elite who would create the authentic Irish nation ... in the pagan Celtic archetype. His heroes and heroines were mystical aristocrats who, by sacrificing themselves, were able to redeem a fallen people" (135). As early as 1891 Yeats had begun to combine his mythic, nationalist and occult interests in an attempt to awaken "ancient fires," and forge a new post-colonial consciousness for the Irish race (Ellmann, *Masks* 86–134). Influenced by Wagner's *Parsifal*, by Celtic mythology, and by the French Order of the Rosy Cross of the Temple and of the Grail, he imagined a new Irish system which would have as its focal point a "symbolic fabric" centering on the four sacred talismans of the Tuatha Dé Danann ("The People of the Goddess Danu"), chief of which is the "cauldron" of the Goddess, the Celtic prototype for the Grail (Yeats, *Memoirs* 125; Raine 177–246). "A time will come for [the Tuatha Dé Danann] also," Yeats declares in "Rosa Alchemica," "but they cannot build their temples again till there have been martyrdoms and victories" (*Mythologies* 281). Precisely the same body of Celtic myth that supplied the central images for Yeats's work provided the framework for the amalgam of tales that came to be known in twelfth-century France as the Grail myth. In both mythic systems the symbolism of the Celtic quest myth is inverted. In fact, both systems are palimpsests in which are inscribed two radically divergent cultural scripts: one, the conceptualizing discourse of logos, the Word made flesh, and the other, the occulted discourse of motherhood, the flesh made word. The process of narrative colonization functions in different ways in each myth. Whereas in the christianized Grail myth the Celtic concept of female sacrality is repressed and male blood and violence are canonized as the primary source of life, in Yeats's *Cathleen Ni Houlihan*, a central political text in neocolonial Ireland (Deane 147), the female image is retained, and used to provide legitimization for the nationalist ideology of cultural paternity. A harbinger of violence and destruction, Yeats's Cathleen demands blood-sacrifice for the rebirth of the Motherland.

Like thirst-ravaged vampires, Joyce's parodic Cathleens, the sinister sisterhood of the "Gaptoothed Kathleen" (*U* 9.36–7), and their cohorts, the brotherhood of the "bloodfadder" (*FW* 496.26), stalk through the pages of *Ulysses* in quest of blood. In "Circe" one sister inquires, "(with expectation) Is he bleeding!" (*U* 15.4778). This quest for regeneration through sacrificial male blood is juxtaposed throughout *Ulysses* with a quest for regeneration through maternal love: "*Amor matris*, subjective and objective genitive . . . the only true thing in life" (*U* 9.842–3). The endless oscillation between these

two quests in *Ulysses* de-privileges the canonical nationalist myth
and enables us to view the Grail as at once the sacrificial blood of a
male victim and savior and as the regenerative blood of the mother.
The fault line, as it were, around which this revisionary Grail myth
is constructed occupies scarcely two lines in *Ulysses*:

> On the altarstone Mrs Mina Purefoy, goddess of unreason, lies, naked, fettered, a
> chalice resting on her swollen belly. (U 15.4691–3)

The dialogized chalice, represented here by an amalgam of the
Eucharistic chalice and the womb-chalice of Mina, also serves as a
parergon, or enclosing frame, for Joyce's text.[1] Mulligan's shaving
bowl, a parodic Eucharistic chalice, frames the opening consecra-
tion in "Telemachus," and Molly's womb, her "chalice" of menstrual blood, dominates "Penelope." "Telemachus" begins an
immense pivoting so that its subtext, the occulted voice of the old
Celtic Goddess (the milkwoman who speaks not a word of her own
language) dominates "Penelope." In other words, Joyce's dialogized Grail myth has a dynamic and reversible structure. Viewed
from the perspective of the canonical (masculinist) Grail myth, it
reinforces the structure of Western patriarchy, but turned on its
head, as it were, and viewed from the perspective of the occulted
Celtic myth, it subverts that same structure.[2]

    If we are to uncover the subversive force of Joyce's dialogized
Grail myth in *Ulysses*, we need first to uncover the occulted discourse
it sets out to retrieve. Thus, before it reaches its subject, my discussion here will require a brief preamble: a review of the main lines of
interconnection between the christianized Grail myth and – to use
Joyce's words – the "matt*her* of Erryn" (emphasis added), those
"grandest gynecollege histories" (*FW* 389.6–9).[3] As Arthur C. L.
Brown points out in *The Origins of the Grail Legend*, the work of
Chrétien, the French poet who wrote one of the first christianized
versions of the Grail myth in the twelfth century, draws heavily on
Celtic mythic motifs. Chrétien's story of Perceval's parentage and
boyhood deeds (*Perceval le gallois ou Le Conte du graal*), he claims, had
its remote origins in the *Machníomhartha Finn* (*The Boyhood Deeds of
Fionn*). Precisely the same theme, the quest for a mysterious caul-
dron of regeneration, is central to both tales; however, the form this
vessel takes differs radically in each version of the myth. Whereas
Chrétien's Perceval journeys out in search of the "graal" (Barber 5),
Fionn mac Cumhaill (represented here as a descendant of Bran-

Nuadu, the chief god of the Tuatha Dé Danann) searches for the crane bag (*corrbolg*), a strange vessel of poetic inspiration made from crane skin. The pedigree of Fionn's mysterious bag, which James MacKillop links with "the beginnings of the insular alphabet, ogham" (21), is given in "The Crane Bag," a brief poem which appears in the *Duanaire Finn (The Book of the Lays of Fionn)*. In answer to the question "to whom did the good Crane-bag belong that Cumhall son of Tréanmhór had?," the poet is told that the bag belonged to Manannán Mac Lir (Mac Neill 119). The Irish literary journal *The Crane Bag* summarizes the story as follows:

Mananaan the god of the sea ... wishing to punish his wife Aoife, transformed her into a crane. She retaliated by ensuring that his secret alphabet of wisdom, which he treasured, would be shared with the populace. Consequently, whenever cranes are in flight they form images in the sky of the secret alphabet for all to read. (5)

After Aoife's death, Mananaan apparently made the crane bag (*corrbolg*) of her skin, and in it he kept "every precious thing" he owned (Mac Neill 119). When Jessie Weston – Joyce's "Westend Woman" (*FW* 292.6) – dismissed the theory of the Celtic origins of the Grail legend, she was obviously unaware of the legend of the crane bag. The Celtic cauldron, she argues, is merely "a food providing" vessel, whereas the Christian Grail, in contrast, is surrounded by an atmosphere of "sanctity" befitting the holiest of relics (73). But the crane bag of Fionn mac Cumhaill and the Fianna is much more than a mere "food providing" vessel. Made from the skin of a woman, symbol of fertility and regeneration, source of language and poetic wisdom, it is a feminine pre-Christian counterpart for the Christian Grail chalice.

The old Celtic voyage tales (*Immrama*), which tell of a series of journeys to the Otherworld, a mysterious Land of Women (*Tír na m-Ban*) where, as Brown observes, "sex is no sin," served as the basis for the marvelous adventures of Iwain in Chrétien's work (Brown 3–7). Bran Mac Febail, closely related to "Bran the Blessed" ("god of the sacred cauldron") in Welsh mythology, is the hero of the oldest of the voyage tales, *The Voyage of Bran*.[4] He apparently acquired his sacred cauldron on his voyage to the Land of Women. This otherworld is given a variety of names and assumes a variety of different forms in Celtic myth. Representing, on one level, a submerged state of consciousness (akin, in some senses, to Julia Kristeva's semiotic *chora*), it is almost always situated in distant islands, beneath the sea, or beneath the mounds of the *Síd*. As Proinsias Mac Cana notes, it may be reached through a mist, or through a cave, or "simply through the granting of a sudden insight" (125). In some myths, as Mac Cana points out, it appears as a revolving wheel or castle symbolic of the turning world; in others, it is represented as a tower of glass (*turris vitrea*) or a fortress of glass (*Caer Wydyr*) (129). In others still, it is *Tír na n-óg*, the land of the dead and the land of the ever young. Ultimately, whatever form or name it takes, the Celtic Otherworld – "Tear-nan-Ogre," as Joyce puts it in *Finnegans Wake* (479.2) – is, in its very essence, the opening "tear" to otherness, difference, alterity.

The apple, sacred symbol of Venus, figures largely in the Celtic myths of the otherworld. In fact, Avalon, the Otherworld of Arthurian mythology, is, quite literally, the "Apple-Land" of immortality (Walker 479). In *The Voyage of Bran*, as in many of the Celtic voyage myths, a woman bearing a golden apple bough guides the hero to the Otherworld. Other symbols frequently associated with the Celtic Goddess are blood and milk. As several critics have remarked, Medb of Cruachain, "Naif Cruachan" (*FW* 526.20), the fertility goddess/ heroine of the ancient Irish epic *Táin Bó Cuailnge* (*The Cattle Raid of Cuailnge*), was quite possibly the only woman to menstruate in Irish literature before Molly Bloom. Medb's blood, which flows to form a river at the end of the great cattle raid, is a vivid symbol of female creative power. Significantly, it is Medb's daughter Finnabair who served as the prototype for Guinevere in the Arthurian legends. Milk is one of the chief symbols of the goddess Brigid (one of the prototypes for Biddy the hen in *Finnegans Wake*) in her role as Cow Goddess. The milk of the sacred cow, as Mary Condren points out, was "one of the earliest sacred foods throughout the world, equivalent to our present day communion" (58). Indeed, so powerful was the symbolism associated with the Cow Goddess in ancient Ireland that it was not until the Synod of Cashel in 1172 that the use of milk in baptism was finally banned (Condren 177).

The final set of mythic symbols I will consider here are drawn from the central tales in *Lebor Gabala* (*The Book of Invasions*): the battles of Mag Tuired. These battles were fought between Nuadu, king of the Tuatha Dé Danann, and the Fomorians for possession of a queen, Ériu, and for her four sacred talismans: spear, stone, sword, and cauldron. Because it was *geis* (taboo) for a man with a physical or psychological blemish to rule the country,

Nuadu, who lost an arm in the first battle of Mag Tuired, is forced to relinquish his kingship to Bres, his Fomorian enemy. Bres, however, lacks *fír flaitheman* (which Mac Cana translates as "truth of the ruler"); thus the land becomes a Waste Land, and the queen (a personification of the land) grows ugly and haggard. The Waste Land is redeemed only when the Goddess is reunited sexually with a spiritually and physically worthy spouse. In fact, sexuality plays a major role in the inauguration rite, known as the *banfheis rígi* (the wife feast of kingship) of the sacral king. This ceremony involves two ritual acts: the female offers a golden cup containing a red drink to her chosen spouse, and this symbolic offering is then followed by sexual intercourse between the king and the "sovereignty" (Mac Cana 114–21). In the Arthurian myths, only one of Nuadu's aspects, that of reigning king, is transferred to King Arthur. His second aspect, that of a wounded (or impotent) god kept alive by the magic talismans of the Goddess, is represented by the Fisher King.

In almost every instance, the motifs and symbols which appear in the "matther of Erryn" correspond closely with those which appear in the later christianized versions of the myth. There is, however, one glaring exception. Whereas in Celtic myth the cauldron belongs to the Goddess, the Christian Grail has a decidedly masculine lineage; in fact, no woman may even hear of it (Weston 137). In the christianized versions of the myth a new world vision is constructed in which all generativity and creativity fall to God, the spiritual father, rather than to the female. With the same masterful stroke, sexuality, now projected onto the female, is assigned to the realm of the sinful. Whereas the quest for a woman's love is a central feature in the mythology of the Celts, we hear no mention of such love in Robert de Boron's *Roman de l'estoire dou graal*, a work which appeared almost contemporaneously with Chrétien's *Perceval*. In de Boron's work – which links the *matière de Bretagne* with the legend of Joseph of Arimathea – the Grail is represented as the cup used to collect the redeeming blood, the *sang real*, which flowed from the wounds of the crucified Christ. The cup is brought by Joseph of Arimathea to Glastonbury in England (the reputed burial place of Arthur and Guinevere), and, thereafter, it becomes the object of knightly quests that can be achieved only by those who are chaste.[5]

In the "Matter of Brettaine," which Joyce links with "brut fierce" in *Finnegans Wake* (292.34), male friendship receives priority.

Malory's fifteenth-century version of the Grail myth, *Morte d'Arthur*, presents a world dominated by battles, civil wars and tournaments. Here, love is a subordinate interest, and the comitatus, the fraternal bond between man and man, replaces the bond between man and woman. Several hundred years later, in *Parsifal*, Richard Wagner's operatic rerendering of the German poet Wolfram von Eschenbach's work, celibacy is again exalted, and the Grail is once again linked with the blood-filled chalice of the Eucharist. Apparently, Wagner's work so influenced Adolf Hitler that he adopted as his insignum the swastika, the age-old symbol of renewal in the Thule Grail mysteries (Whitmont 161).[6]

Beginning in the mists of Celtic prehistory and moving inexorably forward through Chrétien's *Perceval*, Robert de Boron's *Roman de L'estoire dou graal*, Gottfried von Strassburg's *Tristan and Isolde*, Wolfram von Eschenbach's *Parzival*, Sir Thomas Malory's *Morte d'Arthur*, Alfred Tennyson's *Idylls of the King*, and Richard Wagner's *Parsifal* and *Tristan und Isolde* (to name but a few versions of the myth), the language, symbolism, and ideology of the Grail myth has had a profound influence on our civilization and culture. In Yeats's *Cathleen Ni Houlihan*, the Grail myth came full circle. Here the powerful Celtic mother figure, the original bearer of the Grail, is de-sexualized and harnessed to the service of an ideology that has at its center not the life-giving blood of the mother, but the sacrificial blood of a male victim-savior. So, by a "commodius vicus of recirculation" (*FW* 3.2), we return now to Joyce's work, where we find ourselves confronted with a dialogized Grail and a decentered nationalist vision. Pervading the entire text we find almost all of the symbols and motifs from the Celtic Grail myth: the Waste Land, the Grail Castle (the Crystal Palace), the otherworldly Apple Land, the wounded Fisher King, the Loathly Lady, the Gold Cup, and the questing Knight.

Ulysses's Ireland is a Waste Land (*U* 14.476–83). The fields are barren, the cattle are diseased, and women, disparagingly referred to as "cowflesh" (*U* 14.807), have difficulty giving birth (*U* 14.114–17). The actual drought in June 1904 is reflected in the spiritual paralysis of the people, a paralysis manifestly evident in "Oxen of the Sun" where the agony of Mina (Joyce's everywoman) in "that allhardest of woman hour" is counterpointed by the raucous laughter of Buck Mulligan and his cronies. "I shudder to think of the future of a race," the young "learningknight" Dixon states, "where the seeds of such malice have been sown and where no right reverence is rendered to mother and maid in house of Horne" (*U* 14.832–4). The attitude of the callous "medicals," whose discussion centers around such topics as abortion, contraception, their sexual triumphs with women, and their losses in the Gold Cup Race, is explicitly contrasted with the reverential treatment of the mother in Celtic society (*U* 14.33–49). We are reminded of the Waste Land theme in Celtic myth, and, indeed, in Chrétien's *Perceval*, where the desecration of the Grail country is caused by the violation of the Grail maiden and the theft of her gold cup (the gold cup, as Weston points out, is yet another name for the Grail chalice). Significantly, references to a gold cup echo like a Wagnerian leitmotif throughout *Ulysses*. Represented in the parodic framework of the Gold Cup Race at Ascot, Joyce's "gold cup" theme, like that of Chrétien, is closely associated with the idea of the betrayal of love.

In an ironic inversion of the symbolism of the Christian Grail myth, the Eucharistic chalice emerges in *Ulysses* as one of the major emblems of the Waste Land. In "Telemachus," the blood-filled chalice – a key symbol in the rhetoric of Irish nationalism – is explicitly linked with war and death. Here, Mulligan stands on the gunrest of a tower built for defense in time of war, as he holds aloft his "chalice," a shaving bowl, in an age-old gesture of ritual appeasement. "For this, O dearly beloved," he declares, "is the genuine christine: body and soul and blood and ouns" (*U* 1.21–2). A tissue of allusions links Malachi, whose "plump shadowed face and sullen oval jowl recalled a prelate, patron of the arts in the middle ages" (*U* 1.31–3), with St. Malachy, the celibate Cistercian monk who died in the arms of his friend and biographer St. Bernard, the spiritual father of the Knights Templars (the original Grail Knights). Malachy was responsible for the introduction of Roman ecclesiastical discipline into the Irish Church, thus effectively bringing an end to Celtic Christianity (a system more closely aligned with Gnosticism than with Pauline and Latin Christianity). In thus threatening the power of the British crown in Ireland, he was also in part responsible for the papal bull entitled *Laudabiliter* by which the Englishman, Pope Adrian IV, granted Ireland to Henry II of England in 1155. Thus, it was Malachy – whose greatest enemy was, significantly, King Stephen of England – and not, as the misogynistic Deasy suggests, "a faithless woman," who was responsible for bringing "strangers" to Ireland's shores. As a result of the profound changes introduced by St. Malachy into the Irish Church, the Celtic Mother Goddess was dispossessed of her spiritual power, and her womb/chalice of life-giving blood was framed by the blood-filled chalice of the Father.

St. Malachy's triumph over the Celtic Cow Goddess is mirrored in "Telemachus," where Mulligan dismisses the old milkwoman's can as a urinal: "Can you recall, brother," he asks Stephen, "is mother Grogan's tea and water pot spoken of in the Mabinogion or is it in the Upanishads?" (*U* 1.370–1). Mulligan's "omphalos" (*U* 1.544), a Martello tower rented from the secretary of state for war, serves as a type of phallic parergon for *Dumha na Bó* (the Mound of the Cow), the "omphalos" of the Celtic Mother Goddess at *Teamhair* (pronounced "tower") (Condren 58). Indeed, *Ulysses* is rife with examples of such displacement. In Mulligan's world, a world where "hot fresh blood" is "prescribe[d] for decline" (*U* 8.729), and dying martyrs have spectacular erections, a world, moreover, where "commodious milkjugs" are "destined to receive the most precious blood of the most precious victim" (*U* 12.623–4), the once venerated Cow Goddess is reduced to "a wandering crone, lowly form of an immortal serving her conqueror and her gay betrayer" (*U* 1.404–5). Whereas the Celtic Cow Goddess Brigid was patron of *filidecht* (poetry), this milkwoman does not even recognize her own language; her milk – a traditional symbol of female wisdom – is "not hers" (*U* 1.398). Her usurpers, all key exponents of linguistic and cultural nationalism, all "Pretenders" (*U* 3.313) to the throne of Cathleen, and all, in one sense or another, "bloodfadders," invariably take on the life-centered imagery of the "milkmudder" (*FW* 496.26). In "Circe," Mananaan Mac Lir (alias the "sacrificial butter" [9.64]: the dairy expert, and nationalist sympathizer, A.E.), vehemently and somewhat incongruously insists that he is "the dreamery creamery butter" (*U* 15.2275–6). Not to be outdone, Malachi Mulligan weeps "tears of molten butter" (*U* 15.4179), and, with imperial hauteur, his cohort Haines, the Gaelic-speaking Oxonian, the "Britisher" who shares the citizen's goal of bringing "once more into honour among mortal men the winged speech of the seadivided Gael" (*U* 12.1188–9), demands to know if the milk in his tea is "real Irish cream." "I don't want to be imposed on," he adds (*U* 10.1094–5). The irony is telling.

In many early Celtic myths, the Waste Land is redeemed only by a quest into the otherworldly Apple Land of Women. In *Ulysses*, a text where almost everything contains "two thinks at a time" (*FW* 583.7), no such singular solutions are forthcoming. Here even the apple, the traditional passport to the Otherworld, is dialogized. Joyce's "Applewoman" makes her first appearance in "Lestrygonians" where she hawks her imported "glazed" wares "Two for a penny!" (*U* 8.69–70). She reappears in "Circe" as a supporter of the nationalist cause. In a parody of the traditional role of the Celtic Goddess as emissary to the Otherworld, she joins the chorus of voices urging Bloom to assume his role as successor to Parnell, hero-martyr for the motherland: "He's a man like Ireland wants," she says (*U* 15.1540). Although it is impossible to determine whether the Applewoman calls Bloom to a Christian hell or a pagan heaven, her counterpart, Old Gummy Granny, who propositions Stephen in "Circe," places her bid for sacrifice in an explicitly Christian context: "At 8.35 a.m.," she promises, "you will be in heaven and Ireland will be free" (*U* 15.4737–8). Joyce's intertextual layering of Christian and Celtic motifs here points to an aporia or double-bind in nationalist rhetoric. In the ancient Irish myths from which the nationalists took their myth of origin – myths where, as Stephen discovered, there is "no trace of hell," where the "moral idea seems lacking, the sense of destiny, of retribution" (*U* 10.1082–4) – the apple is the passport to eternal life. In the Christian myth from which their doctrine of sacrificial renewal derives, however, the apple is the forbidden fruit, the cause of the fall, and the emblem of (woman's) original sin: our "grandam," as Stephen puts it – drawing, appropriately enough, on the work of St. Bernard and St. Augustine – "sold us all, seed, breed and generation, for a penny pippin" (*U* 14.300–1). The Applewoman's wares in *Ulysses*, the fruit at once of redemption and damnation, straddle, as it were, the strategic fault-line between two antithetical narrative paradigms. The result is a dialogism that mocks simultaneously the nationalist concept of a monological voice of culture, and the Christian concept of an authoritative narrative of origin.

Like the apples of wisdom, Joyce's parodic Otherworld, his *Caer Wydyr* (crystal palace), is hopelessly convoluted and divided. There is some irony in the fact that the crystal palace makes its first appearance in the "Cyclops" episode, an episode resonant with references to blood-sacrifice – "a genuinely instructive treat" (*U* 12.551) – cattle-disease, pornography, and, significantly, misinformation with regard to the winner of the "gold cup" (*U* 12.1898).

The irony is compounded by the fact that the episode is presided over by the misogynistic, xenophobic "Citizen," the self-styled champion of "Kathleen ni Houlihan" (*U* 12.1375), for whom woman is, paradoxically, one of the chief representatives of cultural "otherness." "A dishonoured wife," he states, "that's what's the cause of all our misfortunes" (*U* 12.1163–4). His obsessive catch cry is "*Sinn Fein . . . Sinn Fein amhain*" (*U* 12.523). In a text where the axis of otherness is constantly being displaced, his doctrine of political and cultural separatism is constantly being mocked. Consider, for example, the paragraph in which the crystal palace appears:

> In Inisfail the fair there lies a land, the land of holy Michan. There rises a watchtower beheld of men afar. There sleep the mighty dead as in life they slept, warriors and princes of high renown . . . Lovely maidens sit in close proximity to the roots of the lovely trees singing the most lovely songs . . . And heroes voyage from afar to woo them . . . princes, the sons of kings. And there rises a shining palace whose crystal glittering roof is seen by mariners who traverse the extensive sea in barks built expressly for that purpose . . . (*U* 12.68–89)

The passage evokes the romantic imagery typical of nationalist rhetoric; however, the crystal palace-Inisfail-questing hero complex of images, which gives it its distinctly Celtic resonance, is framed by an imperialist context. As Weldon Thornton observes, the paragraph almost certainly derives from James Clarence Mangan's translation of "Prince Alfred's Itinerary through Ireland" (257). Joyce's intertextual dialogism here unsettles the idealist quest for meaning (selfhood) that belong to "Sinn Fein," Ourselves Alone. Indeed, even the crystal palace reference itself is a type of Trojan horse. In the context of the Celtic myth, it represents the Otherworld, but it might also refer to the British Crystal Palace, the icon of imperialism erected in Hyde Park, London, for the Great Exhibition in 1851 (Thornton 258). The connotation of the word Inisfail (a traditional name for Ireland) is also open to question, since the stone from which it derives its name, the *Lia Fáil* (the Stone of Fál or "stone of destiny," one of the four sacred symbols of the Tuatha Dé Danann), is itself colonized. Apparently the "Liam Fail" – as Joyce puts it in *Finnegans Wake* – now rests under the Coronation throne in "Westmunster" Abbey (*FW* 131.10–11). The blurred demarcations between the self and the other, the carefully controlled counterpoint between antithetical (imperial and Celtic) motifs and quest myths, here exemplify Joyce's dialogic practice in destabilizing hegemonic nationalist and, moreover, imperialist, narrative forms.

Let us turn our attention now to Joyce's two potential knights, the two "Seekers on the great quest . . . East of the sun, west of the moon: *Tír na n-óg*" (*U* 9.411–13). Both Sir Leopold, "bedight in sable armour" (*U* 12.215), and – to use Biddy the Clap's words – "yon sable knight" (*U* 15.4636) Stephen Dedalus are cast in two quest myths simultaneously. One of the structuring features of Joyce's dialogized Grail myth, as I suggested earlier, is the opposition of blood-filled chalice and the womb. As we trace the threads of this theme as it relates to Stephen through *Ulysses*, we see a new pattern emerging, one in which both chalice and womb are equated as purveyors of death. If the bloody "cup" offered to him by Cathleen Ni Houlihan, alias Old Gummy Granny (*U* 15.4736), represents for Stephen the nightmare of Irish history from which he is trying to escape, the mother is the "Womb of sin" (*U* 3.44), the "allwombing tomb" (*U* 3.402); to both he says "*Non serviam!*" (*U* 15.4228).

In Joyce's treatment of Stephen's relationship with his mother, we find a recapitulation of themes and motifs from a number of Grail myths, particularly Chrétien's *Perceval*. Stephen's quest, like that of Perceval, revolves around the motif of the question, and like Perceval too, he is obsessed with guilt at the plight of his sister and the death of his mother: "They say I killed you, mother," he screams, "choking with fright, remorse and horror" in "Circe." "Cancer did it," he pleads, "not I. Destiny" (*U* 15.4186–7). As Emma Jung and Marie-Louise von Franz have remarked, the failure of Perceval's quest in Chrétien's work is due to an offence against the emotional, spiritual side of the self represented by the mother. Perceval, they state, "did not attend to his mother and he did not ask about the Grail – and the latter offence is actually described as a consequence of the former." "As its primal image," they add, "the Grail takes the place of the mother" (181). In *Ulysses* too, Stephen's quest and his neglect of the mother are inextricably intertwined. In fact, the question which haunts him throughout *Ulysses* is posed directly to the mother: "Tell me the word, mother," he begs at the climax of the novel in "Circe," "if you know now. The word known to all men" (*U* 15.4192–3). Significantly, no answer is forthcoming. The motif of the unanswered question (a motif found in a number of Grail myths) is closely bound up with the notion that "meaning" cannot be imposed by an external authority. Rather, it must be sought within the self. Stephen's quest for the word of the mother, then, is both an inversion and an interiorization of his quest for the Word of the Father. Whereas the nationalist (and Christian) quest myth centers around a quest for a defined "good" – the rejuvenation of a political abstraction called Cathleen Ni Houlihan – and the attendant defeat of an "evil" other, these polar oppositions are interiorized in the quest which centers around the mother. In his drunken state in "Circe," Stephen is dimly aware of the fact that it is in his own consciousness that he must kill the scapegoated other: "the priest and the king" (*U* 15.4437). It is in himself too, as the reader discovers in "Scylla and Charybdis," that Stephen has buried the Grail of love (the repressed "woid" of the mother) that will heal the Waste Land of the spirit (*U* 9.429–30).

That the Celtic quest myth is, in its very essence, a narrative detailing the growth of individual consciousness is evident from the fact that in several versions of the myth the Otherworld may be reached "simply through the granting of a sudden insight" (MacCana 125). In *A Portrait of the Artist as a Young Man*, Stephen, the fledgling poet, had a fleeting vision of this hidden world: he heard "a voice from beyond the world" (*P* 167) and saw a woman, a "strange and beautiful seabird" with legs "delicate as a crane's" (*P* 171). "Her eyes had called to him," but he turned away from her and dedicated himself to the "old father, old artificer" whose name he bore. This link between the would-be poet and the crane woman is particularly significant since, as I have already pointed out, the Grail of Fionn, the poet of the Fianna, is a mysterious bag of poetic wisdom made from the skin of the crane woman, Aoife. In rejecting the visionary woman for the Father, Stephen rejected the Grail he so desperately sought, committing himself instead to the very paralysis he struggles to escape from in *Ulysses*. Trapped in a selfish aesthet-icism, fearful of death and the fluidity of the feminine, he remains at the end of *Ulysses* "the eternal son and ever virgin" (*U* 14.342–3). The meaning of love, like the apples of wisdom and self-knowledge (*U* 3.432), remains for him a "bitter mystery" (*U* 15.4190).

Like Stephen Dedalus, Bloom, the would-be architect of "Bloom-usalem," an otherworldly New Jerusalem "with crystal roof" (*U* 15.1548), is cast in two quest myths simultaneously: he is at once Joyce's Christian Fisher of men and his pagan Fisher King. The "cod-eyed" Bloom (*U* 15.1871), the "last sardine of summer" (*U* 11.1220–1), whose nickname, by the way, is "Mackerel" (*U* 8.405), is, as the Citizen so eloquently puts it, "[a] fellow that's neither fish nor flesh" (*U* 12.1055–6). Sex, the key to renewal in the pagan quest myth and an impediment to renewal in the Christian quest myth, is the aporia on which Bloom's dialogized Grail quest rests. He may be "the very truest knight of the world one that ever did minion service to lady" (*U* 14.184–5), yet, from the perspective of his wife, his "service" leaves something to be desired. Molly resents the fact that she has been cast in the role of the Loathly Lady: "its a wonder Im not an old shrivelled hag before my time," she complains, "living with him so cold never embracing me except sometimes when hes asleep the wrong end of me" (*U* 18.1399–1401). This "new apostle to the gentiles" (*U* 12.1489), who has not had sexual intercourse with Molly since the death of their only son almost eleven years before, is, it seems, a celibate (of sorts). Appropriately enough, he assumes the role of the chaste redeemer in "Circe" where, wearing "a seamless garment marked I.H.S.," he burns "amid phoenix flames" (*U* 15.1935–6). Bloom's credentials as a Christian redeemer, however, are somewhat sullied by the fact that, like the Fisher King of the Grail castle, his celibacy is due to impotence (of a sort). Fearful of the feminine, which he associates with death and corruption, this middle-aged Tristan looks to virgins for consolation, to "Green apples" (*U* 13.1086), and to the cold curves of stone "goddesses" (*U* 8.922). In "Lestrygonians," he imagines these plaster virgins as immortals drinking nectar from "golden dishes" (*U* 8.925–6). Conscious of his own mortality, he envies them their fleshless state. The icons in Bloom's *salle aux images*, the statue of Venus in the National Gallery (*U* 8.1180–1), the various pornographic "Venus in Furs" figures that populate his daydreams, the disgruntled nymph framed over his bed, the immature Gerty MacDowell, the mysterious Martha Clifford, and, most importantly, Cathleen Ni Houlihan – the sterile icon of the militant nationalist group he is reputed to have been instrumental in founding – are the psychological equivalent of the condom he carries in his pocketbook. They enable him to indulge his erotic desires, yet, at the same time, they shield him from the (for him) horrors of female fecundity, and its corollary, death.

Nationalist, freemason, Jew, Christ figure, advocate of universal love, and self-cuckolded lover, Bloom is the personification of Joyce's indeterminacy principle. Although he has apparently immersed himself in a new type of fatherhood, the regenerative fatherhood of Sinn Féin (*U* 18.1227–9), he, nevertheless, rejects the

nationalist ethic of justice and domination in favor of an ethic of
care and responsibility. "Force, hatred, history, all that," he
argues, offers no "life for men and women." "And everybody
knows," he points out, "that it's the very opposite of that that is
really life" (U 12.1481–5): Love. Throughout *Ulysses*, Bloom
searches ceaselessly for "that other world" (U 13.1262–3). His
quest, which begins in what might be described as the "Perilous
Chapel" in "Hades" and ends in Molly's "Perilous bed," "a lair or
ambush of lust or adders" (U 17.2116–18), in "Penelope," reaches
its climax in "Circe." In this dream-world of dissolving identities
and blurred boundaries, the dual-gendered Bello/Bella serves as his
guide on his journey to the otherworldly "womancity" (U
15.1327). "For such favours," she claims, "knights of old laid down
their lives" (U 15.3080–1). Here, Bloom comes face to face with all
the debased images of women that have appeared throughout
Ulysses. He unveils the virginal nymph who "flees from him
unveiled, her plaster cracking, a cloud of stench escaping from the
cracks" (U 15.3469–70). Gummy Granny in her role as the blood-
thirsty Cathleen is also banished. Finally, in the Black Mass scene
at the end of "Circe," the diffuse thematic pattern of this post-
modernist Grail myth reaches its climax. Bloom has a vision of the
dialogized Grail:

*On an eminence, the centre of the earth, rises the fieldaltar of Saint Barbara. Black
candles rise from its gospel and epistle horns … On the altarstone Mrs Mina
Purefoy, goddess of unreason, lies, naked, fettered, a chalice resting on her swollen
belly.* (U 15.4688–93)

In German legend, as Jung and von Franz point out, the "round
mountain of St. Barbara" is the home of the Knight of the Swan
(Lohengrin). Here, it is said, "Venus lives in the Grail" (121).
    If *Ulysses* begins with an image of a colonized "Mother Ireland,"
"Silk of the kine and poor old woman" (U 1.403), it ends, like
Yeats's *Cathleen Ni Houlihan*, with an image of a revivified Mother
Goddess. Whereas Yeats's Cathleen is rejuvenated by heroic sacri-
fice, we find no mention of sacrificial martyrdom in "Penelope";
whereas the maternal embodiment of the nation in the discourse of
Irish nationalism was rigorously chaste and virginal, Joyce's "Gea
Tellus" is a sexually active woman. Molly Bloom has no patience
with the "trash and nonsense" (U 18.384) of "Sinner Fein or the
freemasons" (U 18.1227). In the place of dogmatic nationalism, she

offers "plurabilities"; in the place of sacrificial death, she offers a vision of cyclical life.

The two powerful female icons Molly tries to transcend in *Ulysses* are the sexless Cathleen, the Grail of the Nationalists, and the Virgin Mother, the chaste icon of the Templars, the first Christian Grail Knights.[7] Appropriately enough, Molly, the daughter of a Templar, shares both the name and the birthday of the Virgin. Yet, although she is herself a bereaved mother famous for her stirring rendition of Rossini's *Stabat Mater*, Molly Bloom recalls not the Christian *Mater dolorosa*, but Isis, the Sacred Moon Cow, the prototype not only for the Virgin Mother but also for the Celtic Cow Goddess, Brigid. According to the Isis myth (possibly the earliest version of the Grail story) the origins of life are not male but female. Isis was originally the mother/wife of Osiris, the earliest resurrected god. The pagan myth, Barbara Walker notes, was copied by Christianity, "except for one vital point: the agent of Osiris's resurrection was not the heavenly father," but the mother (216).

A rejuvenated Sacred Cow Goddess, "Marion of the bountiful bosoms" (*U* 12.1006–7), presides over Joyce's otherworldly "Apple Land" in "Penelope." Her blood-filled commode is, significantly, "totally covered by square cretonne cutting, apple design" (*U* 17.2102–3). Molly is, as she herself puts it, "a mixture of plum and apple" (*U* 18.1535). The proliferation of O's in her language points to the Irish *ubhal* (apple), a word which, Harold Bayley – the Scottish scholar of symbolism whose work influenced Yeats – points out, "resolves itself into iabel, the 'orb of god,' oko, 'the great O'" (303). Furthermore, Molly's curiosity about the "capital initial of the name of a city in Canada, Quebec" (*U* 17.679–80), an interest linked to her fascination with Irish "hieroglyphics," points to the Q, the letter of the *Quert* (apple) in the Oghamic tree alphabet. In the "penelopean patience" of "Penelope," as Anna Livia observes in *Finnegans Wake*, the "feminine libido" is represented by "those interbranching ogham sex upandinsweeps" (*FW* 123.4–9).

The final passages in "Penelope" are awash with images of fertility and regeneration. Blazes Boylan, Bloom's rival for the affections of Molly, has lost his bet on the Gold Cup Race, and he has also lost the affections of Molly. In spite of the size of his "tremendous big red brute of a thing" (*U* 18.144), Boylan, it seems, lacks *fír flaitheman*. Molly is convinced that Bloom "has more spunk in him" (*U* 18.168); she believes, moreover, that "he understood or felt what a woman is" (*U* 18.1578–9). Bloom did not, of course, place a bet on the Gold Cup Race, he is no "winner"; yet, as Molly observes, "if anyone asked could he ride the steeplechase for the gold cup hed say yes" (*U* 18.955–6). In her "snakespiral" (*U* 17.2116) bed, her omphalos – a symbol of the mystery of nonduality – Molly is planning to initiate Bloom into the life-empowering mysteries of love; she is planning what is, in effect, a *banfheis rígi*. Yes, she will give him "one more chance" (*U* 18.1498). "I suppose hed like my nice cream too" (*U* 18.1506), she thinks, as she plans her early morning shopping trip to her local crystal palace (the Dublin fruit and vegetable market). She will "throw him up his tea" in an imitation Crown Derby cup, and she will serve him eggs (the sacred symbol of Isis) while he sits in bed "like the king of the country" (*U* 18.931).

Although the title of the final illustration in Sebastian Evans's translation of *The High History of the Holy Graal* (one of Joyce's main sources for the Grail theme) is "Perceval Winneth the Golden Cup," the final chapter in *Ulysses* offers no such Telos; here "nought nowhere [is] never reached" (*U* 17.1068–9). Even as Molly determines to effect changes in her relationship with Bloom, her "new womanly man" is asleep at "the wrong end" of her; in short, Bloom still views the feminine from an inverted perspective. His dilemma, like that of all Grail knights – Bran-Nuadu, Arthur, Perceval, Gawain – when faced with *la vieille ogresse*, the "old shrivelled hag" (*U* 18.1399), who embodies the ever-revolving cycle of life-in-death and death-in-life, centers on the question of vision. As long as he fears death – which he projects onto the feminine – he will reject Molly, and the Waste Land will prevail. But if he can accept her as she is, if he can restore the phallic spear (as in Wagner's *Parsifal*) to her Grail/womb, he will – in mythopoeic terminology – achieve kingship in her timeless realm, and the Waste Land will be fruitful once more.

In the introduction to this essay I suggested that Joyce sets out in *Ulysses* to decenter the nationalist myth of sacrificial renewal by confronting it with an opposing voice. This type of "ideological decentering," as Bakhtin points out, will occur only when a national culture, or a national myth is dialogized: when it "loses its sealed-off and self-sufficient character, when it becomes conscious of itself as only one among *other* cultures and languages" (370). In *Ulysses*, Joyce achieves his purpose by initiating a dialogic exchange

between the hegemonic nationalist Grail myth and its *own* occulted
Celtic prototype. Thus, in the place of a monological myth of origin
in *Ulysses*, we find two versions of the same myth – to use Bakhtin's
words – "mutually animating one another." In the earlier myth, a
moral and humanitarian principle of love, represented symbolically
by *"Amor matris"* (*U* 9.842–3), is represented as the source of life,
spiritual and physical; in its successor, patriotic martyrdoms and
war take the place of love. In one myth, dualism is emphasized; in
the other, we find a recognition of the positive values of otherness
and difference that have been suppressed by the hegemony of logos.
The endless oscillations between these two Grails in *Ulysses* ensure
that meaning is never final but is in a constant process of metamor-
phosis. Here, there are no "winners," but only the constant whirling
of antithetical impulses. As Joyce puts it in *Finnegans Wake*,

there are two signs to turn to, the yest and the ist, the wright side and the
wronged side ... It is a sot of a swigswag, systomy dystomy, which
everabody you ever anywhere at all doze. Why? Such me. (597.10–22)

NOTES

1 The word "parergon" is used here and elsewhere in the essay in the
  Kantian/Derridian sense of the term. For an interesting discussion of
  "parergonal logic" – to use Derrida's term – see Barbara Johnson's "The
  Frame of Reference: Poe, Lacan, Derrida" (Young 225–43).
2 Richard Ellmann's catalogue of Joyce's library in *The Consciousness of
  Joyce* provides ample evidence of Joyce's interest in the Grail myth while
  writing *Ulysses*. The library includes such works as Sebastian Evans's
  translation of *The High History of the Holy Graal* (112), Lady Charlotte
  Guest's translation of the Welsh *Mabinogion* (118) – described as the
  "Welsh Greal" in the introduction to Evans's work – a heavily annotated copy of Francis Hueffer's *The Troubadours: A History of Provençal Life
  and Literature in the Middle Ages* (112), Joseph Bédier's *Le Roman de Tristan
  et Iseut* (101), several of Richard Wagner's works, and an assortment of
  titles on Celtic themes by various members of the Irish Literary
  Renaissance.
  One of the earliest studies of the Celtic roots of the Grail legend to
  which Joyce had access in Dublin was a summary of A. C. L. Brown's
  Iwain: A Study of the Origin of Arthurian Romance, which appeared in the
  November–December 1903 issue of *Celtia* (the journal of the St.
  Stephen's Green Celtic Association). Contrary to popular opinion,
  Joyce's access to Celtic manuscript materials was in no sense restricted
  when he left Ireland. In fact, during both of his sojourns in Paris (1902–3
  and 1920–39), he had access not only to the Celtic materials in the

Bibliothèque Nationale but also to the extensive holdings in the library
of the Ecole Pratique des Hautes Etudes of the Sorbonne. The materials
in the Sorbonne library range from relatively obscure journals such as
Celtia, to facsimile copies of rare manuscripts such as *The Book of Ballymote*
(this contains several hundred Ogham cipher-alphabets), to translations
of old Irish poetry like the *Duanaire Finn*. The library also contains a
comprehensive collection of scholarly works on Celtic mythology,
history, religion, and the Celtic languages, including – to name but a few
– Alfred Nutt's *Studies in the Legend of the Holy Grail*, Kuno Meyer and
Nutt's *The Voyage of Bran* (the latter includes an interesting discussion of
the relationship between the Greek and Celtic doctrines of metempsychosis), John Rhys's *Lectures on the Origin and Growth of Religion as Illustrated by Celtic Heathendom*, and Eugene O'Curry's *Lectures on the Manuscript
Materials of Ancient Irish History*. Both Rhys's and O'Curry's works
provide extensive background information on all aspects of Celtic
culture, history, and literature, and both touch on such Grail-related
motifs and topics as the voyage theme, the apple motif, the stone of Fál,
and the Otherworld of women.

3 The Grail myth, the creation of centuries of accretion of religious and
mythological themes, contains elements from several different traditions,
including Celtic mythology, Anglo-Saxon and French courtly traditions,
Christian iconography, alchemical lore, classical myth, Arabic poetry,
and Sufi teaching (Whitmont 153). Symbols and motifs from several of
these traditions are threaded throughout *Ulysses*, *Finnegans Wake*, and
Joyce's earlier works as well. A discussion of the significance of the Grail
myth for the entire Joycean *œuvre* – a topic well beyond the scope of this
essay – is the subject of a book-length work in progress.

4 For a brief, yet comprehensive survey of the various cycles of Celtic myth
discussed here, see Mac Cana.

5 For a chronological list of Arthurian literature since 1800, see Taylor
and Brewer 324–60.

6 Hitler is quoted in the work of the German historian Wilfried Daim as
having said:

> You ought to understand Parzifal differently from the way it is generally
> interpreted. Behind the trivial Christian dressing of the external story, with its
> Good Friday magic, this profound drama has a quite different content. It is not a
> Christian, Schopenhauerian religion of compassion, but the pure, aristocratic
> blood that is glorified ... The eternal life that is the gift of the Grail is only for the
> truly pure and noble ... How is one to stop racial decay? Politically we have
> acted: no equality no democracy. But what about the masses of the People? ...
> Should we form an elect group of real initiates? An order of templars around the
> grail of the pure blood? (Daim 140; quoted in Whitmont 162–3)

Hitler found in the Grail myth a justification for one of the most horrific
bloodbaths in human history. Although the goals of the Nazi "templars"
were in no sense analogous to those of Yeats and the Irish nationalists, it

is significant that many of the same mechanisms they exploited to incite Germany's collective madness in the Jewish holocaust were used to unify the emerging nationalist movement in Ireland. Both systems were marked by a union of religious and military force; both were predicated on the deliberate manipulation of an alienated people through the exploitation of the archetypes of universal history contained in the Grail myth; in both systems the mother archetype (represented by Ostara in Germany, Cathleen in Ireland) was coopted by a patriarchal system hostile to women and nature; and, finally, in both systems this mother archetype was virginized.

7 The link between the Templars, the Grail, and the cult of the Virgin can be traced back to "Bernardus" (biographer and friend of St. Malachy), the authority on Christian doctrine to whom Stephen refers in "Oxen of the Sun" when he points to the apple, Eve's "penny pippin," as the emblem of the fall (*U* 14.299–301). St. Bernard was not only personally responsible for the phenomenal increase in the popularity of the cult of the Virgin which took place in the twelfth century, but, primarily, through his eighty-six sermons on Solomon's "Song of Songs" (*U* 17.729–30), he lent doctrinal authority to the beliefs put forward by one of the leaders of the First Crusade – the Muslim Prester John (*U* 12.190) – beliefs that linked the Temple of Solomon with the Grail. "Salmonson," as Joyce puts it in *Finnegans Wake*, "set his seel on a hexengown" (297.3–4). Bernard himself preached the Second Crusade and wrote the rule of the Order of the Templars, commending the celibate warrior Knights (who took their name from the Temple of Solomon) to the protection of the Virgin in their bloody quest for the New Jerusalem, the *Visio Pacis* flowing with milk and honey. The last depository of the Templar tradition in the twentieth century, as Arthur Edward Waite points out, is the Masonic order, an all male sect (to which Bloom, it seems, also belongs) whose avowed vocation it is to use mathematics to rebuild Solomon's Temple of the soul (235–9). In fact, it is precisely here, in this Faustian quest to control nature and create a New Jerusalem of the spirit, that Molly's two male protectors, her Templar father and her Mason husband, find common ground.

On St. Bernard's influence on the Grail legend see Cleland 39–61. On St. Bernard and the cult of the Virgin, see Julia Kristeva's "Stabat Mater" in *The Kristeva Reader*.

WORKS CITED

Bakhtin, M. M. *The Dialogic Imagination*. Trans. Caryl Emerson and Michael Holquist. Ed. Michael Holquist. Austin: University of Texas Press, 1981.

Barber, Richard. *The Arthurian Legends*. New York: Bedrick, 1979.

Bayley, Harold. *The Lost Language of Symbolism*. Secaucus, N.J.: Citadel, 1988.

Brown, Arthur C. L. *The Origin of the Grail Legend*. 1943. Rpt. New York: Russell, 1966.

Celtia: A Pan Celtic Monthly Magazine. [Dublin.] 111:8 (October 1903).

Cleland, John. "Bernardian Ideas in Wolfram's *Parzival* about Christian War and Human Development." *The Chimera of His Age: Studies on Bernard of Clairvaux*. Cistercian Studies Series 63. Kalamazoo, Mich.: Cistercian, 1980.

Condren, Mary. *The Serpent and the Goddess: Women, Religion, and Power in Celtic Ireland*. San Francisco: Harper, 1989.

The Crane Bag 4.1 (1980).

Daim, Wilfried. *Der Mann, der Hitler die Ideen gab*. Vienna: Institut für politische Psychologie, 1958.

Deane, Seamus. *A Short History of Irish Literature*. London: Hutchinson, 1986.

Ellmann, Richard. *The Consciousness of Joyce*. London: Faber, 1977.

Yeats: The Man and the Masks. 1948. New York: Dutton, 1958.

Evans, Sebastian, trans. *The High History of the Holy Graal*. London: Dent, 1910.

Hutchinson, John. *The Dynamics of Cultural Nationalism: The Gaelic Revival and the Creation of the Irish Nation State*. London: Allen, 1987.

Joyce, James. *The Critical Writings of James Joyce*. Ed. Ellsworth Mason and Richard Ellmann. New York: Viking, 1959.

Finnegans Wake. New York: Viking, 1939.

"A Portrait of the Artist as a Young Man": Text, Criticism, and Notes. Ed. Chester G. Anderson. New York: Viking, 1968.

Ulysses: The Corrected Text. Ed. Hans Walter Gabler et al. New York: Random, 1986.

Jung, Emma, and Marie-Louise von Franz. *The Grail Legend*. 2nd edn. Trans. Andrea Dykes. Boston: Sigo, 1986.

Kristeva, Julia. *The Kristeva Reader*. Ed. Toril Moi. Oxford: Blackwell, 1986.

Mac Cana, Proinsias. *Celtic Mythology*. Harmondsworth: Newnes, 1983.

MacKillop, James. *Fionn mac Cumhaill: Celtic Myth in English Literature*. Syracuse, N.Y.: Syracuse University Press, 1986.

Mac Mathúna, Séamus. *Immram Brain: Bran's Journey to the Otherworld*. Tübingen: Niemeyer, 1983.

Mac Neill, Eoin, ed. and trans. *Duanaire Finn I: The Book of the Lays of Fionn*. Irish Texts Society 7. London: Nutt, 1908.

Meyer, Kuno, and Alfred Nutt. *The Voyage of Bran*. 2 vols. Grimm Library Series. London: Nutt, 1895-7.

Nutt, Alfred. *Studies in the Legend of the Holy Grail*. London: Nutt, 1897.

O'Brien, Conor Cruise. "A Lost Chance to Save the Jews." *New York Review of Books* 27 April 1989: 27+.

O'Curry, Eugene. *Lectures on the Manuscript Materials of Ancient Irish History*. 1873. Rpt. *Celtic Review* 1 (1904-5).

Raine, Kathleen. *Yeats the Initiate: Essays on Certain Themes in the Work of W. B. Yeats*. London: Allen, 1986.

Rhys, John. *Lectures on the Origin and Growth of Religion as Illustrated by Celtic Heathendom: The Hibbert Lectures for 1886*. London: Williams, 1888.

Taylor, Beverly, and Elisabeth Brewer. *The Return of King Arthur: British and American Arthurian Literature since 1900*. Totowa, N.J.: Barnes, 1983.

Thornton, Weldon. *Allusions in "Ulysses": An Annotated List*. Chapel Hill: University of North Carolina Press, 1968.

Waite, Arthur Edward. *A New Encyclopaedia of Freemasonry*. London: Rider, 1921.

Walker, Barbara G. *The Woman's Dictionary of Symbols and Sacred Objects*. San Francisco: Harper, 1988.

Weston, Jessie L. *From Ritual to Romance*. Garden City, N.Y.: Doubleday, 1957.

Whitmont, Edward C. *The Return of the Goddess*. New York: Crossroad, 1987.

Yeats, William Butler. *Memoirs*. Ed. Denis Donoghue. London: Macmillan, 1972.

Mythologies. London: Macmillan, 1959.

Young, Robert, ed. *Untying the Text: A Post-Structuralist Reader*. Boston: Routledge, 1981.

CHAPTER 8

Joyce and Michelet: why watch Molly menstruate?

Bonnie Kime Scott

Both Joyce and deconstructionist philosophers have taught us to follow the merest trace in order to detect the way that discourse works. In this essay, I take as my trace a flickering memory of Paris that passes through the mind of Stephen Dedalus, walking down Sandymount Strand in the "Proteus" chapter of *Ulysses*:

About the nature of women he read in Michelet. (*U* 3.166–7)

It is an easy statement to discredit. The reader is not Stephen (himself much discredited on the subject of woman in feminist criticism),[1] but Patrice Egan. Egan is a bunny-faced young man of dubious appetite,[2] the son of a powerless Fenian émigré, whom Stephen knew in Paris. Stephen's approval of the Michelet text is far from assured. He volunteers nothing about having read or discussed it, though we know of his penchant for male intellectual debate from *Stephen Hero*, *A Portrait*, and "Scylla and Charybdis." Still, I propose to follow this mere trace, not toward an understanding of women, but toward an understanding of *discourse* on the nature of women. This project includes woman *as* nature, and the viewing of women – specifically the gaze – as a defining act. Michelet, filtered through the continuing essentialist discourse on woman as nature, the burgeoning theory of the gaze,[3] and the text of *Ulysses*, provides a new angle on our specular activities as readers of self and other.

The allusion to Michelet is more valuable as an intertext than as an allusion. As we shall see, it connects to other episodes of *Ulysses* – most notably "Calypso," "Nausicaa," "Circe" and "Penelope" – and to French feminist and psychoanalytic theory, where we can call upon Roland Barthes and Marguerite Duras as appropriators of Michelet.[4] For philosophy of history, Michelet connects with Giambattista Vico, whom he translated into French, to the direct benefit of James Joyce. "Proteus" provides rare glimpses of Stephen in the foreign territory of France, conversing in the French language. It is a promising connection in view of the fact that French feminist theory has been most affirmative in its apprehension of Joyce as a writer of the feminine in language.

Michelet will never assume favored-author status for Joyce, amid figures like Shakespeare, Ibsen, Swift, Blake, Vico, or even Freud, all of whom are culled in Joyce's notebooks and clearly referred to in multiple allusions. Though his concern with the body from the standpoints of disease and sexuality compares to that of Baudelaire, it is the poet and not Michelet who has typically arisen in critical comparison to Joyce – possibly because Baudelaire was easier to accommodate to canonical theories of modernism than was the romanticist Michelet. None of Michelet's books remained in Joyce's Trieste collection for later scholarly perusal at Texas. Ellmann makes no reference to him in the biography, even for the sake of comparison.

Michelet tends to enter Joycean discussion as the provider of the translation of Vico's *La scienza nuova* used by Joyce; it has been argued that Michelet's distorted Vico became a structuring device for *Finnegans Wake* (Hughes). Joyce apparently owned the book during his mature years in Paris, as Constantine Curran reports that Joyce took a copy from his bookshelf to lend him in 1921 (Curran 86–7, 121). Joyce could have read Michelet's Vico in Dublin; the National Library has a copy that would have been there in Joyce's day. Mary Reynolds (who located the Dublin Library copy) suggests that Joyce read Michelet as part of his college course in Romance Languages in 1901 (Reynolds 119–20). The Jesuit Fathers are not expansive on language and literature or modern historical studies in their account of Joyce's era at the Royal University, and what if any Michelet he read there remains unsubstantiated to me in memoirs and records. The classically-oriented Jesuits do note that the demand for modern languages came mostly from the women's colleges – a fact that places Joyce and perhaps Michelet in the women's studies of Joyce's day (Fathers of the Society of Jesus 211–12). Michelet was not in academic favor generally when Joyce was in the university, as it was an era privileging more positivistic accounts (Kippur 224). One suspects that Joyce encountered his writings, and certainly the works on woman, informally, when he was first in Paris in 1902. The allusion to Michelet in "Proteus" is followed closely by names of popular periodicals retained by Stephen when he hastily leaves Paris to return to his dying mother:

Le Tutu and *Pantalon Blanc et Culotte Rouge* (*U* 3.196–7). Despite their sources in real weeklies, the names evoke female dress, with the emphasis upon underwear, a favorite Joyce fetish.[5] The periodicals and Michelet on women may have qualified as prurient private reading for the adolescent male. Medical reading at this stage may have offered similar private diversion, offering the even more invasive view of the speculum, which Luce Irigaray describes as seeing with "men's eyes" (144).

Annotators have found only three references to Michelet, two in *Ulysses*, one in *Finnegans Wake*. Joyce's primary allusion in "Proteus" (cited above) includes no titles. Since the work clearly concerns women, Weldon Thornton supplies the Michelet titles *La Femme, Les Femmes de la révolution* and *L'Amour*, also citing the Vico translation and, as Michelet's greatest work, *Histoire de France*. Don Gifford offers only *La Femme* in annotating the "Proteus" allusion. In his revised annotations Gifford adds a range of quotations representing Michelet's sense of woman (for example) as a "religion," "a reflection of love on a groundwork of purity," to be "cultivated by man" and become "superior to him," though not "strong" (53). Richard Brown cites one more book on women to our building list, but he offers a negative, sardonic summary of Michelet on women:

Michelet, in *La Femme, L'Amour* and *Priests, Women and Families*, does indeed describe the nature of women: their weakness and unsuitability for work; the tragedy that results if they are separated from domestic and maternal duties; the fact that men should marry even though the prospect seems unappealing. (98)

Brown passes over Michelet as the enthusiasm of Patrice Egan, suggesting that "Stephen is critical of the naivety or anti-feminism of others" (98), Patrice's "plump bunny's face" helping in the indictment.

It is easy enough to identify the limiting determinisms of *La Femme*'s domestic utopia of worldly, doting, instructing husband and religious, fragile, wife and mother, whose milk, blood and body are suited to nurture and reproduction. "Woman, sacred lifegiver," the phrase from "Circe" that Gifford adds to his 1988 notes as an evocation of "the way Michelet idealized woman," is quickly undermined in the text (*U* 15.4648–9; Gifford 525). Bloom uses this epithet in speaking to Cissy Caffrey, hoping she will save Stephen's neck in his dispute with Privates Compton and Carr. In failing completely, it too is discredited. An accumulation of Micheletian values for the female can be read in ironic subversion in the evocation of Mina Purefoy that follows a page later: "*On the altarstone Mrs Mina Purefoy, goddess of unreason, lies, naked, fettered, a chalice resting on her swollen belly*" (*U* 15.4691–3).

Over a lifetime, there is considerable variation in Michelet's reactions to and treatment of women. Like Joyce, he experienced his mother's death at an early age (sixteen, in his case), with a sense of guilt and horror. The sort of ambivalence toward his female contemporaries that is noted in Joyce by Stanislaus Joyce is evident in Michelet's recently published journal extracts, meaningfully titled *Mother Death* (Orr 79). A thorough list of Michelet's relevant writings should include, in addition to those primarily domestic works cited by Thornton and Brown, *La Sorcière* (published 1862), Michelet's sympathetic treatment of witches in the context of medieval history and the church. It is apparent in this work, as well as in *Du Prêtre, de la femme, de la famille* (published 1845, title cited in English by Brown), that Michelet anticipated Joyce's own criticism of the inordinate control exerted over women by the Church, though like Michelet, Joyce wanted to substitute a man in his own image as her confessor. In *Stephen Hero* and *A Portrait*, Stephen's gaze is particularly troubled by Emma Clery's interviews with Father Moran (*SH* 65, *P* 215), and in *Stephen Hero* he follows this up with the expressed desire to become her confessor (Scott, *Joyce and Feminism* 141). The exploration of sexual roles and maternal nurture is sustained in Michelet's "nature" books, *L'Insecte* (published 1858), *La Mer* (published 1861), and *L'Oiseau* (published 1867), which along with *L'Amour* and *La Femme* became his best-sellers.

Michelet's writings on woman and nature are usually connected with the era of his happy second marriage to Athénaise. Like Joyce upon his union with Nora Barnacle in 1904, Michelet had a woman he could observe at close range, questioning intimately, and attempting to instruct. But by this time, Michelet was an elderly husband, twenty-eight years his bride's senior, and his sexual vigor does not compare with the forms and level of arousal apparent in Joyce's infamous 1909 letters to Nora. More like Joyce's late creation, HCE, he fantasized father–daughter incest (Orr 83, Kippur 192).

As a philosopher of history, Michelet's statements on gender remain current with contemporary feminist writing, like Julia

Kristeva's "Women's Time," where linear time is equated with the male; cursive and monumental time, with the female.

The man passes from drama to drama, not one of which resembles another, from experience to experience, from battle to battle. History goes forth, ever far-reaching and continually crying to him: "Forward."
    The woman, on the contrary, follows the noble and serene epic that Nature charts in her harmonious cycles, repeating herself with a touching grace of constancy and fidelity. These refrains in her lofty song bestow peace, and, if I may say so, a relative changelessness. This is why the study of nature never wearies, never jades; and woman can trustingly give herself up to it, for Nature is a woman. History, which we very foolishly put in the feminine gender, is a rough, savage male, a sun-burnt, dusty traveler. (*Woman* [trans. of *La Femme*] 104–5)

    Michelet, like Joyce, was an admirer of Viconian historical cycles, and perhaps for some of the same gender-laden reasons. Peter Hughes has suggested that Joyce built upon Michelet's tradition of misreading Vico, transforming a history of events into one of narrative. Hughes detects three Micheletian distortions of Vico. Of these, the most significant is the *ricorso*, "to flood with words 'les silences de l'histoire'" – so much more Joycean than the more accurate rendering of Vico's "course the nations run" (Hughes 86). There is another affinity of Michelet taken up by Joyce – Michelet's colleague Edgar Quinet, whose sequence on flowers that flourish on the ruins of culture became a primary motif of *Finnegans Wake*. The feminine is part of both cycle and floral survival. The Michelet–Vico–Quinet connection is textualized in the nominal allusion to Michelet that appears, in stuttered form, amid the names of Quinet, the Christian avatar John the Baptist, and another philosopher central to Joyce's reworking of historical form, Giordano Bruno: "From quiqui quinet to michemiche chelet and a jambebatiste to a brulobrulo" (*FW* 117.11–12). It occurs in one of the *Wake*'s repetitions of the Quinet sequence, which in this instance is full of references to names and roles of women, to death and renewal, and to varieties of language.

    It is evident in Gifford's annotation that Michelet was controversial in his manner of writing history. Gifford informs us that Michelet is "noted not for his objectivity but for picturesque, impressionistic, and emotional history" (52). He mixes history with popular genres read by women, particularly the novel. This judgment of him surfaces in a novel by Colette, one of Joyce's most important female contemporaries in France. In *Claudine at School*, a novel of female development that bears comparison to *A Portrait of the Artist as a Young Man*, the adolescent Claudine is not uncritical of Michelet, but she can take refuge in him. When she has a cold, she reports, "I stay in Papa's library, reading Michelet's absurd *History of France*, written in alexandrines. (Am I exaggerating a bit?) I'm not in the least bored, curled up in this big armchair, surrounded by books, with my beautiful Fanchette for company" (149). Admittedly, the cat Fanchette gets more space in what follows than does Michelet, but the unconventional historian is part of the atmosphere of paternal comfort; he is amusing for his peculiarity of form. When it comes to her history examinations, Claudine shocks her examiner by responding to a question on "Louis XV (1742)" with the remark, "That was the period when Madame de la Tournelle was exercising a deplorable influence over him . . . " When told that "You're not being asked about that!" she replies that "it's the simple truth" offered by "the best historians," supplying "I read it in Michelet – with full details" when the authority probes further. The examiner does not share her opinion of Michelet: "Michelet! but this is madness! Michelet, get this into your head, wrote a historical novel in twenty volumes and he dared to call that the *History of France!*" (199). Michelet's debasement of the historic genre is not to be borne in academe. Furthermore, Michelet writes domestic space and female influence into history. Colette defies the academy and defines the feminine reader as a force.

Michelet's historical treatment of women as witches in medieval times, and his focus upon menstruation are useful to Marguerite Duras and Xavière Gauthier, as they discuss difference in the female body:

x.g.*um . . . what's specific to woman is pregnancy and – I know that in general you're not supposed to say the word, but her period is also something that belongs to woman . . .*

m.d.Yes, really. For teenage boys, a period is always traumatic. It's an excess, an overfullness that's thrown out of the body, rejected by the body . . . (113)

It is when the denial of speech to women comes up that Duras recalls Michelet, though menstruation undoubtedly stirred thought in his direction:

At the same time it might be good to recall what Michelet said about witches . . . It's in his book *La Sorcière*. By the way, I wanted to tell you earlier that he was the one ... do you remember his book on women when he talks about menstruation, but for him it was a ... a source of eroticism? Yes, he said that in the high Middle Ages, women were alone on their farms, in the forest, while the lord was away at war – whenever I can, I tell this story; I think it's sublime – and so they were extremely bored, alone on their farms, and they were hungry, with the man away on the Crusades or in the lord's war, and that's how women began to talk, alone, to the foxes and squirrels, to the birds, to the trees. And when the husband came back, they continued to do so. I have to add that otherwise no one would have noticed anything; but it was the men who found them speaking alone in the forest ... and then they burned them. To stop it, block up the madness, block up feminine speech. (119–20)

Feminine speech here is associated with nature and female desertion by men – a situation not inappropriate to Molly's final monologue, accompanied as it is by menstruation.[6]

Roland Barthes participated in his own revival of Michelet in the mid 1950s,[7] writing an important essay on *La Sorcière*, and organizing a "pre-critical" collection of Michelet's "organized network of obsessions" (3). A biographical "Memorandum" lists "LOVES" (three women, including both wives, featured) between "INFLUENCES" and "IDEOLOGY." Barthes provides his own headings and summaries for seven thematically grouped sections of quotations. Gender is a dominant interest of this Michelet/Barthes hybrid, being featured in four sections: "History, which we so stupidly decline in the feminine," "Flower of Blood," "Her Majesty the Woman," and "The Ultra-Sex" (a section that develops Michelet's concept of androgyny).

Barthes is as interested as Duras in Michelet's writing on menstruation:

woman's regular period identifies her with a totally natural object, and thereby contrasts her entirely with man. Man, without crisis and without renewal, without turns and returns of weakness – except for the insignificant shedding of skin and emptying of the intestines – man participates only in a quotidian, not a sidereal time; his biology has no relation with the transmutation of the great elements. (Barthes 148)

The ultimate feminine moment for Michelet/Barthes is menstruation, and his erotics "takes no account of the pleasures of orgasm, whereas it attributes a considerable importance to Woman in crisis, i.e. to Woman humiliated. This is an erotics of seeing, not of possession, and Michelet in love, Michelet fulfilled, is none other than Michelet-as-voyeur" (Barthes 150). To achieve this voyeurism Michelet becomes woman, lesbian: "since it is generally the male who is kept away, by a kind of genetic taboo, from Woman's sanguinary crisis, Michelet seeks to strip the genitor away from himself; and since this crisis is made a spectacle exclusively for other women, for companions, mothers, sisters, nurses, and servants, Michelet turns himself into a woman, mother, nurse, the bride's companion. In order to force his way into the gynaeceum more surely, not as a ravisher but as a spectator, the old lion puts on a skirt, attaches himself amorously to Woman by a veritable lesbianism, and finally conceives of marriage only as a kind of sororal couple" (Barthes 153). Elsewhere, Barthes sees it as Michelet's goal to serve as her chambermaid (162–3). It is interesting to me that Barthes is restive when Michelet actually puts on the "language-as-nurse" to "speak of Woman" (157) – an experiment we might compare to Joyce's stylistic variations, particularly the "language-as-fashion-model" of "Nausicaa." Barthes's construction of Michelet moves the gaze out of heterosexual intersubjectivity, regardless of sex, and attempts to work as well with the dimension of increasing age.

Stephen Dedalus is able to demonstrate the sexual ambivalences that are basic to adolescent experience of women and gender, particularly in the richly intertextual situation of "Proteus." For his adolescent experience of women, it is useful to go back to his fascination with E.C. in *A Portrait of the Artist as a Young Man*. Despite a sustained asceticism and removal from women, Stephen has theories about woman in the weakness and humiliation of menstruation that resonate with Michelet/Duras.

He began to feel that he had wronged her. A sense of her innocence moved him almost to pity her, an innocence he had never understood till he had come to the knowledge of it through sin, an innocence which she too had not understood while she was innocent or before the strange humiliation of her nature had first come upon her. Then first her soul had begun to live as his soul had when he had first sinned: and a tender compassion filled his heart as he remembered her frail pallor and her eyes, humbled and saddened by the dark shame of womanhood. (222–3)

In "Proteus," Stephen records one gaze directed at a young woman very like E.C.: "The virgin at Hodges Figgis' window ... Keen glance you gave her. Wrist through the braided jesse of her sunshade" (*U* 3.426–9). But, unlike the situation of *A Portrait*, as he walks along the beach, there is no bird girl to meet or return

Stephen's gaze. He no longer indulges in what Laura Mulvey terms "fetishistic scopophilia" – building up the physical beauty of a woman to allay his own castration anxiety. It is a place to test sound, more than sight; the gaze is turned inward, and at moments backward to his ambivalent experience of sexuality in France.

Paris is figured in his imagination as a waking female, and peopled with vaguely disgusting women who "newmake their tumbled beauties, shattering with gold teeth *chaussons* of pastry, their mouths yellowed with the *pus* of *flan breton*," and with "Faces of Paris men ... their wellpleased pleasers, curled *conquistadores*" (3.213–15). Stephen displays Jesuitical asceticism toward pleasures of the body and a strain of Irish prudishness over Continental (Swedish as well as French) sexual mores. The drawing of other Irish (Patrice and Maud Gonne) into French language and sexual relations may heighten his insecurity:

Maud Gonne, beautiful woman, *la Patrie*, M. Millevoye, Félix Faure, know how he died? Licentious men. The *froeken, bonne à tout faire*, who rubs male nakedness in the bath at Upsala. *Moi faire*, she said, *tous les messieurs*. Not this *monsieur*, I said. Most licentious custom. Bath a most private thing. I wouldn't let my brother, not even my own brother, most lascivious thing. Green eyes, I see you. Fang, I feel. Lascivious people. (3.233–8)

Neither Patrice (the reader of Michelet) nor his father Kevin Egan is particularly masculine. The elder is a reminiscing, weak-handed, forgotten Fenian, protected by Patrice from truths about the atheism and socialism of the younger generation. In this, Patrice is a more considerate son than Stephen, who troubled his mother on religion, even on her deathbed. Kevin Egan plays the role of the "spurned lover" (*U* 3.245) in Stephen's imagination, with the bride a cross-dressed male, and his green eyes are reminiscent of expected adventure, turned to sexual deviance in "An Encounter." Patrice is infantile and animal, with a sensual tongue: "he lapped the sweet *lait chaud* with pink young tongue, plump bunny's face" (*U* 3.165). His father has grown a "green fairy's fang" (*U* 3.226), the constant accessory of a glass of absinthe. Homosexuality, suspected in the Egans, mixes with thoughts of sexual contact with women. And again, as Stephen enters a female shoe (a fetish object associated with his mother in *A Portrait*): "But you were delighted when Esther Osvalt's shoe went on you: girl I knew in Paris. *Tiens, quel petit pied*! Staunch friend, a brother soul: Wilde's love that dare not speak its name" (3.449–51).

It is Leopold Bloom who takes over the male gaze and the active defining of women in *Ulysses*, and also explores alternatives to traditional masculine responses, as explored in Michelet/Barthes. Bloom's gazes tend to be more opportunistic and comic than Stephen's. He recalls viewing Lotty Clark at her toilette, using "papa's operaglasses" (*U* 15.3356). Opportunity to gaze at a fine woman mounting an outside car can be subverted maddeningly by the intervention of a passing tram car (*U* 5.91–140). On the extreme end of comedy is Bloom's imagined invitation to watch Boylan going through Molly a few times through the keyhole in "Circe" (*U* 15.3788). One of his first indulgences of the day is voyeuristic pursuit of the "nextdoor girl" (*U* 4.146) on the way back from the pork butcher's: "To catch up and walk behind her if she went slowly, behind her moving hams. Pleasant to see first thing in the morning" (4.171–3). This is a chapter replete with references to blood, usually from consumable meat (including a "stallfed heifer" [4.153]), which fits with the Micheletian complex of blood. Gerty, of course, is the most notable object of Bloom's extended gaze, though the activity is hardly one-sided; "Nausicaa" begins with Gerty as "pruriently viewing subject" and participant in intersubjective gazing (see Devlin, "The Female Eye"). Notably, Bloom guesses that Gerty may be menstruating; he also assigns that part of the female cycle to Martha Clifford, either a terrific coincidence (when we add in Molly menstruating as well) or an obsession with Bloom.

An important way of seeing the operation of Bloom's gaze, however, is in the bed chamber, where he comes and goes several times, serving as Micheletian chambermaid. During their courtship, Bloom had been curious to know the shape of Molly's bedroom (*U* 18.287). In "Calypso" we find that one of Bloom's first concerns is the preparation of Molly's breakfast of toast and tea, as she lies sleepily abed. His first communications with her are gauged so as not to disturb her sleep (better to leave the door ajar than to fetch the latchkey as he leaves for the butcher's). He delivers the mail (not pressing her for details about the mysterious letter from Boylan), clears the chair of "her striped petticoat, tossed soiled linen" (*U* 4.265–6; soiled drawers were the most prized fetishistic objects to Joyce, as we know from the 1909 letters to Nora [*SL* 185]), and serves tea prepared according to her instructions. Bloom is endeared to Molly by his morning ministrations, as we later learn in "Penelope": "I love to hear him falling up the stairs of a morning with the cups rattling on the tray and then play with the cat" (*U* 18.933–4). During their morning interview, Bloom fulfills the educative domestic function Michelet gives to husbands, as he converses with her and defines metempsychosis. He gazes upon a sensual, earthy woman, focusing upon her breasts, enriched by odor, warmth, and animal analogy as he sets down her tray:

> He looked calmly down on her bulk and between her large soft bubs, sloping within her nightdress like a shegoat's udder. The warmth of her couched body rose on the air, mingling with the fragrance of the tea she poured. (*U* 4.304–7)

Joyce's own preferences with the female body are expressed in the 1909 letters. He does not share Bloom's focus upon the breasts; he is more coprophiliac in his admiration of the "arse," though Bloom will demonstrate his attraction to this part of the anatomy in "Ithaca," and he has positive recollections of administering enemas in "Circe" (*U* 15.3397–3400). Interestingly, menstrual fluids seem to be part of the attraction of the "cunt": "The two parts of your body which do dirty things are the loveliest to me. I prefer your arse, darling, to your bubbies because it does such a dirty thing. I love your cunt not so much because it is the part I block but because it does another dirty thing" (*SL* 186). The admiration of fluids is preserved in Bloom's own letters as recalled by Molly, "thinking of him and his mad crazy letters my Precious one everything connected with your glorious Body everything underlined that comes from it is a thing of beauty and of joy for ever something he got out of some nonsensical book that he had me always at myself 4 and 5 times a day" (*U* 18.1175–9). Possibly Bloom is himself a reader of Michelet. Or, since this thought comes immediately after Molly's physical examination for a vaginal infection (featured by a truly unpleasant emission which she mis-words "omission"), it is also possible that Bloom has been reading medical books, his man's eyes to the medical speculum. His possession (like Joyce's) of *Aristotle's Masterpiece* suggests this sort of specular gaze into the womb.

The chambermaid role re-emerges for Bloom as part of his most masochistic phase as womanly man, imposed by Bello in the "Circe" episode:

> By day you will souse and bat our smelling underclothes also when we ladies are unwell, and swab out our latrines with dress pinned up and a dishclout tied to your tail. Won't that be nice? (*U* 15.3065–7)

Here he again deals with soiled underclothes; "unwell" ladies could be menstruating ones; watching Nora defecate (in effect entering a woman's latrine) was one of Joyce's most erotic, voyeuristic recollections in the 1909 letters (*SL* 181), and Bloom has spent a pleasing interval producing stools in the jakes, if not cleaning it.

It is not clear that Bloom remains as chambermaid at the end of *Ulysses*; indeed many interpreters of the fifties wanted to impress the fact that Bloom sets himself up to be the next recipient of breakfast in bed. In "Penelope" Molly recalls his own confinements to bed, and the attentions he received from older women by being "laid up." She resents this as a maneuver "to make himself interesting" (*U* 18.3–4) to Dante Riordan, and she thinks she has detected another woman's strategy in bringing flowers to him – "anything at all to get into a mans bedroom" (*U* 18.28).

Although Molly is entrenched in the bedchamber in her most focal chapters "Calypso," "Ithaca" and "Penelope," she does not rest quietly in the Micheletian woman's role. Molly plays to a non-familial audience and to herself. In the latter capacity, she may satisfy Luce Irigaray's goal of self-specularity, (re)g(u)arding her self (144–5). As a child in her bedchamber, she lifted her short shift to heat herself at the fire, and danced about, aware of the "fellow opposite" watching. But the activity was largely for her own sensual delight, racing back warm to her bed. "I used to love myself then stripped at the washstand dabbing and creaming" (*U* 18.922–3). The "chamber performance" was done in the dark: "I put out the light too so then there were 2 of us goodbye to my sleep for this night anyhow I hope hes not going to get in with those medicals ..." (*U* 18.924–6). The "2" of this stream of thoughts occurs at a juncture that makes it impossible to determine who the "us" are. Though the two are likely to be Molly and Leopold at a later stage in her life, it is tempting to see multiple Mollies. Molly recalls nearly being caught at washing by Penrose, a memory mixed with a "delicate looking student that stopped ... with the Citrons," and with Molly's abundance of milk (*U* 18.570–5). Her milk production is perhaps the most remarkable of Molly's maternal attributes. Bloom clearly served her here, sucking her breasts at her request when they hardened with engorged milk during Molly's weaning, and playfully wanting to milk them into the tea (*U* 18.569–79).

Molly's actual menstruation does not entirely suit the Micheletian glorification of the natural, fertile cycle, the flower of blood.

5 days every 3 or 4 weeks usual monthly auction isnt it simply sickening that night it came on me like that the one and only time we were in a box that Michael Gunn gave him to see Mrs Kendal and her husband at the Gaiety . . . I was fit to be tied though I wouldnt give in with that gentleman of fashion staring down at me with his glasses and him the other side of me talking about Spinoza and his soul thats dead I suppose millions of years ago I smiled the best I could all in a swamp.(*U* 18.1109–16)

Molly recalls a very obvious voyeuristic gaze, and like an actress plays her role with style. The "swamp" works both ways, reminding us of the muck of menstruation in practical terms, while cycling back to life sources on the nature/woman paradigm. Boylan's "poking and rooting and ploughing" (*U* 18.1106) might as well have been performed on the soil. Molly offers a final simile compatible with Michelet's nature writing, particularly in *La Mer*: "have we too much blood up in us or what O patience above its pouring out of me like the sea" (*U* 18.1122–3). The practical dominates Molly in the early hours of June 17, as she faces the problems of sparing clean bed linen, and locating the awkward cloth sanitary napkins of her era in the creaky old press. In this case, there is no audience and no chambermaid. If Molly speaks to anyone, it is to herself, agreeing, and pacing herself with her famous "yes"es. If anyone watches, it is the sympathetic reader, of indeterminate sex, perhaps as the ultimate, voyeuristic, Micheletian chambermaid. We are still learning to live with the nature in us.

NOTES

1 Skepticism over Stephen as an observer of women begins with Florence Howe, who dismissed Joyce's visionary powers on the basis of Stephen's gaze at the bird girl, which she took as mastering measurement that determines male superiority (263–4). Suzette Henke has studied him as a "young misogynist." I have attempted to distinguish between his public (male-centered) and private discourse, which is more open to feminine influence (*James Joyce* 37). On Stephen and Emma Clery, see my *Joyce and Feminism* 133–5.
2 When we first meet Patrice in "Proteus" he is lapping warm milk. In "Circe," close to another Michelet reference, he reappears munching a quince leaf. In the hallucination, he accuses Stephen of one of his own identifications – being a socialist. There is as much doubling as difference between Stephen and Patrice, I feel.
3 I have found useful for the purposes of this essay what film theorist Laura Mulvey terms "fetishistic scopophilia," which in response to castration

anxiety "builds up the physical beauty of the object" (21). Luce Irigaray, on the other hand, by using the term "speculum" reminds us of
medical examination by the "man's eyes." She goes on to a concept of
woman as subject "(re)g(u)arding itself" (144–5). Interestingly, both
Irigaray and Joyce have examined specularity through *Alice through the
Looking Glass.* Kim Devlin has taken up Jacques Lacan's theory of the
intersubjective nature of the gaze. Devlin is alert to the stealthy "pruriently viewing subject," as well as the self-conceived object of the male
gaze ("'See ourselves as others see us'" 138, 135), and has studied the
gaze of women characters, most notably Gerty MacDowell ("Nausicaa") and Issy from *Finnegans Wake.* Devlin goes back to Freud (specifically to his Wolf Man) for sources of Joyce's treatment of the gaze.
Freudian influences are much easier to pinpoint in Joyce's notebooks
and texts than Micheletian ones.

4 I am grateful to Judith Roof, my colleague at the University of Delaware, for alerting me to the connection to Duras, and to the connection
to Colette, which appears later in the essay.

5 For a summary of Joyce's personal fetishes, and a masochistic angle on
the gaze in Joyce, see Restuccia (126–31). Restuccia lists Nora's breasts
as a fetish; Molly's function better in the discourse on woman as nature, I
would argue.

6 Michelet is further recirculated by Gauthier's selection of the title
Sorcières for a journal she inaugurated in 1976.

7 Commentators on Michelet's critical reception generally cite the atten-
tion he received from Lucien Febvre in 1946, the centenary of Michelet's
Le Peuple, and Gaston Bachelard in *Water and Dreams* (published 1942).
See Barthes (221) and Kaplan (xi).

WORKS CITED

Atherton, James S. *The Books at the Wake.* London: Faber, 1959.
Barthes, Roland, ed. *Michelet.* 1954. Trans. Richard Howard. New York:
Hill, 1987.
Brown, Richard. *James Joyce and Sexuality.* Cambridge: Cambridge Univer-
sity Press, 1985.
Colette. *Claudine at School.* Trans. Antonia White. New York: Farrar, 1957.
Curran, C. P. *James Joyce Remembered.* New York: Oxford University Press,
1968.
Devlin, Kimberly J. "The Female Eye: Joyce's Voyeuristic Narcissists." *New
Alliances in Joyce Studies: "When it's Aped to Foul a Delfian."* Ed. Bonnie
Kime Scott. Newark: University of Delaware Press, 1988. 135–43.
"'See ourselves as others see us': Joyce's Look at the Eye of the Other."
PMLA 104 (1989): 882–93.
Duras, Marguerite, and Xavière Gauthier. *Woman to Woman.* Trans.
Katharine A. Jensen. Lincoln: University of Nebraska Press, 1987.

Fathers of the Society of Jesus. *A Page of Irish History: The Story of University College Dublin, 1883–1909.* Dublin: Talbot, 1930.

Gifford, Don, with Robert J. Seidman. *"Ulysses" Annotated: Notes for James Joyce's "Ulysses."* 2nd edn. Berkeley and Los Angeles: University of California Press, 1988.

Henke, Suzette. "Stephen Dedalus and Women: A Portrait of the Artist as a Young Misogynist." *Women in Joyce.* Ed. Suzette Henke and Elaine Unkeless. Urbana: University of Illinois Press, 1982. 82–107.

Howe, Florence. "Feminism and Literature." *Images of Women in Fiction: Feminist Perspectives.* Ed. Susan Koppelman Cornillon. Bowling Green, Ohio: Bowling Green University Popular Press, 1972. 253–77.

Hughes, Peter. "From Allusion to Implosion: Vico, Michelet, Joyce, Beckett." Verene 83–99.

Irigaray, Luce. *Speculum of the Other Woman.* Trans. Gillian C. Gill. Ithaca: Cornell University Press, 1985.

Joyce, James. *Finnegans Wake.* New York: Viking, 1939.
A Portrait of the Artist as a Young Man. New York: Viking, 1964.
Selected Letters. Ed. Richard Ellmann. New York: Viking, 1975.
Stephen Hero. Ed. John J. Slocum and Herbert Cahoon. New York: New Directions, 1963.
Ulysses: A Critical and Synoptic Edition. Ed. Hans Walter Gabler et al. 3 vols. New York: Garland, 1986.

Joyce, Stanislaus. *The Complete Dublin Diary of Stanislaus Joyce.* Ed. George H. Healey. Ithaca: Cornell University Press, 1971.

Kaplan, Edward K. Preface. *Mother Death: The Journal of Jules Michelet, 1815–1850.* Trans. and ed. Kaplan. Amherst: University of Massachusetts Press, 1984. xi–xiii.

Kippur, Stephen A. *Jules Michelet: A Study of Mind and Sensibility.* Albany: State University of New York Press, 1981.

Kristeva, Julia. "Women's Time." Trans. Alice Jardine and Harry Blake. *The Kristeva Reader.* Ed. Toril Moi. New York: Columbia University Press, 1986. 187–213.

Michelet, Jules. *Woman.* Trans. J. W. Palmer. New York: Rudd and Carleton, 1860.

Mulvey, Laura. "Visual Pleasure and Narrative Cinema." *Feminism and Film Theory.* Ed. Constance Penley. New York: Routledge, 1988. 57–68.

Orr, Linda. *Jules Michelet: Nature, History, and Language.* Ithaca: Cornell University Press, 1976.

Restuccia, Frances L. *Joyce and the Law of the Father.* New Haven: Yale University Press, 1989.

Reynolds, Mary T. "The City in Vico, Dante, and Joyce." Verene 110–22.

Scott, Bonnie Kime. *James Joyce.* Brighton: Harvester, 1987.
Joyce and Feminism. Bloomington: Indiana University Press, 1984.

Thornton, Weldon. *Allusions in "Ulysses": An Annotated List.* Chapel Hill: University of North Carolina Press, 1968.

Verene, Donald Phillip, ed. *Vico and Joyce.* Albany: State University of New York Press, 1987.

CHAPTER 9

Re-visioning Joyce's masculine signature

Suzette Henke

> *He war*, it's a counter-signature, it confirms and contradicts, effaces by subscribing. It says "we" and "yes" in the end to the Father or to the Lord who speaks loud, there is scarcely anyone but Him, but it leaves the last word to the woman who in her turn will have said "we" and "yes." Countersigned god, God who countersigneth thyself, God who signeth thyself in us, let us laugh, amen.
>
> (Derrida 158)

How, one might ask, can a "resisting" feminist reader begin to approach the writings of James Joyce? Contemporary critics, male and female alike, have brought charges against him as a chauvinist author, a misogynist, a pornographer, and a champion of patri-archal privilege. One might certainly argue that Joyce, in creating misogynist heroes, was not necessarily himself a misogynist: that he always cast an ironic eye on those woman-haters and female-fearers that populate his fiction. Will that, however, suffice? A genius he was, to be sure. But could he ever transcend the "monk in the man"? Carolyn Heilbrun, Sandra Gilbert, and Susan Gubar think not and castigate him for an abhorrently limited vision of women. The monk was always there, they insist; and if so, can the *Malleus Malificarum* be far behind?[1]

If one searches Joyce's biography (or Nora's) for sins against women, crimes of the heart and mind will not be far to seek. Carolyn Heilbrun, in a recent review of Brenda Maddox's biography of Nora Barnacle, calls him, quite simply, "a shit" ("Sacrificed to Art" 5). But does this kind of graphic epithet clarify our understanding of such a perplexing modern artist? Did Joyce persistently relegate the female to those narrow Catholic categories of virgin/whore, Mary/Eve, angel/temptress that proved so popular and invidious in turn-of-the-century Ireland? Or did he somehow manage to transcend the limits of birth and education, of socialization and temper, to move in the direction of understanding the problems of contemporary sexual politics and the enigma of female desire?

As a young man, Joyce was strongly influenced, like his hero Stephen Dedalus, by the teachings of the Catholic Church and the misogynist theories of Schopenhauer. To a boy schooled in Cartesian dualities, life seemed to entail a Manichean struggle between flesh and spirit, immanent body and transcendent mind. For the artist in pursuit of the world as will and idea, alliances with women meant the perils of "morose delectation" and the possibility of conjugal perdition. The logocentric male eagerly took refuge in intellectual and aesthetic pleasures, avoiding the female as a frightening reminder of physiological process – of menstruation and parturition, of pain, vulnerability, physical deterioration, and death. Yet, paradoxically, despite early misogynist tendencies, Joyce always retained a sense of fascination with female reproductive powers. Like his protagonist Stephen Dedalus, he seemed to believe that "*Amor matris*: subjective and objective genitive" (*U* 2.165–6) might be the "only true thing in life" (*U* 2.143). Throughout his work, Joyce's ostensibly masculine signature is everywhere inscribed on the sexual/textual body of woman represented as mother, muse, ghost, vampire, lover, and symbolic saint.

In the "Telemachus" episode of *Ulysses*, for instance, Stephen Dedalus is perpetually haunted by the maternal specter lurking behind eruptions of melancholia framed by references to the medieval tract *Agenbite of Inwit*. The guilt he associates with May Dedalus' death is founded on a deeply internalized conviction of matricide – responsibility for the death of a parent whose final wishes the Luciferian rebel refused to obey. The ghost of May Goulding haunts Stephen like a lover, a semi-incestuous temptress courting amorous approval and intent on seducing her son into a death-world of Catholic mummery.

Has Stephen changed since we last saw him at the end of *A Portrait*? Our angle of vision is different in *Ulysses*, but Joyce's young man, after an Icarian fall, is still taking flight and soaring on the wings of purple prose and romantic rhetoric. He mythologizes the milkwoman as a symbol of Ireland, "Silk of the kine and poor old woman ... maybe a messenger" (*U* 1.399–403). The message she delivers is of conquest and betrayal, since she symbolically serves as "common cuckquean" (*U* 1.405) to Haines the Englishman and

Mulligan the venal stage-Irishman. Stephen feels contemptuous of the crone who worships a false priest, her medicineman or boneset-ter, rather than the bardic "priest of the eternal imagination" he himself claims to be. Jealous of her child-like attentiveness to Buck's patronizing words, he indicts her as a figure of Mother Eve, whose unclean loins are "made not in God's likeness" (*U* 1.421) because bereft of the primordial patriarchal signifier, the masculine phallus. Deprived of the male generative organ, woman becomes a hole, a cesspool of impurity, a gaping wound prey to penetration by an alien serpent form.

In "Nestor," Stephen tries to bury the ghost of his mother in the nightmare of past history. Like the fox, he continually sequesters her figure in a dead heap of moribund memories, then roots up her skeletal presence amid the shards of a paralyzed past. The pupil Sargent, with a snail-shaped inkstain inscribed on his cheek, reminds Stephen of his own childhood vulnerability and his mother's nurtu-rant role. Like the fiery Columbanus, Joyce's young man bestrode the body of his mother to flee to the aesthetic environs of bohemian Paris. His holy zeal, however, proved futile: he escaped nothing more than a pile of cinders, the remains of a "twig burnt in the fire" giving off a faint "odour of rosewood and wetted ashes" (*U* 2.145–6). Stephen replicates himself as a helpless snail in the mirror of his own imagination, but metamorphoses from mollusk into fox, a rapacious animal whose "merciless bright eyes' (*U* 2.149) seek the lumine-scence of maternal forgiveness. He listens and scrapes, rooting in the earth for the corpse of a "poor soul gone to heaven" (*U* 2.147). Her body becomes a text which cannot lie dormant, a rotting tissue on which he obsessively tries to inscribe a filial aesthetic signature.

The "Nestor" episode unfolds as a riddle, an aporia, a theoretical question concerning the individual's relationship to the past – to personal history and racial history, both of which collapse in a metaphor of female continuity. The mind, examining its past, is like the "fox burying his grandmother under a hollybush" (*U* 2.115), attempting to eschew ties to personal, familial, sexual, and social history by burying the female parent. Woman, as a reminder of the flesh and of physiological processes connected with mortality, must be murdered in the mind of the artist. Her memory needs to be erased, her present figure consigned to a disposable *memoir* – a narrative tale ceaselessly reiterated in order, finally, to be ritualized and forgotten.

And yet, "mother love," untangled from the complex skein of history, may be, in Stephen's words, the "only true thing in life" – the only reality to be salvaged from a competitive, demeaning and hostile battle for survival. *Amor matris* is, after all, the one love identified (by males) as altruistic and self-effacing. All else in phallocentric culture demands violent struggle, as blind bodies clash in the "slush and uproar of battles ... a shout of spearspikes baited with men's bloodied guts" (*U* 2.317–18). Only maternal affection seems to offer sanctuary from the relentless race for survival characteristic of every evolutionary form, from that of the boneless snail to the anthropoid efforts of the poet to subsist on the margins of a competitive, powermongering culture.

Despite Stephen's misogynist fear of women, he knows better than to capitulate to the anti-feminist mentality of a man like Garrett Deasy, representative of the "old wisdom" and of a bigoted tradition. Deasy condemns the Jews for sinning against the light, and he indicts woman as a vessel of sin and the cause of historical destruction. "A woman brought sin into the world ... A faithless wife first brought the strangers to our shore here ... A woman too brought Parnell low" (*U* 2.390–4). Women, Deasy insists, are faithless, adulterous, and guilty of precipitating the fall of nations and the downfall of the race. If men fight over women, then women themselves, he argues, are responsible for the fray. Because Deasy himself is a grass widower, deserted by his wife, he wants to consign the female to a male-written document of religious history that attributes the sins of humankind to Eve and her suffering daughters. In his bigoted mentality, females and Jews prove convenient scapegoats for "the one sin" (*U* 2.395).

Eve/Heva, the eternal temptress, reappears in the "Proteus" episode as "Spouse and helpmate of Adam Kadmon: Heva, naked Eve ... Belly without blemish, bulging big, a buckler of taut vellum, no, whiteheaped corn, orient and immortal, standing from everlasting to everlasting. Womb of sin" (*U* 3.41–4). Stephen's rapturous, lyrical prose ends abruptly with the heavy thud of monosyllabic condemnation: "Womb of sin." The strandentwining cable of all flesh is linked ineluctably to our first mother, a woman who bears, in this incarnation, greater resemblance to Lilith than to the biblical Eve.

Stephen, "wombed in sin darkness" (*U* 3.45), interprets his physicality as a sign of degradation. The poet fosters a myth of self-generation, of transcendence of physical nature and reconstitution of the self through pure, narcissistic postcreation. From a psychological point of view, Stephen's poetic contempt for women may be largely attributable to the guilt he feels over his own mother's impotence, as well as to adolescent fears and puerile shyness. Although he can celebrate the female in rich, voluptuous language and cast blame on mythic Mother Eve, he lacks sufficient courage to approach a real woman of his own class and education. As we learned in *A Portrait*, he has to satisfy amorous longings by visits to the Dublin red-light district or by the more economical measure of "A Honeymoon in the Hand" (*U* 9.1173). He catches voyeuristic glimpses of a widow's stockings, entertains fantasies of "*Naked women*" (*U* 3.134), and courts lascivious reveries stirred by a virgin peering into the window of Hodges Figgis's bookstore. "Sell your soul for that, do, dyed rags pinned round a squaw" (*U* 3.132).

The arrogant poet of *A Portrait* still dreams of erotic transfiguration, but he continues to carry on a narcissistic love affair with his *anima*, the soul "shamewounded by our sins," who clings to the artist as lover and luxuriates in his sinful embrace (*U* 3.422). Stephen imagines himself as both father and mother to the creative self, capable of transcending the *lex eterna* that binds him to the "man with my voice and my eyes and a ghostwoman with ashes on her breath. They clasped and sundered, did the coupler's will" (*U* 3.46–7).

Unsuccessful at bringing a fantasmal projection of the self "beyond the veil" of Platonic idealism, Stephen imagines a more gratifying tryst with a lady of letters clothed in yellow woolen stockings and "curse of God stays" (*U* 3.431). No woman's hand has yet touched Stephen's, and he longs for a tender embrace that will offer emotional sanctuary. "I am lonely here. O, touch me soon, now" (*U* 3.434–5). Sad, longing for the hand and heart of a tangible mistress, the poet impatiently awaits the beloved who will teach him to utter the "word known to all men" (*U* 3.435), the word of love made flesh through sexuality.

Until he meets the female in an actual, rather than a purely possible encounter, Stephen continues to address the *anima* in his flutiest rhetoric and to pine in poetic isolation. His view of woman remains mythic and romantic, on the one hand, yet ominous in its perpetual alterity. Physiological process is terrifying to the young man, who lyrically articulates a neurotic horror of menstrual blood:

"Tides, myriadislanded, within her, blood not mine, *oinopa ponton*, a winedark sea" (*U* 3.393–4). Woman, controlled by irrational lunar cycles, becomes "handmaid of the moon. In sleep the wet sign calls her hour, bids her rise. Bridebed, childbed, bed of death, ghost-candled. *Omnis caro ad te veniet.* He comes, pale vampire, through storm his eyes, his bat sails bloodying the sea, mouth to her mouth's kiss" (*U* 3.395–8).

Stephen mockingly celebrates the vampiric ritual of menstruation in abstract, *fin de siècle* tropes that evoke a grotesque image of female physiology. His lyrical rhetoric is bemusedly pinned down in vapid, unoriginal verses. Stephen is just as convinced as Freud that menstruation is a symbol of the disappointed womb, and his thoughts center on a fetishistic obsession with barrenness. Even the seashore vegetation elicits in the "sigh of leaves and waves" a vision of virginal infertility. The "writhing weeds ... hising up their petticoats" are rapt in melancholia, tearfully "awaiting the fullness of their times ... To no end gathered; vainly then released, forthflowing, wending back: loom of the moon" (*U* 3.461–8). The plants evoke a fantasy of a "naked woman shining in her courts," the wombweary goddess Diana, drawing a "toil of waters" across the surface of the globe (*U* 3.468–9).

The female, symbolic womb and tomb of the race, responds instinctively to the wet sign of blood that rouses her from the sleep of virginity, leads her to bridebed and childbed, and becomes emblematic of that bed of death, ghostcandled, that marks the end of human life. Stephen's vampire poem has usually been dismissed as still another sophomoric attempt by the nascent artist to realize his gift. Almost no one has noticed or commented on the startling misogyny of the lyric. What inspires these imagistic verses is a terror of female physiology and the profound mystery of menstruation.

> *On swift sail flaming*
> *From storm and south*
> *He comes, pale vampire,*
> *Mouth to my mouth.*   (*U* 7.522–5)

The winedark flow of menstrual blood is released from woman's womb by the genital kiss of an unholy vampire, "his bat sails bloodying the sea" (*U* 3.397–8). The dramatic scene suggests a negative, blasphemous rendition of the New Testament celebration of Mary's impregnation by the Holy Spirit, represented in Christian iconography as a dove engendering an incarnate Christ as the "Word made flesh." The word of love, unuttered in fleshly conception, leads to a disappointed womb (like a pier, a disappointed bridge to gestation) made prey to vampiric osculation. The legendary vampire is a profane bloodsucker, raping the virgin's genital mouth with a winedark, sanguinary kiss.[2]

There are, of course, other vampires (and cannibals) in *Ulysses*. In the "Circe" episode, the whoremistress Bella Cohen is transmogrified into a transvestite circus-master who torments Leopold Bloom with sadomasochistic fervor and offers his feminized genitalia for pornographic exchange: "Handle him. This downy skin, these soft muscles, this tender flesh ... Pander to their Gomorrahan vices" (*U* 15.3103–22). Bella/Bello threatens to slaughter and skewer this porcined victim and serve him up "basted and baked like sucking pig" in a non-kosher, cannibalistic feast (*U* 15.2900).

May Dedalus, identified as a corpsechewing Catholic masticating the body and blood of Christ in the Eucharist, returns from the grave in vampiric form and lusts after the life-blood of her son in the full flower of his pagan priesthood. She flagellates him with intimations of filial guilt and enjoins him to return to pietistic observance of the Catholic faith: "Prayer is allpowerful ... Repent" (*U* 15.4197–8). Despite his inebriate hallucinations, Stephen recognizes the phantom as the ghoulish predator that she is: "Raw head and bloody bones" (*U* 15.4214–15), he screams. "Shite! ... *Non Serviam!*" (*U* 15.4223–8). Here Stephen identifies with the rebellious Lucifer and casts the maternal authority figure back to the nether world of hell – or perhaps to the world of his seething artistic consciousness.[3]

In the "Eumaeus" episode, the bawdy sailor D. B. Murphy boasts of acquaintance with an entirely different set of corpsechewers, "maneaters in Peru that eats corpses and the livers of horses" (*U* 16.470–1).

All focussed their attention at ... a group of savage women in striped loincloths, squatted, blinking, suckling, frowning, sleeping amid a swarm of infants ...
—Chews coca all day, the communicative tarpaulin added. Stomachs like breadgraters. Cuts off their diddies when they can't bear no more children. See them sitting there stark ballocknaked eating a dead horse's liver raw. (*U* 16.475–81)

In a grotesque fantasy irrupting from the male unconscious, primitive man (generic) is assimilated to a band of predatory females. These atavistic subjects are photographically represented in lethargic postures of soporific nurture, like lionesses suckling their cubs or satiated animals blinking in the sun amidst a buzzing swarm of progeny. The Amazons resemble outcroppings of an exotic landscape and are so in touch with their maternal functions that postmenopausal women sever superfluous mammaries. Aging crones join a third, androgynous sex whose warrior talents seem limited to feats of degustation: the maceration of opiate coca, the delectation of raw horse's liver, and the possession of alimentary breadgraters that might well be used for castration or cannibalism. This band of meateaters is implicitly a Circean squad of maneaters, and the absence of male phallic authority suggests the breakdown of civilization in a reign of matriarchal chaos.

The only talisman that boggles these intrepid females is, apparently, man-made glass. An inadvertent anthropologist, the superstitious Murphy realizes that primitive peoples, like vampires, often fear the reflection of their images in glass and eschew the kind of specular replication associated with a doubling of the spirit and the soul's vulnerability to appropriation by an enemy. Despite the "lurid story narrated" (*U* 16.491), the postcard bears no message. The primitive world refuses to speak to contemporary civilization – perhaps because we cannot begin to fathom the semiotic system of its gestures.

Leopold Bloom's own notions of exotic travel are circumscribed by fantasies of a voyage to London *via* long sea – a trip that "would benefit health ... especially for a chap whose liver was out of order" (*U* 16.510–12). Bloom is apparently a good "liver" whose liver, nonetheless, is giving him trouble, despite the fact that his abstemious practices preclude the swellings of cirrhosis. If the liver is metaphorically a source of vitality and potency, then the females' consumption of horse's liver suggests symbolic castration, as well as a magical gesture geared to transfer phallic power from the host to its consumer in an atavistic, cannibalistic feast. Clearly, women in "Eumaeus" are to be trusted with neither the bodies of animals nor the souls of men. Without male surveillance, they regress to a state of primordial nakedness, mutilate their bodies, and devour the internal organs of manly/equine mammals. The only recourse for the beleaguered male seems escape by sea to

Odyssean adventure beyond the tribal territory of female sexual difference.

Leopold Bloom, however, does not want to escape. Throughout the text of *Ulysses*, he tries to displace onto the *imago* of his wife Molly the kind of fetishistic wholeness sought in his phallic projections onto Bella/Bello Cohen or through scopophiliac titillation by the silk stockings and deformed leg of a lame Dublin debutante, Gerty MacDowell. Craving maternal valorization of his own unstable subjectivity, Bloom projects onto his supine spouse illusions of psychic coherence associated with pre-oedipal attachment to the Lacanian phallic (M)Other. He fantasizes about her breasts and bottom and about fetishistically milking her "large soft bubs, sloping within her nightdress like a shegoat's udder" (*U* 4.304–5) into his morning tea. As Jane Gallop points out, such needy invocation of the "Phallic Mother is undeniably a fraud, yet one to which we are infantilely susceptible. If the phallus were understood as the veiled attribute of the Mother, then perhaps this logical scandal could expose the joint imposture of both Phallus and Mother" (117).

Molly, for her part, constantly interrogates sexual practice and, in so doing, defers textual climax through an ever-expanding narrative of sexual *jouissance*. She implicitly challenges her spouse's imaginary construction of sexual difference and refuses to tolerate the phallic veiling that hides her genital hole – the "horror of the nothing to see" (Irigaray 26), the yawning gap or specular absence that devours the penis, swallows semen, and magically gives birth to nascent life. Molly dares to articulate female sexuality, to expose the name and nature of the "big hole in the middle of us" (*U* 18.151–2), in defiance of imaginary projections of psychic wholeness onto the (M)Other by male need and erotic longing. As a hole in the scopophiliac lens of male desire, woman's "genitals are simply absent, masked, sewn back up inside their crack" (Irigaray 26) in male-defined discourse. Molly thinks scornfully of the gynecological rhetoric used euphemistically by "that dry old stick Dr Collins ... your vagina he called it ... her vagina and her cochinchina" (*U* 18.1153–7) and insistently names the genital (w)hole and its excrescences – vaginal mucous, menstrual blood, and babies.

In terms of discursive practice, Joyce invites us to read the text of "Penelope" as body, as "that which is not sublimated nor unified but which is open to intercourse" (Gallop 39). Molly's feminine writing flows out of a rich and capacious consciousness in formless, unauthorized mental speech. For Joyce, as for Lacan, woman emerges as the *"pas-tout* (not everything, not all)" who refuses to "sum up, to give a finished representation" (Gallop 49).

Molly, wife and adulteress, voyages in her memories. She wanders, but lying down. In dream. Ruminates. Talks to herself. Woman's voyage: as a *body*. As if she were destined ... to be the nonsocial, nonpolitical, nonhuman half of the living structure. On nature's side of this structure, of course. (Cixous, "Sorties" 66)

Feminist critics like Hélène Cixous enthusiastically praise Molly's fluid, contradictory and subversive discourse as an early example of *écriture féminine*.[4] In "The Laugh of the Medusa," Cixous observes that feminine writing "is precisely working (in) the in-between ... The feminine (as the poets suspected) affirms: '... And yes,' says Molly, carrying *Ulysses* off beyond any book and toward the new writing" (883–4).

There is a bond between woman's libidinal economy – her *jouissance*, the feminine Imaginary – and her way of self-constituting a subjectivity that splits apart without regret ...
She doesn't hold still, she overflows. An outpouring that can be agonizing ... Yet, vertiginous, it can also be intoxicating ...
In a way, feminine writing never stops reverberating ... She *inscribes* what she is saying because she does not deny unconscious drives the unmanageable part they play in speech ...
The Voice sings from a time before the law, before the Symbolic took one's breath away and reappropriated it into language under its authority of separation. (Cixous, "Sorties" 90–5)

Throughout his œuvre, Joyce, like Sigmund Freud before him, assimilates "the otherness of woman into Mother" and is guilty of a "theoretical occulting of femininity by maternity" (Gallop 114). His entire canon centers around a paradoxical flight from woman and an equally ambivalent desire to seize and transform the awesome powers associated with reproductive mystery. Like Dolph and Kev in *Finnegans Wake*, Joyce plays with semiotic echoes from the womb-language of mother and child, creator and created, engendering matriarch and infatuated filial scribe. He peers into the yawning spaces of imagined darkness signified by Anna Livia Plurabelle's gaping womb-delta – a wound, a gap, a scar or invagination on the smooth earth-surface doubled by the *rives* of Anna's flowing river-run. Awestruck and envious, the son (sunny Twimjim) doubles himself in his fictional pictures of Shem and Shaun, Leopold Bloom and Stephen Dedalus, Richard Rowan and Robert Hand, to create a masculine dialogue, a logocentric discourse perpetually deferring to the creative power of the female by embedding its own seminal creations in the heart of a pliable maternal *langue*.

According to this paradigm, writing gains the status of phallocentric project, and woman is the Other whose authority to author human life must be usurped and defused in playful aesthetic transformation. The pen/phallus becomes the primordial signifier capable of inscribing the name of the artist/father in the self-generating text of a fictional *chaosmos*. Fabulation evolves into a generative act that destroys the vitality of life-in-process in order to name a static, immortal world of literary delight. In flight from the irrational forces of corporality, the artist stages a life-long oedipal rebellion against a fantasmatic mother/lover by giving birth to himself through the instantiations of a fabulated text. As poet/priest, he will transubstantiate the bread of everyday experience into the everliving life of art and take refuge, simultaneously, in the authorial persona that inhabits the corpus of his work.

Joyce ends by using the transcendental phallic signifier to inscribe the name of the *mother* even more prominently than that of the father throughout his fiction. The patriarchal signature is ubiquitous: inscribed everywhere in the body of the text, it is everywhere impotent. Consider the powerlessness of males in *Dubliners*; the ironic Icarian flight of Stephen Dedalus; the sexual dysfunction of Leopold Bloom; and the fall, both literal and figurative, of Humphrey Chimpden Earwicker in *Finnegans Wake*.

Joyce both fears and worships woman as erotic temptress and maternal procreator. Even Molly Bloom, that eroticized figure out of Joyce's male imagination, offers motherly solicitude to a spouse who exults in the pleasures of polymorphous perversity. And she eventually returns, at the end of "Penelope," to an amorous reverie that immortalizes her own "mother-love" for her husband Leopold. In a moment of sexual *jouissance*, she gives him her breasts to suck and nurtures him with a pabulum of seedcake and spittle. The male, returning to the womb of woman, is nourished and reborn.

In a passionate epistolary invocation, Joyce pleaded with his wife Nora Barnacle: "Guide me, my saint, my angel. Lead me forward. *Everything* that is noble and exalted and deep and true and moving in what I write comes, I believe, from you. O take me into your soul of souls and then I will become indeed the poet of my race" (*Letters* 2: 248). In another letter to this biographical mother/muse, he fantasized a pre-oedipal return to the *Heimweh* of maternal affection: "O that I could nestle in your womb like a child born of your flesh and blood, be fed by your blood, sleep in the warm secret gloom of your body!" (*SL* 169). Joyce's primary psychosexual obsession, throughout his life, was compulsively pre-oedipal. The virginal figure portrayed in his writing might be defiled in whore-like fashion; but *amor matris* remains for Joyce, sexually speaking, the "only true thing in life" (*U* 2.143).

NOTES

1 See Heilbrun, Afterword. Sandra Gilbert and Susan Gubar observe:

> At bottom, for Joyce, woman's scattered logos is a scatologos, a Swiftian language that issues from the many obscene mouths of the female body . . .
>
> Joyce's puns offer more consistently assertive instances of the ways in which male writers can transform the *materna lingua* into a *patrius sermo*. For, containing the powerful charm of etymological commentary within themselves, such multiple usages suggest not a linguistic *jouissance* rebelliously disrupting the decorum of the text, but a linguistic *puissance* fortifying the writer's sentences with "densest condensation hard." As we do in the presence of all puns, we (laughingly) groan at the author's authoritative neologisms because he has defeated us, even charmed us, by demonstrating his mastery of the mystery of multiple etymologies. (232, 260–1)

2 I am indebted, throughout this paper, to Vincent Cheng's article on "Stephen Dedalus and the Black Panther Vampire." Cheng suggests that the "sea-mother-handmaid-of-the-moon in this passage seems clearly to refer to May Dedalus. It also refers equally, however, to another mother, the Mother Mary" (166). Recalling echoes of Mary's response to the angel Gabriel at the Annunciation, "Behold the handmaid of the Lord" (Luke 1:38), Cheng offers "another parallel interpretation of this violent coupling, mouth to mouth: the sexual violation and destruction, by the vampire-god, of Mary, the mother of God ... 'All flesh shall come to you,' a phrase originally used by David in reference to Yahweh (Psalms 65:2), ... applies to the parallel image of Dracula-God calling his virgin bride to come to him" (166).

3 Stephen, says Cheng, both indicts his mother as "beastly destroyer-vampire" and claims a similar role for himself. Shouting "words of negation and defiance, Stephen makes his break, vaulting himself into the role of *dio boia*, destroyer god, who, like the vampire, destroys sexually and violently" (172–3).

4 For further discussion of Molly Bloom's feminine writing, see Henke, *James Joyce and the Politics of Desire*, ch. 5, "Molly Bloom: The Woman's Story" (126–63).

WORKS CITED

Cheng, Vincent J. "Stephen Dedalus and the Black Panther Vampire." *James Joyce Quarterly* 24 (1987): 161–76.

Cixous, Hélène. "The Laugh of the Medusa." Trans. Keith Cohen and Paula Cohen. *Signs* 1 (1976): 875–93.

"Sorties." *The Newly Born Woman*. By Cixous and Catherine Clément. Trans. Betsy Wing. Minneapolis: University of Minnesota Press, 1986. 63–132.

Derrida, Jacques. "Two Words for Joyce." *Post-Structuralist Joyce: Essays from the French*. Ed. Derek Attridge and Daniel Ferrer. Cambridge: Cambridge University Press, 1984. 145–59.

Gallop, Jane. *Feminism and Psychoanalysis: The Daughter's Seduction*. London: Macmillan, 1982.

Gilbert, Sandra M., and Susan Gubar. *The War of the Words*. Vol. 1 of *No Man's Land: The Place of the Woman Writer in the Twentieth Century*. 2 vols. to date. New Haven: Yale University Press, 1988–.

Heilbrun, Carolyn G. Afterword. *Women in Joyce*. Ed. Suzette Henke and Elaine Unkeless. Urbana: University of Illinois Press, 1982. 215–16.

"Sacrificed to Art." *Women's Review of Books* 5.12 (1988): 5.

Henke, Suzette A. *James Joyce and the Politics of Desire*. New York: Routledge, 1990.

Irigaray, Luce. *This Sex Which Is Not One*. Trans. Catherine Porter with Carolyn Burke. Ithaca: Cornell University Press, 1985.

Joyce, James. *Finnegans Wake*. New York: Viking, 1939.

Letters of James Joyce. 3 vols. Vol. 1, ed. Stuart Gilbert. Vols. 2 and 3, ed. Richard Ellmann. New York: Viking, 1966.

Selected Letters of James Joyce. Ed. Richard Ellmann. New York: Viking, 1975.

Ulysses: The Corrected Text. Ed. Hans Walter Gabler et al. New York: Random, 1986.

Lacan, Jacques. *Feminine Sexuality: Jacques Lacan and the Ecole Freudienne*. Trans. Jacqueline Rose. Ed. Juliet Mitchell and Jacqueline Rose. New York: Norton, 1982.

PART III

ConTexts for Joyce

CHAPTER 10

"Scrupulous meanness" reconsidered: Dubliners as stylistic parody

Roy Gottfried

That Joyce intended to write *Dubliners* in a precise, sparse style has been evident from his own initial description to Grant Richards, the famous pronouncement that "I have written it for the most part in a style of scrupulous meanness" (*Letters* 2: 134). Yet the clarity of this statement of what Joyce calls "my intention" is immediately compromised by the syntax of the sentence, in which that familiar clause is coupled with another by way of seeming explanation: [I have written it] "with the conviction that he is a very bold man who dares to alter in the presentment, still more to deform, whatever he has seen and heard." What Joyce presents, unaltered, by such a clearly defined style is obscured and unstated, what a "mean" style might be and why it should be emulated; even in his first defense of his work, Joyce is careful to conceal as much as to reveal. It is certainly true enough that Joyce wished, as this letter states, to show his country "a chapter of [its] moral history" in the paralyzed features of Dublin; and it is clear enough that he was aware that his work would appear before what he calls an "indifferent public." Yet because all issues of society and morals are first and foremost literary issues for Joyce, the implicit focus of the writing of *Dubliners* is writing itself. The careful attention paid to style, and the concomitant "conviction" that the presentation should be of what is "seen," suggest that the unstated and obscured subject of "scrupulous meanness" is a literary form. What is to be presented and emulated, unaltered, is a certain kind of writing, one that itself may have paralyzed and made indifferent a reading public.

The connection of a distanced, critical realism and a parodic style is present at the very inception of the stories. When George Russell kindly solicited the young Joyce for a piece for his weekly newspaper *The Irish Homestead* that would turn out to be the first story of

Dubliners, he urged him with a series of artistic and financial bland-
ishments: "It is easily earned money if you can write fluently and
don't mind playing to the common understanding and liking for
once in a way" (*Letters* 2: 43). As Russell did, readers have assumed
that Joyce plays down to that understanding with his style of
"scrupulous meanness." Perhaps he had another aim: playing off it.
Joyce would not understand Russell's invitation to "play" as an
attempt to curry favor with and win over the public, any more than
Stephen is willing at Mulligan's suggestion to "play" up to such as
Haines for a quid; for Joyce "play" was the license to mock what the
readers of the weekly would take seriously. In a letter to a friend,
Curran, Joyce announces his plans for the works: "I am writing a
series of epicleti – ten – for a paper. I ... betray the soul of that
hemiplegia or paralysis which many consider a city" (*Letters* 1: 55).
This statement too has directed much critical attention and focus,
yet one part of this announced scheme deserves highlighting, a part
overlooked amid the grander notions and Latin and Greek words:
"I am writing a series ... for a paper." Joyce directly admits that the
appearance and the context of his first stories were to be in a public
medium, and recognizes the fact that in writing for a newspaper he
is writing by necessity in a particular style and for a particular,
indifferent audience: Joyce called Russell's *Homestead* "the pigs'
paper" only partly because of its interest in livestock (*JJ* 164). It
was the common understanding of the reading public that was
Joyce's satiric aim: there lay the indifference to style, or more
exactly a "paralysis" of style, of which his stories were to be the
parodic embodiment.

   The paralysis of which Joyce speaks is not solely caused by
Catholicism, or social mores, but by the unguarded acceptance of
language, a poverty not of persons but of language. In that rather
grandiose plan to write a "series" for a newspaper (and one might
ask whether this is really any more grandiose a claim than the aim to
write "epicleti") is Joyce's recognition, early in his career, that in
the paper-reading public lay only a more blatant commonness (a
dull eye and a duller ear) than that which affected all published
writing, even fiction. Russell's invitation mentioned both money
and the common understanding, a potent middle-class combination;
as a writer and editor, Russell himself was as much the determiner of
what the public wanted as the readers themselves (who, not incidentally, complained about the quality of the three stories of Joyce

that actually appeared in the paper [*JJ* 165]). It was the public context that measured what was considered not only newsworthy but noteworthy; it was there that the consensus formed as to what constituted art, and most particularly what made up the art of the nationalistically revived country.

Some years before, when still a student, Joyce wrote his essay "The Day of the Rabblement" against the riots at the Irish Literary Theatre's 1899 production of *The Countess Cathleen*. Concerned for a growing cosmopolitanism against the "nationalistic" provincialism, the essay takes a disdainful stand against the multitude (a stance attributed to Joyce when he writes the stories). With the assurance that comes from too much youth, Joyce claims: "If an artist courts the favour of the multitude he cannot escape the contagion of its fetichism and deliberate self-deception" (*CW* 71). Perhaps some five years later, when Russell approached him to write for this rabble, and Joyce accepted, he recognized the fact that by writing for the many, in a newspaper no less, he could not escape the contagion of its style by any other means than by making that contagion be the style itself. Despite the seeming turn in intent from disdain for the public in 1899 to begrudging acceptance of it in 1904, the consistency of the metaphor of illness in those years is telling, from contagion to paralysis; what he meant in the essay by the "fetichism" of the audience is probably similar to what Flaubert called *idées reçues*, but it too has a clearly pathological bent. Joyce writes in a style diseased in its adherence to stilted, accepted forms; this is why he claims to Roberts not to alter anything in the "presentment." Despite its being an early written work, *Dubliners* displays the same sense of parody and comedy that Joyce's later writings do. Along with the naturalism and sharp detail of the stories as an indictment of society is a parallel sharpness, the parody of a prevalent literary style which that society had indifferently "read and seen." Its "scrupulous meanness" has been a screen for Joyce to mask the playfulness of his early style under what has appeared to Russell and others as a stern and dispassionate, if youthful, realism. Moreover, in expressing his intention in writing the stories, Joyce may have had an additional reason to leave the object of the mean style unstated to Russell and only made implicit to Roberts; that is because what it emulates and parodies is the literature dear to Russell, published by Roberts, and widely read by the public, the writing of the Literary Revival.

This implicit connection between what Joyce meant by his style of "meanness" and its intended focus on the accepted and unaltered context of a nationalist style is to be found in his own use of the very term. In an unsigned review printed in 1902 in the *Daily Express*, Joyce wrote a piece critical of the verse of one William Rooney, a colleague of Arthur Griffith and a principal contributor to Griffith's *United Irishman*. As might be expected, the volume of poetry was sentimental and nationalistic at the same time, and the youthful reviewer was quite clear in his dislike and very precise in his terminology: "there can be no doubt that little is achieved in these verses, because the writing is so careless, and is yet so studiously mean ... Rooney, indeed, is almost a master in that 'style', which is neither good nor bad" (*CW* 85–6). Joyce would certainly have remembered using the word "mean" when he later wrote to Grant Richards about "meanness," and would hardly wish to describe his own prose in the same terms unless he meant to parody the very style that those like Rooney employed and that the indifferent public, with its common understanding, expected as art. Surely for Joyce to have praised his own work to an as yet unconvinced publisher using this term suggests that this is his particular aim in writing the stories, to "present" without "altering" a style that was uncritically accepted and read by his native audience. Not only does Joyce adopt the context of the public medium of print in writing his first stories, but he also goes further to parody Irish letters.

In both this criticism and in the description of his own work, Joyce would have chosen his words with care. He knew from his beloved Skeat that *mean* is "common, base, or sordid."[1] The N.E.D. notes, as of an artistic production, that it is "poverty of style." "Meanness" makes up a style of an unremarkable kind (like Rooney's, "neither good nor bad," indeed a style of a lack of style), and pitched appropriately to what Russell called the common understanding. It is the flaccid style of the newspaper. Yet "scrupulous meanness" is a style that is also marked by certain features. As a competent Latinist Joyce would know about the *scrupula* which, like the small stone that punctures the foot or the small weight that tips the scale, is the small detail which troubles the surface of the apparently placid prose within that "mean" style. These small features that protrude so sharply are the characteristics of the language of the Literary Revival.

As his review of Rooney demonstrates, Joyce had little interest in the poetry that made up much of the Celtic Twilight. In another letter, to his brother, Joyce attacked a collection of 1904 entitled *A Celtic Christmas*, edited by Russell (Joyce was not one to show favoritism); he singled out for especial blame a maudlin poem by George Roberts: "*What* is wrong with all these Irish writers – what the blazes are they always snivelling about? Isn't it funny to read Roberts' poem about a mother pressing a baby to her breast? O, blind, snivelling, nose-dropping, calumniated Christ wherefore were these young men begotten?" (*Letters* 2: 78).[2] It was humor Joyce found in the thematic and stylistic excesses of the nationalist writers, and in the public acceptance of them. In this letter he makes several criticisms of these young writers, the "Irish Voices," and prompts Stannie to "ask the good young gentlemen can they beat 'Hallow Eve'" (the story "Clay," which was offered to the *Homestead* only to be rejected). Although he would take a sort of literary revenge against this group in "Scylla," he knew he could do better than they because he knew the comic possibilities that lay in their mean style. Early on he had begun to envisage the comic, protean powers of prose. What he did not know in 1904 was the difficulty the self-same George Roberts would give him in the attempt to publish the collection of *Dubliners* (*JJ* 310); perhaps Joyce was getting in an early and preemptive dig at a future betrayer. What Joyce always found comic and the stuff of his art – literary styles and literary commonplaces – other authors and the reading public found assuring and comforting; to parody the accepted was to tread heavily and by necessity on ground the common understanding of readers and editors both would find comfortable, but it was also to present as unaltered what was seen or heard. Even a brief glance at the more famous of these enshrined works reveals the parodic genealogy of Joyce's writing, the unstated object of the style of scrupulous meanness.

Poetry was not Joyce's chosen battleground (one might say his own poems were unintentionally "mean"). Rather his field was prose, and there the ground was as familiar as a bog in which to find what had been accepted by the multitude as its nationalistic art, ground that promised to yield scrupulously good if petrified examples for a comic style. Foremost in the pantheon of nationalist writers is Standish O'Grady with his translations of Irish myth from the Gaelic. His contribution to the sense of national literature was great; in an introduction to an early edition, the ubiquitous Russell remarked on "the neglected bardic literature which O'Grady was the first to reveal in a noble manner" (O'Grady xii). As he was for Joyce's work, Russell was concerned with O'Grady's audience, here somewhat more advanced than the one he promised Joyce; O'Grady had renewed "for a sophisticated people the elemental simplicity and hardihood men had" in Ireland's past, although Russell did demur about the way O'Grady was "not so much concerned with the art of words as with the creation of great images informed with magnificence of spirit" (O'Grady xiii). A short passage, chosen by *sortes Virgilianae*, about the youthful exploits of Cuchulain, suffices as an example of what Russell admitted, for all its energy, was a style that had "faults due to excesses and abundances" (and whose abundances were the sort of scrupulae which Joyce found comic):[3]

For the war-fury ... enwrapped [him] ..., so that his gentle mind became as it were the meeting-place of storms and the confluence of shouting seas. A man ran before him whose *bratta* on the wind roared like fire ... "[B]ut now," said Cuculain, "there ran a man before us. Him I do not see, but what is this herd of monstrous deer, ... as with horns and hoofs of iron ...? Lurid fire plays around them as they flee." "No deer of the earth are they," said Laeg. "They are the enchanted herd of Slieve Fuad, and from their abode subterrene they have come ... " "Pursue and run down those deer." "There is fear upon me," said Laeg. (O'Grady 163)

An uneasy admixture runs through this passage, one in which Irish and "literary" elements remain as separate as oil and water: it is the epitome of a mean style with obtrusive elements (scrupulously so!). The epic quality of Ireland's own material is reinforced by the metaphor of the mind as a storm-tossed sea; yet the self-conscious-ness of O'Grady's attempt to make high literature out of his folk material is certainly indicated by the uneasy qualifier of the epic turn of phrase, "as it were." The declamatory quality of the direct addresses is surely an imitation of the formal rhetoric of such characters as Odysseus and Diomedes in *Iliad* 5 (and this is not unconscious on O'Grady's part: as Russell noted in his introduction, "he is a comrade of Homer" [O'Grady xii]); and their diction (so prominent a feature in this short passage) is certainly directly conned out of school-boy Latin: "lurid fire," "abode subterrene." (This last an epic style by way not only of Virgilian Latin but also of Miltonic inversion.) Commingled with the classic, so as to flavor the pot, is a native diction; inversion, "Him I do not see"; Gaelic idiom, "there is fear upon me"; and strange words, the *bratta* italicized in the text so that its nativeness leaps to the fore. The connections of this style with that of the "Cyclops" chapter are evident, of course; but Joyce did not have to wait for *Ulysses* to mine this lode of strangely preserved material.

Lady Gregory's retelling of the same material was a similar influential prose creation. Here is her version of the very next incident after the one cited above in the youthful exploits of Cuchulain: "So then Ibar [the figure O'Grady calls Laeg] went and brought in the swans, and tied them, and they alive, to the chariot and to the harness" (Gregory 19). A more straightforward, less poetic version, surely, with far less epic and Latinate straining, yet with all the lilt of Gaelic inflection, "and they alive," to give the passage the air of Irish speech known as "Kiltartan." To bring some of the issues back full circle, there is George Moore's judgment of this "Kiltartan" style of Lady Gregory: "[it] consists of no more than a dozen turns of speech dropped into the pages of an English so ordinary" as to "appear in any newspaper without attracting attention" (Kain 32). The nationalistic literature which strives to be art is oddly and finally indistinguishable from the daily press; Joyce was both right and precise to call this style, despite its protruding "literary" features, "mean."

In addition to the comedy latent in the language of these examples, there was another source of influence that provided a direct comic effect, William Carleton's stories of Irish country life which constituted one of the strongest expressions in the mid nineteenth century of Irish writing about Ireland. In an introduction to a selection of his work, Yeats noted that "Carleton recorded ... what the people say to each other on fair-days and high days ... " (Carleton xvi). Yet there, too, is an exaggerated "national" style, a stage-Irish sense of the "poetic." An almost too picturesque Irish lilt and lightness can certainly be heard in this sentence: "The repose of nature in the short nights of this delightful season resembles that of a young virgin of sixteen – still, light, and glowing" (261); and almost all the clichés of Irish song seem to sing from this: "the tear of enthusiastic admiration is warm on my eyelids" (270). One story in particular, from which these examples come, provides another element of what constitutes the general expected comic tone of exaggeration that characterizes all of these examples of Irish fiction, "The Hedge School," a story of the itinerant teachers who provided rural students with their education

despite laws prohibiting Catholics from studying. The story opens
with what appears to be a serious focus and tone, almost those of a
pamphlet: "There was never a more unfounded calumny than that
which would impute to the Irish peasantry an indifference to education" (240). This weighty and contentious start quickly bypasses
serious or even ironic possibilities to fall into broad humor, although
the story closes on a greater point of seriousness, as the schoolteacher
is hanged as an informer.[4] As the text notes, "the youth of Findra-
more were parched for want of the dew of knowledge" (252), and
they were led by teachers like Matt Kavanagh, given over to
imagined knowledge or forgotten learning: to malapropisms, "illo-
cution" (290), and an inflated, highly scholastic and Latinate
diction, largely incorrect: "insuperable turbulentiality" (282), for
example, for the noise of the classroom. What the "hedge school"
stories did, in their long and imitative appeal after the estimable
Carleton, was to educate the reading public in the inflated language
that passes for the learned and the literary, not only (as these
examples show) by the characters in the stories but in the style of the
stories themselves.

    Thus these various prose influences, along with those from poetry,
and the residual issues of the language question (most particularly
what constitutes an Anglo-Irish style) suggest the varied common
expectations of literary style.[5] It should be editorially judgmental to
the point of ponderous (and even pedantic) allusiveness: "Let
[teachers], therefore, put a little of the mother's milk of human
kindness and consideration into their strait-laced systems" (Carleton 281). This sententiousness is the legacy of Victorian didacticism,
the influence of church teachings, and the effect of the press – all
meshing with the middle-class need to be told what to think; the
crowd, Joyce wrote a year before his stories, was "placid" and
"moral" (CW 70). The style should be "high," less in its subject
matter (the peasantry was, after all, still in vogue) than in its
language, "poetic," with felicitous phrases and clearly recognized
rhetorical figures which stand out obtrusively from the rest of the
prose: "Earth quaked to the growling of that ill beast" (O'Grady
51). It should reflect the speech of the nation, to be larded with
Gaelicisms: "'What are you wanting of them now?' said Conchubar.
'I swear by the gods my people swear by,' said the boy, 'I will not
lighten my hand off them ... '" (Gregory 9). However (reflecting
the double bind of the Anglo-Irish), the style must also be that of an

educated writer to an equally educated readership (a mutual flat-tery, that); it must have lofty diction and a large vocabulary most often Latinate, this last as a measure both of learning and of piety: "My head is a complete illucidation of the centrifugle motion" (Carleton 266). Malapropism flatters the reader – and it was, after all, first perfected by an Irishman. Care should be taken, however, to make sure obscure words can be understood, even at the risk of redundancy; "the immature scions of the Red Branch, boys and tender youths, awakened ... " (O'Grady 7).

As this last example clearly shows, there is an uneasiness in much of these writings, an uneasiness due less to the introduction of unfamiliar subject matter than to the style; a balance has to be found: "scions" needs to be explained in a clumsy appositive, embracing both high and low diction and all readerships. This is a style which is "neither good nor bad" but which must include the weight of a small "literary" word for balance, a *scrupula*. Carleton, O'Grady, Gregory and others have provided these features, and the common reading public understood such a style as art and came to like what it had read.

So when Russell asked, Joyce would give just what the common reader liked. When he claims to write in the style of "scrupulous meanness," his aim is to mimic and play off in a rather clever reconstruction just these expected features of the Irish Revival, within the context of what the public thinks of as literary style in the language it had "seen" in the press. He was not only critical of the state to which fiction had come, he was aware of its comic possi-bilities in its uneasy mixture – and it is at that weak point where he works his comic effect. Even at the outset of his career Joyce's habit of comic composition is to parody most closely, most "scrupulously," actual literary matter (and by parodying it suggest his own affection for it in all its weakness). Joyce claims unequivocally to his brother in 1905, as he writes those first stories, "Of course do not think that I consider contemporary Irish writing anything but ill-written ... obtuse formless caricature" (*Letters* 2: 99). Moreover, he foresees that "the Dublin papers will object to my stories as to a caricature of Dublin life ... At times the spirit directing my pen seems to me so plainly mischievous." It is "plainly" so for Joyce, although the status of the stories as caricature, not of Dublin life, but rather of Dublin letters, has been overlooked – in part due to Joyce's implicit statement of his intention. The style of *Dubliners* is so sly, pen in cheek, so well done, as to have passed then to Russell and his readers, and still pass among critics, as precise, realistic, high-minded, and high art.

Moreover, as a sign of a consistent purpose, this parodic tendency obtains not only in the three stories Russell accepted in the paper but throughout the whole collection when it was finally published; as Joyce said to Richards, the stories are written "for the most part" in the "mean" style. Even "The Dead" has comic stylistic elements, although it was composed later and added as an afterthought to the whole. "Scrupulous meanness" is a comic style independent of theme or focus in each story; it is what unites the order of childhood, adolescence, adult and public life.

Here is a passage in description of the character M'Coy from "Grace" that means to give the public what it wants, in filling the bill Russell had prescribed. In it there is the detailed dissection that reveals the social milieu and through it the tone that speaks the determined evaluation in a style apparently "neither good nor bad": "Mr M'Coy had been at one time a tenor of some reputation. His wife, who had been a soprano, still taught young children to play the piano at low terms. His line of life had not been the shortest distance between two points and for short periods he had been driven to live by his wits" (D 158). The declarative sentences convey the measured balance of simple judgment, yet the sentence that follows unravels this judgment and pushes the passage towards parody of that very language; "He had been a clerk in the Midland Railway ... " It is this small sentence, like the *scrupula*, which overturns the apparent balance of the preceding "mean" sentences. Thus "shortest distance," "driven," and "Midland Railway" coalesce into comedy, almost a verbal poke at the naturalism of Zola's *La Bête humaine*. The latent cliché of the "shortest distance," rather than being redeemed from banality, is only made manifest, creating, so to speak, an epiphany of averageness. Such elements as the misplaced phrase "play the piano at low terms" reveal the comic quality of the passage. From scenes of mean life comes a style that is mean, Irish life exceeded in its comedy only by Irish letters.

Like Flaubert, Joyce's best revenge on his audience was to turn their own blunt words against their breasts. And to redeem this metaphor, there is another example of the style of studied sententiousness that gives the public what it wants: from the same story, another passage with axiomatic content:

Everyone had respect for poor Martin Cunningham. He was a thoroughly sensible man, influential and intelligent. His blade of human knowledge, natural astuteness particularised by long association with cases in the police courts, had been tempered by brief immersions in the waters of general philosophy. He was well informed. (*D* 157)

The first sentence seems to provide the touch of the consensual, the average values held in common; but the sentence that tries to make an artful evaluation of Cunningham snaps off when it is unsheathed; this "blade" "tempered in the waters" of thought is dull. And to compound the matter, the appositive phrase "natural astuteness," which modifies Cunningham's knowledge, is drawn on a false and mistaken etymology of *astute* as "keen and penetrating" as a knife rather than as "sagacious" or "clever." Here is pseudo-learning worthy of a hedgeschool master of Carleton. Moreover, the short sentence that follows this artful one, "He was well informed," repeats directly by way of explanation what the preceding one strains at, creating the tautology of high and low style seen in the epic material of O'Grady. (Readers familiar with *Ulysses* will recognize another pun in this last: Cunningham's association with Dublin Castle leads to the suspicion that he is an informer for the viceregal government.)

Thus the style of *Dubliners* is not precise or "astute," it is dull; it is not exact, but banal and bumbling. When the text speaks of a character's growing awareness as "A light began to tremble on the horizon of his mind" (73), it cannot be considered detailed realism in precise prose; it is a hodgepodge of received artistic ideas, ranging from Tennyson's "Ulysses" to Holman Hunt's picture *The Light of the World* and, most pertinent to a Catholic audience, Augustine's *Confessions*: in short, the cultural baggage of the turn of the century. Such sentences as this and the above cannot be taken at face value; in imitating what passes for the average art, the style displays the particular scrupulous feature that makes it nothing other than comic. When the style of "scrupulous meanness" is understood as a parody of language, the stories cannot be read only as serious studies in realism; they are much closer in spirit and method to *Ulysses*, that high paradox of minutely detailed realistic elements with a highly contrived and manipulated style.

Thus the style of the *Dubliners* is comic caricature and parodic posturing ponderousness. A sentence such as the following, which appeared in Russell's paper, poses as moralizing and sententious,

speaking the judgment of the middle class in the tones of Samuel
Smiles: "if he had been so conscious of the labour latent in money"
(44). Yet such a style lifts its own rhetorical skirts to reveal feet
comically clad in Irish brogues; here is a comment on Lenehan, the
sponge in "Two Gallants": "Experience had embittered his heart
against the world. But all hope had not left him ... He might yet be
able to settle down in some snug corner and live happily if he could
only come across some good simple-minded girl with a little of the
ready" (58). The tendentious heights of the first two sentences
descend through the dailiness of hearth and home – "snug corner"
(although a snug is also a feature of the pubs so often frequented by
Lenehan) – to the flatness of the colloquial, "a little of the ready."
The flight of such a sentence, its bathos, reveals the parody of a
writer's wish to cover all ranges of language, to please all parts of an
audience, and the result in almost statistical terms is "mean." Even
the moralizing tone is borrowed from acceptable, even learned
sources; a comment earlier on Lenehan's financial means, "No one
knew how he achieved the stern task of living" (50), owes its turn of
phrase to Dr. Johnson.

To concoct an average style, refer to authority when possible;
when not, refer to the opinions of others: "No one knew ... " The
style of *Dubliners* most often betrays its origins in the newspaper by
the plainness of its frequent appeal to the consensual attitudes of its
middle-class readers. Phrases that seem to judge but only fob off
decision abound: "His friends bowed to his opinions and considered
that his face was like Shakespeare's" (157). A full flowery metaphor
is followed by such a consensual phrase, as in the example above
with the blade of knowledge followed by the sentence "He was well
informed." Here is another such: "His magniloquent western name
was the moral umbrella upon which he balanced the fine problem of
his finances. He was widely respected" (145).

This last example delineates another common characteristic; in
the striving for what is seen by the public as "high" art, the style
comically mixes its metaphors to tip its parodic hand. A moral
umbrella might be construed as protection for debt, but to ask a
parasol to be a balancing rod is to cloud the issue: the metaphor
rather suggests a necessary prop for the character's drunken
support. Other moralizing metaphors are similarly overdrawn: "She
dealt with moral problems as a cleaver deals with meat" (*D* 63).
While this phrase is pertinent to the story (Mrs. Mooney the

estranged wife of a drunken butcher), the metaphor is grotesque; moral issues, at least since Solomon, are not cloven; cleavers do not "deal" with their objects. Metaphors not only mangle meat; of a character's incipient rebellion there is the description, "the barometer of his emotional nature was set for a spell of riot" (91), which compounds a storm with unlicensed behavior, conflates different natures, and also confuses cause and effect. The description of the barometer is itself a signal of that noticeable, scrupulous feature that predicts the presence of the "mean" style.

Both the pomposity of this created style and its calculated comic appeal to the "common understanding" of a flattered readership are captured in the frequent use of Latinate diction in the stories (which, as noted in connection with Carleton, is clearly held by the audience to be a double sign of education and piety). The young boy in "An Encounter" is said to eat "sedulously" (*D* 24), and to remark, "a spirit of unruliness diffused itself among us" (20); the boy in "The Sisters" describes an action by an adult as "inefficacious" (12) and the word *paralysis* as "maleficent" (9). While apparently too elevated a word choice for the children *in* the stories, those critics who explain that the stories are narrated by the older selves of the characters have not bothered to note that the diction is pedantic by any measure, certainly in regard even to the language of the rest of the story. And such elevation is prevalent in stories where there is no age or experiential difference between character and narrator, diction being the measure of the mean style. Evening is said to "invade" an avenue (36); narrow passages in a theatre are "tortuous" (145); a character feels "incipient" pain (153). Not only do these "elevations" flatter both narrator and reader, they comically dilute the details of the supposed naturalist text by a prudery that must appeal to the Mrs. Grundy in all middle-brow readers. An angry man longed "to execrate aloud" (90), cursing being not only anathema but apparently too low in diction; a woman's cheeks are "suffused" (144), where blush would be too suggestive; a pub floor is "tessellated" (151) like a Pompeian villa, rather than being mundanely tiled; a character's lips are "tumid" (184) rather than swollen – the Latinate diction preferable even at the expense of sexual suggestiveness. One might think that in stories of supposed studied realism, a character in poverty brought about by the social conditions of a paralyzed city would unhesitatingly be called "needy," but even here the style blushes and feigns, "the friend . . .

[in] a shabby and necessitous guise" (71). Euphemism and euphony are the characteristics of the style intentionally "mean" and comic.

Yet to be fully "mean" (as Joyce described it, "neither good nor bad") the stories must have colloquial as well as educated language; to make the median balance, there must be a *mélange*. On the same page from "Ivy Day in the Committee Room" can be found Latinate diction, in the sentence "imminent little drops of rain hung at the brim of his hat," alternating with colloquial speech ripe with Gaelic idiom, "Sure, amn't I never done at the drunken bowsy ever since he left school?" (120). Other characters also add a native idiom: "There was nobody but ourselves in the field" ("An Encounter" 24); "We did our best, the dear knows" ("A Mother" 142, a story about the Gaelic League).

The *de rigueur* use of such colloquialisms by the characters suggests that they too are practitioners of the "mean" style. Much critical attention has been focused on how the narrative idiom and perspective are infected with the ideas of the characters.[6] What solves this riddle of which came first, the character or the narrator, however, is a simple stroke through the textual knot: the narrator may adopt the idiom of the characters, but the characters themselves have adopted an idiom which is literary, the style of expected Irish artfulness. Joyce knew that people really do (or at least did) think in a literary way, and not only fictional characters, but even real people very close to him. Joyce's own brother Stanislaus had literary presumptions which Joyce ridiculed, especially after having read his Dublin diary. Later, Joyce shamelessly took Stannie as the model for Mr. Duffy in "A Painful Case" and used some of his judgments committed to the privacy of the diary as those of that character. Yet in the diary Joyce found the ocular proof of an actual "mean" style: there he found, and no doubt long remembered, Stannie's description of Joyce himself surrounded by fawning young women: "The wise virgins delight in the society of the necessitous young genius" (*Dublin Diary* 14). The correctness of "genius" Joyce took at face value; the source of the "wise virgins" he knew was his and his brother's religious heritage; but the word "necessitous" he clearly treasured for the very strained averageness it revealed, and then used in "A Little Cloud," as quoted above ("the friend ... [in] a shabby and necessitous guise" [71]). Stannie's failure at art was Joyce's success in *Dubliners*. In his late reminiscences, Stannie writes about the early years of his brother's writing; of interest here is his

description of the original person from whom the character of
Cunningham in "Grace" is drawn: "His energy and self-confidence
caused him to be regarded ... as very reliable and level-headed, a
solid man" (*My Brother's Keeper* 225). The elements from the passage
already quoted from the story are strikingly similar: "He was ...
intelligent ... He was well informed. His friends bowed to his
opinions." The question as to whether Stanislaus had thought or
written such a passage before Joyce wrote the story, or whether he
adopted the very tone of the story in later years when explaining its
composition, is moot. Joyce knew that real people think and speak
and write in the style of fiction.

If a real person, then how much more so a created character in a
book? When the character Chandler, the aspiring poet, is said to
walk past "the feudal arch ... [and] gaunt spectral mansions in
which the old nobility of Dublin had roistered" (*D* 71–2), the reader
knows, does he not, that this diction comes to him from a reading of
Sir Walter Scott, so widely popular with the average reader? If the
claim can be made that a narrator, not a character, has hold of a
certain passage in a story (as one critic does[7]), the narrator also
conceives of his speech in artful terms. The opening of "Two
Gallants" has just such a "mean" narrative voice: "The grey warm
evening of August had descended upon the city and a mild warm air
... circulated in the streets ... [The lamps] sent up into the warm
grey evening air an unchanging unceasing murmur" (49). The
scene here may be said to be "unchanging" but for that matter so is
its "evocative" purple and sentimental diction: "grey warm
evening, mild warm air," to "warm grey evening air." This passage
may aspire to art, but it is truly stuffy; it is most certainly and
literally a slap at the "Celtic Twilight."

Even a character as painfully self-conscious as Gabriel of "The
Dead" describes his weakness in terms that could easily describe the
narrator of the passage just quoted: "He saw himself as a ludicrous
figure ... a nervous well-meaning sentimentalist, orating to vulgarians ... the pitiable fatuous fellow ... " (*D* 220). The "orating"
within the story involves him in a way that precisely illuminates the
issue of the "mean" style of *Dubliners* (and thus the last story, written
after all the others, is a culmination of the whole collection in
another, new way). Gabriel "glanced at the headings he had made
for his speech. He was undecided about the lines from Robert
Browning for he feared they would be above the heads of his hearers.

Some quotation that they could recognise from Shakespeare or from the Melodies would be better" (179); he too is clearly concerned for the common understanding. The allusions to the "Three Graces" and "Paris" are another gesture to the "educated" author- and readership (like O'Grady's) that portrays Irish life, either epic or domestic, as figures from classical antiquity. Gabriel, like Joyce, writes for the conservative *Daily Express*, the place where Joyce published his review critical of Rooney's "mean" style; yet Gabriel is far less sure of his language than Joyce is. Gabriel is a practitioner of the "mean" style, trapped in the toils of the Irish Revival; Joyce is the exploiter of it. The vulgarians of whom Gabriel speaks are those readers George Russell told Joyce have "common understanding and liking," and the orator (read author) is a well-meaning but fatuous sentimentalist if he aims to give them what they like and expect of art without the irony of knowing that he conscientiously and intentionally constructs his style of "scrupulous meanness."

NOTES

1 Reprint of 1879–82 edition (Oxford: Oxford University Press, 1953).
2 See Torchiana 131ff., for an interesting reading of Little Chandler as a parody of George Roberts, both in his physical person and in his literary presumptions, as he discusses just this poem and the conclusion of the story "A Little Cloud."
3 Kenner (*A Colder Eye* 92) discusses O'Grady's particular style, but does so in reference to its effect on Yeats.
4 The story's uneasiness with both its focus and its audience can be seen in the complexity of its structural elements: the above-mentioned introductory essay material is first followed by a frame tale with the omniscient narrator, then by the comic tale itself.
5 For a detailed treatment of the increasingly polemical press and the persistence of religious publications as factors in the heteroglossia of Dublin discourse, see Herr, especially chs. 1, 2, 6, and 7.
6 See Kenner, *Joyce's Voices* ch. 2, and Riquelme 90.
7 Riquelme 93: "No reader will confuse the mind of Lenehan with the narrative sensibility revealed in this sentence's rhythmical, highly adjectival language."

WORKS CITED

Brandabur, Edward. *A Scrupulous Meanness: A Study of Joyce's Early Work.* Urbana: University of Illinois Press, 1971.

Brown, Homer Obed. *James Joyce's Early Fiction.* Cleveland: Press of Case Western Reserve University, 1972.

Carleton, William. *Stories from Carleton.* London: Scott, n.d. With an introduction by W. B. Yeats.

Ellmann, Richard. *James Joyce.* Rev. edn. New York: Oxford University Press, 1982.

Gregory, Lady Augusta. *Cuchulain of Muirthemne.* 3rd edn. London: Murray, 1907.

Herr, Cheryl. *Joyce's Anatomy of Culture.* Urbana: University of Illinois Press, 1986.

Joyce, James. *The Critical Writings of James Joyce.* Ed. Ellsworth Mason and Richard Ellmann. New York: Viking, 1959.

"Dubliners": Text, Criticism, and Notes. Ed. Robert Scholes and A. Walton Litz. New York: Viking, 1969.

Letters of James Joyce. 3 vols. Vol. 1, ed. Stuart Gilbert. Vols. 2 and 3, ed. Richard Ellmann. New York: Viking, 1966.

Joyce, Stanislaus. *The Complete Dublin Diary.* Ed. George H. Healey. Ithaca: Cornell University Press, 1971.

My Brother's Keeper. Ed. Richard Ellmann. New York: Viking, 1969.

Kain, Richard M. *Dublin in the Age of William Butler Yeats and James Joyce.* Norman: University of Oklahoma Press, 1962.

Kenner, Hugh. *A Colder Eye.* New York: Penguin, 1983.

Joyce's Voices. Berkeley and Los Angeles: University of California Press, 1978.

O'Grady, Standish. *The Coming of Cuculain.* Dublin: Talbot, n.d. With an introduction by A. E.

Riquelme, John Paul. *Teller and Tale in Joyce's Fiction.* Baltimore: Johns Hopkins University Press, 1983.

Torchiana, Donald T. *Backgrounds for Joyce's "Dubliners."* Boston: Allen, 1986.

CHAPTER 11

Joyce and Lacan: the twin narratives of History and His[$]tory in the "Nestor" chapter of Ulysses

Garry M. Leonard

Had Pyrrhus not fallen by a beldam's hand in Argos or Julius Caesar not been knifed to death. They are not to be thought away. Time has branded them and fettered they are lodged in the room of the infinite possibilities they have ousted. But can those have been possible seeing that they never were? Or was that only possible which came to pass? Weave, weaver of the wind.

(U 2.48–53)

[T]he Drama in which the original myths of the City State are produced before its assembled citizens stands in relation to a history which may well be made up of materials, but in which a nation today learns to read the symbols of a destiny on the march.

Jacques Lacan, Speech and Language 17

The "Nestor" chapter opens in medias res on a history lesson that is being conducted indifferently by Stephen Dedalus. The object of a history lesson, as Mr. Deasy might see it, is to acquaint the students with the "facts" of the past so that they might optimize the possibilities of their future. In Deasy's view, history as "what has been" uses "what is" as a fulcrum for elevating "what will be" (which, he insists, eventually leads to "the manifestation of God" [U 2.381]). In direct contrast to Deasy's view, however, Joyce demonstrates in this chapter that "History" is not a record of "what happened," but rather a narrative of selected "actualities" arranged in a fictional construct that masquerades as "Truth." We can see Stephen beginning to resist the narrative of "History" in "Nestor" because he sees it as a dominant discourse that seeks to influence the manner in which he writes his own story (what I am calling "His[$]tory").[1] My presentation of Joyce's view of History in "Nestor" is influenced, in part, by Lacan's idea that the history of a nation, like the history of an individual subject, is always a selection of "actual" events, arranged in a fictional narrative, that promotes the mythical unity and coherence of the "nation" or of the "self" by allowing some facts to represent the sum of "what happened." Individual experiences that challenge the myth of the "self" are repressed, as are those facts in a nation's history that cannot be read as "the symbols of a destiny on the march" (*Speech and Language* 17). Neither the narrative of "History" nor that of "His[$]tory" ousts the possibilities of the past: these fictional narratives only pretend to do so in order to give "meaning" to the present and a sense of predictability to the future. Either of these narratives, once fictionalized as "Truth," serves to limit the possibilities of narratives written in the future. Stephen is anxious to transcend the "actual" limitations set by the narrative of "History" on his as yet unwritten (and therefore still "possible") "His[$]tory."

The fiction of the "self" is a narrative that organizes and interprets the past experiences of a subject (as opposed to that of "a nation") by narrating "a destiny on the march" that guarantees the unity and coherence of what the subject "knows" in the present, which in turn determines what he imagines as the future. Deasy's narration of "His[$]tory," for example, elides his status as a dominated husband by representing, as a monocausal theory of sin, what is in fact a personal commitment to misogyny: "A woman brought sin into the world" (2.390).[2] In a similar fashion, he transforms his powerless status as a writer into an anti-Semitic theory of economics that appears to give a specific cause to his "self"-serving paranoia about "backstairs influence" (2.343–4). According to Lacan, the fictional unity of subjectivity makes the representations of "reality" in language seem real, but "the Real" persists beyond the subject's "knowledge." The "Real," for Lacan, is the uninterpreted residue of actuality which remains after interpretation has reduced the chaos of the world to the fictional coherence of the Word (narrative).[3] The way that a nation depends on "History" for a belief in its "destiny" is similar, for Lacan, to the way a subject depends on a reconstructed memory of an individual past ("His[$]tory") to foster the internal unity of temporalization that permits him to believe in the myth of the "self."

Just as a subject cannot afford to remember every experience, a nation cannot have a coherent "destiny" if it haphazardly records all that has happened (which, in any case, is impossible to do). Both "History" and "His[$]tory" are fictional narratives where the "actualities" that are selected – once woven into narrative – *appear* to have ousted all other possible fictions. "History" is a fiction – one that ousts possibilities *while also* obscuring *some* actualities. This unrepresented actuality (what Lacan calls "the Real") constitutes the margins of the text of a nation, as well as the text of a self. The conflict between "History" and "His[$]tory" occurs when the narrative of a nation whose "destiny" is on the march requires an individual to interpret his or her own past in accordance with this fiction. The fictional narrative of "History" limits the possibilities of an individual's "His[$]tory" – which is equally fictional and therefore easily influenced by the more dominant discourse.

The goal of "History," then, is a more righteous nationalism and the goal of "His[$]tory" is a more secure egotism.[4] We see immediately by the structure of Stephen's lesson that "teaching" History involves memorization rather than any exercise of intuition. Neither Stephen nor his students view recorded "History" as anything but arbitrarily selected facts, imposed from without, that are first memorized and then reformulated into a narrative that constitutes "knowledge" of the event:

– You, Cochrane, what city sent for him?
– Tarentum, sir.
– Very good. Well?
– There was a battle, sir.
– Very good. Where?
     The boy's blank face asked the blank window ...
– I forget the place, sir. 279 B.C.
– Asculum, Stephen said, glancing at the name and date in the gorescarred book. (*U* 2.1–13)

When Cochrane's confusion leads to subjective blankness, we can see "His[$]tory" being dominated by the discourse of "History." But the fact of "the gorescarred book" that Stephen consults, in order to override this sudden stillness, unravels the (fictional) coherency of "History." "Gorescarred" has an archaic meaning of stabbed, and a more contemporary meaning of stained or dirty. Thus, the book that recounts gorescarred events is itself gorescarred by the hands of the forgotten teachers who have passed this information along to students who are equally forgettable. The suspension of Cochrane's subjectivity in the face of forgotten facts places him in a state where the world is, for the moment, more real than he is.

From a Lacanian perspective, both Cochrane's "identity," and the narrative of sequential "History" that has temporarily subsumed it, are imaginary. It is the oscillation between these two imaginary structures – "History" and "His[$]tory" – that generates the centering experience of "reality." One can remember History, or one can re-member the "self," but one cannot do both at the same time. When the past is given an identity, the subject's own unity is put in doubt; inversely, when a subject reasserts his (fictional) unity of self, the reality beyond the "self" is experienced as random and dangerously alien. Struck by the way Cochrane goes blank, Stephen mentally notes that what the boy is failing to recite properly is "History" – an oft-repeated tale "fabled by the daughters of memory" (*U* 2.7). And yet Stephen immediately challenges Blake's dismissal of the past by calling it "a phrase, then, of impatience" since "it [the past] was in some way if not as memory fabled it" (2.7–8). Stephen, of course, wishes to utter phrases of permanence, not impatience. Lacan's concept of the Real is particularly helpful when trying to follow all of the ramifications of Stephen's discovery that one cannot simply dismiss "History" as a fable distorted by memory (as Blake did). Stephen's improvement on Blake is to note that, where there is distortion, there must still be something actual that has been distorted. The Real that remains uninterpreted beyond what is selected as the actual of "History" must be feared by the artist because the resulting "reality" limits the possible formations of "His[$]tory." This, I would suggest, is the idea behind Stephen's formulation of History as a personal nightmare. Stephen's metaphor, in my reading, presents History as a distorted view of the Real that haunts him because it is a fictionalization of the past that controls what he is able to perceive as "reality" in the present. For Stephen, writing "His[$]tory" free from the effects of the fiction of "History" would be like awakening from the frightening distortion of the Real that dictates his "reality."[5]

Previous commentators on the "Nestor" chaptor have suggested that Stephen is hostile to Deasy's linear version of History because this factual way of recounting the past disallows the limitless possibilities of the poetic imagination: "History, then, is seen by Stephen as a usurper and a destroyer of creative potential, a restrictive force which limits other, perhaps more interesting, possibilities" (Cheng 20). My reading, however, suggests that Joyce wished to disarm this notion that "History" is an impersonal and unaccountable force that ousts possibilities by imposing "actualities." By approaching "Nestor" with Lacanian theory in mind, I wish to argue that Joyce insists there is the actual (what Lacan calls the Real), the narrative that *interprets* the actual ("History"), and the subject who views this narrative as "Truth" while constructing a (fictional) unity of the "self" ("His[$]tory"). In the case of the battle of Asculum, the Real might be seen as the actual identity of all the dead bodies on the field whose "His[$]tory" is silence because the "meaning" of their existence has been subsumed by Pyrrhus' felicitous phrase.

It is true, as Cheng notes in his discussion of this chapter, that "if Caesar had not been knifed to death, he might have lived to a ripe old age ... " (Cheng 20). It is equally true, however, that *were he not* Caesar we would not know that he lived, nor when he died, nor to what degree his demise had "ousted" other possibilities. All the men who died at Asculum were as "factual" as Caesar, and yet we know nothing about them because their death has not been fictionalized in a manner that "explains" how the past "inevitably" produces the present. Had Brutus killed Marc Antony, as well as Caesar, might not the death of Caesar be cited by "History" as a necessary step in the recuperation of Rome's glory, rather than a tragic "fact" that cannot be undone? The further question we can ask about Caesar's death, in addition to what might have "actually happened" if Caesar had lived, is this: what alternative fictionalization of the "meaning" of his death might have come to be seen as "the Truth" by future generations if the "fact" of his death were "explained" solely by Brutus? Indeed, in Shakespeare's version of this "actual" event, two *possible* versions of how the event will be imbued with "meaning" are presented to the unruly crowd – Brutus' version followed by Marc Antony's. One version will become "actual" and the other no more than an ousted "possibility," depending on who dominates whom in the upcoming battle. Caesar's death is a "fact" that cannot be undone; but how this "fact" is woven into the narrative of "History" remains a possibility that is only made "actual" by the triumph or failure of someone's individual "His[$]-tory."[6]

In a similar manner, the death of Stephen's mother is a fact that cannot be undone – but whether or not this actuality will destroy Stephen's possibility as an artist still depends on how he weaves the fact of her death into the myth of him"self." Her death is a "fact," but, no matter how he "explains" her death, the uninterpreted residue of this "explanation" will haunt him (not unlike the way Caesar's ghost haunts Brutus). "History" is a metaphorical nightmare for Stephen, but it is the death of his mother that has produced the *actual* nightmare of "His[$]tory." Throughout the day, he is still in dialogue with the "actuality" of her death, trying to control the possibilities that might be ousted from the "room" of "His[$]tory" where he is struggling to make his "destiny" as an artist "actual." Just as nations highlight some "actualities" and ignore others in order to form the narrative of a "destiny on the march," Stephen wishes to see his refusal to take communion as the original event in the "History" of a great writer. What haunts him is that it may, instead, come to signify a miserable step downwards in the "His[$]-tory" of a failed poet (this is already Mulligan's view). For Stephen, there is a danger that all his possibilities as an artist will be ousted by the particular fictionalization of what his mother's death "means." With his Pyrrhic riddles and aphorisms, Stephen wishes to fictionalize him"self" (that is, narrate "His[$]tory") in a way that does not depend on "History." In this way he hopes to evade the limitations that the narrative of "History" imposes on the narrative of "His[$]tory."

Deasy's insistence that God is the ultimate historian makes "History" something above and beyond human consciousness – something that must be submitted to because it has its own mysterious intent. It is this ideology, in essence, that also sanctions Haines's "self"-serving view of "History" as something impersonal that is "to blame" for the actions of his ancestors. But Stephen does not want to be the unfortunate victim of a narrative he is powerless to alter. That is why he wants his phrases to achieve the dominant status of an "His[$]torian" like Pyrrhus – a man who permanently places him"self" as the focal point of any explanation of what happened at the battle of Asculum. Unless Stephen can deconstruct the impersonal and blameful force of "History," the very phrases which he hopes will be retained by "History" are destined instead for Haines's chapbook. Once there, they will serve only to further support Haines's notion that what "happened" to the Irish is an unfortunate "accident" of "History" that can be partially atoned for by his taking a special interest in the witty and whimsical sayings of the Irish. Against the meaningless and fragmented world beyond the word of recorded "History," Stephen posits the fable of his own subjective unity ("His[$]tory"). Both narratives – "History" and

"His[$]tory" – operate upon one another like a see-saw of which the subject is the fulcrum: the privileging of one sets in motion the deconstruction of the other.

Lacan's Real has no ontological foundation, nor does it operate according to the rules of contingency or causality. It is unrepresented in "History," and unconscious in "His[$]tory." In both narratives, it is the nightmare that threatens to expose "reality" and the "self" as fiction. It is what inevitably exists beyond what we know; it is, in fact, what *must* exist, if we are to "know" anything. Put another way, something gets lost in the act of interpretation because the signifier – the Word – crosses through ("murders") the thing signified. Elsewhere Lacan refers to the real as the "non-realized" (*Four Fundamental Concepts* 22) and "essentially the missed encounter" (*Four Fundamental Concepts* 55). A feeling of causality, then, is the central effect on the subject of a narrative that "weaves" a story of "what happened." This illusion of causality permits the subject to view "History" as something possessing its own ontology. But "History" exhibits no sequence illustrated by the past that has not been created by the needs of the subject's own fictional "His[$]tory" of the "self."[7] Lacan sees the subject as a signifier for another signifier, which means that the subject oscillates between those possibilities that have been regulated to the Real by language (symbolization) and those actualities that have been fettered in speech. We cannot directly apprehend it, and so we interpret it by telling stories about it that intersect with the story of our "selves."

The Ireland that Haines and Deasy "understand" does not abolish the Ireland that presses upon Stephen's students. Thus, Stephen mentally supports the young Irish students' indifference to the narration of history: "For them too *history was a tale like any other too often heard, their land a pawnshop*" (*U* 2.46–7, my emphasis). The reference to Ireland as "a pawnshop" suggests that Ireland, by virtue of having been a colony of England, is a land where "infinite possibilities" have been "ousted" by the "actualities" preserved in the narrative of English history. Whether one remembers one's own past, or recounts the events of everyone's past, the intention behind the narration is to present the fiction of what was "in the beginning" as the origin of what "is now, and ever shall be." One recounts "History" in order to endorse a particular action; one recounts "His[$]tory" in order to avoid being acted upon.

The formulation of the past as a support for the direction of the subject's future means that the apparent actuality of "History" is engendered in the present by a subject seeking to interpret the past as leading to the future. Instead of being a narrative that embodies "Truth," the fable of "History" can be seen more simply as a narrative that makes people useful. Since the "self" is a composite of various fictions, the subject does not recall the past, but only reinvents it with an eye towards engendering an originating point that leads to the (supposed) autonomy of the "self." These "facts" are then "remembered" in the form of a fiction of the "self." However, when subjects use the facts of "History" to compose their "His[$]tory," they serve the will of others even as they interpret their past as evidence of their own autonomy. What Stephen admires about Pyrrhus is that he was able to weave his own narrative ("His[$]tory") into the narrative fabric of "History" in such a way that his observation (which has the unsolvable quality of a riddle) dominates and transcends the event that is being observed. No narrative can completely interpret "what happened" (interpretation requires that something be repressed if "meaning" is to be generated), so the issue becomes whose distortion of the Real will dominate the "reality" of future generations.

As the chapter "Scylla and Charybdis" makes clear, whenever Stephen is confronted with an audience he models him"self" after Pyrrhus and searches for a phrase that others will weave into the narrative of their "His[$]tory." He is so terrified of becoming a fictional composite of other people's phrases that he even fears the books in the National Library (because the narratives they contain might dictate "His[$]tory"): "They are still. Once quick in the brains of men. Still: but an itch of death is in them, *to tell me in my ear a maudlin tale, urge me to wreak their will*" (*U* 9.356–8, my emphasis). Once again, Stephen reminds himself that what others know as "History" is really the dominant narrative of those individuals who have succeeded in interpreting events in a manner that makes the "Truth" of their narrative seem inevitable. Just as he earlier imagined the audience of Pyrrhus as "lending ear," Stephen characterizes his listeners in the library as passively accepting his narrative which is intended to urge them to wreak his will: "They list. And in the porches of their ears I pour" (*U* 9.465). Claudius-like, Stephen seeks to dispatch the sleeping narratives of others by pouring into their ears the more dominant narrative of "His[$]tory."

Whether or not he will be remembered in "History" is very much on Stephen's mind because the death of his unfamous mother (who has uttered no phrase the world will remember) is also on his mind. She, for all she will be remembered in future years, might just as well be on that "corpsestrewn plain" with the anonymous soldiers of Pyrrhus' army. While it is true that the felicitous phrase of Pyrrhus has "immortalized" these corpses (they are the carnage that provides the punchline of his phrase), it has only immortalized them as an impressive number of dead bodies. They are "History" without any "His[$]tory." It is Pyrrhus whose "His[$]tory" is constructed at the expense of the forgotten individuality of these fallen men. In essence, he builds his corpus on these corpses.[8] He will be remembered because the dismembered corpses cannot be re-membered. They cannot challenge his phrase with phrases of their own. When Armstrong begins reciting Milton's "Lycidas," Stephen notes that Christ, like Pyrrhus, has been remembered within the narrative of "History" only by virtue of having been an enigmatic narrator whose phrases have been remembered and endlessly interpreted by the world. The triumph of Christ's "His[$]tory" over "History" was so profound that his birth marks the beginning of modern time. Partially by virtue of his phrases, Christ has ascended to the status of a "self" that has no beginning and no end. Whereas Pyrrhus achieved immortality in narrative through the use of paradox, Christ wove his speech into the narrative texture of "History" by pronouncing unfathomable phrases in the form of parables: "To Caesar what is Caesar's, to God what is God's. A long look from dark eyes, *a riddling sentence to be woven and woven on the church's looms*" (*U* 2.86–7, my emphasis). In essence, Stephen seems aware that enigmatic narrative transcends the limitations of someone else's dominant narrative of "History" by providing the basic material later individuals will use to weave the narrative of "His[$]tory." This is the reason, I would suggest, that Stephen speaks in riddles all day – from the incomprehensible riddle he delivers to the class, through the parable of the plums, to the paradoxical replies he gives to Bloom's questions in the "Eumaeus" and "Ithaca" chapters.[9] As Hayden White points out, "the crucial problem, from the perspective of political struggle, is not whose story is the best or the truest, but who has the power to make his story stick as the one that others will choose to live by or in" (12–13). But Stephen's problem – and it is a problem all day – is that no one in any of his various audiences shows any interest in "weaving" his phrases on to their looms.

When Stephen's witty definition of a pier as "a disappointed bridge" goes unheard in the classroom, he reflects to himself, "For Haines's chapbook" (2.42). But far from putting him in a Christ-like position where the "His[$]tory" of British citizens would be entranced by his riddles, he foresees that offering the phrase to Haines's chapbook would make him an anonymous performer: "A jester at the court of his master, indulged and disesteemed, winning a clement master's praise" (*U* 2.43–5). Significantly, one of Stephen's pupils seeks to divert the lesson from the recitation of "facts" by chorusing: "*Tell us a story*, sir" (*U* 2.54, my emphasis). Another student seconds the idea: "O, do, sir. A ghoststory." They are not at all eager for formal "History" – a story too often told and never to their advantage – but for new narrative. Stephen, however, does not tell the students a story because, as I have suggested, he is coming to see himself as a victim of stories. Instead, he offers a riddle that is incomprehensible to the students because it is a private representation of his preoccupation about whether or not he contributed to the death of his mother. "History" is not what happened; it is what happens – again and again – in the narrative of "His[$]tory." The Truth behind a subject's "His[$]tory" – the particular structure of the fiction he misrecognizes as the "Truth" – can only be glimpsed in relation to the way the subject repeats it in the present (this is the basis of psychoanalysis): "What we teach the subject to recognize as his unconscious is his history – that is to say, we help him to perfect the contemporary historization of the facts which have already determined a certain number of the historical turning points in his existence" (Lacan, *Speech and Language* 23). The corpsestrewn plain is behind Pyrrhus' narrative of "what happened," and the corpse of Stephen's mother is behind all the various riddles that Stephen poses to others in an attempt to impose the fiction of him"self."

To conclude, Stephen goes beyond Blake's dismissal by asserting that although "History" is fabled by the daughters of memory, nonetheless *something* happened. Increasingly, however, he is accepting the fact that what he must protect him"self" against is not the actuality of the past – which is chaotic and impossible to recover – but the "Truth" of "History" which is nothing more than a fictional narrative where possibility effectively masquerades as actuality (what "cannot be thought away"). It is this masquerade Stephen must recognize if he is to resist being incorporated into other people's phrases. Much has been made of the historical "errors" in "Nestor," but the necessary relationship between "error" and "Truth" has gone unnoted.[10] As Lacan puts it, "there is no error which does not present and promulgate itself as truth. In short, error is the habitual incarnation of the truth. And if we wanted to be entirely rigorous, we would say that, as long as the truth isn't entirely revealed, that is to say in all probability until the end of time, its nature will be to propagate itself in the form of error" (*Seminar I* 263). The Real that Stephen senses behind "all that has been" is always symbolized by him as the fragmented bodies of forgotten corpses; this is partly because his own corpus depends upon these corpses which compose "His[$]tory" for him. Even the boys' hockey game is envisioned by him as taking place against this back drop: "Jousts, slush and uproar of battles, the frozen death-spew of the slain, *a shout* of spearspikes baited with men's bloodied guts" (*U* 2.317–18, my emphasis).

Stephen intuits that the "body" of knowledge decomposes into "error" in order to compose the body of the subject as the endpoint of whatever happened "in the beginning." That is to say, "errors" from previous accounts are discovered and "corrected," thus giving the appearance of "Progress" in Deasy's sense of the word. In this way, the subject presents "His[$]tory" as a "self"-evident narrative, rather than as a fictional arrangement of selected "facts." But the history lesson that Joyce presents in "Nestor" suggests that all subjects who narrate the past ("History") are actually creating their past ("His[$]tory") in a manner intended to limit the possibilities of other people's future. Stephen's struggle to narrate "His[$]tory," free from the distorting narrative of "History," is the struggle of a terrified sleeper trying to awake from what he knows is not Real, but which nonetheless constitutes all that he knows of "reality."

NOTES

1 "I symbolize the subject by the barred S ... in so far as it is constituted as secondary in relation to the signifier ... [I]t is thus that the subject sees himself duplicated – sees himself as constituted by the reflected, momentary, precarious image of mastery, imagines himself to be a man merely by virtue of the fact that he imagines himself" (Lacan, *Four*

Fundamental Concepts 141–2). I have incorporated Lacan's construction of the barred S into my word "His[Ⱥ]tory" to suggest how the subject becomes secondary to the stories he narrates about "reality" – whether these stories are "objective" (History) or "subjective" (His[Ⱥ]tory). "What we teach the subject to recognize as his unconscious is his history – that is to say, we help him to perfect the contemporary historization of the facts which have already determined a certain number of the historical turning points in his existence. But if they have played this role, it is already as facts of history, that is to say, insofar as they have been recognized in one particular sense or censored in a certain order" (Lacan, *Speech and Language* 23). What I wish to argue in this essay is that just as "a nation" learns to read the symbols of "a destiny on the march" in its past, a subject's supposed "self"-originating autonomy is in fact a fiction that a carefully narrated "His[Ⱥ]tory" comes to represent as "Truth."

2 I am indebted to Robert Spoo's essay "Teleology, Monocausality, and Marriage in *Ulysses*" for my particular use of this term: "Monocausality is a term for the reduction of causal complexity to a single cause or group of causes so simplistic as to be perniciously misleading. This simplified causality then becomes an origin that hopes to transform any number of disparate, opaque events into effortless, transparent 'effects'" ("Teleology" 448).

3 The Real, like all of Lacan's theoretical concepts, is complex and dependent on other terms for its full significance. Ragland-Sullivan's description of the Real in reference to Lacan's seminars on Joyce emphasizes that the Real is beyond representation, even though representation constantly tries to symbolize it. In the context of my essay, this symbolic representation is History in relation to the fiction of "a nation," and His[Ⱥ]tory in relation to the fiction of a subject. "[L]anguage produces a Real which does not have any corresponding reality ... Lacan emphasized that without an internalized representation of a border or an identity limit, a subject is open to the chaos of the Real which wreaks havoc on subjects who have little or no sense of a self that has a name and some characteristic properties. Without our 'legal fictions,' Lacan argued, psychosis waits in the wings, attesting to the human incapacity to think oneself human unless one already has a firm conceptualization of a position in a given Symbolic order ..." (Ragland-Sullivan 79).

4 Seamus Deane describes how all the given "events" of history can be interpreted by the individual in a manner that furthers the goals of nationalism: "Whether it is the history of the Fenians or of the development of English prose, of the history of Dublin or of church dogma or one's own family, the idea of sequence demands that one should conform to the pattern of the past so that in doing so, the pattern becomes extended or fulfilled in oneself" (Deane 101).

5 Although Deane's discussion of Joyce and nationalism is not in any way informed by Lacanian theory, he does speculate about the awareness in Joyce's work of something beyond "reality" that influences "the world of recorded fact": "Below the threshold of complete wakefulness, there is a universe of associative patterns which, in their unofficial way, might be more real or universal or simply more interesting than the world of recorded fact can provide" (Deane 101).

6 Here I am taking up, and offering an initial response to, some of the questions that Jameson poses at the conclusion of his essay "*Ulysses* in History": "Why do we need narrative anyway? What are stories and what is our existential relation to them? Is a non-narrative relationship to the world and to Being possible?" (Jameson 140).

7 Epstein says: "The theme of the 'Nestor' chapter, then, is the problem of the proper way to regard the stream of human history" (Epstein 27). This is a beginning, but the theme is more radical than this because the chapter raises the question: *who* is regarding "human history," and is it a "stream" of sequence and contingency? And is it "human" at all outside of the subject's "self"-serving representation of it?

8 Spoo also identifies Joyce's use of "corpse" as a metaphor for both "the nightmare of history," and the nightmare of his personal past. He quotes a letter from Joyce to Stanislaus that reads in part: "Rome reminds me of a man who lives by exhibiting to travellers his grand-mother's corpse." He draws attention to the similarity of this image to Stephen's riddle about the fox burying his grandmother under a holly bush, and then concludes: "Like the Stephen of 1904, the Joyce of 1906 saw history as a horror, the corpse of a loved one threatening to spurn its graveclothes, all the more ghastly because, as with history, its kinship and intimacy cannot be denied" ("Joyce's Attitude toward History: Rome, 1906–7" 484).

9 McGee states: "Stephen intends to mystify not only his students but himself; by speaking in riddles, he speaks without saying anything, without committing himself to a message that can be decoded" (16). I agree that Stephen is deliberately refusing to be decoded, but in the process he still says quite a bit, even if it is completely obscure to his present audience (and at least partially obscure to himself, as well). I might mention here that Bloom's attempt to define the term "nation," a definition that is generally ridiculed by the Citizen and others, is actually his attempt to expose the hatred and racism embedded in the narrative of History by pointing out the pernicious way it limits and distorts an individual's His[$]tory. What gets ridiculed by the men in the bar is the enigmatic quality of Bloom's definition. The persecution Bloom undergoes for unintentionally speaking in parables adds to his ironic Christ-like stature (which numerous critics have cited as a central motif in this chapter).

10 For a comprehensive list of Deasy's mistakes see Adams 18–26.

WORKS CITED

Adams, Robert Martin. *Surface and Symbol: The Consistency of James Joyce's "Ulysses."* New York: Oxford University Press, 1962.

Cheng, Vincent John. *Shakespeare and Joyce: A Study of "Finnegans Wake."* University Park: Pennsylvania State University Press, 1984.

Deane, Seamus. "Joyce and Nationalism." MacCabe 168–83.

Epstein, E. L. "Nestor." Hart and Hayman 17–28.

Feldstein, Richard, and Henry Sussman, eds. *Psychoanalysis and ...* New York: Routledge, 1990.

Hart, Clive, and David Hayman. *James Joyce's "Ulysses."* Berkeley and Los Angeles: University of California Press, 1974.

Jameson, Fredric. "*Ulysses* in History." McCormack and Stead 126–41.

Joyce, James. *The Critical Writings of James Joyce.* Ed. Ellsworth Mason and Richard Ellmann. New York: Viking, 1959.

Ulysses: The Corrected Text. Ed. Hans Walter Gabler et al. New York: Random, 1986.

Lacan, Jacques. *The Four Fundamental Concepts of Psycho-Analysis.* Trans. Alan Sheridan. Ed. Jacques-Alain Miller. New York: Norton, 1978.

The Seminar of Jacques Lacan, Book I: Freud's Papers on Technique 1953–1954. Trans. John Forrester. Ed. Jacques-Alain Miller. New York: Norton, 1988.

The Seminar of Jacques Lacan, Book II: The Ego in Freud's Theory and in the Technique of Psychoanalysis 1954–1955. Trans. Sylvana Tomaselli. Ed. Jacques-Alain Miller. New York: Norton, 1988.

Speech and Language in Psychoanalysis. Ed. Anthony Wilden. Baltimore: Johns Hopkins University Press, 1968.

MacCabe, Colin, ed. *James Joyce: New Perspectives.* Bloomington: Indiana University Press, 1982.

McCormack, W. J., and Alistair Stead, eds. *James Joyce and Modern Literature.* London: Routledge, 1982.

McGee, Patrick. *Paperspace: Style as Ideology in Joyce's "Ulysses."* Lincoln: University of Nebraska Press, 1988.

Ragland-Sullivan, Ellie. "Lacan's Seminars on James Joyce: Writing as Symptom and 'Singular Solution.'" Feldstein and Sussman 67–86.

Spoo, Robert E. "Joyce's Attitudes toward History: Rome, 1906–7." *Journal of Modern Literature* 14 (1988): 481–97.

"'Nestor' and the Nightmare: The Presence of the Great War in *Ulysses.*" *Twentieth Century Literature* 32 (1986): 137–54.

"Teleology, Monocausality, and Marriage in *Ulysses.*" *ELH* 56 (1989): 439–62.

White, Hayden. "Getting out of History." *Diacritics* 12 (1982): 2–13.

CHAPTER 12

Joyce and Homer: return, disguise, and recognition in "Ithaca"

Constance V. Tagopoulos

Joyce scholarship has termed the Homeric parallels in *Ulysses* incomplete, idiosyncratic, and noninstrumental to the work. With particular reference to "Ithaca," Richard Madtes has argued that "little is to be gained from a study of [the] Homeric references ... Even the very few which establish definite Homeric connections within 'Ithaca' do not, after all, increase the reader's understanding of the episode" (30). But it is precisely the "Ithaca" episode that sets us thinking. For a close reading of this chapter, I will argue, reveals explicit, detailed, and sustained thematic parallels with the *Odyssey*.[1] Organized around the Homeric model of return, disguise, and recognition, these parallels are embedded in the Joycean text by means of stylistic and rhetorical devices which guide our reading and illustrate the way intertextuality with the *Odyssey* illuminates Joyce's novel.

Intertextuality is itself a return. It is the literary memory of a tale or idea returning in a new form. In *Ulysses*, the themes of the *Odyssey* – adultery, identity, heroism, hospitality, marriage, family and sex roles – come back in a new form that through a process of concealing and revealing, in Karen Lawrence's words, through a system of "displacement," "avoidance," "disclosure," and "withholding," seeks to articulate the author's views (182–4). The reader's task is to recognize the traditional representation as disguised in the new text. For indeed, as early as Plato, writing and reading have been defined as a process of disguise and recognition.[2] Established by "isotopies" – semantic bridges created through rhetorical figures – intertextuality, as Laurent Jenny has argued, is a strategy of form (37–40). The function of the intertextual process is critical and playful, to parody or to subvert the text's ideological pinnings in order to systematize new meaning.

Why did Joyce choose the *Odyssey*? The *Odyssey* is a domestic epic, a poem about family which, according to Vico, is the force that moves society. The influence of Vico's *New Science* on Joyce explains the importance Homer's epic had for the author of *Ulysses*. By having Leopold Bloom, a Jew, incarnate Odysseus, the author places his hero twice outside the margins of history, thus seeking to escape the "nightmare of history."[3] Besides, the *Odyssey* tells the story of a father and a son in quest of each other, of a lovely wife surrounded by suitors, of sexual estrangement, of exile, escape, usurpation; it tells of trials and ordeals which the hero overcomes with courage, resourcefulness, and good humor. As Joyce told Budgen, Odysseus was his favorite hero because he is a "complete," "all-around" man who is a father, a husband, a son, a lover, a companion in arms, a warrior, a king, and an astute survivor (*JJ* 435–6). *Ulysses* tells the same story, albeit in a different way and tone – and simultaneously with many other stories. Like the Ithaca books of the Homeric epic, the penultimate episode of *Ulysses* is focused on the hero's homecoming, restating, in Joycean terms, the Viconian argument that basic experiences and situations recur through history. Homecoming, dramatized and validated by disguise and recognition, marks the end of the Odyssean quest, and the returning hero's integration into society after order has been restored. This is also the direction in which the "Ithaca" chapter moves. With a brief outline of the Nostos chapters of the *Odyssey* as our guide, we will identify the Homeric model of return, disguise, and recognition, as applied on both the thematic and stylistic dimensions of Joyce's "Ithaca."

Prudently fearing for his life and following the advice of Agamemnon, who in the underworld had warned Odysseus against women, Homer's hero strategically lands, on his return home, at a secret bay in Ithaca. As a protective measure, the goddess Athena casts a mist over Ithaca's landscape, making the once familiar countryside unrecognizable to Odysseus; then, turning the hero into a beggar, she directs him to his palace by way of Eumaios' hut. As he did during his wanderings, so now in his native land the returning hero has to disguise and thus to give up his name in order to be able to make it anew and repossess it. Before a sense of identity can be achieved, time is needed for readjustment to the changes which have occurred during Odysseus' absence. Caution and a series of recognitions enable him to know his estranged home and family again and to be known by them. First, Odysseus is recognized by his son Telemachus, then by his dog Argos. In the palace, Odysseus' old nurse Euryclea, ordered to wash his feet, recognizes him by the scar in his thigh: as a child, Odysseus had been wounded by a wild boar. Lastly, Penelope identifies her husband after testing his knowledge of the secret of their bed, which Odysseus himself had built around the trunk of an olive tree. The cycle of the Odyssean recognitions is complete with Laertes, Odysseus' father, whom the hero visits the next morning. With this rough outline in mind and guided by the tropes of return, disguise, and recognition, we will attempt through a close textual analysis to trace Bloom's movements from the moment of his arrival home, with Stephen, to the end of the "Ithaca" episode.

In "Ithaca," return is overdetermined both mimetically and linguistically: having lost their keys after a day's wandering about the bars, beaches, and brothels of Dublin, Leopold Bloom and Stephen Dedalus, symbolically a "father" and a "son," find themselves before Bloom's locked door at 7 Eccles Street, literally outsiders, as they are strangers and exiles in their own fatherland. Words like "enter/reenter," "reappear," "return," and "come back" endlessly reproduce themselves textually throughout this chapter. The long chain of returns and entrances, beginning with Bloom's arrival home and his entrance through the back door, continues with Stephen's entrance through the front door, then with Bloom's reentrance from the garden into the house, and finally with Leopold's "entrance" into Molly's bed – after a spectacular entrance into his nightshirt (U 17.2111–12). The chiastic structure of the train passage is an example of rhetorical return: "Retreating, at the terminus of the Great Northern Railway, Amiens street, with constant uniform acceleration, along parallel lines meeting at infinity, if produced: along parallel lines, reproduced from infinity, with constant uniform retardation, at the terminus of the Great Northern Railway, Amiens street, returning" (U 17.2085–9). This passage, reminiscent of the palindromic technique in *Finnegans Wake*, reads the same backwards and forwards. It juxtaposes two almost identical but inverted grammatical constructions separated by a colon. As the part representing retreat is reversed to represent return, the train becomes a train of words drawn now by "retreating," now by "returning." Return along parallel lines meeting at infinity, with which the chapter's opening lines are preoccupied, is thus made possible linguistically.

Facing a locked door and without a key, Bloom ponders: "To enter or not to enter. To knock or not to knock" (*U* 17.82). Besides playfully echoing Hamlet's dilemma, the passage also tells us that Bloom hesitates, if momentarily, to enter his own house. A similar hesitation tormenting Odysseus when he thinks of home ultimately takes him to the underworld to seek Teiresias' prophecy and the foreknowledge of the dead regarding the situation at home and Penelope's faithfulness. In the land of the dead, the shade of Agamemnon cautions Odysseus: "Put thy ship to land in secret, and not openly, on the shore of thy dear country; for there is no more faith in woman" (*Od.* 11.455–6). The example of Agamemnon is to be avoided. For he returns home after the war without delay and enters his palace without hesitation, unprepared to face the changes that have taken place there during his absence. Agamemnon makes a triumphant return – actually "knocks" at the front door – and is murdered by his adulterous wife Clytemnestra and by Aegisthus, the usurper of his throne. In a similar vein, the situation at home has been haunting Bloom all day, and, to match its Homeric counterpart, the Joycean "Hades" episode evokes the Agamemnon theme (*U* 6.926).[4] Molly's infidelity is very much in Bloom's thoughts as he is internally arguing out the wisdom of visiting his daughter Milly unexpectedly: "She mightn't like me to come that way without letting her know. Must be careful about women" (*U* 6.483–4). Both Odysseus and Bloom seem to agree that women and closed doors shouldn't be handled lightly!

The parallel mode of the two heroes' entering demonstrates their ability to use their wits. Like Odysseus, who lands at a secret bay away from the city and arrives at his palace secretly and circuitously, "polytropos" Poldy enters through the back door. He must be experiencing a sense of alienation from the house where his wife went to bed with another man that same afternoon, and he must need time to reconstruct his sense of identity, which has been shaken by the disconcerting experience of a day's life in Dublin aggravated, that particular day, by his wife's betrayal. Bloom's hesitation to visit Milly confirms his preference for a tactician's ways when dealing with a woman: "Must be careful about women. Catch them once with their pants down. Never forgive you after" (*U* 6.484–5). The words describe Molly's act that afternoon and Bloom's reasoning gives the measure of his intention to avoid trouble by checking a spontaneous reaction to an emotional situation. The "stratagem" he devises to enter the house proves his Odysseus-like ability to ease himself out of an awkward position, in other words, to survive.

Disguise is a prelude to recognition. It is a dramatic device without which the crucial revelation would not be possible. Bloom's entrance from the garden into the house sets in motion a series of disguises and recognitions. In knocking his head against the furniture as he re-enters from the garden, he discovers that the furniture had been rearranged earlier that afternoon. Whether moved by Molly or by her lover,[5] the rearranged furniture is a metonymy of Molly's adultery; it represents the change that occurred during Bloom's absence, which the cuckolded husband now acknowledges through "a painful sensation" (*U* 17.1277). Similarly, when he arrives in Ithaca, Odysseus is unable to recognize (*ouden min egno*) his once familiar landscape:

> for around him the goddess [Athena] had shed a mist, ... to the end that she might make him undiscovered [*agnoston*] for that he was, and might expound to him all things ... Each thing showed strange to the lord of the land ... So he started up, and stood and looked upon his native land, and then he made moan withal, and smote on both his thighs with the downstroke of his hands. (*Od.* 13.190–8)

Failure to recognize his once beloved landscape makes Odysseus a stranger (*agnoston*) in his own fatherland. The *egno/agnoston* repetition of the ancient text anticipates the *anagnorisis* that is to follow. The formulaic *peplegeto mero*, "smote on his thighs," acquires particular meaning if related to the wounding in the thigh by the wild boar. In our two texts we have therefore two estranged men returning home and unable to recognize their "disguised" homeland. The change makes them strangers in their native ground and is acknowledged by both through pain as a result of a kind of wounding. In the *Odyssey*, the seme of pain functions as a metaphor for emotional suffering; in *Ulysses* it becomes literal. As Jenny suggests, the transformation of the figurative into literal is one of the techniques of intertextual embedding (41). The contrast between Odysseus' energetic and emotional reaction and Bloom's numb response to the shock throws the latter's solitude and passive enduring into bold relief.

Recognition, the purpose and justification of disguise, is pivotal in the "Ithaca" episode. It enhances characterization and serves self-constituting purposes. "Ithaca" is the chapter which invites us to recognize Bloom in both the physical and psychological aspects of his character. It is in fact only in its penultimate chapter that *Ulysses* offers detailed information on Bloom's appearance and personality. We learn, for instance, that he is a "gent about 40 ... height 5 ft 9½ inches, full build, olive complexion" (*U* 17.2002–3), that his chest measures an impossible 28 inches (*U* 17.1818), and that a size 17 collar is too small for his neck (*U* 17.1431). Moreover, having believed him a Jew, we now hear that he was also a Protestant and a Roman Catholic, three times baptized, and that his father was converted to Protestantism from the Israelitic faith (*U* 17.542, 1637). Additional information also establishes Bloom's conjugal inadequacy and his tendency to leave things incomplete (*U* 17. 372, 417, 513, 598, 765–6, 1445, 2071, 2283). Bloom is "Everyman"; his all-inclusive personality universalizes him, and his endearing imperfections and deformities make this "hero" human and pleasantly accessible to the reader.

Adequate ink has been spilled on Bloom's measurements and their potential contribution to a better understanding of this episode.[6] In the search for meaning one should not lose sight of the fact that Joyce chose to include this information in the one and only chapter of *Ulysses* concerned with recognition. Bloom's grossly disproportionate measurements may be intended simply to pull us into recognizing in him not the heroic stature of Homer's legendary hero but, to use David Hayman words, "a grotesque shadow of the heroic precursor" (64). We are called, in fact, to recognize the comic, life-celebrating instinct in this modern hero. Odysseus is an unconventional hero often presented in a comic light. His mythological ancestry presents him as a trickster figure by inheritance: his direct ancestors were Autolycus, Hermes, and perhaps Sisyphus, all associated with deception and guile. Outside the Homeric representation, Odysseus is often related to the grotesque, carnivalesque aspects of life. The image of the comic doublets, Heracles and Odysseus, as Mikhail Bakhtin notes, was presented in humorous vase decorations with scenes from comedies and symbols of fertility. "The fragments of Aeschylus' satric drama 'The Collectors of Bones' [Ostologoi] contain an episode in which a vile-smelling vessel," that is, a chamber pot full of excrement, "is thrown at the head of Odysseus" (Bakhtin 31, 148). Joyce often spoke of Odysseus' imperfections as defining his humanness; they are flaws that make him, alone among heroes, "all-round, three-dimensional, but not necessarily complete in the sense of being ideal" (*JJ* 436). In burlesquing the heroic

model, the text simply shows without evaluating, without moralizing, the anti-heroic character of modern man.

While the reader is thus called to know Bloom again in "Ithaca,"
the latter's recognition by Stephen remains a murky issue. Once
inside the house, Leopold removes his boots and hat, emblems of
social disguise no longer needed inside his home's protective walls.
The narrator will later test our memory of this disrobing scene.
While waiting for Bloom to open the front door, Stephen "perceives" through the kitchen panes, "a man regulating a gasflame
... a man lighting a candle ... a man removing in turn each of his
two boots, a man leaving the kitchen holding a candle ... [T]he
man reappeared without his hat, with his candle" (*U* 17.110–17).
Although obscured by the pedantry of style, the emphasis placed on
man, candle, and undressing is unmistakable. Passing over the
obvious religious associations triggered by these words, we turn,
once again, to the *Odyssey* for meaning: the word "man," repeated
five times in the passage above, is a predicate of Odysseus and the
English equivalent of the first word, "andra," of the opening hex-
ameter of the *Odyssey*.[7] The repeated reference to Bloom as "a man"
constitutes a suppression of his name. It brings to mind Odysseus
having to give his name away, to become *Outis* in his encounter with
Polyphemus. But what the text does actually say here is that
Stephen is unable to recognize Bloom. The fragmented image
Stephen sees through the glass is not Leopold Bloom but "a man" –
a composite of Christ and Odysseus.

Is Bloom's recognition by Stephen ever achieved? Are the father
and the son in quest of each other finally united in the homecoming
chapter of *Ulysses*? Scholars are skeptical about whether the
"fusion" achieved later in the kitchen, "consubstantially," should
be construed as a successful resolution of the paternal/filial quest.
Phillip Herring argues that, ironically, "the son fails to recognize the
father" (174), and Patrick McGee characterizes the two men's
union as a "missed encounter, a double revelation in which nothing,
the nothing, is revealed" (164–5). The union that undoubtedly takes
place between Bloom and Stephen is certainly the one linguistically
determined in "Stoom" and "Blephen." As in the example of the
train at Amiens station, the language takes over and provides the
solution life is unable to give.

What is Stephen's function, then, in Bloom's house? The intertextuality of *Ulysses* with the *Odyssey* prompts us to look for an answer in

the Homeric theme of host-guest relations as treated by Joyce: the words "host," repeated twice, "guest," six times, and "hospitality," three times, in the kitchen passage alone (*U* 17.359–75), acquire particular importance in view of the centrality of the social institution of hospitality in the *Odyssey*. Stephen's presence in Bloom's house as a guest validates Bloom as a host – the latter can be a host only as long as there is a guest present. Importantly enough, the Greek language uses *xenos* for both "guest" and "stranger." Stephen, whom Bloom gets to know only that same day, is a "stranger," in the Joycean idiom, an Irishman who is an exile in his own fatherland, like Stephen, like Bloom, like the author himself. But he is also the guest who validates Bloom as a master of his house again. Stephen is the opposite of Boylan and of the Homeric suitors. In visiting Bloom's house and sleeping with his wife, Boylan violates the law of hospitality, usurping, like Penelope's suitors, the legitimate host's rights. It is Stephen who, by refusing to stay for the night – refusing Molly whom Bloom has symbolically offered to him more than once – restores Bloom to his Ithaca. If Joyce's hero regains his home on the night of June 16, 1904, it is because Stephen puts a check on Bloom's liberal hospitality, limiting it to a hot cup of cocoa served in the kitchen. By contrast, Boylan's sexual activities in Bloom's house are associated with eating in bed and confirmed by the crumbs and flakes of potted meat Bloom discovers there. Bloom and Stephen may have failed to achieve a union as father and son on the secular level, but in the kitchen scene they confirm each other as guest and host, establishing a relationship between them that in Homer's world defines friendship. This purpose fulfilled, Stephen's prolonged presence has no further function and therefore he can leave.

As the younger man leaves, Bloom unlocks the garden gate by "inserting the barrel of an arruginated male key in the hole of an unstable female lock, obtaining a purchase on the bow ... withdrawing a bolt from its staple, pulling inward spasmodically an obsolescent unhinged door and revealing an aperture for free egress and free ingress ..." (*U* 17.1215–19). These lines echo Penelope's unlocking of the doors of the chamber where Odysseus' bow was kept: "she quickly loosed the strap from the handle of the door, and thrust in the key, and with a straight aim shot back the bolts. And even as the bull roars that is grazing in a meadow, so mightily roared the fair doors smitten by the key; and speedily they flew open before her" (*Od.* 21.45–50).

Both excerpts, the Homeric and the Joycean, are sexually suggest-ive. They serve to build tension in the narrative as they prepare the reader or the audience for a significant turn in the story. The Homeric unlocking forebodes the union of Odysseus and Penelope after a long separation and sexual estrangement, situations which come back in the Molly/Bloom relationship. It is characterized by a climactic tone which stirs emotions in view of the upcoming bow contest anticipated by the oral audience. The Joycean passage (characteristically featuring the word "bow") forebodes a new birth through the union of the male key with the female lock. On the other hand, the complete lack of emotion at the crucial moment of the two men's separation indexes the text. In contrast to the *Odyssey*, the protracted factual description of this anti-climactic unlocking can be seen as a perversion of the reader's anticipations.[8] It is at this juncture that the author chooses to stress Bloom's loneliness and to introduce the substitute for the lost "son." The word "alone" (twice repeated, at 1242 and 1245) gains importance in view of Joyce's own statement to Budgen that his literary hero was Odysseus because he was a complete man and a good man. Surrounded by a family, Odysseus can also be alone, as opposed to Faust, who "can't be complete because he's never alone. Mephistopheles is always hanging round him at his side or heels" (*JJ* 435). "Alone" denotes loneliness but also intimates that special courage and self-sufficiency which make a man a survivor. Community, ubiquitous and control-ling but often supportive in ancient society, is glaringly absent in Bloom's solitary struggle to cope with life.

The reason Bloom "remain(s)" is the apparition of a "visible diffusion of the light of an invisible luminous body, the first golden limb of the resurgent sun perceptible low on the horizon" (*U* 17.1266–8). Punning transforms the rising sun into the lost son. "Luminous body" also describes the moon in its different phases and, symbolically, Molly, "denoted by a visible splendid sign, a lamp" (*U* 17.1178). Molly's lunary/tellurian qualities endow her with the power to renew, to change and also be consistent, "to enamour . . . to render insane" (*U* 17.1157–70). Her affinity with the moon is substantiated by the fact that her mother's name, as we learn from her drowsy confessions in "Penelope," was Lunita (*U* 18.848). So, it is with the appearance of a new celestial body, the sun, and Molly's promising lampshade beckoning to him, that Bloom returns from the garden and re-enters the house. Importantly, it is when a new moon appears that Odysseus returns and regains his palace. He returns at *lykabas*, when "the old moon wanes and the new is born" (*Od.* 14.160–2, 19.305–7), on the day of the festival of Apollo Noumenios (Apollo of the New Moon). As Norman Austin has convincingly shown, the poem's dénouement comes at the "moment of equilibrium between one moon and the next," a moment that also marks the beginning of spring, symbolically a new birth for the returning hero (244–7). Like his ancient counterpart, Bloom is soon to be reborn as "a manchild in the womb."

But before a new cycle of life can begin, order has to be established. Bloom cannot reconstruct his sense of inner order before ordering the spatial and temporal chaos of the external world. Rather than imitate Odysseus' bloody method of revenge, Joyce's hero fights jealousy by ordering his thoughts and purging his emotions. His gentleness, compassion, and common sense articulate the new ideology into which the Homeric concepts of heroism and honor are translated in Joyce's work. The items in the front room and the memories and images of himself are the means and the objects of Bloom's ordering enterprise. In contemplating his wedding presents on the mantelpiece – a timepiece, a dwarf tree and an embalmed owl – Bloom re-evaluates his marriage: all three objects connote endurance through time and represent wisdom. But an attempt to recognize his own face in the mirror almost fails: instead of himself, he sees a solitary man who "had resembled his maternal procreatrix" and "would increasingly resemble his paternal procreator" (*U* 17.1355–6). Bloom can only think in past and future tenses. Present time is blurred in his mind as the "final image" the mirror returns to him, that of the "inverted volumes improperly arranged," is the image of disorder (*U* 17.1358).

Bloom's last act before going to bed involves self-recognition and the quest for a sense of continuity necessary to counteract change. He unbuttons his collar and waistcoat, then removes his collar and necktie, unbuttons his trousers, shirt and vest and lets his fingers, involuntarily exploring the bare area of his stomach, feel "a cicatrice" from a bee sting (*U* 17.1446–9).[9] A "cicatrice" is a scar – Odysseus' scar in verbal disguise – concealed under a cold, impersonal scientific word. The contact of Bloom's fingers with the scar reawakens the memory of the bee sting incident, the way Odysseus' scar touched by Euryclea's fingers revives the story of the boar hunt. To approximate the Homeric *anagnorisis* even more closely, the "Arranger" has Bloom bare his feet as if about to have them washed by an invisible Euryclea: "he disnoded the laceknots, unhooked and loosened the laces, took off each of his two boots for the second time . . . took off his right sock, placed his unclothed right foot on the margin of the seat of the chair, picked at and gently lacerated the protruding part of the great toenail . . ." (*U* 17.1483–9). The words "second time" refer the reader to the almost forgotten first time the protagonist took off "each of his two boots" (*U* 17.111). Two scenes evoking foot-baring are thus linked syntagmatically through the repetition of an identical phrase, "each of his two boots," and stressed by the Interrogator's "for the second time." The "lacerated" toenail (emphasized through repetition, 1489–91) is another instance of mock-wounding. But in Joycean recognition, there is no analogy to Euryclea, nor is there a god to watch gently from afar. Bloom, the modern wanderer, is alone, unhelped by man or god.

As Joyce's protagonist moves from outside to inside,[10] the text takes us from the unlocking scene in the garden to the unlocking of Bloom's private drawers. From public space we are gradually moving into private, intimate space and the wanderings of the mind. The unlocking of the two private drawers takes Bloom's solitary plunge into reconstructive memory one step further. In revealing the contents of the drawers, the author unfolds before us a Homeric catalogue. Among the items Bloom encounters are Milly's and Martha's letters (establishing him as a father and a lover), his birth certificate revealing his second, feminine-sounding name "Paula," the notice of the change of his family name, bank documents, certificates of possession, etc. All are objectifications of his existence, name, assets, and relationships. The anagrams and acrostics Bloom makes with his name evoke the epic theme of making a name and provide yet one more instance of the literalization of the metaphor. The repeated references to Bloom's grandfather and to the change of his name from Virag to Bloom constitute a retelling of the story of Autolycus, who gave his grandson Odysseus his name. Lastly, Bloom comes across a letter from his father, now dead, reading: "To My Dear Son Leopold . . . be kind to Athos" (*U* 17.1881–5). "Athos," the name of Virag's dog, echoes "Argos," the name of Odysseus' beloved hound. But whereas the king of Ithaca restores his identity as a son by visiting his father, Bloom has to search in the contents of a drawer, in the world of memory and the unconscious and among the tokens of the dead, to find a sense of reassurance and some proof that he has been born and loved. Bloom is reaching out to the dead father the way Odysseus tries in vain to embrace the flitting shade of his mother in the Nekyia episode.

The process of accepting reality is often interrupted by attempts to run away from it. Bloom withdraws to his illusory dreamhouse; then, picturing himself stripped of all his possessions, he sets off on an imaginary trip in his desire to escape the mendicant's fate – and his own historicity.[11] His reduction to a beggar is imagined in "descending helotic order" (*U* 17.1936). The use of "helotic order" here is interesting in that it evokes the gynecocratic ancient Spartan society in which there was no adultery. In Sparta the women were in charge of the *oikos* and the economy, whereas the men, most of the time away from home fighting long wars, were respected outsiders. The state's need for warriors made it socially acceptable, even desirable, for a wife to sleep with a helot – a public slave who worked the land – during her husband's absence. Thoughts of this kind must have been in Joyce's mind also since among his unused "Ithaca" notes, as Madtes observes, there is one proclaiming, "Gynecocracy coming" (28). This utopian concept of social structure stands in sharp contrast to the reality that Ithaca, a society constructed around the peacetime institutions of marriage and family, repre-sents. "Helotic order" may be articulating Bloom's masochistic desire for a utopian "order" which, by legitimizing adultery, would allow an escape from oppressive social attitudes and the tyranny of convention. Between the lines, one can also read in this allusion a celebratory freedom from the empty passion of jealous possession that can lead to murder.

But the sense of reassurance Bloom seeks in daydreaming is actually to be found in Molly – symbolically the Great Mother. Peace of mind lies in the complementarity and interdependence that preserves their marriage. The smudging of the boundaries between maleness and femaleness which this chapter promotes produces an impression of such complementarity. As he enters Molly's bedroom, Bloom is struck by the resemblance of her face to "the face of her father, the late Major Brian Cooper Tweedy" (*U* 17.2082), a model of masculinity. The smoothing out of the male/female polarity is maintained by the cross-reference of polytopic words which in Jenny's terms, amplify and "multiply interdiscourse allusions," and admit intertextual elements from the source into the new text (49). As a "drawer of water" (*U* 17.183) Bloom, the "womanly man" of the "Circe" episode, is doubly vested with female attributes, as both words, "water" and "drawer" connote, invoking the element of life and a symbolic container. Another use of the word "drawer" – as in Molly's "drawers" lying on the top of Major Tweedy's "rectangular trunk" (*U* 17.2097–8) – endows her with maleness. On the other hand, "trunk" evokes the trunk of the olive tree around which Odysseus had built his bed. Major Tweedy's association with Molly's bed, which he had brought all the way from Gibraltar,[12] illustrates the way polysemic signifiers scattered throughout the narrative come together to heighten our sense of the contextual and intertextual operation.

Archaic literature is often seen to feminize male heroic characters (or to masculinize heroines) in order to enlarge and expand meaning.[13] Helene Foley has pointed to the effect of the rhetorical figures in the *Odyssey* she calls "reverse similes," which compare Penelope to Odysseus and invert their social roles. The function of these metaphors is to stress the complementarity that guarantees the endurance of the couple's marriage.[14] In Joyce's novel the bond between Leopold and Molly endures, and, for all its emotional and sexual problems, exists as a result of mutual affection and inter-dependence.

Last of all comes Molly's recognition of Bloom, brief and under-stated, as opposed to Penelope's protracted recognition of Odysseus. When at last Bloom "enters" Molly's bed, with Odyssean "circum-spection," "prudently," but also "lightly" and "reverently" (*U* 17.2111–19), his place there is confirmed by Molly's "somnolent recognition" (*U* 17.2248). As in the Homeric epic, the connubial recognition in "Ithaca" is followed by an account of the returning adventurers' wanderings. Bloom buries in silence his erotic experi-ence with Gerty MacDowell in the "Nausicaa" chapter, the way Odysseus leaves the encounter with Nausicaa out of his tale to Penelope. Agamemnon's advice to Odysseus not to give his wife a full account of his story but to tell her only part of it (*Od.* 11.442–3) seems to have worked its way into *Ulysses*. As Penelope helps to restore Odysseus as a husband, recognizing him not by his scar and all the scar stands for, but by the secret of their bed, so Bloom's "recognition" by Molly takes place in bed, symbol of marriage and sexuality. The chapter ends with Bloom regressively assuming a foetal position at Molly's feet, ready for a symbolic rebirth in the womb of Gaia Tellus. Among the descriptions of Gaia Tellus, one should interest us most: "Gaia Tellus: a divinity the same as the earth ... generally represented in the character of Tellus ... She also appeared as holding a scepter in one hand, and a key in the other, ... while at her feet was lying a tame lion without chains ..." (Lempriere 663). While Stephen and Bloom ramble toward an impossible converging of their parallel individual courses, Molly remains the one and only stationary point of return, the very period ending this chapter and all action – the full stop that ends writing. As Penelope is the key to Odysseus' return, so Molly/Tellus holds the key that Bloom lacks when he is away from home and which he uses with mastery when he returns. In sharp contrast with Odysseus, the gore-spattered lion of the famous simile in Book 23 of the *Odyssey*,[15] Poldy enters the bed of the "goddess" meekly and lies at her feet – literally, with his head at her feet – unepic, unheroic, *Leo*pold, a tame lion! In *Ulysses* the heroic code is reinscribed to project a new sense of heroism which celebrates life and is synonymous with modern man's struggle to cope with the limitations of his existence.

Joyce's novel works, of course, on more than the Homeric plane. Its various levels include the symbolic, the literary, the religious, the mythical, the naturalistic, the folkloric. If there is one work, however, which alone can provide and maintain a framework for Joyce's novel, this work is the *Odyssey*. Although the Odyssean order may have been disrupted and telescoped in Joyce's modern epic, the Homeric analogies remain important elements in the forging of meaning throughout the "Ithaca" chapter. Lending itself to modern exploitation, the Homeric tropes of return, disguise and recognition become integral to the structural development of the novel and instrumental to its plot and characterization. Odysseus, a far cry from Achilles, is a new hero who bridges the gap between the tragic and the comic, the ideal and the real. It is exactly this hero's "jocoserious" nature and his capacity to adjust, to endure, and to prevail that make this recasting into the character of Bloom possible. Similarities, antitheses, and reversals produce a critical and playful effect which invests Bloom with epic qualities and makes a modern hero out of Odysseus, illuminating both works. The author replaces, palimpsestically, the mythical and heroic with the pedestrian and commonplace, without erasing the first. Through the intertextual process, concepts such as heroism, adultery, order, marriage and sex roles are modified by means of formal and rhetorical devices and rewritten. After all, return, disguise, and recognition are but metaphors for the very act of reading and writing.

NOTES

1 All English quotations from the *Odyssey* are from the S. H. Butcher and A. Lang prose translation published in 1879. This translation seems to have been the one with which Joyce, not knowing classical Greek, worked. See Seidel 194.

2 Calling attention to the act of reading as a process of revelation, Plato uses the word "anagignosko" (*ana* + *gignosko*), meaning both "reading" and "knowing again," or recognizing. See *Phaedrus* 228e7, 230e5, 234d5.

3 See Baron and Bhattacharya 186–7.

4 Gilbert has pointed to the Parnell/Agamemnon analogy invoked in the "Hades" episode (169).

5 Kenner proposes that it was Boylan who moved the furniture. (See "Molly's Masterstroke" 25.) Rebutting this proposition, Madtes calls attention to Joyce's notes, which proclaim that Molly "will move furniture" (23, 100).

6 On this topic, see Adams 183–4; also, Kenner's essay "Bloom's Chest" and Kimball's "The Measure of Bloom – Again."

7 The relationship between "man" and "wandering" that links the two protagonists in a meaningful way has been pointed out by Senn (127–8).

8 Joyce's tendency in "Ithaca" to "sabotage the climax" is noted by Lawrence (183).

9 More details about the bee incident, vaguely known from previous chapters (*U* 4.483, 6.381, 8.430, 8.625, 13.1143, 15.2412), are now made available to the reader.

10 Seidel has seen an analogy in the parallel motion of Bloom and Odysseus from exterior to interior space (238–49).

11 Teiresias foretells that Odysseus will travel inland after his return to Ithaca. Following Dante, post-Renaissance writers have portrayed the hero as sailing always on a new trip to seek new experiences: "I cannot rest from travel," Tennyson's Ulysses admits; and Nikos Kazantzakis' Odysseus, discontented and uneasy with his quiet life in Ithaca, sails off in quest of freedom.

12 The Molly/Penelope analogy is further enhanced by characteristics the two women have in common. Both come from a sunny place in the South: Penelope from Lacedaemon, Molly from Gibraltar. Both have left their fathers and their warm native birthplace in the Mediterranean to follow their husbands north – Penelope to Ithaca, Molly to

Dublin – and, in keeping with the Joycean spirit, to become themselves exiles in a foreign land. As women, creative and destructive like the Great Mother, they have betrayed a man, the father, to whom they were emotionally attached, to follow another.

13 Typical examples among such heroic figures are Achilles and Heracles, Antigone and Clytemnestra.

14 See Foley 11ff. In one simile Odysseus is compared to a woman weeping over the body of her husband lost in war (*Od.* 8.523–31); in another, Penelope's reputation ("'kleos'" – a word reserved for men) is compared to that of a king (*Od.* 10.108–14); or she is described as a beleaguered lion (*Od.* 4.791–3). Lion similes are otherwise used only for Odysseus.

15 Following the slaughtering of the suitors, Odysseus stands among the bodies of the dead, "stained with blood and soil of battle, like a lion" (*Od.* 23.45–9).

WORKS CITED

Adams, Robert Martin. *Surface and Symbol.* New York: Oxford University Press, 1962.

Austin, Norman. *Archery at the Dark of the Moon: Poetic Problems in Homer's "Odyssey."* Berkeley and Los Angeles: University of California Press, 1975.

Bakhtin, Mikhail. *Rabelais and His World.* Trans. Hélène Iswolsky. Bloomington: Indiana University Press, 1984.

Baron, Naomi S., and Nikhil Bhattacharya. "Vico and Joyce: The Limits of Language." *Vico and Joyce.* Ed. Donald Phillip Verene. Albany: State University of New York Press, 1987. 175–95.

Butcher, S. H., and A. Lang. *The Odyssey of Homer.* London: Macmillan, 1927.

Foley, Helene P. "Reverse Similes and Sex Roles." *Arethusa* 11.1–2 (Spring and Fall 1978): 7–26.

Gilbert, Stuart. *James Joyce's "Ulysses."* New York: Random, 1955.

Hayman, David. *"Ulysses": The Mechanics of Meaning.* Rev. edn. Madison: University of Wisconsin Press, 1982.

Herring, Phillip F. *Joyce's Uncertainty Principle.* Princeton: Princeton University Press, 1987.

Jenny, Laurent. "The Strategy of Form." *French Literary Theory Today.* Trans. R. Carter. Ed. Tzvetan Todorov. Cambridge: Cambridge University Press, 1982. 34–63.

Joyce, James. *Ulysses: The Corrected Text.* Ed. Hans Walter Gabler et al. New York: Random, 1986.

Kazantzakis, Nikos. *The Odyssey: A Modern Sequel.* Trans. Kimon Friar. New York: Simon, 1958.

Kenner, Hugh. "Bloom's Chest." *James Joyce Quarterly* 16 (1979): 505–8.

"Molly's Masterstroke." *"Ulysses": Fifty Years.* Ed. Thomas F. Staley. Bloomington: Indiana University Press, 1974. 19–28.

Kimball, Jean. "The Measure of Bloom – Again." *James Joyce Quarterly* 18 (1981): 201–4.

Lawrence, Karen. *The Odyssey of Style in "Ulysses."* Princeton: Princeton University Press, 1981.

Lempriere, John. *Lempriere's Classical Dictionary*. London: Bracken, 1984.

McGee, Patrick. *Paperspace*. Lincoln: University of Nebraska Press, 1988.

Madtes, Richard E. *The "Ithaca" Chapter of Joyce's "Ulysses."* Ann Arbor: UMI Research Press, 1983.

Plato. *Phaedrus.*

Seidel, Michael. *Epic Geography: James Joyce's "Ulysses."* Princeton: Princeton University Press, 1976.

Senn, Fritz. *Joyce's Dislocations*. Ed. John Paul Riquelme. Baltimore: Johns Hopkins University Press, 1984.

CHAPTER 13

James Joyce and cartoons

Dan Schiff

As a cartoonist interested in the works of James Joyce, I was surprised and delighted to find what appeared to be cartoon characters in the pages of his last two books. When I checked the works of James Atherton, Adaline Glasheen, and other Joyce scholars to see what comments they had made about Ally Sloper and Iky Moses, Mutt and Jeff, Popeye and Olive Oyl, and Mickey and Minnie Mouse, I found little beyond a vague sentence or two. I sought out more about these comic characters and more, generally, about Joyce's ways of drawing on the parallels between comics and characters in his texts. As I researched background material, I found that the information provided about many of these cartoon figures was only partially correct, and that, in some cases, the cartoons had been misidentified.[1] This paper will look at evidence concerning Joyce's exposure to cartoons, examine cartoon characters in *Ulysses* and *Finnegans Wake*, and assess the possible reasons for which Joyce chose to refer to these specific cartoons in his last two novels.

Did James Joyce read the comics? Although there is no sworn deposition from Joyce that he did, there are a few documented instances of Joyce's encounters with cartoons as an adult. On August 19, 1906, a month after he arrived in Rome, Joyce wrote to his brother Stanislaus, "Would you like to see some copies of *L'Asino* – the Italian anti-clerical newspaper" (*Letters* 2: 151). This newspaper was arranged in such a way that anyone reading it would be exposed to the cartoons of Gabriele Galantara. The layout of *L'Asino* is described by Carlo Bigazzi in "Joyce and the Italian Press": "The front and back covers were taken up by two large satirical cartoons in colour, while in the six inner pages the printed texts were interspersed with a number of black-and-white satirical drawings and cartoons" (55). Figure 1 shows another cartoon Joyce mentioned some years later to his brother. In a January 16, 1924, letter

*Warder: " We took you off the oakum picking half an hour ago
and gave you Joyce's " Ulysses " to read. What do you want now ?"
Convict : " More oakum !"*

Figure 1. Cartoon from *Dublin Opinion* January 1924

to Stanislaus, Joyce wrote: "The first caricature of *Ulysses* I saw
appeared in a comic Dublin paper *Dublin Opinion*. A convict has
called the warder. The warder says 'We let you off hard labour and
gave you Joyce's *Ulysses* to read. What do you want now?' The
convict (handing back a large volume): More oakum!" (*Letters*
1: 208).

There is evidence that Joyce was exposed to an American cartoon
through Gilbert Seldes, a popular culture critic who was a supporter
of Joyce's writings and an enthusiast of the comic strip *Krazy Kat*. In
Krazy Kat: The Comic Art of George Herriman, the editors assert:
"Seldes's circle included the renowned literary figures F. Scott
Fitzgerald, e. e. cummings, James Joyce, Ernest Hemingway, and
H. L. Mencken, all of whom were introduced to *Krazy Kat* by
Seldes" (McDonnell 67). An example of Krazy's vocabulary, from a
September 29, 1918, strip, shows the distinctly Wakean flavor of
Krazy's speech: "Thenx 'Mr. Kelly' I will except the infimation
with spid and aleckritty" (McDonnell 137). Critics have noted that

George Herriman's writing style in *Krazy Kat* has similarities to Joyce's work: "He has a way of playing with the meaning and sounds of words which reminds one of James Joyce, not merely for the sake of nonsense, as sometimes intended by the Dadaists, but for the sake of true pleasure in the flexibility of the English language" (Inge 49). Since *Krazy Kat* began as an independent comic strip in October 1913, ten years before Joyce began writing *Finnegans Wake*, one has to list Herriman as a writer whose linguistic experiments prefigure Joyce's.

There are passages in the *Wake* that refer to the cartoon form in general, showing Joyce's awareness of their humor, form and low social standing. A look at earlier draft versions of certain passages indicates that Joyce reworked some sentences in order to include more references to cartoons. For example, the phrase "Such wear a frillick for my comic strip" (*JJA* 60: 75) is expanded into the sentence "Such wear a frillick for my comic strip, Mons Meg's Monthly, comes out aich Fanagan's Weck, to bray at by clownsillies in Donkeybrook Fair" (*FW* 537.33–5). The words "bray" and "clownsillies" underscore the humorous aspects of the comic strip. References to months and weeks suggest the serial nature of the comic strip. Another such phrase is found in the first chapter of *Finnegans Wake*: "Not shabbty little imagettes, pennydirts and dodgemyeyes you buy in the soottee stores" (*FW* 25.2–3). This sentence suggests the "penny dreadfuls," the English nickname for inexpensive comics filled with what some considered small, poorly drawn pictures ("shabbty little imagettes") and hard-to-read type ("dodgemyeyes"). One such "penny dreadful" was the publication *Comic Cuts*, which sold for a halfpenny when it first hit the news-stands in May 1890 (Carpenter 76). This publication was included in the first draft of the passage Joyce wrote (*JJA* 53: 3), and appears as part of a long sentence in the *Wake*: "comic cuts and series exerxeses always were to be capered in Casey's frost book of, page torn on dirty" (*FW* 286.8–10). This passage, like the previous one, refers to both seriality and dirt. One possible reason for the dirt and soot in these passages is that Joyce was making the point that this type of reading material was as common as dirt or considered by many to be filth unsuitable for respectable homes.

One such dirty, disreputable cartoon character is Ally Sloper, who has the distinction of being the only cartoon character who is identified in both *Ulysses* and *Finnegans Wake*. Don Gifford's

"Ulysses" Annotated lists Ally Sloper (and his sidekick Iky Moses) as being "published by Gilbert Dalziel in London on Saturdays in the 1880s and 1890s" (488). While this description is true as far as it goes, it makes Ally Sloper seem more short-lived in popularity than he actually was. The antics of Ally Sloper span forty-seven continuous years of publication, beginning on August 14, 1867, in the *Judy* cartoon, "Some of the Mysteries of the Loan and Discount" (figure 2), and ending with the last of 1,570 issues of *Ally Sloper's Half-Holiday* on May 30, 1914. The *Half-Holiday* was briefly revived in 1914–16 and again in 1922–3 (Carpenter 76). Sloper and Moses were drawn by four different artists over these years. Their originator was Charles Henry Ross, who drew figure 2. Within the year, Ross had his wife Marie Duval ink his drawings. In 1883, Ross sold all published Ally Sloper and Iky Moses material and all rights to their characters outright to publisher Gilbert Dalziel for a single lump sum. Dalziel then began publishing *Ally Sloper's Half-Holiday* on May 3, 1884. American artist W. G. Baxter was hired to draw the covers of the magazine, and the older Ross material was reprinted on the inside. In the 1890s W. F. Thomas took over the job as Ally's artist, and continued in this capacity into the early twentieth century.

Ally had a reputation as a bad egg, a ne'er-do-well, a man who would slope down the alley to avoid paying rent, and particularly as a red-nosed drunk. Figure 3 is a detail of an 1885 W. G. Baxter cartoon found in *Ally Sloper*, a collection of *Half-Holiday* covers. Sloper is drawn in his full alcoholic glory, fully pickled, with a well-oiled head and a sloping brow. Or as the *Wake* puts it, "O little oily head, sloper's brow and prickled ears!" (*FW* 291.26–7). The last phrase may be a reference to the Ally Sloper brand of pickles (one of many items merchandised under the Sloper name), although to my eyes, Ally's nose seems a better candidate for a pickle than his ears (Glasheen 8). It is probably the more exaggerated nose of the type W. G. Baxter drew to which Joyce is referring when he mentions the "Ally Sloper nose" (*U* 15.2152) on the face of a hobgoblin in Nighttown. There are other Ally Sloper references scattered through the *Wake*: "Ali Slupa" (*FW* 319.18), "allied sloopers" (*FW* 288fn.4), "alley english spooker" (*FW* 178.6), "alley loafers" (*FW* 372.20), and "ally croaker" (*FW* 391.15–16), all of which seem to point to this cartoon rogue. Joyce teasingly asks, "Have you got me, Allysloper?" (*FW* 248.10), which is the closest he gets to naming him outright.

As IKY MO and ALLY SLOPER could raise no more
Money on their own account, what was more natural
than that they should start a Loan Office, and lend Money
to Others.

Figure 2. Detail of cartoon by Charles Henry Ross, "Some of the Mysteries of the
Loan and Discount." From *Judy, or the London Serio-Comic Journal* August 14, 1867

With his bald egg-shaped head, Ally Sloper is a cartoon approximation of the Humpty Dumptyish hero of the *Wake*, Humphrey
Chimpden Earwicker. Ally's appearance exclusively in the chapters
that primarily concern HCE's children – "Shem the Penman,"
"The Mime of Mick, Nick and the Maggies," "Nightlessons," and
"Tristan and Isolde" – underscores the perception of Ally as father
figure. And indeed, Ally Sloper in the *Half-Holiday* was made into a
father. As Gifford states in *"Ulysses" Annotated*, "Sloper was represented as constantly embarrassing his family by his bumbling eccen-
tricities and by his predilections for *Friv' girls* and the bottle" (488).
Sloper's disreputable character, combined with his willingness to
try his hand at authoritarian roles such as loan officer, parallels
HCE's fluctuating public persona from hero to villain and back
again.

To the right of Ally, in figures 2 and 3, is Ally's partner in crime,
Isaac Moses or Iky Mo, who got top billing in their first cartoon but
fell eventually to the role of supporting player. Charles Henry Ross

Figure 3. Detail of cartoon by W. G. Baxter, "Some Valentines to Eminent Personages." *Ally Sloper*. Camden: Dalziel Brothers, 1885

first created Iky and Ally with identical noses as figure 2 clearly shows. Later, as W. G. Baxter drew him, Moses has an enlarged nose like Ally, but of a more Semitic bent, and he wears *paot*, the Hasidic sideburns. Iky was a negative Jewish stereotype who hustled money in a slyboots fashion. Figure 3 reveals Iky in a characteristic moment: we see him picking someone's pocket. In *Ulysses* Leopold Bloom is thought by Buck Mulligan to look like Iky Moses. In the National Library, Mulligan picks up Bloom's card and asks, "What's his name? Ikey Moses? Bloom" (*U* 9.607).

Due to the long run of *Ally Sloper's Half-Holiday*, from the time of Joyce's birth through his early thirties, Ally Sloper and Iky Moses are the most likely candidates for cartoon characters Joyce actually saw as a child. It should be noted that although Sir John Tenniel's illustrations in Lewis Carroll's *Alice in Wonderland* were created earlier than the first Ally Sloper, a 1927 letter Joyce wrote to Harriet Shaw Weaver indicates that Joyce was in his forties before encountering the *Alice* books. Of Lewis Carroll, Joyce wrote: "I never read him till Mrs Nutting gave me a book, not *Alice*, a few weeks ago – though, of course, I heard bits and scraps. But then I never read Rabelais either though nobody will believe this. I will read them both when I get back" (*Letters* 1:255). Judging by the abundance of *Alice* material included in the *Wake*, the adult Joyce more than made up for lost time.

Ally Sloper and Iky Moses are not the only cartoon team to appear in *Finnegans Wake*. There are also many variations on the names of American comic strip characters Mutt and Jeff: Jute and Mutt (*FW* 16.10–18.16), Butt and Taff (*FW* 338.5–355.7), Bett and Tipp (*FW* 342.30–1) and Juva and Muta (*FW* 609.24–610.32). Joyce was committed to the use of this comic duo from the very first draft of Book 1's first chapter, which he wrote in 1926 (*JJA* 44: 39). This duo did not start off together, as Sloper and Moses did. First came *A. Mutt*, a strip drawn by H. C. "Bud" Fisher. It began on November 15, 1907, on the racing page of the *San Francisco Chronicle*. For the first months of the strip, Fisher used the same format. In the last panel Mutt would show up at the betting window to wager on a horse, usually one actually running that day at the Emeryville racetrack. In spring of 1908, Mutt was committed to the "bughouse" (a mental institution), where he met a little fellow who was convinced that he was the famous turn-of-the-century boxer Jim

Jeffries. Mutt dubbed the little guy "Jeff," rescued him from the bughouse, and the two have been together ever since.

While Mutt and Jeff were favorites of American papers from this point, the strip did not make it into English or Irish newspapers until the middle of 1918. In an autobiographical piece written for *The Saturday Evening Post*, Bud Fisher recalled how the strip crossed the Atlantic:

The introduction of Mutt and Jeff into London is interesting – at least to me. Ralph D. Blumenfeld, editor of the *London Daily Express*, was in New York, just after the war . . . Mr. Blumenfeld, with some hesitation, agreed to depart from all the accepted customs of British journalism and publish Mutt and Jeff. Waxing enthusiastic myself, I agreed to go to London to start them off, knowing how crazy the English readers are about racing, and feeling I could give them the same sort of stuff I did when I began drawing in San Francisco. In short, this would be tips on the races . . . Having always been interested in racing myself, I felt sure that after studying the English dope sheets a bit I could pick plenty of winners. But I ran into a terrible streak of luck, just the opposite of the great success I had had with my selections in San Francisco. [Blumenfeld] got several violent letters from old subscribers . . . The English write more letters than the readers of American newspapers, and are more vicious about the things they don't like. It eased off some when the *Express* began to publish the straight stuff anglicized . . . Then I undertook to sell Mutt and Jeff to several papers in the British Isles and opened up a syndicate in my vest pocket in London . . . We finally lined up about ten papers in England, Ireland and Scotland, and arranged to have matrices of the strips as they appeared in the *London Daily Express* made and shipped. ("Confession of a Cartoonist" 113–14)

It is more likely that Joyce saw the newspaper strip of Mutt and Jeff from one of these papers than from the harder-to-obtain American ones. And if one looks at the *Mutt and Jeffs* from this time – what Fisher called "the straight stuff anglicized" – a few revealing details emerge. For starters, from the time Mutt and Jeff arrive in London on June 18, 1918, until July 11, 1919, when they receive their discharges, Mutt and Jeff appear in military uniform in virtually every strip. The reason for their uniformed appearance is explained in the June 4, 1918, strip. Jeff says to Mutt: "That was a great idea of ours – me joining the British army and you the American army to promote a good international feeling" (Fisher, "Mutt and Jeff" 7). Joyce's first impression of Mutt and Jeff, if he saw them in English or Irish newspapers, would be that they were cartoon soldiers. The military involvement of Mutt and Jeff during and after the years of the first World War explains the appeal they would have to Joyce as characters who tell the wartime story of Buckley shooting the Russian general (*FW* 338–55). Fisher also mentions Russia and the radical Bolsheviks many times in his strip. For three weeks in March 1919, he ran a strip-within-a-strip entitled "Bolsheviki" in the first panel of the daily *Mutt and Jeff* strip. This tiny strip always had the same punchline: after some minor or imagined offense, Bolsheviki would shoot the person who had produced the insult, screaming "Take that!" (See figure 4 for a detail of a *Mutt and Jeff* strip featuring Bolsheviki, and Mutt and Jeff in military uniform.) The irrational behavior and shooting by a Russian repeated over and over again might have made an impression on Joyce as an additional reason to use Mutt-and-Jeff-like characters for his story of the shooting of a Russian general.

There are other factors that also help explain the appeal of Mutt and Jeff to Joyce. As one of the many variations of opposing brothers Shem and Shaun, Mutt and Jeff represent physical opposites – beanpole Mutt verses little Jeff. The violent physical nature of the strip might have caught Joyce's attention. Fisher often gave the punchline of the joke in the second-to-last panel, and reserved the last panel of the strip for the blackout reaction shot, where Mutt or Jeff, like the central dreaming figure of *Finnegans Wake*, was shown knocked out. Many a Mutt and Jeff strip ended like the conclusion of the "Nightlessons" chapter in *Finnegans Wake*, with one character giving the other a black eye. The association of the strip with the world of horse racing was another appealing element to Joyce. In the second Mutt and Jeff dialogue in the middle of the *Wake*, Joyce alludes to horse racing many times (*FW* 341.21, 342.16–18), and briefly renames the characters "Bett and Tipp" (*FW* 342.30–1). In Book IV, the characters use more betting slang: "*Muta*: Haven money on stablecert? *Juva*: Tempt to wom Outsider!" (*FW* 610.17–18). On the same page the news flash, "Peredos Last in the Grand Natural. Velivision victor. Dubs newstage oldtime turftussle, recalling Winny Willy Widger" (*FW* 610.34–6), makes puns on the names of the famous racehorse Peredos, the Grand National, Waterford amateur jockey J. W. Widger, and calls up images of a horse race with the words "turftussle" and "Winny." All of these racing terms placed in and around the Mutt-and-Jeff-like characters suggest Joyce's familiarity with the comic strip's emphasis on gam-

Figure 4. Detail of a *Mutt and Jeff* cartoon by Bud Fisher, *San Francisco Chronicle* March 22, 1919

bling. It is also a possibility that Joyce featured Mutt and Jeff so prominently because he knew their full names. Figure 5 shows two cartoon strips taken from a series celebrating the forty-fifth anniversary of Mutt and Jeff. An examination of the first and tenth panels reveals the full names of Mutt and Jeff to be Augustus Mutt and James Jeffries. Thus, a conversation between Juva and Muta is between Jeff and Mutt, or, to use their first names, between a James and an Augustus. This coincidence probably would have amused James Augustine Joyce, whose middle name was listed on his birth

Figure 5. Two *Mutt and Jeff* cartoons by Bud Fisher. *Nemo: The Classic Comics Library* December 1984

certificate as Augusta. The wordplay of names makes the conflict
between Mutt and Jeff also a struggle within the name of James
Augustine Joyce. It seems appropriate for the battling twins Shem
and Shaun (which represent two sides of Joyce's personality) to be
given alternative names which simultaneously suggest Joyce. Joyce
might also have been taken with the parallel between Shem and
Shaun, creations of the *Wake*'s central character HCE, and Mutt
and Jeff, creations of *H. C.* Fish*Er* (emphasis mine).

There were other formats besides the comic strip in which Mutt
and Jeff appeared that might have caught Joyce's attention. He
might have seen one of the over 500 silent Mutt and Jeff animated
cartoons produced from 1917 until 1928 (Crafton 198–200). Or
perhaps he saw or heard about the Mutt and Jeff pantomimes that
appeared on the stages of London; this might account for the
script-like format of the Mutt and Jeff dialogues in the book.

Another team of popular American cartoon characters is Mickey
and Minnie Mouse. They are renamed "Micky and Minny Mouse"
in *The Third Census of "Finnegans Wake"* and listed as appearing in the
phrase "Stand up, mickos! Make strake for minnas!" (*FW* 12.24–5).
Was Joyce thinking of what the *Census* dourly calls "Disney's dismal
cartoons" when he wrote this phrase (Glasheen 194)? A look at draft
versions of *Finnegans Wake* reveals that Joyce's original phrase was
even closer to the cartoon characters' names: "Stand up, mickies.
Make leave for minnies" (*JJA* 44: 66). He revised the phrase to the
more enthusiastic "Stand up, mickies! Make stray for minnies!"
(*JJA* 44: 116), before settling on his final version, cited above, which
changes the vowels on the ends of the names. Although this evidence
seems to point toward Joyce's awareness of Disney's mice, an
examination of the dates on which the drafts were written tells a
different tale. Joyce refined the phrase between November 1926 and
its appearance in the October 1927 issue of *transition*. The first
appearance of Mickey and Minnie Mouse was in the animated
short, *Steamboat Willie*, which premiered in the United States on
November 28, 1928. The debut of the film in America occurred a
full year *after* Joyce had published his final revision of the phrase.
European movie theaters, where Joyce could have encountered the
cartoons, did not show the first Mickey Mouse cartoons until the
early 1930s. The citation of Mickey and Minnie Mouse in the *Census*
turns out to be an anachronistic – but startlingly coincidental –
misidentification. What Joyce was thinking about when he wrote

Figure 6. A *Thimble Theater* cartoon by Elzie Crisler Segar

the phrase is not known, but it appears impossible that he was thinking about animated mice.

Neither is there an iron-clad case for inclusion of Olive Oyl, Popeye and their cartoon strip *Thimble Theater* within the pages of *Finnegans Wake*. There is a possibility that the listing of this cartoon is a case of misidentification. *The Third Census of "Finnegans Wake"* lists the phrase "thereby adding to the already unhappiness of this our popeyed world, scribblative!" in reference to Popeye of the *Thimble Theater* (Glasheen 237). However, the *James Joyce Archive* indicates that Joyce had written this by 1924 (*JJA* 50: 392). It was January 17, 1929, five years after this sentence was written, that Elzie Crisler Segar first drew Popeye into his strip (see figure 6), so it would be impossible for Joyce to be thinking of the fighting sailor in this instance. As the *Annotations to "Finnegans Wake"* points out, the other Popeye phrase, "as innocens with anaclete play popeye antipop" (*FW* 13.29–30) also refers to the opposition of Anacletus II, anti-pope to Innocent II, pope (McHugh 13). One could argue that this battle of historical opposites fits better into the theme of Shem and Shaun than a reference to a comic strip character. Popeye's famous expression "I yam what I yam" can be found in the phrase "I yam as I yam" (*FW* 604.23), but as the *Census* notes, it could just as easily be a reference to "I am what I am," proclamations made by Jehovah and Shakespeare. "And a bodikin a boss in the Thimble Theatre" (*FW* 268.15–16) not only refers to the comic strip by name, but also the 1920s New York City experimental dance troupe Thimble Theatre. Joyce could have learned the name from this context through his daughter Lucia or one of her dance associates. In Issy's long footnote (*FW* 279fn.21–3) is the sentence, "How Olive d'Oyly and Winnie Carr, bejupers, they reized the dressing of a salandmon and how a peeper coster and a salt sailor med a mustied poet atwaimen." While this sentence seems to refer to Olive Oyl, a character in *Thimble Theater*, there is an argument that the sentence is an inventory of items in a salad, and the name is a personification of the salad ingredient olive oil.

On the other hand, there are many reasons to think that aside from the 1924 Popeye reference, Joyce was aware that he was incorporating *Thimble Theater* characters into the *Wake*. A look at the *James Joyce Archive* shows that Joyce had plenty of time to discover the *Thimble Theater* and work it into his novel. "And a bodikin a boss in the Thimble Theatre" was written in 1934 (*JJA*

51: 64), fifteen years after the strip first appeared. "How Olive D'Oyly and Winnie Carr bejupers they reized a saladmon and how a peeper coster and a salt sailor med a mustied poet atwaimen" (*JJA* 52: 233) was also written in 1934, five years after Popeye courted and won the heart of Olive Oyl. Although he added a few words to the sentence, the first draft version contains "Olive D'Oyly" and "a salt sailor" together, which strongly indicates to this writer that Joyce was aware of the courtship between the two cartoon characters. The words "popeye antipop" (*JJA* 44: 304) were added to the text between 1937 and 1938, eight to nine years after Popeye's first appearance in the strip. "I yam as I yam" (*JJA* 63: 138) was added during the same time period, which was nearly ten years after Popeye first uttered the phrase on November 6, 1929, and three to four years after the September 29, 1933, debut of "I Yam what I Yam," the first of 105 Fleischer animated Popeye cartoons (Cabarga 181).

Yet another indication that Joyce was thinking about cartoons when he wrote these *Thimble Theater*-related phrases is the placement of these phrases in chapters that contain other cartoon references. In the *Wake*, Joyce would often place similar material close together so that the aggregation of items would make an impression on the reader. "Popeye antipop" (*FW* 13.30) is placed less than three pages away from the first Mutt and Jeff dialogue (*FW* 16.10), and "I yam as I yam" is positioned within five pages of the last one (609.24). The other two phrases are found in Book II, chapter 2, which contains more allusions to different cartoons than any other chapter in the *Wake*.

There are aspects of the *Thimble Theater* that nicely parallel themes in *Finnegans Wake*. Like the *Wake*, *Thimble Theater* centered itself on the exploits of a single family. The *Wake* features the Earwickers; *Thimble Theater* details the comic antics of the Oyl clan. Most people are familiar with Olive Oyl, who was a central part of the strip from the beginning, but she was only the tip of the Oyl iceberg. Olive had a brother, Castor Oyl (who had a wife, Cylinda Oyl), mother Nana Oyl (short for "Banana Oil" – 1920s slang for nonsense), father Cole Oyl, and a boyfriend Ham Gravy. This central cast of characters had a liquidity of name that might have appealed to Joyce, whose Anna Livia is frequently depicted as a river. Joyce placed two of the *Thimble Theater* allusions following the chapter that concerns the children's pantomime. There are theatrical conceits in the strip that help reinforce Joyce's dramatic motif. The daily *Thimble Theater* strips would always run a theatrical title, letting one know what was "Now Showing" and the title of tomorrow's strip, which was the comic-strip equivalent of coming attractions shown in movie houses. Early on, Popeye looked and acted like a cross between the Wakean figures of the Norwegian sailor and the cad with the pipe. Within a matter of months, Popeye stole Olive Oyl away from a ten-year romance with Ham Gravy. In the twenties and early thirties, Popeye spent none of his time on spinach. He preferred shooting craps, cursing, lying and punching anything that moved. In short, the Popeye of the early years had more in common with the lowlife world of Ally Sloper and Mutt and Jeff than the all-American hero he became in later years.

Looking at the cartoon characters Joyce chose to include in his books, a few common denominators can be found. Firstly, the cartoon characters he picked were all humor (as opposed to adventure) strips that were extremely popular with the general public for many decades. The wide popularity of the strips Joyce chose helped to make sure that readers noticed these funny cartoon characters within the difficult chaotic wordplay of the *Wake*. As one reviewer of the *Wake* put it, "In the first section there is a dialogue between two primitive men, Mutt and Jute, whose names relate them, characteristically, to the simple humours of the comic strip" (Glendinning 79). It should be noted that *Krazy Kat*, shown to Joyce by Gilbert Seldes, although a critical success, never had the mass appeal of Ally Sloper, Mutt and Jeff or *Thimble Theater*. This difference might explain why Krazy never materialized in the pages of the *Wake*.

The second common denominator of these cartoons is that each was an important innovator in the medium. Ally Sloper is cited as the first regular character to appear in the British comics, and the 1873 collection of cartoons, *Ally Sloper: A Moral Lesson*, is credited as the first comic book (Carpenter 73). *A. Mutt* had the distinction of being the very first American comic strip to run seven days a week (Blackbeard and Williams 15), and as Bud Fisher noted above, the first American comic strip to appear in English papers. E. C. Segar was a pioneer of the comic "continuity strip," or to put it in Wakean vocabulary, Segar told a "Tobecontinued's tale" (*FW* 626.18) that would contain a joke per day while telling a story with a plot that would last for weeks or months. Comic strip historian Bill Blackbeard cites Popeye as the first cartoon superhero, but adds that of "far greater interest to Segar and most of his readers was Popeye's scrappiness and cheerful contempt for most social conventions, including 'correck' speech" (Blackbeard 96). Like Krazy Kat's lingo, Popeye's humorous, not-quite-English vocabulary is a cartoon approximation of Wakean language. Joyce's use of groundbreaking comic strips in the *Wake* seems appropriate for a work that pioneered new linguistic experiments.

The third common feature of all these cartoons is that each one features adults, not children, as their protagonists. Considering that Victorian and early twentieth-century comics on both sides of the Atlantic were dominated by child-related material (*The Yellow Kid, Buster Brown, Little Nemo in Slumberland, The Katzenjammer Kids, Max and Moritz, Ted and Tod* etc.), one realizes that Joyce carefully picked "adult" cartoons for his last two books. One can postulate a few reasons for his choices. First of all, in relation to *Mutt and Jeff* and *Thimble Theater*, it makes sense that Joyce, when reading comic strips for his own enjoyment, would seek out strips that were written for adults instead of the ones geared for children exclusively. Beyond that, as most of the references to comics are clustered in chapters of the *Wake* which feature the children of HCE, the choice of adult cartoon characters underscores the theme of adult authorities as comic figures.

Lastly, a word concerning the heavy concentration of cartoon references in Book II, chapter 2, of the *Wake*, the "Nightlessons" chapter. To briefly review what was found in this chapter: *Thimble Theater* references on 268.15 and 279fn.21–3, Ally Sloper references on 288 fn.4 and 291.26–7, Mutt and Jeff on 273.18, *Comic Cuts* on 286.8. This chapter also contains more graphics than any other in the book: a bar of music on page 272, a geometrical diagram on page 293, the Doodles family on the bottom of 299, and an open hand and thumb and crossbones at the bottom of 308, the last page of the chapter. The theme of the chapter is education of the children of HCE. The large amount of graphics in the chapter reminds us that children learn from pictures as easily as words. While on one level, the chapter is filled with classical knowledge, there is an equal amount of material focusing on "forbidden knowledge," such as how people procreate. One general drift of the chapter suggests that children can ignore the education that their elders consider worthwhile, and gravitate towards subversive knowledge from which their parents wish to protect them. The picture of the thumbed nose at the end of the chapter expresses much the same contempt for authority as do the cartoons that Joyce chose to highlight in *Finnegans Wake*. All the cartoon characters Joyce selected give their readers the information that adults fight, drink, gamble, cheat, curse, steal and lie. In this way, Ally Sloper and Iky Moses, Mutt and Jeff and the *Thimble Theater* are ideal subversive educators from which HCE's children seem to have learned about the dark side of adult behavior.

NOTE

1 Thanks to the San Francisco Academy of Comic Art, John Lauritz, Mary Alice Wilson of Dark Star Books, Rick Wilson, and Grace Eckley for their assistance in my research.

WORKS CITED

Bigazzi, Carlo. "Joyce and the Italian Press." *Joyce in Rome*. Ed. Giorgio Melchiori. Rome: Bulzoni, 1984. 52–64.

Blackbeard, Bill. "The First (Arf! Arf!) Superhero of Them All." *All in Color for a Dime*. Ed. Dick Lupoff and Don Thompson. New York: Ace, 1970. 96–112.

Blackbeard, Bill, and Martin Williams. *The Smithsonian Collection of Newspaper Comics*. Washington, D.C.: Smithsonian Institution Press, 1986.

Cabarga, Leslie. *The Fleischer Story*. New York: Nostalgia, 1976.

Carpenter, Kevin. *Penny Dreadfuls and Comics*. London: Victoria and Albert Museum, 1983.

Crafton, Donald. *Before Mickey: The Animated Film 1898–1928*. Cambridge, Mass.: MIT Press, 1984.

Fisher, Bud. "Confession of a Cartoonist." *Saturday Evening Post* Aug. 4, 1928: 26ff.

"Mutt and Jeff." Cartoon. *San Francisco Chronicle* June 4, 1918: 7.

Gifford, Don, with Robert J. Seidman. *"Ulysses" Annotated: Notes for James Joyce's "Ulysses."* 2nd edn. Berkeley and Los Angeles: University of California Press, 1988.

Glasheen, Adaline. *Third Census of "Finnegans Wake."* Berkeley and Los Angeles: University of California Press, 1977.

Glendinning, A. "Commentary: *Finnegans Wake*." Review of *Finnegans Wake*, by James Joyce. *Nineteenth Century and After* July 1939: 73–82.

Inge, M. Thomas. *Comics as Culture*. Jackson: University Press of Mississippi, 1990.

The James Joyce Archive. Ed. Michael Groden et al. 63 vols. New York: Garland, 1978.

Joyce, James. *Finnegans Wake*. New York: Viking, 1939.

   Letters of James Joyce. 3 vols. Vol. 1, ed. Stuart Gilbert. Vols. 2 and 3, ed. Richard Ellmann. New York: Viking, 1966.

Ulysses: The Corrected Text. Ed. Hans Walter Gabler et al. New York: Random, 1986.

McDonnell, Patrick, Karen O'Connell, and Georgia Riley de Havenon. *Krazy Kat: The Comic Art of George Herriman.* New York: Abrams, 1986.

McHugh, Roland. *Annotations to "Finnegans Wake."* Baltimore: Johns Hopkins University Press, 1980.

PART IV

Re-reading Joyce: Joyce in his own context

CHAPTER 14

Refining himself out of existence: the evolution of Joyce's aesthetic theory and the drafts of A Portrait

Ian Crump

The aesthetic theory that Stephen Dedalus expounds to Lynch in *A Portrait of the Artist as a Young Man* is James Joyce's most complete expression of the ideas that he first promulgated in his Paris Note-book in March 1903, supplemented in his Pola Notebook in November 1904, and then revised and placed in Stephen Daedalus' mouth in *Stephen Hero* during the spring of 1905. As he prepared the final version, Joyce not only consolidated and amplified these three earlier versions but also redefined the figure of the artist: while in *Stephen Hero* Stephen describes a "man of letters" who regards the other with his "spiritual eye" until it "is epiphanised" in "a sudden spiritual manifestation" (*SH* 211), in *A Portrait* he likens the artist to "the God of the creation [who] remains within or behind or beyond or above his handiwork, invisible, refined out of existence, indifferent, paring his fingernails" (*P* 215). These two figures demarcate the evolution, between "Dublin 1904 / Trieste 1914" (*P* 253), in Joyce's aesthetic ability, which enabled him to fulfill, in the fictional *Portrait*, the intention that he had articulated in his autobiographical essay, "A Portrait of the Artist": to represent his past selves' "individuating rhythm, ... [their] curve of ... emotion," in "a fluid succession of presents" (*JJA* 7: 71).

I

The relation of Stephen's aesthetic theory to *A Portrait* has long been a conundrum for critics, but their efforts to resolve it often reveal more about their own narrative theories than about either Joyce's theory or his novel.[1] Wayne C. Booth, for example, in *The Rhetoric of Fiction*, renews his complaint about the "Confusion of Distance" in the novel (311), which is caused, he believes, by Joyce's pursuit of the impersonality that Stephen advocates. In trying to redeem the "hodge-podge of irreconcilables" of *Stephen Hero* by effacing "the immature narrator" and writing the "authorless" *Portrait*, Joyce took a "way out [that] seems inevitable, but [that] seems a retreat nonetheless: simply present the 'reality' and let the reader judge. Cut all of the author's judgments, cut all of the adjectives, produce one long, ambiguous epiphany" (332–3, 326, 332–3). Booth objects to the chaos of conflicting readings occasioned by Joyce's decisions to provide no warning about his use of irony, to imbue his ironic narrator with his own "subtle and private" norms, and to win our sympathy for Stephen by "bind[ing] the reader tightly to the consciousness of this ambiguously misguided protagonist" (324). Reiterating his belief that "no work, not even the shortest lyric, can be written in complete moral, intellectual and aesthetic neutrality" (329–30), Booth refuses to accept "the absurd assumption that Joyce had in reality purged himself of all judgment by the time he completed his final draft" and accuses him, in effect, of having willfully "resign[ed] his public position" as an author when he revised *Stephen Hero* into *A Portrait*, a work in which "many of the refinements he intended ... are, for most of us, permanently lost" (335, 311, 335–6).

In *Teller and Tale in Joyce's Fiction: Oscillating Perspectives*, John Paul Riquelme tries to resolve Booth's complaint by locating an authority in *A Portrait*. He argues that critics have long misunderstood Stephen's idea of the impersonal or invisible artist-God; all narration requires a "teller," or narrator, and "Impersonality is simply one among [his] many possible disguises" (131). In *A Portrait*, Riquelme writes, "The narrator is *not* invisible" or impersonal, he merely merges with the character (93, 60): as "the teller of his own story," Stephen Dedalus is, "like the purloined letter of Poe's story, ... well-hidden out in the open, where anyone who cares to look can find him" (51–2).

This merging of narrator and character is accomplished, for Riquelme, in "the style which shifts from psycho-narration narrowly conceived toward narrated monologue" and occasionally detours into quoted monologue (54).[2] Reading this style, as it shifts increasingly towards narrated monologue, "The reader translates the third person into 'I,'" yet remains aware of the narrator who renders the character's consciousness in the third person (54). Although an "ambiguous merger of voices [can make] it difficult, even impossible, for the reader to distinguish between the cunningly combined voices of character and narrator" (54), this style allows us to experience Stephen as actor and as writer simultaneously. Riquelme believes that this "subtle intermingling of third- and first-person perspectives that Joyce effects in *A Portrait* is the most significant change in the style of his autobiographical work, one that differentiates it clearly from *Stephen Hero*"(48).[3]

A shared assumption about the nature of narrative underlies Booth's faulting Joyce for rewriting *A Portrait* without the adjectives that would reveal his true judgment of Stephen and Riquelme's foisting an older, more mature Stephen on the novel as a "teller" who resembles Marcel in *A la recherche du temps perdu* (Riquelme 51). They misread this novel precisely because they impose on it their belief that narrative is an act of discourse uttered by a speaker (the author) to an addressee (the reader). Their desire for authority compels them to dismiss or distort Stephen's theory without properly understanding it or its importance for *A Portrait*. Because they do not regard speaking and writing as distinct linguistic acts, as Joyce learned to do when he studied Flaubert's and Mallarmé's aesthetic pronouncements while developing his own,[4] they fail to understand that, by means of writing, an author is able to circumvent the authority of the "I," whose speech is directed at a "you" and confined to the present moment (Banfield, *Unspeakable Sentences* 144), or, as Joyce himself announced in 1903, that "when the Bard begins to write he intellectualises himself" (S. Joyce, *Dublin Diary* 15). Following Flaubert, Mallarmé, and Joyce, theorists interested in the conjunction of linguistics and philosophy, including Roland Barthes, Maurice Blanchot, and Ann Banfield, have continued to elaborate this distinction between speaking and writing, or what they call *écriture*.[5] To understand the relation of Joyce's aesthetic theory to *A Portrait*, then, we must first examine the evolution of the theory to see how he revised, amplified, and clarified it so that it would participate in, but also shape, this larger theoretical tradition.

In *A Portrait*, Stephen's aesthetic theory divides into three parts. In the first part, a streamlined version of the ideas Joyce worked out in the Paris notebook, he defines aesthetic and unaesthetic emotions and reveals, while distinguishing between the arts that elicit these emotions, his distaste for rhetorical art. Like Joyce, Stephen considers desire and loathing to be unaesthetic emotions because they are kinetic ("Desire urges us to possess, to go to something; loathing urges us to abandon, to go from something" [*P* 205]) and the arts which excite such emotions, whether by didactic exhortation or pornographic appeal, to be improper. Pity and terror, on the other hand, are static, and thus aesthetic, emotions because they arrest and raise the mind above desire and loathing, and the art which awakens these emotions is proper (*P* 205–6). In defining proper art, Joyce may have thought of Flaubert's "book about nothing" (154); certainly he anticipated Banfield's "objectivized text" (*Unspeakable Sentences* 222) and Blanchot's "work of art [that] exists all by itself, an unreal thing, ... an imaginary object" free of all props or moorings, which both author and audience apprehend with the passive interest of distance, "A disinterested interest" (137, 136).

   In the second part of his theory, Stephen argues that the beauty of proper art "is beheld by the imagination which is appeased by the most satisfying relations of the sensible ... [thus] The first step in the direction of beauty is to understand the frame and scope of the imagination, to comprehend the act itself of esthetic apprehension" (*P* 208). This act, which entails the three stages or activities whereby the aesthetic object or image creates what Joyce called "the indiffer- ent public" (*SL* 83), appears in three different versions in his works, but only in the third version does the final activity correspond to the stasis that proper art induces. Joyce founded the first version on a phrase from Thomas Aquinas, "*Pulchra sunt quae visa placent*," which he translated as "Those things are beautiful the apprehension of which pleases" (*CW* 147); it concentrates on the pleasure or satisfac- tion experienced by the audience: "the act of apprehension involves ... the activity of cognition or simple perception ... the activity of recognition ... [and] the activity of satisfaction" (*CW* 148). By the time he incorporated the act of apprehension into *Stephen Hero* and, later, into *A Portrait*, he had based it on another phrase from Aquinas, "*ad pulcritudinem tria requiruntur, integritas, consonantia, clari- tas*," which Stephen renders as "*Three things are needed for beauty, wholeness, harmony and radiance*" (*P* 212). He added this second phrase to the first because it enabled him to detail the act more fully and to balance the audience's satisfaction with the qualities inherent in the object. In *Stephen Hero*, Stephen tells Cranly that "First we recognize that the object is *one* integral thing [*integritas*], then we recognize that it is an organised composite structure, a *thing* in fact [*con- sonantia*]: finally, when the relation of the parts is exquisite, when the parts are adjusted to the special point, we recognise that it is *that* thing which it is [*claritas*]" (*SH* 213). He then yokes this *claritas* to the epiphany: when the audience reaches the third activity, recognizing the object for that which it is, "Its soul, its whatness [*quidditas*], leaps to us from the vestment of its appearance. The soul of the commonest object, the structure of which is so adjusted, seems to us radiant. The object achieves its epiphany" (*SH* 213). Yet by including the epiphany here, Joyce distorted the meaning of the act of apprehension: by definition, the epiphany focuses on the "sudden spiritual manifestation" of the other, while "the man of letters" effaces himself so that he might record this manifestation "with extreme care" (*SH* 211); yet in recording his epiphanies, Joyce found, as I will show below, that they betray the egoistic authority that the "man of letters" (*SH* 208) imposes on this other and then mistakes for its *quidditas*. Thus, when he revised this act of apprehension for *A Portrait*, Joyce allowed Stephen to elaborate the three activities he outlines in *Stephen Hero*, but had him replace the epiphany with a biological simile: as the captivated mind apprehends "that supreme quality of beauty, the clear radiance of the esthetic image," it experiences "the luminous silent stasis of esthetic pleasure, a spiritual state very like to that cardiac condition which the Italian physiologist Luigi Galvani ... called the enchantment of the heart" (*P* 213). Galvani coined this phrase to describe the death-like state produced in a frog when a needle inserted in its spinal cord momentarily stops its heartbeat (Gifford 254). In this final version of the act of aesthetic apprehension, then, the "disinterested interest" that the image awakens in its audience becomes a kind of death, which mirrors the impersonality – or "death," as Barthes terms it – of the artist.

In the third part of his theory, Stephen distinguishes the three forms of art and traces the artist's growing impersonality in each form. He begins by announcing that because the aesthetic image

must be set between the mind or senses of the artist himself and the mind or senses of others ... art necessarily divides itself into three forms progressing from one to the next. These forms are: the lyrical form, the form wherein the artist presents his image in immediate relation to himself; the epical form, the form wherein he presents his image in mediate relation to himself and to others; the dramatic form, the form wherein he presents his image in immediate relation to others. (*P* 213–14)

By the phrase "his image," Stephen means "The personality of the artist," which is implicit in every aesthetic image that he tries "slowly and humbly and constantly to express, to press out again, from the gross earth or what it brings forth, from sound and shape and colour which are the prison gates of our soul" (P 215, 207). Following Flaubert, who proclaimed that, into *Madame Bovary*, "I put none of my own feelings and nothing from my own life. The illusion [of truth] (if there is one) comes . . . from the *impersonality* of the work . . . The artist in his work must be like God in his creation – invisible and all-powerful: he must be everywhere felt, but nowhere seen" (229–30), and Mallarmé, who wrote that "The pure work . . . implies the elocutionary disappearance of the poet, who yields place to the words" (Symons 73), Stephen asserts, in a passage which first appeared in the final version of the theory, that, as the artist progresses through the three forms, his personality becomes increasingly impersonal in, or absent from, the aesthetic image that he presents in increasingly immediate relation to "the indifferent public." In the most personal of the three forms, the lyrical, this personality is "a cry or a cadence or a mood"; in the epical form, it "passes into the narration itself, flowing round and round the persons and the action like a vital sea"; and in the dramatic form, the vitality of this personality, "which has flowed and eddied round each person" in the epical form, "refines itself out of existence" as it "fills every person with such vital force that he or she assumes a proper and intangible . . . life" (P 215).

We can clarify Stephen's definitions of his three forms by correlating his progression from authority to impersonality with the process that Barthes and Blanchot separately describe an author undergoing when he writes "he" rather than "I." Stephen's characterization of the lyrical form as "the simplest verbal vesture of an instant of emotion, a rhythmical cry," which, like the opening verses of the "old English ballad *Turpin Hero*," the artist "utters" in the first person (P 214–15), establishes it as discourse.[6] As such, it resembles what Barthes calls transparent classical writing, "through which there passes only the intention to speak" (*Writing* 3, 19), and what Blanchot terms "a bad tale," marred by "an authoritarian and complacent 'I' still anchored in life and barging in without restraint" (134). By writing "he" instead of "I" in the epical form, Stephen's artist progresses, in effect, from discourse to narration, which has a "centre of emotional gravity [that] is equidistant from the artist himself and from others" (P 214–15), but he does not succeed in transcending his authority and becoming impersonal.

Narration is less personal than discourse because it is neither spoken nor heard and cannot be situated with temporal deictics, and so it is used to recount objective knowledge (Banfield, *Unspeakable Sentences* 166, 171, 270), yet as Barthes observes in another context, the author who merely exchanges pronouns attains no more than "the castrating objectivity of the realist novelist" ("Death" 143).

In the dramatic form, Stephen declares, the artist becomes like an invisible and indifferent god who infuses his creations with life. Similarly, Barthes believes that the author who deliberately uses the third person "enters his own death" and creates a writing in which language itself speaks ("Death" 142–3), while Blanchot argues that this author simultaneously accepts his "essential solitude"[7] and develops a writing in which the "he" divides itself: it "becomes the impersonal coherence of a *story* which is performed in the thought of a demiurge ... and in a more visible way it marks the intrusion of character" into the narrative (135).[8] The initial "he" indicates "the *objective* reality" of the narrative which "exists on its own" and is spoken by the other, which cannot speak; the second "he" fills this objective reality with "a constellation of individual lives, *subjectivities*," which Blanchot playfully terms "little 'egos'" (136, 135). Banfield identifies this kind of writing as represented speech and thought (*"Ecriture"* 5–6).[9] Like narration, represented speech and thought has neither a speaker nor an addressee, but, unlike narration, it employs present-time deictics cotemporally with verbs in the past tense (see Banfield, *Unspeakable Sentences* 65ff.). When using represented speech and thought, an author relinquishes his or her authority to the self whose past subjective knowledge he or she apprehends and then re-presents, or makes present again (Banfield, *Unspeakable Sentences* 268); the author thus succeeds in breathing "a proper and intangible life" into this self and in becoming, in the resulting text, as intellectualized – or as impersonalized – to his or her readers as Shakespeare is to his audiences.[10]

II

Although he boasted in 1903 that "when the Bard begins to write he intellectualises himself," Joyce was prevented by his "ineradicable egoism" from putting this belief into practice in his initial attempts to represent his past selves (*JJA* 7: 73). By both provoking him to subvert his own efforts to transcend the succession of presents and the curve of emotion that linked his present self to his past selves and instilling a desire in him to assert his artistic authority by adopting a series of poses, this egoism kept him, as he worked on "A Portrait of the Artist" and then on *Stephen Hero* in 1904 and 1905, from apprehending these selves with the "perfect vision and an angelic dispassionateness" of another dramatist, Ibsen (*CW* 65).

In his first significant pose, which he assumed between 1900 and 1904 when he was copying down his epiphanies, Joyce regarded himself as "a man of letters" (*SH* 208) who, in imitation of Carlyle's hero-poet who possesses such "a great power of vision" that he can "[pierce] as it were down into the heart of Being" (*On Heroes* 121), "seeks to adjust [the] vision" of his "spiritual eye" "to [the] exact focus" at which he can "pierce to the significant heart of" the other, and it "is epiphanised" "in the vulgarity of speech or of gesture or in a memorable phase of the mind itself. He believed that it was for the man of letters to record these epiphanies with extreme care, seeing that they themselves are the most delicate and evanescent of moments" (*SH* 211, 33, 211).

In the following epiphany, Joyce strives to efface himself as the addressee so that he might record Eva Leslie's "vulgarity of speech" "with extreme care":

> [London: in a house at Kennington]
> Eva Leslie – Yes, Maudie Leslie's my sister an' Fred Leslie's my brother – yev 'eard of Fred Leslie? .... (*musing*) ... O, 'e's a whoitearsed bugger ... 'E's awoy at present.......
>   (*later*)
> I told you someum went with me ten toimes one noight .... That's Fred – my own brother Fred .... (*musing*) ... 'E is 'andsome ... O I *do* love Fred .... (*JJA* 7: 35)

Eva's speech here is coarse and contradictory; in recording this epiphany, Joyce must have thought that he had captured the "*quidditas*" of an uneducated prostitute. Yet in it he betrays his egoistic authority which he imposes on her: as the present, but silent "you," he not only listens to but encourages the discursiveness of the "I," while as the recorder, he reveals, in his choice – and exclusion – of information, his preconceived desire to apprehend Eva as coarse and contradictory.

By January 7, 1904, when he scrawled out "A Portrait of the Artist" in his sister's copybook in Dublin, he had revised this pose into that of "The poet" who, as "the intense centre of the life of his age," brings "spiritual renewal" to his nation by "absorbing in himself the life that surrounds him and ... flinging it abroad again amid planetary music" (*SH* 80, 192, 80). He remained fond of this new pose for several years, writing to Nora in 1912 that "I am one of the writers of this generation who are perhaps creating at last a conscience in the soul of this wretched race" (*SL* 204), yet it marred his efforts to represent his past selves in "A Portrait of the Artist" and *Stephen Hero*.

In trying to represent, in his essay, "the natural sensibility of the subject of this portrait" (*JJA* 7: 71), Joyce hoped to intellectualize himself by grammatically distancing his present self from his past selves: he writes of them in the third person and uses passive constructions and indistinct assertions: "About this period the enigma of a manner was put up at all corners to protect the crisis"; "It was part of that ineradicable egoism which he was afterwards to call redeemer that he imagined converging to the deeds and thoughts of the microcosm" (*JJA* 7: 72–3). Yet although he begins by using present-time deictics with verbs in the past tense ("He *was* quick enough *now* to see that he must disentangle his affairs in secrecy and reserve had ever been a light penance" [*JJA* 7: 73; my emphases]), his artificial intellectualization disintegrates before he finishes the essay. First, during his past self's apostrophe to the girl on the strand, he lapses into discourse – thus collapsing the temporal distance between his past and present selves, while maintaining their common curve of emotion – because he still could not represent this moment without reliving it: "Dearest of Mortals! ... How could he thank *thee* for that enrichment of soul by *thee* consummated? ... A kiss: and they *leap* together ... Again, beloved! Again, *thou* bride! Again, ere life *is ours!*" (*JJA* 7: 81–2; my emphases). Then, in the last lines of the essay, he tries to forge the uncreated conscience of his race by appealing kinetically to his Irish readers: "Man and woman, out of you comes the nation that is to come, the lightning [sic] of your masses in travail" (*JJA* 7: 84).

Less than a month later, on the night of his birthday, Joyce informed his brother that he was planning to rewrite this essay, which the editors of *Dana* had rejected, as narrative fiction (*JJ* 147). As he began the novel, *Stephen Hero*, he tried to overcome the problems he had had with his discursive authority in the essay simply by transforming the anonymous "he" into Stephen Daedalus and by using represented speech and thought with increased skill.

Throughout the extant manuscript, he consistently matches present-time deictics with past-tense verbs and, except for a sentence in the Mullingar episode, the earliest written section of this manuscript, which he writes as discourse (*"you are* ... to conceive Stephen Daedalus packed in the corner of a third-class carriage and contributing the thin fumes of his cigarettes to the already reeking atmosphere" [*SH* 237–8; my emphasis]), his few errors are either lapses which he crossed out (a sentence in which he wrote "us" [*SH* 79]) or experiments: he uses the second person in a paragraph on pages 205–6 in an attempt to represent Stephen's impression of the speeches of the "embassy of nimble pleaders" the Church sends him (*SH* 204), while in the following paragraph, he tries to represent pronunciation ("Cranly occasionally swore at his *flamin'* cue" [*SH* 207; my emphasis]).[11]

Yet despite these efforts, Joyce still could not intellectualize himself. Stung by the rejection of his essay, which merely reinforced his image of himself as the solitary artist, mocked and misunderstood by the very people he believed he could spiritually renew, he found solace by subsuming his identity into his protagonist's. According to Stanislaus, he began what he called his "lying autobiography and raking satire" (*Dublin Diary* 25), "half in anger, to show that in writing about himself he has a subject of more interest than [the] aimless discussion" of the editors of *Dana* (quoted in *JJ* 147).[12] He further identified himself with Stephen by freely plundering the essay of sentences and scenes for the novel: when he writes of Stephen's timidly liberal schoolmates, "They admired Gladstone, physical science and the tragedies of Shakespeare: and they believed in the adjustment of Catholic teaching to everyday needs, in the Church diplomatic" (*SH* 172), he repeats the irony that he had directed at his own fellow students in "A Portrait of the Artist" (*JJA* 7: 74); the anonymous injunction, in the essay, against a student's attending a performance of *Othello* because "There are some coarse expressions in it" [*JJA* 7: 75]), he attributes, in the novel, to the president of the college (*SH* 29); and to elucidate Stephen's situation among his peers, he appropriates an image which he had applied to himself not only in the essay but in "The Holy Office" as well: "Behind the rapidly indurating shield the sensitive answered: Let the pack of enmities come tumbling and sniffling to my highlands after their game. There was his ground and he flung them disdain from flashing antlers" (*SH* 34–5).[13] Joyce completed his self-reinvention as "his hero [when] he announced his intention of appending to the end of the novel the signature, *Stephanus Daedalus Pinxit*" (*My Brother's Keeper* 244).[14]

In adopting this newest pose as he worked on *Stephen Hero*, Joyce once again collapsed the temporal distance between his past and present selves, while maintaining their shared curve of emotion. This collapsing often caused him to confuse his present moment of consciousness with the past moments that he intended to represent as Stephen's. With a change of verb tense in a sentence added in pencil to the beginning of chapter 24,[15] for example, he unwittingly reveals that he has adopted his protagonist's misogyny: "Stephen *wished* to avenge himself on Irish women who, he *says*, *are* the cause of all the moral suicide in the island" (*SH* 200; my emphases). Because of this confusion of consciousnesses, Stephen's consciousness ceases, at many points, to be the novel's controlling structural principle, as in the passage on pages 210–11 in which Joyce represents Stephen's uncomprehending anger at women, his belated vengeance on Emma for rejecting his offer to "live one night together" (*SH* 198), and his discovery of the method of the epiphany. While writing this passage, he proved so unwilling to investigate the fears implicit in his protagonist's – and, hence, his own – ideas about "marsupials" that he abruptly altered its direction by representing Stephen's desire for an end to "the misty Irish spring" and then his reaction to the colloquy, overheard in Eccles Street, that inspires him to write "a 'Vilanelle [sic] of the Temptress'" (*SH* 211). Yet reminded by this colloquy of the theory of the epiphany, Joyce again altered the direction of the paragraph by having Stephen – who is suddenly transported across the Liffey to the Ballast Office – detail it for Cranly. In the meantime, Joyce forgot to have him quote the villanelle.

The pose that caused this confusion of consciousnesses ultimately led Joyce to confuse his narrative authority with the authority arrogated by Stephen, who brashly asserts, "My own mind ... is more interesting to me than the entire country" (*SH* 248). Throughout *Stephen Hero*, Joyce legitimates Stephen's opinions as objective knowledge by using narration to recount them. Here, for instance, is the description of Mr. Hughes, the Irish language teacher:

He never lost an opportunity of sneering at seoninism and at those who would not learn their native tongue. He said that Beurla was the language of commerce and Irish the speech of the soul ... Everyone regarded Mr

Hughes as a great enthusiast and some thought he had a great career before him as an orator. On Friday nights when there was a public meeting of the League he often spoke but as he did not know enough Irish he always excused himself at the beginning of his speech for having to speak to the audience in the language of the ... "Spiritual Saxon." (*SH* 59–60)

In exposing Mr. Hughes's intellectual hypocrisy, Joyce neglects to indicate that this is Stephen's view of the man; in fact, he does not even make clear whether Stephen is in the classroom, observing Hughes, at the moment of this narration.

In the late summer of 1907, Joyce decided to rewrite *Stephen Hero*, which he had put aside two years earlier when its problems had become insurmountable, as the five-chapter *Portrait*. Because there are no surviving manuscripts that can be conclusively dated to between 1907 and 1911, when, according to Hans Walter Gabler, Joyce threw what was probably "an intermediate manuscript of *Portrait*" into the family stove (*JJA* 8: ix), and because, between 1911 and 1914, he apparently destroyed these "charred remains of the MS" (*SL* 247) after copying them out, with probable revisions, as the final holograph manuscript,[16] we cannot determine what "agonies of Art" he may have suffered while drafting *A Portrait* (Flaubert 179). We can only guess that he formulated the simile of the artist-God and added it to the novel after 1909, since he does not mention it in his "Alphabetical Notebook," and before the fall of 1912, when, because of his work on his *Hamlet* lectures, he began to be interested in Shakespeare as a figure for the artist.

When he likened the artist to, rather than identifying him as, "the God of the creation," Joyce did not assume yet another pose, that of the authoritarian Yahweh; rather, he indicated that he had transcended his egoism and achieved the intellectualization that he had first imagined for himself in 1903. While writing the final draft of *A Portrait* in Trieste, he refined himself out of existence so that he could disinterestedly apprehend his past selves' consciousness and then relied almost exclusively on the authority-less technique of represented speech and thought to re-present this past consciousness, in "a fluid succession of presents," as that of the fictional Stephen Dedalus:[17] "*Now* that the play *was* over his nerves *cried* for some further adventure"; "*Now*, as never before, his strange name *seemed* to him a prophecy"; "Cranly, *now* grave again, *slowed* his pace ... " (*P* 85, 168, 247; my emphases). He even used this technique when he wrote the inquit-tags because he wished to represent how Stephen hears speech: note, for example, the childlike repetition of the interlocutors' names when Nasty Roche asks Stephen about his name and his father (*P* 9).

Joyce decided, however, not to limit himself to represented speech and thought as he represented Stephen's consciousness in a style which modulates to conform accurately to both its growth and its mutability. Instead, he shifts from represented speech and thought to interior monologue, an authority-less technique that is structured discursively, but is not discursive, to indicate, as Chester G. Anderson points out, "the disturbance that ... enuresis causes in the stream of Stephen's consciousness" (146): "When *you wet* the bed first it *is* warm then it *gets* cold" (*P* 7; my emphases). He also filters Father Arnall's second sermon through Stephen's imagination to reveal its impact on him: he feels "Every word of it was for him" (*P* 115).[18] And he presents Stephen's thoughts as discourse whenever he wants to show him talking to himself ("She too wants me to catch hold of her, he thought" [*P* 70]) and concludes the novel with Stephen's diary to show that, as an artist, he remains doubly ensnared by his desire to be a discursive authority and his inability to communicate with anyone other than himself.[19]

It is precisely because Joyce employed represented speech and thought when he wrote *A Portrait* that readers such as Booth and Riquelme have difficulty with it. By using this authority-less technique, he succeeded, after ten years, in producing a novel which no longer permits us, its readers, to receive the author's univocal or definitive message, but rather forces us to apprehend, or interpret, the multiple, and often conflicting and unconscious, messages that emanate from Stephen's unstable authority. Joyce worked so long to restructure literary authority in *A Portrait* – or, to borrow Stephen's language, to detonate in his novel "the first of [his esthetic] explosives" (*SH* 81) – because he believed that the Irish could only achieve true political independence once they had achieved their independence as readers. And in learning to employ these authority-less techniques in *A Portrait*, Joyce prepared the groundwork for the even more subversive techniques of *Ulysses* and *Finnegans Wake*.

NOTES

1 For a recent discussion of the "aesthetic distance" controversy that has focused on this relationship, see Mahaffey 26–9 and 55–6n.
2 Riquelme borrows these terms from Cohn, who coined them to

differentiate among "the three modes of presentation of consciousness
... in the context of third-person narration" (14). Psycho-narration
refers to "the narrator's discourse about a character's consciousness"; it
is often used with inarticulate characters because it can render, "in a
narrator's knowing words, what the character 'knows,' without
knowing how to put it into words" (14, 46). Narrated monologue
renders "a character's thought in his own idiom while maintaining the
third-person reference and the basic tense of narration" (100). Quoted
monologue is her term for "a character's mental discourse" which
occurs in the first person and in the present tense (14; Riquelme 54).
3 Reinhart, another critic who adopts Cohn's terminology, argues that
the apparent "shift from the omniscient narrator's point of view in
[Stephen Hero] to Stephen's point of view in [A Portrait] ... is only
partially true" for, despite our "clear feeling that in Stephen Hero
Stephen speaks in the narrator's language while in Portrait it is the
narrator who speaks in Stephen's language," "the narrator uses the
same style as his character in both texts" (63, 74).
4 Between 1899 and 1904, Joyce read Flaubert's correspondence, Arthur
Symons's The Symbolist Movement in Literature, and at least some of
Mallarmé's essays. From the correspondence he realized that writing
need not be referential: "What seems beautiful to me, what I should
like to write, is a book about nothing, a book dependent on nothing
external, which would be held together by the strength of its style, just
as the earth, suspended in the void, depends on nothing external for its
support" (Flaubert 154). In Symons, he read that the Symbolists
desired "to spiritualise literature, to evade the old bondage of rhetoric
... Description is banished that beautiful things may be evoked" (5)
and that Mallarmé intended "To evoke, by some elaborate,
instantaneous magic of language, without the formality of an after all
impossible description; to be, rather than to express" (71). Joyce
probably also knew Mallarmé's assertion, "Nommer un objet, c'est
supprimer les trois-quarts de la jouissance du poème qui est faite de
deviner peu à peu: le suggérer, voilà le rêve" (quoted by Hayman 1: 51).
See Hayman, especially 1: 51–69, for a discussion of Mallarmé's influence on Joyce's early writings.
5 See Barthes, Writing Degree Zero and "The Death of the Author";
Blanchot, "From Dread to Language," "The Essential Solitude," and
"The Narrative Voice (the 'he,' the neuter)" in The Gaze of Orpheus;
and Banfield, Unspeakable Sentences and "Écriture, Narration and the
Grammar of French."
   These three theorists share the assumption that writing is not equiv-
alent to speech. Barthes writes, "All modes of writing have in common
the fact of being 'closed' and thus different from spoken language.
Writing is in no way an instrument for communication" (Writing 19).
Blanchot argues that the narrative voice belongs to the other, which

cannot speak, since "when the other speaks, no one is speaking, because the other ... is never precisely the other, rather it is neither one thing nor the other, and the neuter [the "he"] that indicates it withdraws it from both, as from the unity, always establishing it outside the term, the act, or the subject where it claims to exist ... It is the narrative voice, a neuter voice that speaks the work from that place-less place in which the work is silent" (141). For Banfield, "It is writing which frees language from [the present] moment and [the] communicative relationship and which allows the creation of a fictional NOW completely separate from the real linguistic act which creates it and creation of a fictional SELF separate from any writing *I*. This is because the present of the writer and presence of his linguistic point of view may be silenced in writing" (*Unspeakable Sentences* 242).

6 Although lyric art and the improper arts are both discursive, lyric art is apostrophic, or "*over*heard," to borrow Mill's description of poetry (109), whereas the improper arts are rhetorical – they urge their audience to an action.

7 Blanchot describes the author's "essential solitude" as neither the solitude he experiences as he writes, which is "self-communion," nor the solitude of "I am alone," which is an act of communication; rather, it is the solitude he attains when, by inscribing "he" instead of "I," he relinquishes all authority over his writing and loses the power to speak or to make others speak (63, 3, 69).

8 Barthes also uses this metaphor of the demiurge (*Writing* 30) for what Blanchot calls "The narrative (I do not say narrating) voice" (141).

9 Other names for represented speech and thought are *style indirect libre*, or free indirect discourse, *erlebte Rede* ("experienced speech"), and Cohn's "narrated monologue"; Banfield rejects these terms as inadequate (*Unspeakable Sentences* 277–8n).

10 Joyce presumably used "the Bard" as a figure for the impersonal artist because readers have long searched his works in vain for his opinions on monarchism, Jews, the Irish question and other contemporary issues. In *Ulysses*, he redefined Shakespeare as a figure for the artist who is scriptively present and authorially absent in his art.

11 Banfield argues that, because represented speech is written and silent, it "can make no attempt to render the phonetic"; she dismisses examples such as "flamin'" as "cases of partial quotation ... without the quotation marks" (*Unspeakable Sentences* 249, 115).

12 For a discussion of *Stephen Hero* as autobiography, see Tobin.

13 In the essay, Joyce writes, "But behind the rapidly indurating shield the sensitive answered. Let the pack of enmities come tumbling and sniffling to the highlands after their game – there was his ground: and he flung them disdain from flashing antlers. There was evident self-flattery in the image but a danger of complacence too" (*JJA* 7: 73). As part of his identification with his protagonist, he omitted this last,

238   IAN CRUMP

harshly self-analytical sentence from *Stephen Hero*. In "The Holy
Office," he writes: "I stand the self-doomed, unafraid, / Unfellowed,
friendless and alone, / Indifferent as the herring-bone, / Firm as the
mountain-ridges where / I flash my antlers on the air" (*CW* 152).

14 Joyce also signed several letters during the summer of 1904 with his
protagonist's name or initials (see *SL* 21–2).

15 This chapter number appears as 25 in the New Directions edition of
Stephen Hero because Theodore Spencer, the editor, misnumbered the
chapters as [15] to 26 rather than as [15] to 25 (see Gabler, "Seven Lost
Years" 55).

16 There is no agreement on the compositional chronology of *A Portrait*.
According to Ellmann, Joyce completed the first three chapters of *A
Portrait* by April 1908, but he did not finish the final two chapters until
early 1914 (*JJ* 270, 355). On the other hand, Gabler claims that the
novel "reached the state of an intermediary manuscript during 1907 to
1911," when it was burned; then, "In 1913–14, the novel was completed" ("Seven Lost Years" 25).

17 For other discussions of authority in *A Portrait*, see Lane and Mahaffey,
especially 15–16 and 53–103.

18 Joyce's use of the second person and the present tense in the following
sentence from the sermon does not violate the rules of represented
speech and thought because, again, it is discourse heard by Stephen:
"*O you* hypocrites, O *you* whited sepulchres, O *you* who *present* a smooth
smiling face to the world while *your* soul within *is* a foul swamp of sin,
how will it fare with *you* in that terrible day?" (*P* 114; my emphases).

19 For another reading of Joyce's apprenticeship, see Brown.

WORKS CITED

Anderson, Chester G. "Baby Tuckoo: Joyce's 'Features of Infancy.'"
Approaches to Joyce's "Portrait": Ten Essays. Ed. Thomas F. Staley and
Bernard Benstock. Pittsburgh: University of Pittsburgh Press, 1976.
135–69.
Banfield, Ann. "*Ecriture,* Narration and the Grammar of French." *Narra-
tive: From Malory to Motion Pictures.* Ed. Jeremy Hawthorne. London:
Arnold, 1985. 1–22.
Unspeakable Sentences: Narration and Representation in the Language of Fiction.
Boston: Routledge, 1982.
Barthes, Roland. "The Death of the Author." *Image-Music-Text.* Trans.
and ed. Stephen Heath. New York: Hill, 1977. 142–8.
Writing Degree Zero. Trans. Annette Lavers and Colin Smith. New York:
Hill, 1967.
Blanchot, Maurice. *The Gaze of Orpheus and Other Literary Essays.* Trans.
Lydia Davis. Ed. P. Adams Sitney. Barrytown, N.Y.: Station Hill,
1981.

Booth, Wayne C. *The Rhetoric of Fiction.* 2nd edn. Chicago: University of Chicago Press, 1983.
Brown, Homer Obed. *James Joyce's Early Fiction: The Biography of a Form.* 1972. Hamden, Conn.: Archon Books, 1975.
Carlyle, Thomas. *On Heroes, Hero-Worship and the Heroic in History.* London: Oxford University Press, 1904.
Cohn, Dorrit. *Transparent Minds: Narrative Modes for Presenting Consciousness in Fiction.* Princeton: Princeton University Press, 1978.
Ellmann, Richard. *James Joyce.* Rev. edn. New York: Oxford University Press, 1982.
Flaubert, Gustave. *The Letters of Gustave Flaubert, 1830–1857.* Trans. and ed. Francis Steegmuller. Cambridge, Mass.: Harvard University Press, 1980.
Gabler, Hans Walter, ed. *"A Portrait of the Artist as a Young Man": A Facsimile of Epiphanies, Notes, Manuscripts, and Typescripts.* Vol. 7 of *The James Joyce Archive.* 63 vols. New York: Garland, 1978.
    ed. *"A Portrait of the Artist as a Young Man": A Facsimile of Manuscript Fragments of "Stephen Hero."* Vol. 8 of *The James Joyce Archive.* 63 vols. New York: Garland, 1978.
    "The Seven Lost Years of *A Portrait of the Artist as a Young Man.*" *Approaches to Joyce's "Portrait": Ten Essays.* Ed. Thomas F. Staley and Bernard Benstock. Pittsburgh: University of Pittsburgh Press, 1976. 25–60.
Gifford, Don. *Joyce Annotated: Notes for "Dubliners" and "A Portrait of the Artist as a Young Man."* 2nd edn. Berkeley and Los Angeles: University of California Press, 1982.
Hayman, David. *Joyce et Mallarmé.* 2 vols. Paris: Lettres modernes, 1956. Vol. 1.
Joyce, James. *The Critical Writings of James Joyce.* Ed. Ellsworth Mason and Richard Ellmann. New York: Viking, 1959.
    A Portrait of the Artist as a Young Man. New York: Viking, 1964.
    Selected Letters of James Joyce. Ed. Richard Ellmann. New York: Viking, 1975.
    Stephen Hero. Ed. John J. Slocum and Herbert Cahoon. New York: New Directions, 1963.
Joyce, Stanislaus. *The Dublin Diary.* Ed. George Harris Healey. Ithaca: Cornell University Press, 1962.
    My Brother's Keeper. Ed. Richard Ellmann. New York: Viking, 1958.
Lane, Jeremy. "His Master's Voice? The Questioning of Authority in Literature." *The Modern English Novel: The Reader, the Writer, and the Work.* Ed. Gabriel Josipovici. London: Open, 1976. 113–29.
Mahaffey, Vicki. *Reauthorizing Joyce.* Cambridge: Cambridge University Press, 1988.
Mill, John Stuart. *Mill's Essays on Literature and Society.* Ed. J. B. Schneewind. New York: Collier, 1965.

Reinhart, Tanya. "Reported Consciousness and Point of View: A Comparison between Joyce's *Stephen Hero* and *A Portrait of the Artist as a Young Man*." *PTL: A Journal for Descriptive Poetics and the Theory of Literature* 4 (1979): 63–75.

Riquelme, John Paul. *Teller and Tale in Joyce's Fiction: Oscillating Perspectives*. Baltimore: Johns Hopkins University Press, 1983.

Symons, Arthur. *The Symbolist Movement in Literature*. New York: Dutton, 1958.

Tobin, Patricia. "A Portrait of the Artist as Autobiographer: Joyce's *Stephen Hero*." *Genre* 6 (1973): 189–203.

CHAPTER 15

Entering the lists: sampling early catalogues

Fritz Senn

Most epic works contain, at some point or other, lists of various kinds where, often, the action is halted to take time out for stocktaking or for pertinent information, all in one separate place. Some works are known for their lists and insertions: the *Iliad* with its ships' catalogue or Rabelais come to mind. Joyce is a modernist addition to *that* list. Occasionally catalogues threaten to take over and to usurp the narrative.

One might generalize that Joyce's works became more cataloguic as he went along. It is easy to find catalogues proliferating in the second half of *Ulysses* – think of the interpolations in "Cyclops," the many splurges in "Circe," and of course most of "Ithaca." In *Finnegans Wake* they thrive no less: one whole chapter (1.6) is arranged as twelve strange questions and twelve odd answers, of which the first one amounts to the longest list in the whole canon. One might say, in strategic exaggeration, that *Finnegans Wake* sets off with a catalogue of "not yets" in its second paragraph, and that its end formally drifts into a list formed on a phonetic pattern: "A way a lone a last [a lost][1] a loved a long the." *Ulysses* and *Finnegans Wake* are among the first modern works, certainly prose works, to become cataloguized into Word Lists, Concordances, Handlists. They were, it seems, asking for it.

The field is wide and promising, it expands in pace with our curiosity and involvement. For the present purpose, this probe or quick survey limits itself to a few observations *en passant*; they are wholly empirical, marks on a page, so to speak, about early Joycean listings, without even trying to define what a catalogue (list, enumeration, inventory, etc.) may be, but with questioning glances at the border lines. Therefore the far more rewarding area of conspicuous and attention-clamoring catalogues in the more parodistic, later, chapters of *Ulysses* and those of *Finnegans Wake* is left aside, in favor of the much simpler but already exemplary ones in the less "experimental," less extravagant earlier works and passages. No methodical approach has been attempted, but cautious and provisional generalizations are possible.

You do not expect many lists in Joyce's poetry, or in the epiphanies, nor do they abound in *Dubliners*. A minor cluster in *Chamber Music* poem 15 may qualify, but it will hardly be experienced as a catalogue:

> From dewy dreams, my soul, arise,
> From love's deep slumber and from death.

Still, there it is, a small list of items, with alliterative connection: dewy dreams, love's deep slumber, and death. Three items, and it probably takes at least three of them to make up a list; so maybe the serial adverbs in the third stanza can be adduced:

> While sweetly, gently, secretly,
> The flowery bells of morn are stirred
> And the wise choirs of faery
> Begin (innumerous!) to be heard.   (*CP* 23)

After "sweetly, gently, secretly" the stanza becomes a trifle anticlimactic, the prominent anteposition has ironic (perhaps intended?) effects: so much emphasis detracts from the nature of "gently"; while "secretly" appears to get more highlight than befits its meaning. The parenthetical "innumerous" with its exclamation in the last line draws attention to enumeration itself, which has mutely invaded the poem.

We find the minimally required three items in other lists; in "An Encounter" Joe Dillon "had a little library made up of old numbers of *The Union Jack, Pluck* and *The Halfpenny Marvel*" (*D* 19). A short list, but possibly a complete one, matched by the paper-covered books in the house of North Richmond Street: "*The Abbot*, by Walter Scott, *The Devout Communicant* and *The Memoirs of Vidocq*" (*D* 29). Those belonged to a priest about whom we know next to nothing; but the reading list tempts us to guess at some personal profile. Lists of possessions characterize. "A Painful Case" sets the scene with an itemization of Mr. Duffy's monastic interior: "a black iron bedstead, an iron washstand, four cane chairs, a clothes-rack, a coal-scuttle, a fender and irons and a square table on which lay a double desk" (*D* 107). Few superfluities, no decoration; the bare list evokes a room as well as a way of life. On the whole, lists in *Dubliners* – like the singers of the past in "The Dead": "Tietjens, Ilma de Murzka, Campanini, the great Trebelli, Giuglini, Ravelli, Aramburo" (*D* 199) – do not tend to distract us from the stories themselves. Few seem to come to mind at once; they are integrated into the stories; we have to look for them. One, at least, is implied but out of sight. Mrs. Kearney is adept at the "disposing of items for a programme": "She knew what *artistes* should go into capitals and what *artistes* should go into small type" (*D* 138). Catalogues are a matter of "disposing of items," including their shape and, above all, their order.

In *A Portrait*, in contrast, several catalogues call out for attention and are neatly separable from their surroundings. The names of Christian Brothers form a first, short, list of clergy (and of possible Irish fates and futures):

> – Brother Hickey.
> Brother Quaid.
> Brother MacArdle.
> Brother Keogh. (*P* 166)

From a collective of such names, unique ones like "Dedalus" "Stephanos" or even "Bous Stephanoumenos" can take off all the more portentously. The next list in line is a "box of pawntickets" in the squalid kitchen, at the opening of chapter 5, as Stephen idly takes up

> in his greasy fingers the blue and white dockets, scrawled and sanded and creased and bearing the name of the pledger as Daly or MacEvoy.
> 1 Pair Buskins.
> 1 D. Coat.
> 3 Articles and White.
> 1 Man's Pants. (*P* 174)

That reading would be enough to bring any fledgling Daedalus after his ecstatic outburst, the climax of the preceding chapter, down to earth again. Following the discovery of his own mythical auspicious name, the assumed cover identities in a pawnshop, Daly and MacEvoy, cheap disguises, may be no less disenchanting.[2] This particular catalogue tells its story of poverty, each docket freezes a minor domestic calamity ("buskin" has overtones of tragedy). A tacit escalation takes us from more dispensable items like shoes and coat to pants, a vital garment no man would ever like to be without. Lists may have their own code, here a vocabulary of pawning with the abbreviation "D." or "Articles and White." "3 Articles" indicates a subsidiary list not worth detailed specification.

Stephen, with an active sense of humor, is the inventor of one of the most amusing parts within the whole novel, in answer to Cranly's "What was he?"

Stephen began to enumerate glibly his father's attributes.
– A medical student, an oarsman, a tenor, an amateur actor, a shouting politician, a small landlord, a small investor, a drinker, a good fellow, a storyteller, somebody's secretary, something in a distillery, a taxgatherer, a bankrupt and at present a praiser of his own past. (*P* 241)

Stephen's paternal catalogue is devised for effect (and is received well: "The distillery is damn good"): it moves from potential professions to habits and roles or idiosyncrasies. The individual items tend to get longer; the modifiers function quite differently ("shouting" is definitely not in line with "medical," "amateur" or "small"). We find patterns and subpatterns, a cluster of echoing word forms: "tenor, actor, investor" trailing into "drinker, storyteller, taxgatherer, praiser"; there are internal links ("small landlord – small investor," "somebody's ... something"), repetition as well as variation: "taxgatherer" seems to clash with "bankrupt." Then there is the typical provective[3] increase towards the end; the concluding item, introduced by the habitual "and" at the end of a list, comprises more words and is of a different build (pitting "present" against "past"). As we know from the novel's first line, Simon Dedalus initiates the novel *as* a story-teller and proves himself, within it, a praiser of times past: "Once upon a time and a very good time it was ..." More comic potential emerges once we remember that some entries would also apply to the author himself, who certainly became a recorder of his own past, or its recreator. The work we read is a result.

The terminal phrase is the adaptation of a classical tag, Horace's "*laudator temporis acti*" from the *Art of Poetry*. Stephen's enumeration acquires another dimension when we realize that Horace's well worn phrase in turn occurs *within* a catalogue of its own. The subject is the "manners/characteristics of each age" (*aetatis cuiusque ... mores*); they are then elaborated, Old Age coming naturally last: "many ills encompass an old man"; the subsequent list of them includes a string of nouns and adjectives: "*dilator ... iners avidusque futuri, difficilis, querulus, laudator temporis acti se puero, castigator censorque minorum*" (he is "dilatory ... sluggish and greedy for longer life, peevish, surly, given to praising the days he spent as a young boy, and to reproving and condemning the young"). So Horace's listing of the ages of man, with its sketchy portrait of an old man *for* the artist, is plugged into Stephen's improvised series. Even more appropriately, the whole divergence serves the purpose of telling poets to note these manners of each age and, technically, to give "a befitting tone to shifting natures and their years" – "*aetatis cuiusque notandi sunt tibi mores, / mobilibusque decor naturis dandus et annis*" (*Ars Poetica* 462–5).[4] In other words, Horace's precept is precisely what Joyce did to his own evocation of the attributes of each age, up to the state of "a young man" – and did so with unaccustomed, radical, literalness, adapting diction and style and point of view to each single phase.[5] By calling up classical quotation, the wording "a praiser of his own past" celebrates its own literary descent.

Not all catalogues are formally visible and as easily detachable. It would be a matter of definition whether the following listing deserves the label; it is, if anything, a submerged catalogue in narrative dispersion:

On all sides distorted reflections of her image started from his memory: the flowergirl in the ragged dress with damp coarse hair and a hoyden's face who had called herself his own girl and begged his handsel, the kitchengirl in the next house who sang over the clatter of her plates with the drawl of a country singer the first bars of *By Killarney's Lakes and Fells*, a girl who had laughed gaily to see him stumble when the iron grating in the footpath near Cork Hill had caught the broken sole of his shoe, a girl he had glanced at, attracted by her small ripe mouth as she passed out of Jacob's biscuit factory, who had cried to him over her shoulder:
– Do you like what you seen of me, straight hair and curly eyebrows? (*P* 220)

This moves from frustration over the addressee of the villanelle ("her image") to a review of past encounters, under some unstated heading of "girl" or "woman remembered." Something analogous will happen later in "Proteus" at the sight of two women which induces a diffused list of womanhood in multiple variations: "*Frauenzimmer* ... mighty mother ... midwife's bag ... Mrs Florence MacCabe, relict ... Bride Street ... sisterhood" all the way to "Heva, naked Eve" (*U* 3.30–41). Progressively this was to lead to the widest dispersion, all those thematic chapter colorings of vocabulary, the concurrent overlays, that put wind into "Aeolus," music into "Sirens," or river names into ALP.

If we want, we can interpret the Hell Fire Sermon, as detailed in chapter 3, as a carefully constructed catalogue of infernal atrocities, with a methodical composition of place, all rhetorically amplified and embellished. One of its consequences on Stephen is the devoted translation of each whole week into a spatial and devout order and disposition: "Sunday was dedicated to the mystery of the Holy Trinity, Monday to the Holy Ghost, Tuesday to the Guardian Angels, Wednesday to Saint Joseph, Thursday to the Most Blessed Sacrament of the Altar, Friday to the Suffering Jesus, Saturday to the Blessed Virgin Mary" (*P* 147). Such rigid dedication is not likely to last long, and chapter 4 is in turn dedicated to the breakdown of the compulsive order in favor of presumed freedom and creation. At a decisive stage, the transition from "planting his steps scrupulously in the spaces of the patchwork of the footpath" to "then timing their fall to the fall of verses" (*P* 164) seems to illustrate the direction from space to time, from scrupulous[6] steps to falls, from patchwork to verses, in later terminology from spatial *Shaunitas* to temporal *Shemness*. Typically, when Stephen then meets what looks like the spectre of a past that is to be put behind, a squad of Christian Brothers, marching orderly, in "two by two," he relegates them to the dull list of names (of next-to-no individualities) which was mentioned above (*P* 166).

Literary works may well start out of lists, jottings of material perhaps to be used. Joyce's often did, as many volumes of notes for *Ulysses* and for *Finnegans Wake* testify. Some of this process is rehearsed in *A Portrait*, when the incipient artist awakes from troubled sleep to an instant of morning inspiration, and three lines of verse pass "from his mind to his lips" and, later, on to the cardboard surface of a pack of cigarettes. Once the resolution is made to extend them to a villanelle, a number of technical problems arise since the verse form requires a repetitive auditory grid. Stephen has already matched "ardent ways" with "enchanted days"; and this, as though by itself, leads to a tiny repertoire of possible echoes within the language: "The roselike glow sent forth its rays of rhyme; ways, days, blaze, praise, raise. Its rays burned up the world" (*P* 218). Imperceptibly the "rays" sent forth in the introductory phrase have become part of the subsequent list, and are carried on after its closure. Sound alone determines the candidates for the catalogue: "That is how poets write, the similar sounds" (*U* 8.64). All of the rhyme words will in fact be assimilated into the finished poem, whose step-by-step composition seems to illustrate how artefacts may depend on spontaneous inspiration and on systematic efforts.

The catalogues in the early parts of *Ulysses*, those of the so-called "initial style," with "realistic" intent and appearance, are low key and relatively short, at least when contrasted with the grotesque outgrowths of the chapters with conspicuous stylistic programs. Some are integrated into the action, or taken from the environment, as when Bloom, looking at his *Freeman's Journal*, is "scanning the deaths: Callan, Coleman, Dignam, Fawcett, Lowry, Naumann, Peake, what Peake is that? is it the chap was in Crosbie and Alleyne's? no, Sexton, Urbright" (*U* 6.157–60). The list of the deaths is neat, factual, presumably complete, unembroidered, therefore uneventful in itself and in the likeness of alphabetic obituary notices – disrupted only, but remarkably, by Bloom's intrusive attempt to identify one of the names. True-to-life lists often need some such diversion to avoid inherent monotony. Typically, Bloom has no great curiosity about the "deaths" but uses them to occupy himself in momentary embarrassment, after a failure to be accepted by his funeral companions. Ordinary, everyday, purely informative catalogues are easily tedious, intended as they are for consultation at need rather than leisurely reading; for literary uses they have to be livened up.

The Homeric equivalent to the "Hades" chapter, the *Nekuyia* (book 11), is well known for its long catalogues, when Odysseus reports about all the famous dead heroes he has seen. Such sprawling catalogues always invite critical speculation, also because epic interest tends to lag, and in this case some scholars consider them inferior, later interpolations, suitable as they are for practically unlimited insertions. This has been a view in particular about the List of Famous Women in Hades ("and the women came") where there is a uniform pattern ("and then I saw Antiope") etc. followed by biographical sketches of various length; this for more than a hundred verses (*Od.* 11. 225–332). Readers may (and will) skip them. Joyce does not imitate these long lists, which take up practically the greater bulk of the *Nekuyia* (he makes up for that in "Ithaca"); Bloom's scanning of the deaths seems to be the only analogy, a rather muted one at that, together with some casual reading of gravestone inscriptions.

The various names, however, may come in useful as material for

fictitious sub-epics. When Bloom covers his letter to Martha Clifford
with a businesslike front, "Messrs Callan, Coleman and Co,
limited" (*U* 11.896), he summons a company that conveniently
arises from the dead. Many of Joyce's fictions, we know, have grown
out of newspapers, or out of that indispensable compendium of the
British Empire, Ireland, and Dublin that consists of nothing but
catalogues, *Thom's Dublin Directory*.

Some pristine embedded lists hardly register, as when Mulligan
ceremoniously blesses "thrice the tower, the surrounding land
[country] and the awaking mountains" (*U* 1.10–11). The more
artful ones are memorable, and once more Buck Mulligan starts the
game, in priest's tone introducing "the genuine christine: body and
soul and blood and ouns" (*U* 1.21–2). This may make us wonder
whether a double pairing is meant with subgroups ("body and soul"
added to "blood and ouns") or a fourfold enumeration. In typical
manner, the last item tends to be slightly odd for dramatic effect:
"ouns" is unfamiliar, obsolete, lexically different, a truncated form
(from "wounds"), occurring mainly in oaths; it may well need a
gloss – a deviation from the pattern already established. It is also
what breathes life into the series. Without special knowledge, it may
often not be possible to distinguish ingredients in a catalogue from
subgroups. In "The oval equine faces, Temple, Buck Mulligan,
Foxy Campbell, Lanternjaws" (*U* 3.111–12), we may surmise four
different persons. Only a passage in *A Portrait*, "the face of one of the
jesuits whom some of the boys called Lantern Jaws and others Foxy
Campbell" (*P* 161), can tell us that the last two are alternatives. The
string of three persons in four designations contains submerged lists
of potential contours, like "faces – Temple – jaws"; or an ecclesiastical current in "Temple – Buck Mulligan (his role at the book's
opening)" and the twice nicknamed jesuit. A possible or even likely
mistake in identification fits the Protean concern with deceitful,
dissimilar appearances for the same entity. The internal organization of lists is not always immediately evident.

Memory often comes in the shape of nascent enumeration:
"Folded away in the memory of nature with her toys ... Her glass of
water ... A cored apple ... Her shapely fingernails" (*U* 1.265–8). A
more extended catalogue occurs in the evocation of the church with
its pomp and its heretics:

A horde of heresies fleeing with mitres awry: Photius and the brood of
mockers of whom Mulligan was one, and Arius, warring his life long upon

the consubstantiality of the Son with the Father, and Valentine, spurning Christ's terrene body, and the subtle African heresiarch Sabellius who held that the Father was Himself His own Son. (*U* 1.656–60)

We find a structure parallel to the conventional windup: the last item getting more weight, a distinctive flourish. Sabellius is equipped with the epithet and title "the subtle heresiarch" – not just a heretic, but a ruler over them – and he gets the only relative clause to himself. These are conventional devices that signal a rhetorical closure.

In the "Nestor" chapter, more catalogues surface, understandably in connection with History, the presiding Muse and schematic Art of the episode. Historical sources are often lists of heroes, conquests, achievements – or debts. Stephen mentally runs through his:

Mulligan, nine pounds, three pairs of socks, one pair brogues, ties. Curran, ten guineas. McCann, one guinea. Fred Ryan, two shillings. Temple, two lunches. Russell, one guinea, Cousins, ten shillings, Bob Reynolds, half a guinea, Koehler, three guineas, Mrs MacKernan, five weeks' board. (*U* 2.255–9)

In some sense, the "one pair brogues" continues and modifies "1 Man's Pants" from the listing of pawning tickets in the previous work, wearing apparel given in pawn or had on loan. Certain things, it appears, do not change easily.

Mr. Deasy, expert on historical causes, comes up with a neatly analogous fourfold catalogue of the Evil Doings of Woman:

A woman brought sin into the world. For a woman who was no better than she should be, Helen, the runaway wife of Menelaus, ten years the Greeks made war on Troy. A faithless wife first brought the strangers to our shore here, MacMurrough's wife and her leman, O'Rourke, prince of Breffni. A woman too brought Parnell low. (*U* 2.390–4)

The list is well constructed, the last sentence echoing the initial one. There is enough variation to counteract monotony: the second sentence changes subject, verb (departing from "brought") and word order; the third one substitutes "wife" for "woman." It is as though Mr. Deasy were to supplement Hesiod's *Catalogue of Women* ("Pardoned a classical allusion") with that of his own, Famous Guilty Women. A few chapters later the attentive reader may come to add a fifth character to the chain, Mrs. Deasy: "and I knew his wife too. The bloodiest old tartar God ever made" (*U* 7.532–3); her

nomination is due to history of a sort: "The night she threw the soup
in the waiter's face" (*U* 7.534). She may be the underlying cause for
Deasy's catalogue of causation, which retrospectively turns out to
be, whatever else, an extended *argumentum ad feminam*. Poetic justice
seems to be exerted when Mr. Deasy's letter, unquestionably a
discursive one with all the garrulous embroidery of which we get
glimpses, is practically reduced to a catalogue in Stephen's hasty
scanning: "May I trespass ... Our cattle trade. The way of all our
old industries ... European conflagration ... Rinderpest ... Mr
Henry Blackwood Price ... Allimportant question ..." (*U*
2.324–36). In like manner Bloom first glances "down the page" of
Milly's letter: "Thanks: new tam: Mr Coghlan: lough Owel picnic:
young student: Blazes Boylan's seaside girls" (*U* 4.280–2), before he
reads it slowly and with care later on.

Mr. Deasy, a lover of horses like *Nestor hippodamos* (*Od.* 3.17, et
passim), sports "vanished horses" on his wall for Stephen to read:
"lord Hastings' *Repulse*, the duke of Westminster's *Shotover*, the duke
of Beaufort's *Ceylon, prix de Paris*, 1866 (*U* 2.300–3). The listing tells
its story of racing triumphs, as well as that of wealth, aristocracy and
British ascendancy, and is also a reflection on Irish history. By a
coincidence of names, "*prix de Paris*" links the race horse to the
mythical causation of the Trojan war, behind the story of Helen
herself, who was the prize awarded to Paris, heroine of a classical
French triangle. At a critical moment, she stood outside the Trojan
horse and nearly jeopardized the Greek strategy (*Od.* 4.271–89).

No Helen has been awarded to Stephen yet, and even his young
well-to-do students may be better off: "With envy he watched their
faces: Edith, Ethel, Gerty, Lily" (*U* 2.36). The mini-list of imaginary companions is patterned: all names are dissyllabic, the first two
beginning with the letter which, the *Portrait* told us, is a meaningful
initial for Stephen, the last two having the same (common) ending.
Similarly, Bloom tries to guess at the meaning of a pen name:
"A. E.: what does that mean? Initials perhaps. Albert Edward,
Arthur Edmund, Alphonsus Eb Ed El Esquire" (*U* 8.527–9). Such
probing lists tend to run through possibilities that come to mind. In
typical manner, Stephen's is artfully constructed (frustration turned
into a pleasing shape), Bloom's inceptive, inquisitive, experimental.
By their catalogues shalt thou know them.

Bloom, after all, is introduced to us *by* a list, that of his food
preferences: "the inner organs of beasts and fowls. He liked thick

giblet soup, nutty gizzards, a stuffed roast heart, liverslices fried with crustcrumbs, fried hencods' roes. Most of all he liked grilled mutton kidneys" (*U* 4.1–4). If you try to articulate this menu you will find that your tongue in your palate has to move around those consonant clusters as if you were to taste these delicacies – the list is imitative, gustatory. Again, the last item is given special limelight by constituting a separate sentence, with an unexpected final tang: "Most of all he liked grilled mutton kidneys which gave to his palate a fine tang of faintly[7] scented urine" (*U* 4.3–5). Bloom, incidentally, also exits from the book in a catalogue, a conspicuous one which takes us from "Sinbad the Sailor" all the way to "Xinbad the Phthailer" (*U* 17.2322–6), a farewell example of a catalogue *per se*, in self-perpetuating permutation. Joyce introduced Odysseus to Frank Budgen through a catalogue of applied versatility: "Ulysses is son to Laertes, but he is father to Telemachus, husband to Penelope, lover of Calypso, companion in arms of the Greek warriors around Troy and king of Ithaca ... Don't forget that he was a war dodger ... But once at the war the conscientious objector became a jusqu'auboutist ... he was the first gentleman in Europe ... He was an inventor too" (Budgen 16–17).

Catalogues may be external – Bloom appears to read street legends: "Towers, Battersby, North, MacArthur: parlour windows plastered with bills" (*U* 4.236–7) – or internal: he mentally composes a list of "the cities of the plain: Sodom, Gomorrah, Edom" (*U* 4.222). A factually "correct" and complete list would borrow three more cities from Genesis (14: 2–3) and omit Edom, the odd one. Bloom is of course not answering an exam question but shifts from Sodom, it seems, to an Old Testament place of similar sounds. Edom is biblically connected with the cities of the plain, through "Also Edom shall be a desolation ... As in the overthrow of Sodom and Gomorrah and the neighbour cities thereof, saith the Lord" (Jer. 49: 17–18): so some knowledge is in Bloom's mind, the transition makes sense. Internal catalogues branch out in all directions.

The interior monologue has no obligation to the supposed heading of a list. "God wants blood victim. Birth, hymen, martyr, war, foundation of a building, sacrifice, kidney burntoffering, druids' altars" (*U* 8.11–13). A mental recall of examples may deviate and change tracks. By the end of an enumeration, its earlier purpose may have been lost sight of; "kidney burntoffering" or "druids' altars" may or may not have something to do with blood, in

historical fact or in Bloom's mind ("A kidney oozed bloodgouts ..."
[4.145]). The list has acquired a momentum of its own. At times,
even the much more pedantic and quasi-scientific catalogues of
"Ithaca" behave in similarly psychological manner. Gliding catalogues could be contrasted with rigid ones.

   A simple stocktaking of breakfast requirements – "Kinch, wake
up! Bread, butter, honey ... Where's the sugar? O, jay, there's no
milk" (U 1.334–6) – is hardly noteworthy, except that we get a
glance at the morning's bill of fare and an impression of relative
comfort. More interesting is the tone of the exclamation, which is
not at all obvious until we begin the paragraph following right
afterwards: "Stephen fetched the loaf and the pot of honey and the
buttercooler from the locker." We now realize that Mulligan's
enumeration was not so much an inventory as a command, which
Stephen – oddly enough in light of his tribulations, some moments
before, about becoming the "server of a servant" (U 1.312) – silently
obeys without internal protest. The action of the second paragraph
helps to determine the voice of the one before, an implicit stage
direction is trailing behind.

   In the third chapter, in a mental try-out catalogue Stephen
Dedalus, writer à la recherche du mot juste, is testing near-synonyms
from various languages for the best descriptive effect: "She trudges,
schlepps, trains, drags, trascines her load" (U 3.392–3); arguably
this also reflects on the procedure of the author of "Proteus" himself.
Note is taken of "fourworded wavespeech: seesoo, hrss, rsseeiss,
ooos" and its possible transcription, as well as the literal fixation of
related noise: "flop, slop, slap" (U 3.456–8).

   Of all the early chapters, the seventh, "Aeolus," contains the most
catalogues; it is also the one with most affinities to the second half of
Ulysses: the overtly intruding headlines/captions suggest some sort of
external, editorial, agency that interferes with the established
manner of storytelling. Its action begins, right away, with a parallel
enumeration of possibilities of motion: "Before Nelson's pillar trams
slowed, shunted, changed trolley, started ..." Around a fixed and
stable point, Nelson's pillar, the city's geometrical center, trams
change speed and direction. At another level we may notice that this
is true of Ulysses; after two monolinear tracks that followed first
Stephen, then Bloom, the plot slows, shunts, changes direction, with
new starts and many new personal destinations. But our catalogue
has only just begun, "started" initiates an exfoliating subgroup: "...

for Blackrock, Kingstown and Dalkey, Clonskea, Rathgar and Terenure, Palmerston Park and upper Rathmines, Sandymount Green,
Rathmines, Ringsend and Sandymount Tower, Harold's Cross." A
few lines later we learn that this list is not superimposed, or need not
be, but is what we would hear if we were present, the words of a
"Dublin United Tramway Company's timekeeper" who, by now
hoarse from the exertion, bawls off these names and is to add more
destinations:

– Rathgar and Terenure!
– Come on, Sandymount Green! (*U* 7.1–9)

The double triad of the first six chapters has been highlighting one
individual character each; "Aeolus" now focuses on the city and on
collectivity. Cities consist of areas and suburbs that have to be
connected; traffic may be more noticeable than single people. No
one character is on scene during the whole episode. It does not seem
to matter whether the initial cluster of names would actually be
heard by anyone standing by, or whether a suburban inventory is
silently called up by the narrative itself. The view is a wide-angle
one, and lists are one of its suitable expressions. The chapter implies
that there are usually numerous alternatives (the timekeeper's
options indicate, for example, that there is more than one way to
reach Rathmines), and so it puts them on the map. The chapter
doubles back on itself, towards the end, the initial catalogue is
balanced by a corresponding one, this time in neutral third-person
narrative:

At various points along the eight lines tramcars with motionless trolleys
stood in their tracks, bound for or from Rathmines, Rathfarnham, Blackrock, Kingstown and Dalkey, Sandymount Green, Ringsend and Sandymount Tower, Donnybrook, Palmerston Park and Upper Rathmines, all
still, becalmed in short circuit.

This is "circuit" indeed, a recirculation of most, though not all,
destinations, but a short circuit that paralyzes motion. In pointed
contrast to the "motionless trolleys," a list of vehicles that are not
dependent on electricity, the great technological advance of the
period, and are therefore able to move, is appended: "Hackney cars,
cabs, delivery waggons, mailvans, private broughams, aerated
mineral water floats with rattling crates of bottles, rattled, rolled,
horsedrawn, rapidly"[8] (*U* 7.1043–9). Catalogues of this sort

(especially with phonetic effects forming a sublist: "rattling ... bottles, rattled, rolled ... rapidly") can give an impression of bustling metropolitan traffic that is perceived mainly as a series in quick succession. Likewise lists are generally skimmed over without too much detailed concentration, unless one particular stands out, such as the heavily burdened "aerated mineral water floats with rattling crates of bottles" (significantly, again, the list within the list), the noisiest vehicle of them all. This is a close-up full of slightly jarring oddities; it is not of course the floats that are aerated, but the mineral water they carry; the air contained in "aerated" does not surround the float but is carbon dioxide within the bottles within the crates on the floats; the collocation "water floats" may be momentarily distracting. Perhaps the "Hackney cars" that open the enumeration make us remember a characteristic of the chapter in which tired or common use has been made of the venerable rhetorical forms of the past, and of language in general.

So the seventh chapter is inflated with catalogues; after the tramlines and their southern directions, we find another vital communicative service with even more far-flung destinations: "... His Majesty's vermilion mailcars ... received loudly flung sacks of letters, postcards, lettercards, parcels, insured and paid, for local, provincial, British and overseas delivery" (U 7.16–19). The four possible deliveries seem to repeat the official wording as it might be visible on letter boxes, they form a neat classification of the entire known world, a systematic and all-inclusive list. "Aeolus" makes a show of all-inclusiveness. One section, entitled "OMNIUM GATHERUM," is devoted to it: "All the talents ... Law, the classics ... The turf ... Literature, the press ... The gentle art of advertisement ... And Madame Bloom ... The vocal muse" (U 7.605–9). The daily press aims to be comprehensive, including "Nature notes. Cartoons. Phil Blake's weekly Pat and Bull story. Uncle Toby's page for tiny tots. Country bumpkin's queries. Dear Mr Editor, what is a good cure for flatulence? ... The personal note. M.A.P. Mainly all pictures. Shapely bathers on golden strand. World's biggest balloon. Double marriage of sisters celebrated ..." (U 7.94–9). As the editor emphasizes: "Put us all into it, damn its soul. Father, Son and Holy Ghost and Jakes M'Carthy" (U 7.621–2). Clearly the identification of Jakes M'Carthy (as a minor Irish journalist of the time, it appears) is far less relevant than the animation his name lends to the Holy Trinity, which is already supremely complete in itself, and the sidelight a word like "Jakes" can throw on it. Ritual texts spell out the same: "And then the lamb and the cat and the dog and the stick and the water and the butcher. And then the angel of death kills the butcher and he kills the ox and the dog kills the cat" (*U* 7.210–13).

Most appropriately for this episode, when a vision is put into words and a professional press man asks for a title, no less than three are offered for choice – "Call it: *Deus nobis haec otia fecit. –* No ... I call it *A Pisgah Sight of Palestine* or *The Parable of the Plums*" (*U* 7.1056–8) – and each one of the alternatives can give the story a different direction and co-determine its meaning. On a smaller scale, a faint humorous effect depends on a string of synonyms, Lenehan's "Reflect, ponder, excogitate, reply" (*U* 7.514–15), almost in parody of the chapter's penchant for enumeration. Professor MacHugh provides a series of derivatives, "Rome, imperial, imperious, imperative" (*U* 7.485–6),[9] and then a comparative study of "Material domination. *Domine!* Lord! ... Lord Jesus? Lord Salisbury? ... *Kyrios!* Shining word! ... *Kyrie!* ... *Kyrie eleison!*" (*U* 7.557–64). Stephen again marshals rhyme words ("South, pout, out, shout, drouth. Rhymes ... *pace* ... *piace* ... *tace*") and personifies them: "by three, approaching girls, in green, in rose, in russet, entwining" (*U* 7.715–21). Dan Dawson's speech, critically commented on, could be seen as a concatenation of stereotypes, some of them predictable. Useful handbooks were in circulation that listed impressive turns of speech and poetical phrases.

As is common knowledge by now, Joyce in turn infused the episode with close to a hundred rhetorical figures, as handed down from antiquity, something for which he would have to have recourse to one of their many listings. After the fact, Joyce collaborated with Stuart Gilbert on such a list, a fitting way to explain some of the chapter's aspirations. One of these figures, termed "Synathroesmus," is glossed as "accumulation by enumeration"; its example is, naturally, the listing of "Law, the classics, literature, the press" etc. (as adduced above [7.605–7]).[10] Quintilian, the arch-cataloguer, briefly refers to "the figure styled συναθροισμος," where "a number of different things are accumulated – *plurum rerum est congeries*" (3: 278–9). A number of different things are in fact accumulated in "Aeolus," that most confusing chapter for novices (who might well be helped by a list of all the characters passing through its pages).

The Aeolean subheadings themselves, chancy and off-center and

256 FRITZ SENN

unreliable as they may be, can serve as a device to handle the whole chapter into a list.

Some final remarks on the last chapter. Though it does not qualify as "early," it looks like a nostos to the initial manner, it is also the most homogeneous of all. In pointed contrast to the preceding "Ithaca" chapter, which strives towards becoming all cataloguic, "Penelope" does not. It does not seem to afford the breaks, the necessary pauses that often separate a list from its surroundings, or its single items from each other. In Joyce's distribution of roles, list-making seems to be a male activity, men are cataloguers; "duumvirate," after all, put its pompous mark on the "Ithaca" chapter in the second question already. Male fascination with the power of imposing order is mimicked. Not that Molly could not generate lists too, say about strange names:

Dedalus I wonder its like those names in Gibraltar Delapaz Delagracia they had the devils queer names there father Vilaplana of Santa Maria that gave me the rosary Rosales y OReilly in the Calle las Siete Revueltas and Pisimbo and Mrs Opisso in Governor street O what a name Id go and drown myself in the first river if I had a name like her O my and all the bits of streets Paradise ramp and Bedlam ramp and Rodgers ramp and Crutchetts ramp and the devils gap steps. (U 18.1463–9)

The efforts do not get very far, there is constant interference of comment and exclamation with an energetic gush that works against the uniformity of systematic catalogues. Molly never descends to mere enumeration, her vitality infuses even a string of persons linked by "and": "I was thinking of so many things he didnt know of Mulvey and Mr Stanhope and Hester and father and old captain Groves and the sailors playing all birds fly" (U 18.1582–4). Her monologue ends with rhapsodic lists that are experienced more as rhapsody than as lists, "O and the sea the sea crimson sometimes like fire and the glorious sunsets and the figtrees in the Alameda gardens yes and all the queer little streets and the pink and blue and yellow houses and the rosegardens and the jessamine and geraniums and cactuses and Gibraltar" (U 18.1598–1602). A representative and basic list pattern hardly has a chance to emerge, and no monotonous regularity ever takes over, and of course it is almost impossible to separate a catalogue neatly from its surroundings, which was, after all, one of the characteristics throughout.

The sampling given has been sketchy, a mere first glance round, assembling the kind of passages that one might underline and provide with marginal notes as a start. The notes would have to be sifted and arranged in some order. Joycean catalogues could and no doubt will be classified according to, for example, their function and formal properties. There are isolated, clearly visible – "boxed" – kinds, and others that need to be disentangled. Some are integrated, others stand out, some are predetermined or closed (like the seven days of the week), others inherently open-ended, wholly expandable. One might investigate what separates the various items, and the closure devices. Some catalogues are straightforward and consistent, others preen themselves in playful contortions, many slip into their own parodies.

This then is an invitation to other scholars with more systematic minds to enter the lists.

NOTES

1 The end was changed from "and then a walk along the" to "A way a lone a lost a last a loved a long the"; and then to the version we know in print "A way a lone a last a loved a long the" in successive stages of typescript (*JJA* 63: 233, 243, 262). Along the way "a lost" got lost – transmissional oversight or authorial tightening?

2 Compare "bearing the name of the pledger" with the previous proud soaring phrase "the great artificer whose name he bore" (*P* 170).

3 "*Provective*": connected with the private technical term provection, by which a movement typical for Joyce's development is circumscribed, a movement characterized by exaggeration, by increase and deviation from whatever pattern it is that we may have provisionally deduced. The ascent from "oarsman" or "tenor" to the alliterative pinnacle "at present a praiser of his own past" is an illustration.

4 See lines 156–74 of *Ars Poetica*.

5 Other translations could just as well be taken to refer to the technicalities of *A Portrait*: "you must observe the characteristics of each age and assign a fitting grace to natures that shift with the years" (trans. Blakeney in *The Complete Works of Horace* 402); "Make careful note of the way each age group behaves, / And apply the right tone to their changeable natures and years" (*The Satires and Epistles of Horace*, trans. Bovie 277); "Correctly represent the marks of every phase of life, / and give your characters what suits their varying years" (*Horace's Satires and Epistles*, trans. Fuchs 88); "you must note the behaviour of people of different ages, and give the right kind of manners to characters of varying dispositions and years" (*Classical Literary Criticism*, trans. Dorsch 84).

6 "Scrupulously" may of course remind us of Father Flynn in "The Sisters": "He was too scrupulous always," his sister judges (*D* 17), "The duties of the priesthood was too much for him"; that may have caused

his decline. In the previous section of *A Portrait*, Stephen has been invited to take "the duties of the priesthood" upon himself.

7 This odd collocation seems to qualify Joyce's previous use of one of his favorite adverbs in *Chamber Music*, *A Portrait*, etc., as well as its orchestration in *Dubliners*, at the beginning ("lighted in the same way, faintly and evenly") and in the exalted conclusion ("the snow falling faintly through the universe and faintly falling" [*D* 9, 224]).

8 Not surprisingly, this multiple catalogue was added at some secondary stage, during the extensive revision of the "placards." A facsimile page shows the heavy overlay of headings and the "short circuit" insertion, where the "Hackney car . . ." sentence looks like an afterthought to the addition. (See *JJA* 18: 87.)

9 This was triggered off by "*empire*" from a song, which led to "*Imperium romanum*" (7.472, 478).

10 See Gilbert 193. Stuart Gilbert became Joyce's best-known cataloguer, turning all of *Ulysses* into a handy list, the famous Schema of correspondences, a quintessential list, both temptingly convenient and deleteriously reductive. Within Gilbert's (useful) methodical listings, the "Examples of Rhetorical Forms" are a subspecies typical for the chapter.

WORKS CITED

Budgen, Frank. *James Joyce and the Making of "Ulysses."* London: Oxford University Press, 1972.

Classical Literary Criticism. Trans. T. S. Dorsch. Harmondsworth: Penguin, 1965.

Gilbert, Stuart. *James Joyce's "Ulysses."* London: Faber, 1962.

Horace. *The Complete Works of Horace.* Trans. Edward Henry Blakeney. Ed. Casper J. Kraemer, Jr. New York: Random, n.d.

Horace's Satires and Epistles. Trans. Jacob Fuchs. New York: Norton, 1977.

The Satires and Epistles of Horace. Trans. Smith Palmer Bovie. Chicago: University of Chicago Press, 1959.

Satires, Epistles and Ars Poetica. [Latin and English.] Trans. H. Rushton Fairclough. Loeb Classical Library. Cambridge, Mass.: Harvard University Press, 1926.

The James Joyce Archive. Ed. Michael Groden et al. 63 vols. New York: Garland, 1978.

Joyce, James. *Collected Poems.* New York: Viking, 1957.

Dubliners. New York: Viking, 1967.

A Portrait of the Artist as a Young Man. New York: Viking, 1964.

Ulysses: The Corrected Text. Ed. Hans Walter Gabler et al. New York: Random, 1986.

Quintilian. *Institutio Oratoria* [Latin and English.] Trans. H. E. Butler. Loeb Classical Series. 4 vols. Cambridge, Mass.: Harvard University Press, 1921.

CHAPTER 16

Cataloguing in Finnegans Wake: counting counties

Bernard Benstock

Even if Homer did not invent the catalogue (and it would take more than a mere Joycean to prove that he didn't), that time-honored literary device, although of dubious aesthetic value, nonetheless has survived as a standard component in the epic, and Joyce's use of various kinds of lists in both *Ulysses* and *Finnegans Wake* place those texts within the epic tradition. If, furthermore, Joyce's works are more readily classified as "mock-epics," perhaps his prodigious lists might best be classified as "mock-catalogues." For whatever purposes they serve, as tabulations, recapitulations, summations, digressions, commentaries, asides, comic distortions, narrative pauses, they abound in varied forms, from brief intrusions to disproportionate giganticism, and have taken on a distinctly Joycean dimension. Even a casual survey of the vagaries of Joyce's methods of cataloguing in *Ulysses*, as was undertaken in *Who's He When He's at Home*, indicated the enormous range of possibilities, and only the information insisted on by scientists that no two snowflakes look alike assuages the frustration of being unable to superimpose the methodology of one Ulyssean catalogue exactly upon another, although various kinds of superficial similarities could always be found. Where a framing device is apparent, as in the case of trees in the forest wedding (in "Cyclops," lines 1266–95), or where a fixed number of similar items pre-exist Joyce's text, as in a Hebrew *minyan* (minimum of ten, as in "Circe," 3220–4), the variant possibilities become somewhat finite, and the comic depends on a single factor, puns in the first case, the presence of a woman in the second.

More disruptive are the wilder sorts of arrangements, perhaps best characterized by that definitively titled catalogue of "Irish heroes and heroines of antiquity" ("Cyclops," 176–99), where one assumes a legitimate list would be circumscribed by (1) Irishness, (2) heroism, and (3) a placement in the past, while allowing for the representation of both genders. As soon as betrayers and villains and cowards enter the catalogue, much less Italians and Englishmen, multinationals and nondenominated nationals, the "anti-catalogue" is in operation, augmented by non-humans and inexplicable hybrids and compounds. Veering off into tangentials and intangibles at greater and greater distance from the central "control" (Irish Heroes and Heroines of Antiquity), the catalogued entities (ninety in number, although only eighty-seven as catalogued items, counting Adam and Eve, for example, as a single "item") never quite fall apart into a "non-category," but are always linked in a chain by a principle of relationship between any subsequent pair or trio or foursome. Gender, nationality, title, coincidence, status, occupation, or mere parallel construction is enough to hold the mismatched chain together.

By comparison with *Finnegans Wake*, the methods in *Ulysses* seem almost reasonable, if never quite predictable, although we can carry over the methodologies of matching and mismatching, and of parabolic arrangements veering off from a central control mechanism that is almost immediately made inoperative, although it continues to hang on for dear life. The *Wake* has many more catalogues as such, although defining the minimal requirements for a legitimate catalogue worthy of the name is not really possible: does every Tom, Dick, and Harry constitute a catalogue? every appearance or intimation of the Four Old Men? When they display themselves in a quartet of "-ation" words is *that* a catalogue, or does one have to wait for a dozen of them, and even then be suspicious of the impossibility of a catalogue of the same (*single*) item? Are functional catalogues continuous, equally spaced, or dispersed within a reasonably close area? When a whole paragraph consists of twelve sentence fragments that resemble titles, those of the internal Odyssey proper chapters of *Ulysses* (*FW* 229.13–16), then we can assume that the titles of the fifteen stories in *Dubliners* (*FW* 186.13–187.15), separated across three paragraphs and internally hidden in the ongoing narrative, have the same sort of legitimacy.

The varieties of such catalogues fall into three broad areas: those of specific items or articles, those that are people's names, and those that suggest place names or titles, the first group hidden more deeply in the narrative, while those in the last group are often heightened by italicization, the obvious consecutive lists, although often the most disparate, in line with those Irish heroes and heroines of antiquity. The insults hurled at Earwicker, some 114 of them, began as specific appellations (*Firstnighter, Informer,* etc.) but by the eighth item they devolve into a song title, *Yass We've Had His Badannas,* so that titles and names interlink along the entire sequence (*FW* 71.10–72.16). These HCE characteristics are followed by ALP characteristics in the titles for her mamafesta (*FW* 104.5–107.7), perhaps 117 of them, depending on how one counts through the impositions of various commas (and is it significant that whereas the comma is the usual mark separating titles, two semicolons separate the totality into three disproportionate segments?). And whereas all the titles through the penultimate one are of reasonable title proportion, the last long one rambles on through a narrational description. How meager (and somewhat more homogenous), by comparison, is the catalogue of games in the Shem chapter (forty-four of them, *FW* 176.1–18).

By the very nature of its marginal jottings the Lessons chapter offers a particular kind of opportunity for lists, but only toward the very end does it take advantage of that opportunity in a pair of contiguous catalogues that are paralleled by lists in the body of the text. The weeks of the year and the fingers on a pair of hands determine the outside number possible in the two cases, and something approaching coherence determines the fifty-two authors/authorities (of antiquity) that parade down the left columns of the pages (*FW* 306–8), from Cato to Xenophon, neither alphabetical nor chronological, to accompany the trail of essay subjects attributable to them. The "crush" of names, disadvantaged by the narrowness of the margin compared to the line length of the text, results in several instances of accidental couplings, but the Adam and Eve couple only counts as a single entity, and "Pompeius Magnus, Miltiades Strategos" – august as it all sounds – is merely a single Pompey. The subsequent list, by contrast, is narrower in the text than it is in the margins, the inner compound a variation on the first ten numbers and the outer a list of "subjects." In both cases the marginalia is italicized, as were the insulting names, mamafesta titles, and children's games, which would seem to place these among those privileged catalogues, except that they also follow the nature of the preceding marginals, putting into question the "authority" of designated catalogues.

Unemphasized by italicization, one of the longest catalogues in the *Wake* forms the first question in the Riddles chapter (riddles by their very nature offer good possibilities for a string of items, but only the first and the third of the twelve riddles take advantage of the format). Whereas the third question offers two dozen wrong answers in a row, analogous to the baker's dozen of wrong answers to Shem's riddle in the succeeding chapter, the first overwhelming question that calculates the qualities of Finn MacCool lines up an almost uncountable 383, although in this series the separating punctuation is the semi-colon. Each of the 383 characteristics diverts the search for an answer in still another direction, since "direct" answers to each item result in an invisible catalogue of such inferred "heroes of antiquity" as Adam, Wellington, God, James II, Cain, Noah, King Mark, Moses, Parnell, and James Joyce (et al.), and although they all lead to the Finn MacCool of *Finnegans Wake*, they hardly identify the Finn MacCool of Irish heroic antiquity.

Some Wakean catalogues derive rather directly from Ulyssean cataloguing, so that a procession of dignitaries with their acronyms appended after their names is relatively familiar and a grouping of Dublin churches standard procedure. The churches, however, all easily identifiable as actual Dublin edifices, provide two separate catalogues, the first (*FW* 569.5–15) of both R.C. and C. of I. denominations, and the second (*FW* 601.21–8) all Roman Catholic. The first is obviously not all-inclusive, since there are only seventeen of them, and perhaps their bells ("Carilloners will ring their gluckspeels" [*FW* 569.4]) may in some way distinguish them. In turn, "mock" churches that suggest instead the four provinces of Ireland precede the listing (cumulative then of twenty-one, but not all real ones), "S. Presbutt-in-the-North" (Ulster), "S. Mark Underloop" (Munster), "S. Lorenz-by-the-Toolechest" (Leinster), and "S. Nicholas Myre" (Connacht) (*FW* 569.5–6). The twenty-six churches, on the other hand, seem to be more attuned with prevailing numerology in the *Wake*, and that there are only twenty-six in Dublin a limitation that has to be overcome for compliance with the numbers scheme: between the final pair a trio of exclamations intercede ("S. Thomassabbess's and (trema! unloud!! pepet!!!) S. Loellisotoelles!" [*FW* 601.27–8], resulting in an augmentation of items to the significant twenty-nine (Issy as Pepette, the leap year girl). The traditional pairing of Thomas à Becket (declining) and Lawrence O'Toole (ascending) is there, and all of the churches have been feminized to comply with the Girls of St. Bride's. As such, this catalogue satisfies several demands and allows for easier explication:

real items that pre-exist the fictional text, a consistent pattern for the name distortions, and a means of counting that has an existing numerological basis within the text. Few catalogues in the *Wake* are as accommodating.

Is there any predictability as to what will be catalogued in *Finnegans Wake*, once we get past the obvious churches and processionals? A random survey uncovers streets, musical groups, tradesmen, urban residents, hostels, news agencies, newspaper headlines, museum items, eggs, clothing, popes, Irish writers, program credits, horses (and their owners), runners, keepers of the peace, law case contestants, gifts, house junk, letter senders, and various lists of personal names. (This random cataloguing is offered here as one reader's "reading" of the constituent elements of these catalogues and may not necessarily be the headings under which other readers would classify these lists.) In general these are usually blended into the narrative, calling attention to themselves only when the itemization becomes extensive rather than casual, and at other times predictable by their number, like the seven articles of clothing or the twenty-nine Peace Girls or words for death – the latter as ironic counterpoint to the former. And, of course, the twelve customers/jurors in facing complements of six as well.

Nor can the simple division of categories into items, names, and titles retain their discrete existence in the *Wake*, and several expansive catalogues cross differentiating barriers. The very nature of the distribution of gifts by Anna Livia ("her maundy meerschaundize, poor souvenir as per ricorder" [*FW* 210.2–3]) implies a group of recipients ("all for sore aringarung, stinkers and heelers, laggards and primelads, her furzeborn sons and dribbolderry daughters, a thousand and one of them" [*FW* 210.3–5]). The pluralization of daughter into daughters immediately implies augmentation, from the three to the usual 111, while the clear indication of 1001 translates them into the stories of the Arabian Nights. A gift and a recipient constantly in tandem, each couple separated consistently and definitively by semi-colons again (*FW* 210.1–212.19) – yet the first "item" destroys the even balance ("A tinker's bann and a barrow to boil his billy for Gipsy Lee" [210.6–7] – two gifts for one recipient), and soon after a single gift for a trio of recipients, although the gift is subdivided into containing four items: "a jigsaw puzzle of needles and pins and blankets and shins between them for Isabel, Jezebel and Llewelyn Mmarriage" (*FW* 210.11–12). The most scrupulous double-entry bookkeeping may be able to at least account for the actual recipients, the gifts folding into each other too frequently for anything approximating an accurate count, although we probably should be careful not to count gifts disguised as recipients ("Jill, the spoon of a girl, for Jack, the broth of a boy" [*FW* 211.15]). As such recipients seem to total just under 120, and no system of elimination quite gets it down to 111. Nor can we rely on counting semi-colons: that there are seventy-one of them indicates that they separate seventy-two sequences of gifts-cum-recipients, but the method of cataloguing dissolves thereafter with new lists of ten male recipients (but of what?) and over two dozen females, but not quite twenty-eight, although Issy is the final receiver immediately after. A patterned development in these enlarged catalogues seems to mature toward a finite number, but a tendency toward disintegration near the end becomes the operative technique instead, a splaying out of possibilities rather than a fulfillment of a cohesive assemblage.

HOW MANY COUNTIES ARE THERE IN IT? – A DEMONSTRATION

One of the most intriguing catalogues in *Finnegans Wake* actually has its "disintegration" at the beginning rather than at the end, and may therefore be overlooked in a casual search for designated catalogues, although treated as such by Brendan O Hehir (*A Gaelic Lexicon for "Finnegans Wake"* 310–11), Louis Mink (*A "Finnegans Wake" Gazetteer* 183–4), and Roland McHugh (*Annotations to "Finnegans Wake"* 595), each of whom makes a valiant effort to treat it as a *complete* catalogue despite its inherent mysteries. In its main frame it consists of a single (non)sentence:

For korps, for streamfish, for confects, for bullyoungs, for smearsassage, for patates, for steaked pig, for men, for limericks, for waterfowls, for wagsfools, for louts, for cold airs, for late trams, for curries, for curlews, for leekses, for orphalines, for tunnygulls, for clear goldways, for lungfortes, for moonyhaunts, for fairmoneys, for coffins, for tantrums, for armaurs, for waglugs, for rogues comings, for sly goings, for larksmathes, for homdsmeethes, for quailmeathes, kilalooly. (*FW* 595.10–17)

Allowing that the cataloguing indicator here, as in Anna Livia's gift list, is the word "for," thirty-two items are in the forefront, and only a lone tagword breaks the perfect formation, relevant or irrelevant to whatever the subject of the catalogue may be. If the *count* is taken as the determining factor, there is the easy assumption that the thirty-two counties of Ireland are being enumerated, accounting for the logical interest in the sentence taken by O Hehir and Mink. At least from the word "limerick" on, the temptation exists to unpun the key words back into names of the counties of Ireland, all the while aware that a limerick is also something else as well.

And most of the time that process of name-association works only too well, even when compounds intrude, endangering the numerical construction (if "clear goldways" stands for both counties Clare and Galway, the listing should fall short; on the other hand, the final threesome of "larksmathes ... homdsmeethes ... quailsmeathes" is an embarrassment of Meaths, since only two counties have the name, Meath and Westmeath). When two equal one and three equal two the final number is still the correct three, and the conflations and extensions have a logic of their own: Claregalway is also a single city, and historically Royal Meath was divided in the seventeenth century into the two counties, so it may be added on here as a third possibility.

The major element of frustration exists in that disarranged beginning: how do we account for the first eight items that don't call attention to themselves as Irish counties and even defy association with any of the counties not included in the post-limerick sequence? Brendan O Hehir, who begins with Limerick, ends before the Meaths, so he lists ten counties as "missing: Cork, Derry, Down, Dublin, Kilkenny, Mayo, Meath, Tipperary, Tyrone, Westmeath"), but in his next entries he recuperates Meath and Westmeath. His list of counties totals twenty-four. Louis Mink advances on this by beginning with "Korps" as Cork, and only reports as "Missing: Cos Derry, Down, Dublin, Mayo, and Tyrone," since he finds two more outside the framework, accepting "kilalooly" as a ?-prefaced Kilkenny and an unquestioned Tipperary as a word nine lines later, "Deepereras" (*FW* 595.28). (Although tempted by "alpsulumply" [*FW* 595.19] as ?Dublin, he nonetheless keeps Dublin on his Missing list, and his total is twenty-seven.) Roland McHugh does not accept "Korps" as Cork, but does accept "Deepereras" as Tipperary and "kilalooly" as Kilkenny, and consequently comes up with a total of twenty-six. This would indeed be a desirable "alternate" number if it would account for the counties within Eire, and exclude those still in British Ireland, but this neat separation oviously does not work out.

266 BERNARD BENSTOCK

There is no way to avoid the coincidental relationship between the existence of at least a vast majority of the Irish counties and (even *within*) the presence of a thirty-two-part catalogue, yet other numerological indicators are present as introductory elements. Leading into the enumeration is a travelogue-approach to the landscape:

We may plesently heal Geoglyphy's *twentynine* ways to say goodbett an wassing seoosoon liv. With the *forty* wonks winking please me your much as to. With her tup. It's a long long ray to Newirgland's premier. For korps . . . (*FW* 595.6–10, italics added)

The long, long way to Tipperary has indeed a long way to go with no Tipperary in the catalogue and "Deepereras" buried even deeper in the ensuing lines, nor is either twenty-nine or forty an operative directional signal for the counties of Ireland, although familiar enough elsewhere in the *Wake*. A river ("gazelle channel and the bride of the Bryne" [*FW* 595.4–5]) snakes its way through the country, through all the counties, starting with such fish as carp ("korps") and streamfish, which soon give way to other forms of livestock and food. Superimposed on the "counties" format then are two other "primary" structures, animals and edibles, the former taking an evolutionary path in time, from sea to land to air, "korps" and "streamfish" and "bullyoungs" and "pig" and "waterfowl" and (an evolutionary lapse conjuring up flying fish) "tunnygulls" into curlews and larks and quail, while the latter consists of fish and sweetmeats and sausage and potatoes and steak and fowl and curries and leeks and tunafish. It is a country rich in stock and foodstuff, enough to feed all the population of all the counties.

There is no particular order in which the thirty-two counties of Ireland are necessarily arranged, nor a line of progression inimitable to the food products available in Ireland, so if linear descent applies as a structuring concept in Wakean cataloguing only the evolutionary process gives direction to this particularly complex scheme. The position of "men" is significant in the pattern: sea and land creatures are separated from the airborne by the position of "men" in the ordered arrangement, but these "men" also separate what might be determined as two discrete catalogue subjects, the gastronomic from the geographical: every item preceding "men" is in the culinary line, every item thereafter is an identifiable county – beginning with the one that exists linguistically as untampered with,

Limerick. Progression, in effect, is implied in the context, the shift from night to morning, the anticipation of dawn, as the first light touches the prehistoric stone markers built in Ireland by the Druids – as in Newgrange – ("The spearspid of dawnfire totouches ain the tablestoane ath the centre of the great circle of the macroliths" [*FW* 594.21–2]), and any disruption of such progression is immediately frowned upon: "But why pit the cur afore the noxe?" (*FW* 594.29).

What is always disruptive in any Joycean catalogue is the inherent potential for tangential development, a suggestive process that allows Captain Moonlight and Captain Boycott to be linked together, for an Italian like Dante to spawn a fellow in Columbus, for Saints Fursa and Brendan to march in lockstep, or Sidney Parade to succeed Dolly Mount, only to be followed by Ben Howth, making a travesty of Irish heroes and heroines of antiquity. The proximity of sound pattern as well as propinquity of environs accounts logically for "waterfowls" and "wagsfools" (read Waterford and Wexford), while "curries" and "curlews" are strictly sound-oriented; Donegal and Galway naturally link end-to-front, but the existence of the town of Claregalway intrudes to separate rather than join "tunnygulls" and "clear goldways"; Fermanagh and Monaghan also link easily end-to-front, but instead are lined up chiasmatically as "moonyhaunts" and "fairmoneys," as different as moonlit night and fair day. Any alternate linkage naturally intrudes and interrupts in a constant series of comings and goings ("rogues comings" and "sly goings") in amoebic separations and coalescences, following an internal logic often at odds with the overall external logic, punwheels within punwheels.

Picking apart the crosshatchings of patterns in *Finnegans Wake* results in various catalogues-within-catalogues, and any constrictive assumption that a single *primary* catalogue somehow takes precedence over whatever else has fallen into place may not be the relevant critical approach to the cataloguing method in the *Wake* – or to other areas of allusions and "pun possibilities." Yet the nagging urge for comprehensiveness in this all-Irish web early in the Dawn chapter does not allow for compromise solutions or easy near-victories: the thirty-two items, a vast majority of which point much too directly toward specific counties, seem to insist upon some attempt at completion. That a homogenous catalogue can spill over several paragraphs has been observed in the *Dubliners* titles, much as we may prefer the continuous presentation of the middle-*Ulysses* titles, so "kilalooly" can perhaps be allowed for Kilkenny and "Deepereras" for Tipperary. For purists, however, all thirty-two counties should be conjured up within the infrastructure of the thirty-two items prefaced by the word "For" – or what are patterns for? The remaining problem, then, is to align the following items (in order of appearance in the text) with the corresponding county (arbitrarily listed in alphabetical order):

streamfish	Derry
confects	Down
bullyoungs	Dublin
smearsassage	Kilkenny
patates	Mayo
steaked pig	Tipperary
men	Tyrone

To dispense with the obvious, let us accept James Joyce's assumption that Dublin is famous for its men (the one item most difficult to account for in the catalogue). That pleasantry aside, it then only requires the information retrievable from an agricultural survey to determine which of the remaining six counties produces fish, confections, cattle, sausages, potatoes and pigs in abundance (quite predictable Irish fare), and the two catalogues can fuse into one. Conversely, we might prefer the observation that Ireland is a divided nation of fish, flesh and fowl, humans and animals, and that the political division between Southern Ireland and Northern Ireland is only the most obvious example of divisiveness within the "nation," as witness the otherwise arbitrary distinctions between the anticipated, but somehow unrecuperable, twenty-six and those outside the Irish Republic. As seems usual throughout the extended catalogue lists (insults, mamafesta titles, children), the specific number remains tantalizingly vague, as the roulette ball hovers among possible numbers once the rotating wheel slows down toward closure.

WORKS CITED

Benstock, Shari, and Bernard Benstock. *Who's He When He's at Home: A James Joyce Directory*. Urbana: University of Illinois Press, 1980.
Joyce, James. *Finnegans Wake*. New York: Viking, 1939.
  Ulysses: The Corrected Text. Ed. Hans Walter Gabler et al. New York: Random, 1986.

McHugh, Roland. *Annotations to "Finnegans Wake."* Baltimore: Johns Hopkins University Press, 1980.
Mink, Louis O. *A "Finnegans Wake" Gazetteer.* Bloomington: Indiana University Press, 1978.
O Hehir, Brendan. *A Gaelic Lexicon for "Finnegans Wake."* Berkeley and Los Angeles: University of California Press, 1967.

CHAPTER 17

Translating Ulysses, East and West

Di Jin

The unique achievements of James Joyce's art in *Ulysses* put his translator in a peculiar position. There is no choice before him or her: one has to try to preserve its artistic integrity as closely as possible.

So much cannot be said of all works of art. Without going into details about evaluation and marketing, no translator would want to spend too much time on stuff which is clearly trash though in demand. Even with serious literature there is a possibility of doing what may be described as "transwriting" instead of translation proper. Edward FitzGerald produced his famous *Rubáiyát of Omar Khayyám* not by really translating Omar Khayyám, but by rewriting the Persian songs in English, adopting what ideas, sentiments and rhythms *he* liked from the original texts. Loyalty to the author was out of the question because the transwriter was working from a position of dominant English culture where he felt free to pick and choose what he found interesting or useful in an exotic culture. The same underlying stance is found in Lin Shu, the famous Chinese writer whose over 170 "translations" in classical Chinese brought European literature to the "Central Empire" around the turn of the century, though in his case the transference was *from* English and other European sources. One example which I have discussed in *On Translation* (83) will suffice to illustrate the situation. The passage is taken from Charles Dickens's *Nicholas Nickleby*, followed by my back-translation of Lin's Chinese version, with salient differences italicized by me in both:

Dickens's text
Miss Knag laughed, and after that cried. "For fifteen years," exclaimed Miss Knag, *sobbing in a most affecting manner*, "for fifteen years have I been *the credit and ornament* of this room and the one upstairs. Thank God," said Miss Knag, stamping first her right foot and then her left with remarkable

energy, "I have never in all that time, till now, been exposed to the arts, the vile arts, of *a creature, who disgraces us with all her proceedings, and makes proper people blush for themselves.* But I feel it, I do feel it, although I am disgusted."

Back translation of Lin's version[1]
Knag ... first laughed, but finally cried *in a voice which suggested a singsong chant.* "Alas!" she said, "I have been here for fifteen years, and everybody in this establishment has said *I am as beautiful as a glorious flower,*" – stamping her left foot while chanting, she cried, "Alas, Heavens!" Then she stamped her right foot and continued: "Alas, Heavens! I have never been slighted in all those fifteen years, and now *this coquettish vixen dares to dash in front of me and humiliate me!* O how it makes my liver and intestines tremble!"

To be sure Lin's prose runs full of life, but it is a life Charles Dickens did not know. The Miss Knag of Dickens presents herself as a conscientious and reliable forewoman furious against a scheming upstart; the Knag of Lin is a shrew whose jealousy has been violently roused because she finds her beauty overshadowed by a "coquettish vixen," and she vents her emotions not just in exclamations, but by means of a stream of loud melodious denunciation, as was the wont among shrewish wives of the lower classes in feudal China. As to niceties like which foot Miss Knag stamped first, or subtleties such as might be observed in the distinction between disgust and feeling, or hints such as might be carried in names like Knag, they were simply beneath the attention of the masterly transwriter.

Clearly that type of "translation," while it may serve the purpose of extending the literary bounds of the language in which it appears, is not meant to be a substitute for the original work of art, as is the goal of literary translation proper. If the atmosphere, the characterization, the fine artistic touches in a piece of serious literature are often features essential to its identity as a work of art, then how particularly true this is of a work of such consummate complexity and finish as *Ulysses*! They are the very life of the work. The path of transwriting is simply closed to any one attempting a translation of a masterpiece of this calibre.

That was an unspoken premise when I accepted the challenge of translating *Ulysses* into Chinese, in full or in part. As a matter of fact, I believe that that is the very reason for which the task is considered to be a formidable challenge, for otherwise why should it need so much ado? And I thought I understood thoroughly why Joyce had in 1936 told a prospective translator "not to alter a single word" (*JJ* 692).

But wait: "not to alter a single word"? Was he not a master of languages who ought to have known how languages differ from each other? Is it not in the nature of things that a translator – any translator – is bound to alter words or, as in many cases, *all* the words in the text?

Evidently Joyce was again, typically, expecting people to understand what he did not say. And I was delighted, when I was granted a Beinecke fellowship at Yale University in early 1989, to have the opportunity of seeing other translations of *Ulysses*, which I knew are available in the Beinecke Rare Book and Manuscript Library. Now I could find out how others had managed to do the job "without altering a single word."

The special restriction imposed by the art of *Ulysses* on all its translators lends the comparison of versions an unusual pertinency and meaning. The ideal goal of producing a work of art which can be enjoyed as a perfect substitute for the original may be unattainable in practice, yet when everybody works at this common goal it becomes more feasible to compare the relative efficacy of various approaches, and that in turn will help bring the goal closer than ever. What follows is a selection of the results of the comparative study of various language translations I conducted at the Beinecke Library. I think it sheds light on the difficult art of translation and helps to give body to the usually elusive ideas of losses and gains in its execution.

Some loss in translation is inevitable, objectively speaking, but one can avoid unnecessary loss or provide appropriate compensation by adopting the right kind of principles. Some literary translators like to talk about their occupation as an art beyond principles, but the truth is every choice one makes in diction, rhythm or syntax involves some principle. There is no question about there being principles in any translation: the only question is whether they are consciously or unconsciously employed, and whether they are good or bad principles. The greater the artistic complexity is in the original work, the more pressing is the translator's need to have good flexible principles at his command.

The rendering of names, for instance, usually poses no special difficulty. It is true that you have more freedom in literary translation than in other interlingual communication, for it is your option to retain more or less of the alien flavor of the personal and other names. You can either simply reproduce the original or replace them with meaningful words to represent the ideas behind them. But with Joyce's names one may be obliged to do neither or both at the same time. One such example is "Miss Dubedatandshedidbe-dad" (*U* 15.4354–5).

One look at this name is sufficient for most translators to decide that ordinary methods for rendering names would not do here, but it takes a great deal of thinking to find an adequate solution. The first part of the name, "Dubedat," could be regarded as a not too extraordinary proper name, but the long tag "andshedidbedad," with its obviously meaningful elements, refuses a straightforward treatment. These elements have first appeared separately in Bloom's musings in "Lestrygonians":

Wouldn't mind being a waiter in a swell hotel. Tips, evening dress, halfnaked ladies. May I tempt you to a little more filleted lemon sole, miss Dubedat? Yes, do bedad. And she did bedad. Huguenot name I expect that. A miss Dubedat lived in Killiney, I remember. (*U* 8.887–90)

And now in "Circe," the combination pops up as a newly formed name in the long list of pursuers that run after him:

After him freshfound the hue and cry zigzag gallops in hot pursuit of follow my leader: ... John Wyse Nolan, handsomemarriedwomanrubbedagainst-widebehindinClonskeatram, the bookseller of *Sweets of Sin*, Miss Dubed-atandshedidbedad ... (*U* 15.4335–55)

The Joycean Bloomish humor cries out for proper representation. Among the translations I compared, I found three distinct methods of treatment:

(1) Simple reproduction of the whole name, such as in the early German version:

Fräulein Dubedatandshedidbedad (Goyert 2: 270)

The translator seems to expect the German readers to guess the play of possible meaning in "Dubedat," for he has rendered the passage where the name first appears in "Lestrygonians" like this:

Fräulein Dubedat? Ja, in der tat. Und sie tat es in der tat. (Goyert 1: 284)

It is true that *there* this rendering does convey the fun to an extent, for there is some sort of linkage between "Dubedat" and "in der tat" on the strength of the rhythmic pattern and the rhyme. But would it not be asking too much to expect the reader to remember that association hundreds of pages later in "Circe," where he does not have the phrase "in der tat" before his eyes? If he did not remember that, as probably is the case with most readers, then what would he be able to make out of this long string of alien syllables?

Now this is Joyce's instruction "not to alter a single word" carried out to the syllable. But one may well wonder whether it catches the spirit. The price for this complete identity between the translation and the original is perhaps an all-but-complete loss of the intended comicality.

(2) Partial copying plus partial meaningful translation, as in the Danish version:

Dubedatoghuntogfat (Boisen 565)

The tag "oghuntogfat" (meaning something like "and she did get hold of it") is probably as amusing in itself as the original tag, and its rhyming end gives it some connection with "Dubedat" (as the German version is only able to do in "Lestrygonians"). But since that is nothing but a phonetic pattern, can one be quite certain that a Danish reader not familiar with English would see the semantic similarity? The equivalence (or rather identity) of the proper name Dubedat seems to be maintained at some expense of the comical effect.

(3) Total reconstruction of the name, as in the French version:

Miss Saint-Prixetellenpritsapristi (Morel 650)

There is hardly any phonetic or semantic semblance between the French "Saint-Prix" and the original "Dubedat," but the French readers must have as much fun in seeing it expand into "etellenpritsapristi" as the English do with "andshedidbedad." In fact they might even derive more amusement from this conglomeration of syllables because of the witty play on the sounds and ideas of four words: "prix" (price), "prie" (pray), "prit" (took) and "sapristi" (for goodness' sake; damnation), something which has been fully evolved in Bloom's stream of consciousness in "Lestrygonians":

... Mademoiselle de Saintprix? Je vous en prie. Et elle en prit sapristi ... (Morel 197)

Although the name "Dubedat" has been replaced, the interplay of the four "pri" words represents the same tenor of a little tableside conversation plus a humorous comment as is found in the original.

This is the equivalent effect the translator achieves through a transformation of form and content.

It does not follow as a matter of course that a total reconstruction or transformation will always bring about an equivalent effect. The Spanish version I compared, "la señorita Delbidetysidelbided" (Subirat 619), involves a transformation even more thoroughgoing than the French. In itself it may be able to afford some amusement to Spanish readers, and the joke could even be regarded as Joycean in character, but one finds it out of place in its context, a situation which is still more conspicuous in "Lestrygonians":

... señorita Delbidet? Sí, del bidet. Y ella se, bidet. (Subirat 187)

The wordplay on "bidet" moves the environment from a restaurant into a toilet, and that seems to bring in an element of illogicality and unnaturalness alien to Bloom's mind. Perhaps this may be compared to Lin Shu's replacement of an upstart by a "coquettish vixen."

My Chinese version does not shine with such witty brilliance, French or Spanish, but it happens to have been constructed along lines similar to the French in abandoning simple equivalence for the sake of a larger equivalence:

莫推兹而她也真不推辞小姐 (Jin 167)

The Chinese words, which literally mean "Miss Do-not-decline-and-she-indeed-did-not-decline," employ a double negative instead of the emphatic affirmative implied in the original because that gives the first part (莫推兹, pronounced *mo-tui-zi*) the verisimilitude of a name (like "Dubedat"). A similar consideration may have been in the French translator's mind when he added "Saint." But in comparison with the French version this Chinese name, curious as it is, misses the element of exclamation brought in by the mild curse "sapristi." It is not in any of the other language versions either, but I think the French word translates "bedad" wonderfully well in its context, showing a certain roguishness in Bloom's stream of consciousness. Perhaps I should try to work something similar to it into my Chinese in a later edition.

If "Dubedatandshedidbedad" may be called an exceptional case because of its queer formation, the same cannot be said of some very commonplace names which tax the translators' ingenuity even more with their complexity of meanings. One of those is "Coffey" in Father Coffey. I knew his name was like a coffin. (*U* 6.595)

The meaningless name assumes some unexpected meaning because its sound suggests to Bloom an association with the funeral ritual that is taking place and with the priest's duty to deal with bodies in coffins. Again, the French and German versions I compared represent two different approaches:

French version
Le Père Serqueux. Je savais qu'il y avait du cercueil dans son nom. (Morel 115)

German version
Pater Coffey. Wusste doch, dass sein Name an coffin (Sarg) erinnerte. (Goyert 1:169)

This time the German translator, who again reproduces the original name, provides a parenthesis to show the connection between the sounds and the idea, but since the sounds are alien to a German ear, the connection cannot but sound far-fetched. What is more, the appearance of a foreign word with a parenthesis to explain its meaning may give rise to an impression that Bloom is playing with an exotic idea, which is of course not what the original text gives English readers at all.

The resemblance between the French "Serqueux" and the English "Coffey," on the other hand, is so indirect and flimsy that they can hardly be considered equivalents, but the French readers can easily see the association between "Serqueux" and "cercueil," more or less in the same way as English readers do with "Coffey" and "coffin." The transformation of the name enables the French readers to see the naturalness of the sentence following it and, together with that, what is more important, a glimpse of Bloom's mind, which after all is what Joyce meant to show in this passage. At the expense of the simple equivalence of the name itself, the French version achieves the closest approximation in total effect.

My Chinese version again happens to have been contrived along similar lines:

关采神父. 早知道了, 他的姓氏象棺材 (Jin 63)

The name 关采 (pronounced *guan cai*) sounds very different from the original, but it easily suggests the idea of 棺材, meaning "coffin," the words being homophones with just a little tonal variation.

That Joyce himself took an active part in preparing, and gave his approval for, both the French and the 1930 German versions is a fact particularly interesting in this connection. Many theorists have suggested that an ideal translation would be one produced by the author writing in the target language. A very laudable ideal, but there must be a premise: that the author should be able to write with a conscious suspension of his mastery of his own language! For otherwise he would be apt to say things perfectly clear to himself but not really comprehensible to his new readers. By the same token, an author who knows the target languages well may not be the best judge of the accuracy of the translations unless he has trained himself for that specific purpose. What he regards as a correct representation of his idea may not convey the same thing to the new readers when it involves some element (linguistic or extralinguistic) familiar to him but not to them. The ultimate correctness of a translation does not lie in its expressing the same thing to people who know the source language, for otherwise the only correct translation would be the original text itself ("not a single word altered," indeed). It lies in its expressing the same or the closest possible thing to people who do *not* know the source language.

It is only in this light that Joyce's instruction to his translator can make sense. What is not to be altered is not the words themselves, which *must* be altered, but the ideas, sentiments, images and implications they carry and suggest. By his emphasis on "not a single word," Joyce was trying to protect the shades of meaning he put half-concealed behind the words and the hints he built into his text, either between the lines or between the episodes. He was demanding that the translation should be capable of producing an effect on its readers which would be an *exact* copy of what *Ulysses* in its original produces on its English readership.

God knows that ever since He created the chaos on the construction site of Babel no such copy has been produced for any book, and in all probability none will ever be. But Joyce's instruction manifests the wish of an ultra-ardent artist to counteract that linguistic havoc in accomplishing his mission, and it rings in harmony with the aspiration of a serious translator. An exact copy of the effect of the original is impossible, just as gold of 100 percent purity is impossible, but whether you work toward that ideal or not makes all the difference. The translator's hope lies in the fact that despite the disastrous disruption of languages, human beings share common sensibilities, and proper adjustments can be made in the text to suit the new linguistic environment so that very similar effects can be produced on the new audience.

The translator must first be a researcher–connoisseur in the source language who can fully appreciate every subtlety in the text; then he needs to be an artist with a creative imagination and a delicate touch comparable to the author's but expressible in the new language. Joyce's difficult art makes the first an arduous role and the second exasperatingly demanding, though ultimately rewarding (one hopes) in pleasures of genuine creation. In order to produce an equivalent effect on the new readers, one has to be extremely sensitive to their particular receptor capacity. The nuances one has managed to catch in the source language may easily get lost in the transfer because they involve elements inaccessible through the new channel, and such nuances are innumerable in Joyce.

As a rule a translator cannot be satisfied with words and expressions which seem to have equivalent denotative values in the target language. If those "equivalents" do not ramify in the target language with the nuances their counterpart carries in the original, and if the ramifications are the real point of the text, then the translator will usually try to improve the situation by modifying those words or expressions at the expense of their equivalent values. That is a balance of effects every translator has to manipulate. But sometimes, as in the cases discussed so far, and this happens often in translating *Ulysses*, those local equivalent values are in direct conflict with the ramifications in the context. Then the translator is faced with an important matter of principle, though he or she may not be conscious of it. The early German translator stuck to the simple verbal equivalences, thus foregoing the ramifications which would constitute a larger equivalence. The French translator gave up those equivalences and created something which does not look equivalent to the original, but which ramifies in the translation in such a way as to produce a total effect comparable to the original. The French translator, one might say, succeeded in approximating the original more closely by moving away from it.

In the case of a translator working in a language as distant as Chinese, understandably his difficulty is more than doubled. Not to mention the special syntactical and stylistic features which are Joycean wonders in English but which sometimes are nightmares to the poor translator, even the rendering of the simplest of words can cause headaches unknown to his European-language colleagues. It took me, for instance, days of cogitation (musing, wavering, analyzing and synthesizing, often muttering to myself to call in the help of more senses, when not cursing one language or the other or both) to decide what to do with the little word "yes" in the final episode. Where all European translators can comfortably repeat their respective *oui, si, ja*, etc. with beautiful consistency, I had to devise a way which might allow for consistency and variation at the same time. The consistency is necessary to convey Joyce's express emphasis and artistic play in repeating the word so many times throughout the episode, but if pushed as far as in the English text it would ruin the Chinese translation completely. Since there is not one Chinese word or phrase which can translate "yes" on all occasions and stand all those repetitions, that kind of "consistency" would either weaken the text hopelessly or turn it into ridiculous nonsense.

Once in a while, however, the very distance of the Chinese language seems to give it a freedom not found in languages close to English. A case in point is the translation of this passage in the black mass in "Circe":

THE VOICE OF ALL THE DAMNED
Htengier Tnetopinmo Dog Drol eht rof, Aiulella!
(From on high the voice of Adonai calls.)

ADONAI
Dooooooooooog!   (*U* 15.4707–11)

All European translators are constrained to use the inversions of their respective words for "God". Thus:
   (French): Uuuuuuuuuuueid! (Morel 663)
   (German): Ttoooooooooog! (Goyert 2: 285)
   (Spanish): Soooooooooooid! (Subirat 632)
   (Dutch): Dooooooooooog! (Vandenberg 663)
   (Danish): Duuuuuuuuuuug! (Boisen 575)
With the exception of the Dutch "Dooooooooooog," which means something similar to the English but is really different because the same word in Dutch refers to a mastiff or bulldog instead of the generic dog, they carry no semantic meaning or appear to denote something quite unrelated. The Danish "Dug," for example, refers to cloth or dew. The Spanish "Soid" can suggest "só," an interjection to stop a horse, and in that sense produces an effect closer to the

original than the others, though this suggestion does not seem to carry much implication of profanity. Apart from those more or less irrelevant complications, these translations are mainly faithful to the original in form only: they represent the respective words for God inverted, and they repeat the vowels the same number of times, eleven, but they do not sound as bad a blasphemy as the glaring original. The problem seems to be rooted in the target languages, where in each case the word for "God" is fixed, with little room left for manipulation.

The exotic Chinese, however, is full of homophonic word-charac-ters. I had learned from a Chinese Catholic bishop that the Catho-lics have a term for God which is different from the one Chinese Protestants use. The Catholic term is 天主, pronounced *tian zhu* and meaning literally "heavenly master" or "lord in heaven." The inversion of those two word-characters would be 主天, *zhu tian*, which could mean "lord heaven" or "rule heaven." But the first of these, 主 *zhu*, is identical in sound (with a tonal variation) to the word for "pig" 猪. Thus I thought I was entitled to use a pun in translating the original "dog" and produce this version:

猪猪猪猪猪天 (Jin 183)

(*zhu zhu zhu zhu zhu tian,*
meaning "pig pig pig pig pig heaven")

Although the animal is different, it represents the same blasphe-mous culmination of the black mass. It gave me a rare moment of consolation when I compared this bit of Chinese maneuver with the European versions. The total stranger who most of the time can only envy their intimacy seems to have caught a point the close relatives have missed.

Linguistic kinship or the lack of it, however, does not constitute a decisive factor in producing equivalent or non-equivalent effect. Much depends on the approach the translator chooses for either to become an advantage. One approach can shorten the distance and another may further widen it. The early Japanese translators, using a language equally distant from English, did not even try to produce an inversion of their translation of "God," which is a kanji character 神, pronounced *kami* in Japanese, and whose inversion would con-ceivably be something like *"mika"* or *"imak."* They just gave a string of Japanese syllable-characters which may be represented by these English transliterations: "do-o-o-o-o-o-o-o-o-o-o-gu."[2] While the

European translations can at least produce an impression of inverted order, it may be doubted whether any Japanese reader who has no knowledge of English would have an inkling that this string of letters is meant to be "God" upside down.

So the translation of *Ulysses* requires a conscious application of principle even in the case of syllables and letters. In fact it would be very instructive to study the translation of phrases like "H. E. L. Y' S" and "Bloo ... Me?" I will confine myself to just one such example, which I hope can counteract a misleading impression the above discussion might have caused.

   The point in question is that the principle of "the closest approximation in total effect" does not imply, as the examples cited above might seem to imply, that a transformation always produces a better effect. Far from it. The simple equivalence is still the first choice wherever it does not involve factors adverse to the total effect. A pertinent case is the translation of the postcard Mrs. Breen shows Bloom in "Lestrygonians":

– What is it? Mr Bloom asked, taking the card. U. P.?
– U. p: up, she said. (*U* 8.257–8)

French version
– Qu'est-ce que c'est? demande M. Bloom en prenant la carte. Fou. Tu.
– Fou. Tu.: foutu, dit-elle. (Morel 177)

German version
«Was ist das?» fragte Bloom und nahm die Karte. P-L-E-M?
«P-L-E-M: plem,» sagte sie. (Goyert 1: 254)

   Both French and German translators rendered the term with the basic sense of dementedness, which is probably based on the fictional character J. J. O'Molloy's interpretation that "it implies that he is not *compos mentis*" (*U* 12.1043–4). But there is one significant difference: the German version sticks to some formal features of the original which the French ignores. Firstly, "P-L-E-M" appears as separate letters just as "U. p." does in the original. Secondly, "plem" is not clear in meaning, or at least not immediately clear because it is only a segment of the colloquial "plemplem," again to some extent like "up" which is felt to be part of some phrase. Now the pivot of the mini-comedy around the postcard, it seems to me, does not rest on the exact meaning of the two letters "U. p.," but rather on their apparent lack of exact meaning, for that is the element which makes Mr. Breen's fussy attempts to start a lawsuit appear so comical as well as pathetic. Therefore the German preservation of those formal features, which gives the postcard a somewhat mysterious appearance, plays a positive role in presenting the Joycean comedy. The French version with its more thorough-going transformation is an admirable rendering too, being pregnant with the volatile and insulting implications of "fou" and "foutu"; but compared with the German version it appears to involve a relative reduction of mystery and uncertainty.

The preservation of formal features, which is often simplistically identified with "faithfulness to the original text," can easily go too far, however. Both the Japanese versions I compared preserve *all* the formal features of the original in this instance: they simply reproduce the English letters "U. P." The impression these absolutely unaltered letters give the Japanese readers may perhaps be classified under "mystery" too, but since that mystery does not come with an uncertainty of meaning but rather with a total blank of meaning, even more so than the German reproduction of "Dubedatandshedidbedad," it cannot but entail a total loss of the mini-comedy.

"U. P.: up" is only one of the many hard nuts I have not come around to crack yet, but this research has cleared my mind and I think I know what I will do and what I will not. I will not succumb to the lack of affinity between the two languages by following the easy path of "faithfully" reproducing the English letters. I will do my utmost, by searching for and giving play to peculiar potentialities of the Chinese language which may help in this particular situation, to present the mini-comedy to the Chinese readers in such a way that there will be as much room for the play of their imagination as the English readers enjoy.

I have already spotted a feature on which I think I can try to get closer than the European versions. It is the range of possible interpretations for the postcard message. The lawyerly remark by O'Molloy in "Cyclops" quoted above may indeed be regarded as a somewhat authoritative interpretation, yet the two letters "U. p." standing by themselves on the postcard by no means give the addressee or anybody who sees it (and the readers of the book) such a clear-cut impression. A good rendering of the message ought to be as enigmatic as those letters appear to be when the postcard is received. While its linkage with O'Molloy's learned interpretation need not be quite so obvious, ample room should be provided for wilder guesses, including all the other interpretations suggested by Robert M. Adams (192) and more. I have a feeling that by invoking the peculiar genius of the Chinese language, it may be possible to contrive such a version as will help in "almosting" Joyce's own tragicomical interlude.

That prospect, however, remains yet to be realized. And even when the possibility becomes an actuality it will only be one tiny portion of the tremendous task. Although I have included some of my own renderings in the comparative study, there is one principal respect in which I cannot thus far compare with any of the other translators: they have all completed their translations, while I am still struggling with mine, having only published portions of it.[3] But this little study has strengthened an optimism which has sometimes been wobbling. It has confirmed my belief that a literary translator should always work for the closest approximation in total effect. That principle will demand the utmost exertion from the translator but will also bring out the best in him or her as an artist, which is an absolute necessity in translating works that are among the highest achievements of human art.

What is more, this study has shown that the great linguistic and cultural distance between the East and the West is not insuperable. Joyce's art has Daedalian wings.

NOTES

1 Lin Shu's Chinese version (quoted from Qian 68):
   …那格…始笑而终哭, 哭声似带讴歌. 曰: "嗟呼! 吾来十五年, 楼中咸谓我如名花之鲜艳"— 歌时, 顿其左足, 曰: "嗟夫天!" 又顿其右足, 曰: "嗟夫天! 十五年中未被人轻贱. 竟有骚狐奔我前, 辱我令我肝肠颤!"

2 The hyphens are mine to indicate the separate syllable-characters in Japanese. See Itô et al. 2 (1934): 306. Also Morita et al. 4 (1932): 341.

3 The latest Chinese version I have published is the book, listed at the end of the Works Cited below, published by the Hundred Flowers Literature and Art Press in Tianjin, 1988, which contains five episodes, three of them in full and two in excerpts.

WORKS CITED

Adams, Robert Martin. *Surface and Symbol.* New York: Oxford University Press, 1967.
Ellmann, Richard. *James Joyce.* Rev. edn. New York: Oxford University Press, 1982.

Jin, Di, and Eugene A. Nida. *On Translation*. Beijing: China Translation and Publishing Corporation, 1984.

Joyce, James. *Ulises*. [Spanish.] Trans. J. Salas Subirat. Buenos Aires: Rueda, 1945.

Ulysse. [French.] Trans. Auguste Morel. Paris: Gallimard, 1946.

Ulysses. [German.] Trans. Georg Goyert. 2 vols. Zurich: Rhein, 1930.

Ulysses. [Japanese.] Trans. Morita et al. Tokyo, 1932.

Ulysses. [Japanese.] Trans. Itô et al. Tokyo, 1931–4.

Ulysses. [Danish.] Trans. Mogens Boisen. Copenhagen: Martin, 1949.

Ulysses. [Dutch.] Trans. John Vandenbergh. New York: Oliemeulen, 1969.

Ulysses: The Corrected Text. Ed. Hans Walter Gabler et al. New York: Random, 1986.

Yulixisi Xuanyi. [Chinese, selected episodes.] Trans. Jin Di. Tianjin, 1988.

Qian, Zhongshu. *Jiu wen si pian*. (Four old essays.) Shanghai: Guji Chubanshe, 1979.

Index

285